THE MODERN STUDY OF THE MISHNAH

EDITED BY

JACOB NEUSNER

Wipf and Stock Publishers
EUGENE, OREGON

Wipf and Stock Publishers
199 West 8th Avenue, Suite 3
Eugene, Oregon 97401

The Modern Study of the Mishnah
By Neusner, Jacob
Copyright© January, 1973 by Neusner, Jacob
ISBN: 1-59244-217-X
Publication date: April, 2003
Previously published by E. J. Brill, January, 1973

For
Geza Vermes

TABLE OF CONTENTS

Preface IX
Foreword
    JACOB NEUSNER XI
List of Abbreviations XXV
Transliterations XXVII

I. The Traditional Study of the Mishnah
    JOEL H. ZAIMAN 1

PART I
THE ACHIEVEMENT OF JACOB N. EPSTEIN

II. Jacob N. Epstein's *Introduction to the Text of the Mishnah*
    BARUCH MICAH BOKSER 13
III. Jacob N. Epstein on the Formation of the Mishnah
    BARUCH MICAH BOKSER 37

PART II
THE BEGINNING OF CRITICAL STUDY

IV. The Pioneer: Zecharias Frankel
    JOEL GEREBOFF 59
V. Jacob Brüll: The Mishnah as a Law-Code
    GARY G. PORTON 76
VI. Hirsch Mendel Pineles: The First Critical Exegete
    JOEL GEREBOFF 90

PART III
THE HISTORIANS AND THE MISHNAH

VII. The Talmudic Historians: N. Krochmal, H. Graetz, I. H. Weiss, and Z. Jawitz
    WILLIAM SCOTT GREEN 107
VIII. David Hoffmann's *The First Mishnah*
    CHARLES PRIMUS 122

TABLE OF CONTENTS

IX. Y. I. Halevy
    BARUCH MICAH BOKSER 135
X. Joachim Oppenheim
    JOEL GEREBOFF 155

PART IV

LITERARY CRITICS

XI. J. S. Zuri
    WILLIAM SCOTT GREEN 169
XII. David Weiss Halivni on the Mishnah
    JOEL GEREBOFF 180
XIII. Abraham Weiss
    CHARLES PRIMUS 197

PART V

RECENT ISRAEL CONTRIBUTIONS

XIV. Ḥanokh Albeck on the Mishnah
    GARY G. PORTON 209
XV. Abraham Goldberg
    WILLIAM SCOTT GREEN 225
XVI. Benjamin DeVries
    CHARLES PRIMUS 242

Bibliography 256
Index of Talmudic Passages 270
General Index 273

PREFACE

The editor and authors thank Brown University for bearing the costs of preparing the manuscript for press and of the indices. The Department of Religious Studies at Brown University has so devoted its resources to the study of the History of Religions: Judaism that we might do our work together. We know no words fully to convey our gratitude to our University.

We appreciate the inclusion of our work in this series and its publication, in the usual handsome form, by E. J. Brill. The director, Mr. F. C. Wieder, Jr., encouraged us to plan and execute this volume as a companion to *The Formation of the Babylonian Talmud. Studies in the Achievements of Late Nineteenth and Twentieth Century Historical and Literary-Critical Research* (Leiden, 1970: E. J. Brill. *Studia Post-biblica, Volumen Septimum Decimum*).

Dr. Geza Vermes, Oxford University, Visiting Professor of Religious Studies at Brown University in 1970-1971, provided valuable instruction for most of the students represented here. Like Professors Wendell S. Dietrich and Horst R. Moehring, to whom the earlier studies were dedicated, he made an important contribution to the development of the graduate program in History of Religions: Judaism at Brown University. It was therefore thought appropriate to dedicate this volume to this valued friend and teacher.

J. N.

Providence, Rhode Island
July 28, 1972
17 Av 5732

FOREWORD

JACOB NEUSNER

The Mishnah of Judah the Patriarch, produced about 200 A.D., not only stood at the end of approximately a hundred and thirty years of rabbinic legal study, but also laid the foundations for the next three hundred in the Palestinian and Babylonian rabbinic circles, and so provided the structure for the Palestinian and Babylonian Talmuds. It is a deceptive document. Because of the simplicity of its construction and the lucid style of its expression, the Mishnah seems more open and easily understood than it really is. The earliest generations of Palestinian and Babylonian Amoraim, moreover, accomplished so much in the analysis and exegesis of the Mishnah that later on attention turned to other documents and problems. Consequently people have assumed more is known about the Mishnah, its meaning and its history, than is actually the case. When, moreover, the evidence of Tosefta, not to mention that in the Tannaitic Midrashim, the Tannaitic sayings in the Palestinian *Gemara*, and the *beraitot* in the Babylonian *Gemara*, was taken into account, it was supposed that one knew about the Mishnah pretty much everything one needed. From the third to the nineteenth century, therefore, the Mishnah was read in the light of the *Gemarot*, particularly of Babylonia, and rarely formed the focus of attention on its own. Only in the nineteenth century did scholars, with Hirsch M. Pineles at the start, begin to elucidate the Mishnah in its own terms—without first attending to the opinions of the Amoraim and later commentators—and even they had great difficulty first in articulating and then in breaking free of the traditional presuppositions.

Traditional study of the Mishnah, as of other ancient holy books of rabbinic Judaism, pays close attention to the exegesis of individual words and sentences, to the interpretation of their meaning, and to the application of that meaning to legal problems. The problems emerge chiefly from the contents of the text; and solutions are weighed by criteria internal to the text.

A second form of study of the Mishnah is historical. Historical study stands outside of the Mishnah and asks questions extrinsic to the individual sentences and to their meanings. Historical study begins with questions about the Mishnah as a whole, its origins, and the development of its law.

When, however, the answers to historical and literary questions are arrived at from other criteria in addition to the information supplied by the early students of the Mishnah on the basis of their theological presuppositions, and when that information is critically evaluated in the light of the motives behind it and the external evidence, then we have entered the modern era in the study of the ancient text. What is "modern" about the modern study of the Mishnah is not merely an interest in historical, as opposed to exegetical and legal, problems, but the critical evaluation of the evidence. The first and greatest historian of the Talmud was Sherira Gaon, who lived in the ninth century; one cannot say that with him began the "modern" age in Mishnah-study. But because of his historical interests he stands as the most important precurser to the modern study of the Mishnah. In the nineteenth century Sherira's picture retained influence far out of proportion to its credibility. It was taken for granted, never tested against internal evidence. Sherira so shaped the imagination of the nineteenth century historians that the questions they raised were more or less identical to those thought important—and answerable—by Sherira. The main lines of his "history of the Mishnah" were as follows.

Sherira was asked how the Mishnah was written down? Who began to write it? Was it the "Men of the Great Assembly" which began the work, so that each succeeding generation added to it? Sherira thus is asked a fundamentally historical question, and he goes about answering it by composing narrative history: the story of the Mishnah, as revealed in the pertinent, historical-narrative sayings in the Mishnah itself, supplemented by sayings and stories in other Talmudic documents. Sherira answers that Judah the Patriarch was responsible for the Mishnah as we have it. But the later rabbis in the chain ending with Judah accurately preserved what the earlier ones had handed on. The early generations, however, were not named; only the leaders of each generation left their names on the laws. Initially the laws were fully understood and everyone grasped the reasons for them. Therefore no disputes 'marred' the oral Torah. The first difference in law had to do with 'laying on of hands' (M. Ḥag. 2:2). After the destruction of the Temple, the masters tended to vary their language while teaching the laws. This, together with upheavals of war and poor discipleship, tended to produce disputes the laws and the reasons behind them. Sherira then reviews the several generations after 70, which were supposed to be responsible for organizing and preserving what they had received from the former generations. In the course of his narrative he alludes to a number of Talmudic stories, all of which he takes at face as accurate accounts of what actually was said and done on the several occasions they allude to. The disciples of 'Aqiba were ultimately responsible for preserving the whole, in particular, Meir. Judah the Patriarch studied with the masters of Meir's generation. The traditions were preserved in the names of individuals or of the majority, but nothing was lost. Nothing was written down until the time of Judah the Patriarch. But the oral traditions were carefully preserved. Each master taught exactly what his master had given him, in the precise words of the master, back to the Great Assembly. Nevertheless, for the reasons given above, differences among traditions developed, and Judah the Patriarch determined to produce a single consistent document. Judah the Patriarch therefore gathered all the traditions, and, in times of peace, was able to produce the Mishnah as the corpus and summary of the antecedent traditions. It was written down lest it be forgotten in times of stress (B. M. Lewin, ed., *Iggeret Rav Sherira Ga'on* [Haifa, 1921], pp. 4-35).

Sherira, it is widely supposed, shaped his account of the history of the "Oral Torah" to defend the rabbinic tradition from the attack of Qaraism. Therefore he stressed the perfection of the rabbinic process of formulating and transmitting traditions, claiming that the Oral Torah of rabbinism went back, without interruption, to the Men of the Great Assembly, and thence to Sinai. But the alleged formative, tendentious factors in Sherira's history were not taken into account by later scholars, who in one way or another mostly repeated the details he supplied and replicated his viewpoint.

What is of interest is Sherira's formulation of the questions and his method of answering them. His questions take for granted that the Mishnah is a unitary document, with a one-dimensional history; that it is wholly the work of a single line of masters, who, one after the other, carefully preserved what had gone before; that it has a history recovered in the pertinent stories contained in Talmudic literature. His answers therefore are reached by collecting the Talmudic stories and putting them into a simple chronological order. His presuppositions are that (1) the whole corpus of traditions was memorized; (2) the system of master-disciple relationships was permanent and extended back into remote antiquity; (3) all traditions were everywhere available; (4) Judah the Patriarch was the single authority responsible for the final compilation; and (5) Judah produced a single document with no important textual problems.

Clearly, an interest in historical questions is not unique to modern scholars. Those who told historical and biographical stories in Talmudic times and those who later on composed histories based on such stories obviously wanted to reconstruct the past. But until the nineteenth century—and, for Talmudic studies, until the last third of the twentieth century—it was routinely taken for granted that any story in a holy book accurately portrays exactly what happened. The story itself *has* no "history," but it *is* history. No special interests or viewpoints are to be found in a given historical account. Everything is taken at face value. To pious historians it was unthinkable that anyone would either lie or make up a story for his own partisan purposes. They never asked, *Cui bono?* To whose interest is it to tell a given story? But in modern times—beginning long before the Enlightenment—people learned to take a skeptical position *vis à vis* the sacred histories and holy biographies of the earlier generations. They asked about the tendencies of stories and the point the story teller wished to make, and wondered not only about whether the events reported in a story "really" happened, but also about the situation from which a given story had arisen and about which it might supply accurate testimony. They asked how the story teller knew the facts of the case. Who told him? If he was an eye-witness, on whose side did he stand in a situation of conflict? No reporters were present to take down verbatim what was said and done at the various incidents recorded in the rabbinic traditions. Therefore all we have are, at best, *traditions* about such events, given both form and substance on some other, later occasion than that of which they speak. But often we have not *traditions* but mere legends, fabrications quite unrelated to the events they purport to relate.

Such a skeptical attitude had been well established in New Testament and *Tanakh* studies by the early nineteenth century. Scholarship in these and related fields showed the necessity of analyzing the components of stories and asking how each element took shape and where and when the several elements were put together. But with rabbinic materials, aside from some reservations about obvious miracles, one rarely discerns, among nineteenth or even most twentieth century scholars, any desire to go beyond the Talmudic stories in attempting to understand the historical background of texts. And when rabbinic scholars did try to question the presuppositions of

FOREWORD

the texts, they did so unsystematically, chiefly for exegetical, not historical purposes. Only in recent times have various scholars of rabbinic literature in different ways shown that one must recognize the hidden historical motives and the complex literary situation of rabbinic literature.

Those motives and that situation make it impossible to read the texts as completely reliable historical witnesses. They require that we ask about the Mishnah a number of new questions. First, is the Mishnah a unitary document, or is it a collection of many documents, not all of them of the same sort, but deriving from different sources? Second, can we rightly speak of a single editor who stands behind the compilation as a whole? Third, do we actually have a single, *original* Mishnah-text, which we may recover among the various, often conflicting textual testimonies? Or is "The Mishnah" an artificial construct, concealing the many Mishnahs—in part or in the whole—available in antiquity? Fourth, does the Mishnah stand at the end of a single line of development, or is it the confluent of many streams of tradition and growth? Are its contents the work of a single group, or party, in ancient Judaism, or must we make distinctions among various types of law and suggest which types are produced by one sort of political party, social group or historical process, which by another? If the "sages," meaning the Pharisees, did not govern pre-70 Palestine, then how shall we account for those Mishnaic laws which probably come from the period before 70, but deal with areas of public life not then subject to Pharisaic control? Was there a common law in ancient Palestine, to which all groups subjected themselves, and which in time entered the rabbinic tradition? How were the several types of traditions formulated and transmitted? Can we take for granted the historical accuracy of the rabbinic picture of a master's formulating a sentence and orally teaching it to his disciple, who then memorized the sentence and in time passed it on the same way to his disciple? Or were there a number of different means by which materials were formulated in their final stage and handed on to the next generation?

In asking these questions, we have moved a very long way from the historical agenda laid down by Sherira. These too are historical questions, but they are not questions of narrative and cannot be answered by a retelling the thrice-told stories and sayings in rabbinic literature that would seem to provide pertinent information. For the critical scholar such stories and sayings reveal primarily the situations of the people who made them up, and normally we know who those people were. They do not stand as unimpeachable evidence about the Mishnah's own history. They tell us only what later generations thought to claim about that history. One need not, therefore, refute in detail histories made up on the basis of Talmudic tales. One need only point out that such histories are wholly uncritical, omit all reference to the internal evidence revealed by Mishnah itself, and generally exclude from discussion the literary evidences available in cognate literature, particularly Tosefta. Nor need one refute the nineteenth and twentieth century histories of the Mishnah which, using the Talmudic materials, go on to reinterpret them, to invent new "postulates" about their meaning, to reject one detail of a story in favor of another—in all, to lay claim to a "critical" position towards a literature whose historical usefulness is never in the end called into question or criticized. In such histories we have the pretense of critical scholarship but not its substance. The bulk of the work of nineteenth and twentieth century historians of the Mishnah must be regarded as pseudo-critical, critical in rhetoric but wholly traditional in all its presuppositions and, in the main, primitive and puerile. Like the "critical" fundamentalists, who postulate that the whale did not really swallow Jonah, but only kept him in his cheek, and like the pseudorthodox who say it was for three hours, not for three days—the "critical" scholars of the modern period have scarcely improved upon the traditional picture. They have merely rearranged some of its elements. Nothing has changed, but much is made of the changes.

Sherira's questions and presuppositions predominate throughout the modern study of the Mishnah, with only two exceptions. The first, and greatest, is not treated here at all. Saul Lieberman's *Tosefta Kifshutah* and *Tosefet Rishonim* constitute the greatest commentaries to Mishnaic literature ever written. Since Lieberman concentrates on Tosefta, however, the Mishnah is elucidated only as part of a larger framework. This is as it should be, for the Mishnah and Tosefta constitute a single literature—Lieberman demonstrates this on virtually every page of his work—and cannot be studied except in relationship to one another. Lieberman further demonstrates that Tosefta represents the hinge on which all Talmudic 'doors' must turn, so he includes all pertinent materials from the Palestinian Talmud and the Babylonian Talmud's *beraitot*. What is of interest here is that Lieberman as yet has produced no "introduction" to Mishnah-Tosefta. One reviewer criticized his failure to write an "introduction to

FOREWORD

Tosefta," explaining when the document was written, by whom, for what purpose, and the like. But Lieberman wisely prefers to await the conclusion of his detailed and thorough researches into Mishnah-Tosefta. Only at the end will the accumulated, internal evidence permit him to speculate about the literary and historical traits of the whole compilation. This sage reserve and close attention to internal evidence, not to mention the extraordinary thoroughness, exegetical lucidity, stylistic taste, and prudent judgment, set Lieberman's work apart from anything ever done or ever likely to be done. He has raised scholarship on Mishnah-Tosefta to an entirely new level of achievement. Many generations will profit from his work. But since we have chosen to concentrate on works devoted primarily to the Mishnah, and since Lieberman's work is not yet complete for the whole Tosefta and still lacks the required general introduction, we choose to postpone our account of it.

The second exception to the pseudo-critical rule is J. N. Epstein. Epstein asks a deceptively simple question: What is the requirement for a "critical text" of the Mishnah? He shows that such a critical text is hardly possible. Indeed, the textual situation was so fluid, right from the outset, that one may probably have to abandon the concept of *the Mishnah* as a single corpus of readings and traditions. Rather, he shows, from the beginning the Mishnah was constituted by a not-precisely-limited collection of formulations. The earliest Amoraim did not hesitate to revise what they had received, to produce "the Mishnah" in accordance with their own conceptions of what Rabbi ought to have produced. They did not merely study a received, fixed text; they worked, so to speak, in creative partnership with the founder(s) of the Mishnah(s) in establishing the text(s) they thought viable. Epstein not only showed the fluidity of the Mishnah's text from Rabbi's time onward, but also demonstrated the complexity of the materials received by Rabbi and shaped into the Mishnah. Rabbi drew upon many different sources, and these several sources were themselves characterized by considerable variation in both style and substance. The exact words attributed to earlier authorities might change from one source to the next. Conflicts already existed in the various sources used and preserved by Rabbi. And there were other collections of ancient legal traditions, produced both at the same time and afterward. Internal inconsistencies, successive recensions, distinct collections produced a mass of varying interpretations and alternative readings, and on this basis later masters doctored the Mishnah they had received. So the Mishnah as we now have it cannot be said accurately to preserve *the* Mishnah-text of the Talmudic period. One must then wonder whether we may accurately speak of a single Mishnah-text of any period, even of the period in which "the Mishnah" was actually taking shape. Here, obviously, we are far indeed from the presuppositions and consequent questions of Sherira Gaon.

Epstein's monumental conception and the execution of his work may be contrasted with the questions framed by Sherira. Sherira asked, How was the Mishnah written down? What is its history? Epstein begins with the question, What are the evidences for a single, essentially static Mishnah-text? Can we speak of "The Mishnah" at all? He further raises the question of the variety and multiplicity of sources behind the Mishnah. He brings us a long way indeed from the simple account of Sherira. In the light of Epstein's achievements, one may no longer take seriously the questions posed by Sherira, for those questions no longer relate to the document as we now know it.

Zecharias Frankel, the founder of the modern study of the Mishnah, appears in comparison to Epstein to belong to the distant past. It would, indeed, be unnecessary to criticize his ideas at all, were they not still taken seriously, as shown by the reprinting of his books and their use in contemporary Israeli scholarship to this day. Frankel operates in a world of private definitions, circular reasoning, and capricious postulates. For him it is unnecessary to prove much, for one may, through *defining* things properly, obviate the need for proof. He thinks medieval commentaries constitute primary sources for the study of the Mishnah. He furthermore claims that *Seder Toharot* is old because it is the *largest* order (!), that the ancient Jews were *all* students of the rabbinic Torah, that the structure of the Mishnah was revealed by divine inspiration; and he reveals numerous other marvels. In what way then is he to be regarded as "modern"? The reception of his book supplies the answer. His enemies accused him of treating the Mishnah in a secular spirit and not as a divinely revealed document, the Oral Torah. They said he regarded the Mishnah as the work of men and as a time-bound document. He even explained Mishnaic laws in other ways than by reference to the Babylonian Talmud. For this Frankel was condemned, and correctly so, by the traditionalists of his day, who quite rightly saw in his work a threat to their presuppositions. That his work today is taken seriously among traditionalists tells us that what is said in the name of tradition changes from one century to the next. But scarcely a line of his

Darkhé HaMishnah can be taken seriously. The same may be said of Brüll, who follows closely on Frankel's path.

Ḥ. Albeck looks upon the Mishnah as the culmination of the process of "oral tradition" beginning in ancient times. He takes for granted that anything not reflective of Scriptural tradition, whether in biblical or apocryphal, pseudepigraphical, or Septuagintal literature, is a reflection of *The Oral Tradition* of Pharisaic-Rabbinic Judaism. That it might have been invented never enters his head—and he supposes any "oral tradition" must be "the" oral tradition of Pharisaic and rabbinic Judaism. While Albeck is critical of earlier students of the history of the oral Torah, he does not depart from their frame of reference. Indeed, he takes pretty much the position of Sherira, altering details but not the main points. The scholarly agenda formulated by Sherira remain uncriticized and unchanged: "When was the Mishnah written?" He extensively reviews and criticizes the ideas of earlier scholars, as if they had supplied him with viable agenda. So we find ourselves once again in the midst of debates on the work of the Men of the Great Assembly, as if we had the slightest shred of evidence about what they had actually done, let alone a document produced by them or in their days. While Epstein demonstrated, for example, that the tractate ʿEduyyot was produced by the disciples of ʿAqiba at Usha—they are explicitly named throughout—Albeck takes seriously what the traditions from Talmudic times allege, that ʿEduyyot was produced at Yavneh: "It was ordered according to the name of the sages and the work was done at Yavneh." But he never proves this is so. One may easily show that ʿEduyyot is *different* from other tractates, but that difference does not mean it is *earlier* than the others. Whatever a Talmudic tradition alleges about a tractate is taken as fact. Unlike Epstein, Albeck seldom looks in a thorough and critical way for internal evidence. Again and again one finds circular reasoning. For example, he holds that Rabbi arranged the material he had received according to a single principle: content. He did not change anything he had received. How do we know this? Because any material not collected according to this principle was formed into units *before* Rabbi received it. But how do we know the units were formed before Rabbi received them? *Because* Rabbi ordered his material only according to the content of the laws. Likewise, Rabbi did not change any of the material he received, because the sources are not changed. We know the sources are not changed because Rabbi did not change any of the sources. And so forth. While aware of variant readings, Albeck further disputes the view of Epstein that the Mishnah yielded numerous variations in texts. He says once the Mishnah was edited, it was never again changed. There was only one correct version of *the* Mishnah. I am not clear on how Albeck understood the work of the Amoraim, for they seem not only to have changed the Mishnah, but to have stated explicitly that they changed the Mishnah.

In his essay on the *Scriptores Historiae Augustae* (*Studies in Historiography* [N.Y., 1966], pp. 149-150), A. D. Momigliano states, "The discussion of the *Historia Augusta* provides a classic example of a discussion in progress about forgeries. In this discussion I can perhaps claim the distinction, which must be almost unique among the students of the *Historia Augusta*, of not having any theory to propound about it. I have not found it either necessary or possible to formulate any new theory. What I think I can do is to apply to the study of the *Historia Augusta* the method of Simple Simon — who, when he had no penny, told the pieman that he had not any. Too many of the arguments which have been offered, especially in very recent years, about the *Historia Augusta* are imaginary pennies." Momigliano's judgment applies to the study of the history of the Mishnah and especially to the works of those who, without testing the evidence, presumed, on the basis of how they believed or imagined things had to have been, to write that history. Time and again our sole criticism of the theories of the several historians is simply, "There is no evidence," or "The evidence adduced is inadequate." Now that may not seem a particularly weighty criticism, especially in the face of elaborate theories and theologically well-grounded notions. But so far as historical, and not theological, problems are at hand, one's only significant criticism must focus on the nature and the use of historical evidence, and wisdom consists in mature skepticism.

Why then did we take the trouble to criticize the works before us and to call attention to their inadequacy as history? At the outset it was not our intention to do so. Our earlier studies had made us well aware of the severe limitations of the historical method and results achieved by modern Talmudic scholarship. We had already encountered the arbitrary definitions, the circular arguments, the loose and often slovenly formulations, and the highly theological framework of discourse exhibited in most, though not all, nineteenth and twentieth century studies. We had hoped to find and draw attention to solid results. But, as noted, apart from Jacob N. Epstein, such results were difficult to come by. The larger number of books at hand, however, have been reprinted and are widely read to this day, not for the history of modern *scholarship* on the Mishnah but for the history of the Mishnah itself. Seminary and university courses on Talmudic literature still take for granted the usefulness of the results of Frankel, Hoffmann, and the other pioneers, not to mention Albeck, DeVries, and the like. Studies on the history of the Mishnah as "the Oral Torah" still begin with Ezra or with Simeon the Righteous. The Mishnah is still regarded as primarily the work of pre-70 Pharisaism, and Ezra's or Simeon's or Hillel's foundation of the Mishnah remains part of the scholarly picture. While seeking permanently valid results, therefore, we found it necessary to point out the major flaws in concept and method in the several works before us, so that obsolete works might be honorably laid to rest, and new inquiries might begin.

These papers were originally prepared for my seminar in Talmudic Judaism at Brown University and then were revised for publication. They form a complementary study to *The Formation of the Babylonian Talmud. Studies in the Achievements of Late Nineteenth and Twentieth Century Historical and Literary-Critical Research.* Having considered how modern scholars have dealt with a specific, and important historical-literary problem, namely, the editing of the Babylonian Talmud, we decided to broaden our frame of reference. We asked, How have modern scholars dealt with a major rabbinic document as a whole? What did they consider to be the important issues pertaining to that document? What was the nature of their "introductions" to the Mishnah? What did they think an "introduction" should introduce and discuss? How did they formulate the problems posed by the Mishnah? Since no survey of the history of scholarship on the various problems and documents of rabbinic literature is available, we decided to undertake some of the preliminary work on modern Mishnah-studies. We cannot claim to supply a full and wide-ranging account of the present state of the question, but we do hope to have given a responsible and careful account of some of the more important contributions to its study. In the bibliography we have, moreover, briefly described a number of studies which did not seem to us to warrant more extensive consideration.

We noticed that while the scholars of the Mishnah addressed themselves to the historical and literary-critical *issues* raised in university studies of the humanities in general, and of the Bible in particular, their primitive *methods* and answers tended to derive chiefly from the (more enlightened) Yeshivot of their day. The modern study of the Mishnah has not proved to be an enterprise based on universities, but rather has remained primarily an exercise in Judaic theology. None of the scholars before us taught in a non-Jewish setting, either in a secular university or in research institute. Indeed, except for those at the Hebrew University, Epstein, Goldberg, and Albeck, and DeVries at Tel Aviv University in his very last years, most of the scholars before us never held university posts at all. They were rabbis or teachers in various communities or synagogues, or in a few instances they taught, full- or part-time, in Jewish seminaries. If therefore, they had received university doctorates and attempted to meet the critical requirements of modern, secular scholarship in ancient literature, most did not do their work within the critical discipline or framework of discourse of universities and did not have access to continuing interchange with university scholars in Semitics, ancient history, philology, and theology. That fact helps account for the insularity and methodologically primitive conceptions of most of the scholars whose work we shall examine.

But it also helps account for the generally incompetent work on rabbinic sources produced by Christian seminary professors and university scholars. With noteworthy exceptions, by ignoring the experts on Judaic studies whom they might have consulted and by excluding them from university life, they insured that scholarship on ancient Judaism would be narrow-minded, uninformed, and derivative. The inevitable result was childish reliance upon dubious compilations of rabbinic materials thought pertinent to New Testament and the necessarily consequent misinterpretation of New Testament and other matters to which such materials were thought to pertain. Both sides paid a heavy price in ignorance and retrograde scholarship because they were deprived of one another's presence.

In America this situation has greatly changed. My graduate students in Brown University are able to study the early Christian literature, not to mention theology and history, with sophisticated scholars and so are brought abreast of scholarly issues and critical achievements, which both in method and in substance help to illumine the study of ancient rabbinic Judaism. They are learning to speak in a common conceptual language of, and to formulate issues in a way proved sound by, scholarship in related areas of ancient history and literature. Our hope is that in showing some of the important results in modern studies of the Mishnah, we may make available to colleagues in related fields a way of entry into Mishnaic and cognate studies. So we may reciprocate the valuable gifts we have received by opening to others the literary treasures hitherto not easily studied by them. If Talmudic studies of various kinds are to make their contribution to humanistic scholarship in universities, as I believe is required for the benefit both of the humanities and of Talmudic studies, then we shall have to strive for a clear picture of the history and promise of Talmudic scholarship. It is my hope that the present writers have not wholly failed in giving a glimpse of a small, but not unimportant part of that picture.

It also is our hope that this study may be one of those which fairly represent, in respect of their origin, the beginning of a new stage in rabbinic studies. May this expression of work now being done at Brown University contribute to mutual understanding among scholars at work on closely related documents and the history of not dissimilar religious traditions.

LIST OF ABBREVIATIONS

Ah.	=	Ahilot
Ant.	=	Josephus, *Antiquities*
ʿArakh.	=	ʿArakhin
ARN	=	Avot de Rabbi Natan
A.Z.	=	ʿAvodah Zarah
b.	=	Bavli, Babylonian Talmud
b.	=	ben
B.B.	=	Bava Batra
B.M.	=	Bava Meṣiʿaʾ
B.Q.	=	Bava Qamma
Ber.	=	Berakhot
Beṣ.	=	Beṣah
Bik.	=	Bikkurim
BT	=	Babylonian Talmud (b.)
Dem.	=	Demai
Development	=	*Development of a Legend: Studies on the Traditions Concerning Yoḥanan ben Zakkai* (Leiden, 1970)
ʿEd.	=	ʿEduyyot
ʿEruv.	=	ʿEruvin
Giṭ.	=	Giṭṭin
Ḥag.	=	Ḥagigah
Ḥal.	=	Ḥallah
Halivni, *Meqorot*	=	David Weiss Halivni, *Meqorot uMesorot* (Tel Aviv, 1968)
HaMadaʿ	=	J. N. Epstein, "HaMadaʿ HaTalmudi veṢorkhav," *Proceedings of the Academy of Jewish Studies* (Jerusalem) 2, 1935, pp. 5-22.
Hor.	=	Horayot
HUCA	=	*Hebrew Union College Annual*
Ḥul.	=	Ḥullin
IAL	=	J. N. Epstein, *Introductions to Amoraic Literature* (Mevoʾot leSifrut HaʾAmoraʾim [Jerusalem, 1962])
ITM	=	J. N. Epstein, *Introduction to the Text of the Mishnah* (Mavo leNusaḥ HaMishnah [Jerusalem, 1964²])
ITL	=	J. N. Epstein, *Introductions to Tannaitic Literature* (Mevoʾot leSifrut HaTannaʾim [Jerusalem, 1957])
JQR	=	*Jewish Quarterly Review*
Kel.	=	Kelim
Ker.	=	Keritot
Ket.	=	Ketuvot
Kil.	=	Kilaʾim
M.	=	Mishnah
MGWJ	=	*Monatsschrift für Geschichte und Wissenschaft des Judentums*
M.Q.	=	Moʿed Qatan
M.S.	=	Maʿaser Sheni
M.T.	=	Midrash Tannaʾim
Ma.	=	Maʿaserot
Mak.	=	Makkot

LIST OF ABBREVIATIONS

Maksh.	=	Makshirin
Me.	=	Meʿilah
Meg.	=	Megillah
Mekh.	=	Mekhilta
Men.	=	Menaḥot
Mid.	=	Middot
Miq.	=	Miqvaʾot
Naz.	=	Nazir
Ned.	=	Nedarim
Neg.	=	Negaʿim
Neusner, *Pharisees*	=	*The Rabbinic Traditions about the Pharisees before 70* (Leiden, 1971) Vols. I-III.
Nez.	=	Nezirot
Nid.	=	Niddah
Oh.	=	Ohalot
ʿOrl.	=	ʿOrlah
Par.	=	Parah
Pes.	=	Pesaḥim
PT	=	Palestinian Talmud (y.)
Qid.	=	Qiddushin
R.	=	Rabbi
Rabbi	=	Rabbi Judah the Patriarch
REJ	=	*Revue des études juives*
R.H.	=	Rosh Hashanah
Sam.	=	Samuel
Sanh.	=	Sanhedrin
Shab.	=	Shabbat
Shav.	=	Shavuʿot
Sheq.	=	Sheqalim
Shev.	=	Sheviʿit
Soṭ.	=	Soṭah
Suk.	=	Sukkah
Ta.	=	Taʿanit
Tem.	=	Temurah
Ter.	=	Terumot
TK	=	*Tosefta Kifshuṭah* (N.Y., 1955ff.)
Ṭoh.	=	Ṭoharot
Tos.	=	Tosefta
Ṭ.Y.	=	Ṭevul Yom
ʿUqṣ.	=	ʿUqṣin
y.	=	Yerushalmi, Palestinian Talmud
Y.Ṭ.	=	Yom Ṭov
Yad.	=	Yadaim
Yev.	=	Yevamot
Zab.	=	Zabim
Zer.	=	Zeraʿim
Zev.	=	Zevaḥim

TRANSLITERATIONS

א	=	ʾ	מ ם	= M
ב	= B		נ ן	= N
ג	= G		ס	= S
ד	= D		ע	= ʿ
ה	= H		פ ף	= P
ו	= W		צ	= Ṣ
ז	= Z		ק	= Q
ח	= Ḥ		ר	= R
ט	= Ṭ		שׁ	= Š
י	= Y		שׂ	= Ś
כ ך	= K		ת	= T
ל	= L			

CHAPTER ONE

THE TRADITIONAL STUDY OF THE MISHNAH

JOEL H. ZAIMAN

i

Herbert Danby defines the Mishnah "as a deposit for centuries of Jewish religious and cultural activity in Palestine, beginning at some uncertain date (possibly during the early half of the second century B.C.) and ending with the close of the second century A.D."[1] For the tradition, however, the Mishnah was the first collection of oral Torah to be written down, and, like the written Torah itself, became a holy book:

> The central myth of classical Judaism is the belief that the ancient Scriptures constitute a divine revelation, but only a part of it. At Sinai, God handed down a dual revelation: the written part known to one and all, but also the oral part preserved by the great Scriptural heroes, passed on by prophets to various ancestors in the obscure past, finally and most openly handed down to the rabbis who created the Palestinian and Babylonian Talmuds. The 'whole Torah' thus consisted of both written and oral parts. The rabbis taught that the 'whole Torah' was studied by David, augmented by Ezekiel, legislated by Ezra, and embodied in the schools and by the sages of every period in Israelite history from Moses to the present.[2]

This myth underlies the following exegesis of Ex. 24 : 12 quoted by R. Levi bar Hamma in the name of R. Simeon b. Laqish:

> What is it that is written: ... *and I will give thee tables of stone and a law and commandments which I have written that thou mayest teach them? Tables* are the ten commandments, a *law* is the Pentateuch, commandments are the Mishnah, *which I have written* is the Prophets and the Hagiographa, *that thou mayest teach them* is the Talmud. This teaches that all were given to Moses on Sinai.
>
> (b. Ber. 5a)

---

[1] Herbert Danby, *The Mishnah*. (London, 1933) p. III.
[2] Jacob Neusner, *The Way of Torah: An Introduction to Judaism*. (Belmont, 1970) p. 35.

The oral part of divine revelation, the Mishnah and the Talmud, as well as the written part, the Ten Commandments and Pentateuch, were given at Sinai. Likewise:

> When God revealed Himself at Sinai to give the Torah to Israel, He communicated it to Moses in order: Scripture, Mishnah, Talmud, and Haggadah, as it says, *And God spoke all these words.* (Ex. 20 : 1). Even the question a pupil asks his teacher, God told Moses at that time.
>
> (Ex. R. 47 : 1)

How was this myth of dual revelation understood and how did it function once it was accepted? Over a thousand years later, Rabbi Aryeh Leib Ha-Cohen, in the introduction to his work, *Ketzot Haḥoshen*, offers the following justification for his enterprise:

> For the primary purpose of the creation was the Torah, and man, with his human mind, cannot perceive veritable truth ... To this the Lord replied that it was His will that truth come forth from the earth and that truth should be as agreed by the sages with their human mind ... It has already been said in the *Gemara* that the Lord made a Covenant with Israel for the sake of the oral law only ... that He gave us the oral law as an absolute gift ... as the sages may decide ... And they said in the Talmud that the larger part of the Torah is oral and lesser part is written; for if all were in writing, we would still be foreign to it, for how can the human mind understand the Torah of the Lord, but the oral law is of our very own ... The oral law was given to be decided by the sages ...³

The Psalmist had said (85 : 9): "Truth springs forth from the earth," and the sages saw themselves as the guardians of that truth. The myth of a dual revelation was enunciated by the rabbis, from the end of the first century onward, who further taught that they were its legitimate bearers in an unbroken chain of transmission from Sinai. The rabbi developed and explained the revelation of Sinai and the product of his efforts was, for practical purposes, as important as that written revelation to Moses. It was for the sake of the activities of the rabbis that God had given the written Torah to begin with.⁴ Indeed, "the words of the rabbis are dearer (*ḤBYBYN YWTR*) than the words of Torah."⁵

---

³ Quoted by Izhak Englard, "The Problem of Jewish Law in a Jewish State" in Haim Cohn, *Jewish Law in Ancient and Modern Israel.* (New York, 1971) p. 146.
⁴ b. Git. 60b.
⁵ y. Ber. 1 : 7.

ii

In terms of tradition the Mishnah was, by definition, authoritative and binding from the day it was published.[6] The task then became to comment upon the Mishnah, even as the Pentateuch had been commented upon. This commentary was known as the *Gemara*. In the traditional study of the Mishnah, it was understood only as part of the Talmud, the whole being the effort to discover the oral Torah. There was, in fact, no break, nor did tradition envisage a break, in this process.

This fact gave rise to an interesting phenomenon. The Mishnah, as the first example of oral Torah, became its most important statement. Even as with Scripture itself, it could not be contradicted. Yet from the practical standpoint, the Mishnah hardly had an independent existence. On the one hand, though oral Torah become written, it still retained its theological status as oral; on the other, it could not be properly understood without the *Gemara*. As such the process of *Gemara* is what occupied the early post-Mishnaic teachers, and the importance of the Mishnah was that it formed the basis for such discussions. "Even if one has learned Scripture and Mishnah, if he has not ministered to the disciples of the wise, he is an *'am ha'areṣ*."[7] Knowing the written Torah and the first and most important publication of the oral Torah was not enough, for the process of commentary did not stop there, and the Mishnah is integrally connected with Talmud.

It is significant that some thought that the study of Mishnah was neglected in favor of the study of Talmud, even during the time of Rabbi. It was undoubtedly true by the time of Rabbi Yoḥanan, the leading Palestinian Amora of the second generation (250-280 C.E.).

> Our rabbis taught: They who occupy themselves with Scripture (alone) are but of indifferent merit; with Mishnah, are indeed meritorious, and are rewarded for it; with Talmud there can be nothing more meritorious; yet always run to the Mishnah more than to the Talmud.
>
> Now, this is self-contradictory. You say, with Talmud—there can be nothing more meritorious." And then you say, "Yet always run to the Mishnah more than to the *Gemara*!"

---

[6] Saul Lieberman states, "When the Mishnah was committed to memory and the *Tannaim* recited it in the college, it was thereby published ..." *Hellenism in Jewish Palestine*. (New York, 1950) p. 88.

[7] b. Ber. 47b.

Said R. Yoḥanan, "This teaching was taught in the days of Rabbi; thereupon, everyone forsook the Mishnah and went to the *Gemara*; hence he subsequently taught them, "yet run always to the Mishnah more than to the *Gemara*."

(b. B.M. 33a-b)

The Mishnah, authoritative and binding, thus did not have an independent existence. It became part of Talmud.

iii

The first commentary to the Mishnah therefore is the *Gemara*, and it has remained the commentary *par excellence*. When the process of *Gemara* came to a close (ca. 500-700), commentaries on it were considered as explanations of the Mishnah as well. Consequently, the first commentaries to the Mishnah were on those tractates for which there was no *Gemara*. When the Mishnah was originally published, a sizeable portion had no practical bearing on religious practice. This explains the absence of *Gemara* in the Babylonian Talmud for Seder Zeraʿim, save for Tractate Berakhot, and Seder Toharot, save for Tractate Niddah. Precisely because these Tractates had no *Gemara*, the early Mishnah commentaries were written for them and them alone. These commentaries supplied the missing *Gemara*. While the *Gemara* had several complete commentaries by the end of the eleventh century, for example those of R. Ḥananel (990-c. 1055) and Rashi (1040-1105), commentaries on the Mishnah were not only rare, but fragmentary. The oldest extant commentary is a compilation of Geonic materials relating only to Seder Toharot; it deals almost entirely with textual difficulties and lexical questions. Isaac b. Malkiṣedeq of Siponto (c. 1110-1170) wrote a commentary to Zeraʿim, printed in full in the Vilna Rom edition of the Talmud and to Toharot, which is quoted extensively by others. His commentary to Zeraʿim relies heavily on the Palestinian Talmud which, unlike the Babylonian, has *Gemara* for the entire Order.[8]

[8] See Hanoch Albeck, *Mavo la-Mishnah*. (Jerusalem, 1959) pp. 237-257, and Zechariah Frankel, *Darkhé haMishnah*, (Berlin, 1923) pp. 317-340. Twersky remarks: "Contemporaneously, there are several other scholars dedicating themselves to Mishnah study—almost as if there had been a prearranged plan to 'redeem' the Mishnah: Shemaya, Rashi's disciple; Moses b. Abraham of Pontoise, R. Tam's disciple; Isaac b. Melkizedek, the well-known scholar from Siponto; Samson of Sens, the noted Tosafist." *Rabad of Posquières*. (Cambridge, 1962) p. 107, note 6.

THE TRADITIONAL STUDY OF THE MISHNAH

Maimonides (1135-1204) composed the first commentary on the entire Mishnah. Completed in Egypt when he was thirty-three, it was written in Arabic. Maimonides attempted to detach the Mishnah from its later commentaries, to make it an independent subject of study. "What prompted me to compose this composition," writes Maimonides, in his *Introduction to Seder Zera'im*, "is that I have seen that the Talmud makes of the Mishnah a matter that will never be able to be logically grasped ..." He then proceeds to enumerate four great benefits which will accrue from his commentary on the entire Mishnah: "One, that we will teach the correct explanation of each Mishnah ... Two, I shall clearly provide the Halakhah and according to whose view it was decided. Three, it will serve as an introduction to all who begin an investigation of wisdom (B'YWN HHKMH) ... and four, it will serve as a record (MZKRT) for him who has studied and understood Scripture so that what he has studied will be always set before him and his Mishnah and Talmud can be ordered on the basis of it." Maimonides' goal was to synthesize, systematize, abridge and condense. A modern student describes the goal of Maimonides in the following way:

> Maimonides ... desired to condense the rambling Talmudic explanations and distill the quintessence from the lengthy discussions. He would manipulate, refashion, and recast these conclusions and insights in the form of a self-contained commentary on a self-contained literary unit. His expressed aim was to render the Mishnah an independent cadre, which would provide a worthwhile subject of study.⁹

He succeeded. The first printed edition of the Mishnah (Naples 1492 and following) contained a Hebrew translation of the commentary of Maimonides. Future commentators would rely heavily on his substance, while ignoring his form.

A contemporary of Maimonides, Abraham b. David of Posquiéres in France (1120-1198) known as Rabad, wrote commentaries on the treatises of *Edduyot* and *Kinnim* and Samson b. Abraham of Sens, (c. 1150-1230) prepared his on Seder Zera'im, except for Berakhot, and on Seder Toharot, except for Niddah — those tractates which had no *Gemara* in the Babylonian Talmud. Twersky describes Rabad's method and goal:

---

⁹ *Ibid.*, p. 109.

> He is both methodical and comprehensive. He cites alternative explanations, weighs them, and decides between them. He occasionally reverts to a passage in order to add yet another interpretation. Passages explained elsewhere in Talmudic literature are dismissed with a cross reference, for his is not an elementary commentary but an advanced work for competent students who can find their way in the Talmud ...
>
> Rabad was intrigued by Mishnah study because it was baffling and difficult; he wanted to supplement what the Amoraim had omitted, to elucidate the uninterpreted sections of the Mishnah, but not to detach it completely from the Talmud. His commentaries gave the Mishnah a modicum of literary independence, but the cross references to the Talmud caused the two to remain substantially interwoven.[10]

The result was that no one who could not well navigate the sea of Talmud could benefit in the least from Rabad's commentary. As in the past, one came to Mishnah through Talmud. Unlike Maimonides, Rabad was not concerned with the independent study of Mishnah.

Samson of Sens', a famous French tosafist, exercised the greatest influence, after R. Tam and Isaac b. Samuel, upon Talmudic studies in France and Germany during the thirteenth century. His Mishnah commentary was written after he had compiled most of his *Tosafot*. E. E. Urbach describes his commentaries:

> ... and from the perspective of method and approach they are in essence *Tosafot* for Zera'im and Toharot ... The primary and major source in the explanations of Samson of Sens' is 'our Talmud.' At times he merely provides a cross reference to the Babylonian Talmud, where an explanation of the Mishnah can be found ... Indeed there is hardly a chapter in his commentary which does not contain *sugyot* from the Babylonian Talmud which he explains.[11]

First published by D. Bomberg in 1523, it has since appeared in almost all editions of the Talmud.

Asher b. Yehiel (c. 1250-1328) continued this pattern, writing a commentary for those tractates wanting Talmud. His method was to briefly summarize previous commentators adding his own remarks. Excerpts of his commentary were first printed in the Amsterdam edition of the Talmud (1715), later to be printed in full in the Altona edition (1735). It is significant to note that most Mishnah commentaries were first printed as part of an edition of the Talmud.

---

[10] *Ibid.*, pp. 108-109.
[11] Ephraim Urbach, *Ba'alé HaTosafot.* (Jerusalem, 1963) pp. 247-251.

THE TRADITIONAL STUDY OF THE MISHNAH

It was not expected that Mishnah would be studied as an independent discipline.

iv

The Venice edition of the Mishnah, published in 1548, contained the commentary of Obadiah ben Abraham of Bertinoro (b. ca. 1500) on the complete Mishnah. Unlike Maimonides, he attempted no introduction, nor was his purpose to provide general rules and principles. He followed Rashi's commentary on the Talmud where available, more often than not using his identical wording. Where Rashi was unavailable, that is, for those Tractates for which there was no *Gemara* in the Babylonian Talmud, he followed the commentaries of Samson of Sens' and Maimonides. Bertinoro was probably well aware that one of the functions of his commentary was to reattach the Mishnah to the *Gemara*, and once again render it impossible to study the Mishnah independently of the Talmud. Though now printed in separate editions, so that technically it was easier to study Mishnah independently, the apparatus provided to facilitate such study, that is Bertinoro's commentary, once again made the Mishnah subservient to the Talmud.

R. Yom Tob Lippman Heller (1579-1654) then composed *Tosafot Yom Tob* on the Mishnah, actually on Bertinoro's commentary to the Mishnah. He writes concerning Bertinoro's decision to write a commentary after Maimonides had already written a commentary:

> What is clear to me is that he did not compose a commentary simply because at times he explains a matter contrary to an explanation of Maimonides, for if this were the case, he had but to provide glosses. Rather he clearly recognized that Maimonides' method of explaining the Mishnah was to establish general rules and principles summarizing its contents and joining them together, and this is not the way and method of Rashi, who analyzes the Mishnah into its single parts and short dicta. His method has generally been adopted, as we can see from the fact his commentaries on Scripture and *Gemara* have spread. For this crucial reason Bertinoro prepared a complete commentary on the Mishnah.

It was to improve on that commentary and again further acceptance of that approach that R. Heller wrote his elaborate and erudite commentary. Mishnah and *Gemara* were again bound together. In traditional study, the Mishnah was refracted through the Talmud and the process of oral Torah, of commentary, at least in France and Germany, was to analyze, detail and expand.

Israel Lipschütz (1782-1860) also used the commentary of Bertinoro as the starting point of his own commentary to the entire Mishnah, *Tiferet Yisrael*. His purpose, after briefly explaining each Mishnah and offering new explanations for difficult sections, was to teach *halakhah*. To accomplish this he often quoted from the *Shulḥan ʿArukh* and its commentaries. "I also promise," he writes in his introduction, "that for each Mishnah which contains a law applicable today, I will briefly provide the development of the law according to the *halakhah*." Elsewhere Lipschütz suggests that for the student of his commentary "the words of the holy Mishnah will become as a *shulḥan ʿarukh*." Clearly, this is not an attempt to treat the Mishnah as an independent corpus for study. The measure of independence given the Mishnah by Lipschütz's commentary is that he provides the accepted *halakhah*, so that one need not search elsewhere. This only frees the person who is studying Mishnah with *Tiferet Yisrael*, from looking in other books, but it attaches the study of the Mishnah and its importance, to all the commentaries and codes developed since the Mishnah became the first evidence of oral Torah.

Short commentaries based primarily on the works of Rashi, Maimonides, Bertinoro and Heller, found their way into printed editions of the Mishnah. Eclectic works, they exerted no influence on the manner in which Mishnah was studied. Among such works are those of: Isaac ibn Gabbai, *Kaf Naḥat* (Venice, 1609f.); Jacob ben Samuel Hagiz, *ʿEṣ Ḥayyim* (Verona 1650 and Leghorn 1653f.); Elisha ben Abraham of Grodno; *Kab We-naqi* (Amsterdam 1697) and Shneior Pheibush ben Jacob, *Melo Kaf Naḥat*.[12]

Of special note are the commentaries of Elijah ben Solomon, the Vilna Gaon (1720-1797). At a time when the study of Hebrew grammar, Scripture and Mishna were largely neglected, he taught them to his students. He also introduced them to other Tannaitic literature such as the *Sifra, Sifré, Mekhilta* and *Tosefta*. The Gaon's Mishnah commentairies—*Shenot Eliyahu on Zeraʿim* (Lemberg, 1799), *Eliyahu Rabbah on Toharot* (Brunn, 1802)—were highly original, as he brought to bear his extensive knowledge of all rabbinic sources and the beginnings of a critical examination of the text itself.

---

[12] Hermann Strack, *Introduction to the Talmud and Midrash*. (Philadelphia, 1931) pp. 145-149.

V

Who studied Mishnah? M. Avot 5 : 21 suggests that schooling began at the age of five. An Amoraic source required waiting until the child was six before beginning formal instruction.[13] In the twelfth century seven was deemed appropriate for starting school.[14] Avot suggests a five year cycle. The first five years were to be spent in the study of Scripture, the next five in the study of Mishnah, and at fifteen one began the study of Talmud.

It is impossible to determine whether the suggestion to spend the years between ten and fifteen were indeed spent in the study of Mishnah. There is the Amoraic dictum that one-third of one's time should be spent in the study of Scripture, another third devoted to the study of Mishnah, and the last third should be used for studying the Talmud.[15] But by the twelfth century, the study of Talmud itself was regarded as complying with this Talmudic saying, since the Babylonian Talmud is "a compound of Scripture, Mishnah and *Gemara*."[16] One source, accepting the tri-part suggestion of Avot, describes a high rate of attrition. "A thousand pupils begin the study of Bible, and a hundred succeed. The hundred continue with the study of Mishnah, and ten succeed. The ten proceed to study Talmud and one succeeds."[17] Everyone, it would seem, studied Scripture and a goodly number continued with the study of Mishnah, but only a few were able to study the Talmud.

A similar rate of failure is noted by Jacob Katz in his evaluation of the *Ḥeder* over a thousand years later:

> The critics of the *Ḥeder* attributed its lack of success in teaching partly to the fact that teachers failed to attune their syllabus to the pupils' age and mental capacity. In the light of these criteria, they should have taken as their goal a thorough knowledge of the Bible and familiarity with the Mishnah. Instead, these goals were regarded merely as preparation for the ultimate aim of education: to turn the pupil into a scholar (Talmid Ḥakham), with a thorough training in Talmud, who eventually mastered its contents and the work of its codifiers ... Though the *Ḥeder* was a

---

[13] b. Ket. 50a.
[14] Maimonides, *Hilkhot Talmud Torah* 2 : 2 and *Schulḥan ʿArukh*, *Yoreh Deʿah* 245 : 5.
[15] b. Qid. 30a; b. A.Z. 19b.
[16] See *Tosafot* to b. Sanh. 24a and Maimonides, *Hilkhot Talmud Torah* 1 : 11; *Shulḥan ʿArukh*, *Yoreh Deʿah* 246 : 4.
[17] Lev. R. 2 : 1.

popular educational institution, it was forced to cater to the aims of the minority. Before the pupils had acquired a fundamental knowledge of the Bible, or even of the Pentateuch, they started to study the Talmud.[18]

Since the goal of traditional Jewish education was always to reach the level of studying *Gemara*, all education before that was mere preparation for that goal.

In the traditional context, Mishnah *qua* Mishnah was not studied. When the text of the Mishnah was utilized, it was used either by children preparing for advanced study, that is of *Gemara*, or by those adults who were not able to study *Gemara*. The *Hevra Mishnayot* of the last century are often spoken of, though hardly any literature of consequence concerning them is available. What they are remembered for is not their learning, but their dedication to *Talmud Torah* as a central ritual of their religion. The *Hevra Mishnayot* consisted of men who wished to express their piety through study, and were not able, for intellectual reasons, to join the *Hevra Shas*, that group of laymen which spent their time studying the six orders, which no longer referred, as once it did, to the Mishnah, but to the *Gemara*, which was its traditional commentary *par excellence*.

Modern study of the Mishnah begins, in a real sense, with Maimonides, for what characterizes modern study is that the Mishnah is regarded as an independent document and not seen merely through the perspective of *Gemara*. Since Maimonides' commentary to the Mishnah was written originally in Arabic, it did not have an immediate impact on the world of rabbinic scholarship. Yet even when it did appear in its entirety in Hebrew (1492), its impact and influence were due to its substance and not to its form. Later commentators understood that form and the method which produced it, and consciously rejected the validity of such an enterprise. Mishnah was to remain bound to the *Gemara*, its first commentary.

---

[18] Jacob Katz, *Tradition and Crisis*. (New York, 1961) p. 191.

PART I

THE ACHIEVEMENT OF JACOB N. EPSTEIN

CHAPTER TWO

JACOB N. EPSTEIN'S *INTRODUCTION TO THE TEXT OF THE MISHNAH*

BARUCH MICAH BOKSER

i

Jacob Naḥum ha-Levi Epstein was born in Lithuania in 1878. After receiving a traditional *yeshiva* training in his youth, he turned to study Semitics in 1907 in the Universities, first of Vienna, and then of Berne. He received his doctorate in 1913. He lived in Berlin until 1925, when he moved to Jerusalem to take the professorship of Talmudic Studies at the Hebrew University—a post he held until his death in 1952. Epstein wrote many articles on Talmudic and post-Talmudic literature.[1] His *Introduction to the Text of the Mishnah*, 1948, hereafter *ITM*, was his only book that he saw published.[2] Three other volumes on Talmudic literature, based on Epstein's lecture notes, appeared posthumously, edited by his pupil E. Z. Melamed,[3] who also edited the second edition of the *ITM*, published in 1964. The *ITM* has changed the nature of all subsequent scholarly study of the Mishnah. The following pages attempt to explain why. I shall first examine Epstein's main thesis, his method and proofs, then summarize the *ITM*, discuss several other points, and conclude with an assessment of the overall importance of this volume.

The *ITM* contains 1308 pages, indexed only in the second edition, and does not read easily. It is composed of eighteen chapters, each of which exhaustively deals with various aspects of the Mishnah and its

---

[1] For a biographical and bibliographical account and references, see Robert Goldenberg, "J. N. Epstein," in J. Neusner, ed., *The Formation of the Babylonian Talmud* (Leiden, 1970: E. J. Brill), pp. 75-6.

[2] He also edited a Geonic commentary on the Mishnah and a medieval rabbinic commentary on the Talmud, *Commentary of the Geonim on Seder Toharot*. (German introduction, Berlin, 1915); (Hebrew edition, introduction and text, Berlin, 1921-1924); *Commentaries of R. Judah b. Natan to Ketuvot* [Hebrew] (Vienna, 1933; Jerusalem, 1933).

[3] On these volumes, see below pp. 37-55.

text. Chapters One through Seven chronologically cover this material from the time of the pre-Mishnah collections through the end of the Talmudic period. Chapter Eight concerns the Mishnah-text used by the Talmudic rabbis, while Chapters Nine and Ten deal with quotations of the Mishnah and their terms. Chapters Eleven through Eighteen examine the written traditions of the Mishnah, including the texts of the Mishnah from the Talmudic and post-Talmudic period, their origin and peculiarities, variants and orthography. As indicated, I shall summarize this material below.

The chapters flow into each other, from point to point. Except for short prefaces and summaries of several chapters, we find no synthetic presentation and evaluation of the material, no statement of thesis or method. Epstein nowhere states what he considers to be the importance of the book as a whole, nor a conception that might unite the diverse chapters. Nevertheless, Epstein's main thesis *is* clear: There is no such thing as *a Mishnah text* with a capital M. Many texts circulated, in the time of its author (whom he identifies as Rabbi Judah the Patriarch,[4] henceforth Rabbi) and afterwards. This can be attributed to three factors.

First, Epstein particularly repeats the following factor in various forms and places:[5] The Mishnah is made up of different sources, taken from earlier Mishnayot and Tannaitic collections. Variations existed among these sources due to differences in style, in the authoritative legal view, and in the evidence of what the earlier authorities had in fact said. From here, Rabbi extracted material and produced his Mishnah. He thus produced inconsistencies within his own work on the bases of the already existing conflicts in the various sources he used and preserved.

Second, Rabbi produced several editions of the Mishnah and also taught his own personal view.

Third, other collections existed both at the same time as, and after, Rabbi. Individual rabbis taught their views of the law on the bases of these collections, or of their particular "authoritative version" of Rabbi's Mishnah. Only when the Mishnah of Rabbi was later accepted as the final authority did the Mishnah become *The Mishnah,* so far as law was concerned. But the existence of internal inconsistencies, several recensions, and distinct collections had already produced

---

[4] See his remarks in his *Introduction to Tannaitic Literature* (Jerusalem, 1957), pp. 200-24. (Henceforth: *ITL*).

[5] He opens his work with these remarks, p. 1.

interpretations and alternative readings, on the basis of which oral reciters of the Mishnah and later scribes doctored the Mishnah text. Furthermore, the written traditions of the Mishnah complicate the matter, for they do not accurately preserve the Mishnah-text of the Talmudic period. Epstein nowhere states that this conception is his thesis. It emerges from the points he makes and the discrete analyses of individual pericopae.

Epstein's method varies. He generally collects, categorizes, and analyzes all texts of a certain kind. Often he does not prove his point but demonstrates the viability of his interpretation. At times he merely alludes to texts, as if they were self-evident and clearly showed his point. Elsewhere, particularly where he explains a Talmudic usage or term, he fully cites texts and analyzes them, bringing all parallels and variants, attempting to explain the differences, especially where different traditions concerning the same statement or event exist. Yet his detailed analyses often go beyond what his point necessitates; the point he makes often does not depend on the validity of his literary and philological conclusions.

ii

Let us now turn to the main thesis. In dealing with the evidence of the disputes before Rabbi about traditions of early masters and of the formation of early Tannaitic collections, Epstein only surveys and cites texts, rarely representing and examining them. Perhaps he later added this material for the sake of completeness of his presentation.[6] Consequently, we do not clearly know Epstein's views on the proper use of sources not contemporary with the events and statements that they record. Thus, in our case, how shall we use the Mishnah, edited ca. 200 C.E., and other extant Tannaitic collections to understand events and personalities of 100 years earlier? This important historical and methodological problem is only now being systematically investigated.[7] To demonstrate the existence of differences among early collections in disputes of the House of Shammai and the House of Hillel, Epstein refers to Tos. M.S. 2 : 12 (Lieberman ed. p. 253, 1. 69):

[6] Only pages 5-7 deal with this material. Significantly, he thoroughly covers this material in his *ITL*, pp. 21-180. Perhaps he had already projected this longer treatment when he published the *ITM*.

[7] See Jacob Neusner, *Development of a Legend* (Leiden, 1970); and *The Rabbinic Traditions About the Pharisees Before 70* (Leiden, 1971).

R. Yosi said, "This [the above text in the Tos., = M. M.S. 3 : 7] is the Mishnah of R. ʿAqiba, but the first Mishnah [mišnah rišonah, is] . . . ."

This text would indicate that people at the time of R. Yosi recognized the existence of both an early corpus and a later corpus of R. ʿAqiba's teachings—each presenting a different construction of a Houses' dispute. But what does this say concerning the nature of the First Mishnah (mišnah rišonah), which Epstein refers to in quotes but nowhere defines? Significantly, Lieberman's edition has mišnat rišonah, literally "the Mishnah of the First," and he suggests that the original reading is "the Mishnah of the First Ones" (mišnat rišonim). He further points out that the PT parallel reads "but the words of the sages" (ʾaval divre-ḥakhamim), and therefore suggests that Yosi is not really referring to (a/the) "early Mishnah," but merely to the view of the rabbis. He uses this formula here in a praiseworthy fashion, for the law follows their position.[8]

Epstein's other references to disputes between the Mishnah of R. ʿAqiba and the Mishnah of the Sages, between the students of R. ʿAqiba, Meir and Judah, Yosi and Simeon, are of the same fashion. Thus Epstein's point, that before Rabbi disputes existed concerning the views of early masters, is not really controversial. But he hardly makes an exhaustive presentation.

Epstein argues that these differences of what the early masters had said and those of language and style became embedded in separate collections, which Rabbi used and which thereby caused inner inconsistencies in the Mishnah. He underscores the meaning of Talmudic remarks that refer to these phenomena. He then argues that these varied sources exist elsewhere, even where not stated by the Talmuds. Thus for the presence of different sources in the Mishnah, he refers to M. Ḥal. 1 : 6:

> Flour paste [MʿYSH = boiling water in dough].
> The House of Shammai declare free [from the requirement to give Ḥallah].
> And the House of Hillel make liable.
> Dumplings [ḥalyta—flour paste in boiling water].
> The House of Shammai make liable.
> And the House of Hillel declare free.

Epstein points out that no actual difference exists between the flour paste and the dumplings—only the order of placing the boiling

[8] *Tosetta Kifshutah* (New York, 1955), II, pp. 740-41. (Henceforth: *TK*).

water—and therefore the same law should apply to both. He then refers to Talmudic passages, y. Ḥal. 1 : 6, 58a, b. Pes. 37b, that recognize that the text represents two Tannaitic views. The first part follows the Mishnah of R. Yosi, who includes flour paste as one of the leniencies of the House of Shammai, as it is stated in M. ʿEd. 5 : 2:

> R. Yosi says, "[The following] six things are among the leniencies of the House of Shammai and among the stringencies of the House of Hillel:
> . . .
> Flour paste (HMʿYŚH).
> The House of Shammai declare free.
> And the House of Hillel declare liable."

The second half of the Mishnah comes from the corpus of R. Meir who considers flour paste one of the stringencies of the House of Shammai. The Mishnah elsewhere also contains his view; M. ʿEd. ch. 4, which lists leniencies of the House of Shammai and the stringencies of the House of Hillel, does not include flour paste. In fact, it is to this list that R. Yosi had made his addition.[9]

Epstein's many examples of the use of variant language in the different collections, Mishnah and Tosefta, Mishnah and *Halakhic Midrashim*, and within the Mishnah itself, show that we are dealing with distinct collections and sources. The following example is representative: Two Mishnayot concerning the same object use two different words, reflecting the fact that each is based on a different source. Suk. 4 : 10 calls the vessel for the Water Libation a "golden jar" (*ḥavit šel zahav*), while Me. 3 : 7 calls it a "golden pitcher" (*kad šel zahav*).[10] We may observe, however, that when different collections use different language they do not always reflect different sources. Thus Tosefta uses many Greek terms whose equivalents in Mishnah are Hebrew words. Does this mean that Tosefta uses a different source from Mishnah? Or does Tosefta better reflect the language of the time when it was composed or edited, indicating the increased use of Greek? The latter would argue that the Mishnah was either edited earlier, or that it preserves the language already found in its sources.[11]

---

[9] *ITM*, pp. 2, 7. See *TK*, II, pp. 791-91. The previous reference to Ḥal. 1 : 6 is dealt with on *ITM*, p. 5. For a full study of the Houses' disputes, see Neusner, *The Rabbinic Traditions, op. cit.*

[10] *ITM*, p. 3.

[11] The latter would also mean that less Greek was spoken in the first two centuries than later. This is consistent with Fitzmyer's warning not to judge the nature of the language of the first century on the bases of second and third century—and later—sources. See J. A. Fitzmyer, "The Language of Palestine in the First Century

Epstein has thus further refined source criticism of Mishnah—the attempt to get behind the text and to reconstruct its sources. One cannot accept a text at face value and understand it both literally and historically, without first establishing what were the original forms of the statements and how they were shaped and adapted to fit into the Mishnah.

In the first chapter, Epstein demonstrates in great length the continued presence of separate collections and describes their relation to Rabbi's Mishnah. These collections complement or supplement the Mishnah, or sometimes their authors seem totally unaware of the Mishnah of Rabbi—with laws following a different construction and pattern of *Beraitot*. Epstein continually refers to and demonstrates how the Talmuds contrast and explicitly recognize the distinct individuality of these collections—by commenting on how a particular *baraita*, for example, that of R. Ḥiyya, complements or disputes the Mishnah. The former is done with the phrase 'the Mishnah needs the *baraita*, and the *baraita* needs the Mishnah.' One typical example is y. Shab. 1 : 5, 3a:

> A man should not sit before the barber near *Minḥah* time until he prays. We learn "near *Minḥah*." R. Ḥiyya teaches "near darkness."

> Our Mishnah needs the Mishnah of R. Ḥiyya. The Mishnah of R. Ḥiyya. needs our Mishnah. If Ḥiyya taught and we did not learn ours . . . . Or if we learn ours, and R. Ḥiyya did not teach, we would say . . . . In that we taught "*Minḥah*" and R. Ḥiyya taught "darkness" . . . .

Epstein notes that the PT includes a second interpretation of the relationship of these two texts—an interpretation which also underlines the distinct nature of "our Mishnah" and that of R. Ḥiyya. This is the interpretation of the Caesarean rabbis who identify the view of the Mishnah as following R. Judah, and that of R. Ḥiyya, the sages, both views known from elsewhere.[12] Epstein thus grounded his thesis on internal proof—the existence of different language and legal views in the Mishnah and in other collections; and on indirect testimony—the use of language by the Talmud in quoting and in referring to *beraitot* "that would not be used of [different] readings of our Mishnah."[13]

A.D.", *CBQ* 32 (1970), pp. 501-31. Would it also mean, though, that Mishnah may reflect the earlier period? See L. Ginzberg, "The Mishnah Tamid," *Journal of Jewish Law and Philosophy*, 1 (1919), 33ff.; and *ITL*, pp. 27-31, 34-5, 39-40, 44, and 46.

[12] *ITM*, pp. 32-3. See S. Lieberman, *Hayerushalmi Kiphshuto* (Jerusalem, 1934), pp. 18-9. (Henceforth: *YK*.)

[13] *ITM*, p. 164.

Epstein further argues that although these collections do not enlighten us about the Mishnah's original readings, they are indirectly important for establishing the correct text, because the oral reciters and copyists later changed the Mishnah texts on the bases of these *beraitot*. The only direct source that Epstein points to that would indicate that the reciters did doctor the Mishnah text is M. Zev. 14 : 3 and its BT comments, b. Zev. 114b:

> An offering whose time was not yet come [may be such] either by virtue of itself or of its owner. Which is an offering whose time is not yet come by virtue of its owner? If the owner was a man or a woman that had a flux or a woman after childbirth or a leper, and they offered their Sin-offering or their Guilt-offering outside [before its appointed time], they are not culpable. If they offered their Whole-offering or their Peace-offering outside, they are culpable.
>
> [trans. Danby p. 489]

> And are not men and women who had a flux or a woman who gave birth liable to Guilt-offerings?
> Ze'iri said, "Recite (*teni*) 'leper' among them."
> "Whole-offerings and Peace-offerings," And are not these liable for Peace-offerings?
> R. Sheshet said, "Recite (*teni*), 'Nazarean' among them." That of Ze'iri the reciters fixed (*qab'ua*), that of Sheshet the reciters did not fix in the Mishnah.

Here the BT records two "emendations" and the anonymous Talmud remarks that the reciters, indeed, entered one into the Mishnah and not the other. Epstein notes that all the texts and manuscripts of the Mishnah, except for three, contain Ze'iri's reading. Thus the Mishnah was emended on the basis of the BT.[14] He feels this text provides a dating for Mishnah doctoring—from the time of Ze'iri, but before Sheshet, for the "emendation" of Ze'iri was included and not that of Sheshet. But Epstein himself shows that "recite" (*teni*) may refer to reciting in the Mishnah-corpus or legal teachings of the spokesman himself, and not necessarily in the Mishnah of Rabbi. Therefore, this is not necessarily an emendation.[15] Perhaps Ze'iri and Sheshet did not emend the Mishnah but taught its laws differently in their own collections.[16]

---

[14] *Ibid.*, pp. 436-37.
[15] *Ibid.*, p. 177. See below pp. 30-32.
[16] See H. Albeck, *Studies in Baraita and Tosefta* (Jerusalem, 1944) (Hebrew), pp. 24-5; and *Introduction to the Talmuds* (Tel-Aviv, 1969), p. 419.

Secondly, the anonymous observation of the BT can date from as late as Saboraic times. It only indicates the then-present situation. In addition, the mere fact that our present Mishnah-text contains the first "emendation" and not the second need not mean that the doctoring had to occur before the second "emendation" was offered. For if one can find a rationale for the superiority of one reading and "emendation" over the other—which Epstein himself refers to—could that not account for the presence of that reading and the lack of the other? Could that not explain why a later reciter doctored the Mishnah only on the basis of that "emendation"? Epstein has thus shown only that reciters doctored the Mishnah text, but not when they did so. In addition, he offers strong evidence that scribes added to the Mishnah. By comparing manuscripts to printed editions, we note that such additions often stand out, especially when the Talmudic discussion presupposes the lack of a clause or a less complete clause. Some manuscripts even indicate the presence of an addition with a notation "an addition" (TWŚPH as in M. Ket. 7 : 6.[17]

Epstein quite often assumes the presence of a doctored text in his textual analyses.[18] I believe he does so too often, and other factors can at times explain the Mishnah readings. When the two Talmuds quote separate *beraitot*, each reflecting a different Mishnah recension, and the Mishnah in the BT or in the PT reads in accord with one of the *beraitot* and/or a single Amoraic view, despite a discussion in the Talmud that might presuppose a different reading, cannot that Mishnah reading reflect one of these *baraita* traditions or that of the single Amora? Must the Mishnah always have been doctored? In addition, we must remember that we cannot automatically consider the Mishnah of the BT and of the PT to be the Mishnah the Amoraim actually used.[19] Furthermore, one may rely on this assumption too often in explaining a reading. Indeed, Epstein presents us with no canons for its use and limitations. When shall we maintain that such a doctoring took place? Or when shall we say that the Mishnah-text may merely reflect one of the readings and interpretations cited within the Talmud itself? One such criterion suggests itself to the present writer: When the Mishnah reads unsmoothly, with a mixed reading

---

[17] *ITM*, p. 950. See pp. 419, 946-79. See D. Halivni, *Meqorot*, p. 215.
[18] E. g., pp. 22, 25, 27, 48, 58, 75-6, 78, 94, 112, 127-28, 132, and 198.
[19] See p. 100. Compare pp. 171, 191 with 673-726, 897-946, and 1269-84. Perhaps Epstein was partially motivated by his apparent conception of separate Babylonian and Palestinian Mishnah traditions. See below, pp. 33-34.

evident, one should look for the possibility of a doctored text.[20] Epstein has thus proven the existence of doctored texts.

iii

Epstein was interested in collecting all the materials that shed light on the knowledge of the Mishnah and its role in different generations and places. In order to appreciate the breadth of his work, I shall survey and summarize the material he has covered.

There was not one Codex of Mishnah. Different traditions existed of what the early Tannaim had said, not variants of a single text. Rabbi on the basis of these variant sources wove the Mishnah, selecting clauses from different Tannaitic collections, each with its own style, thus producing a text in which various sorts of style proliferate. Rabbi published the Mishnah several times,[21] and expounded his own personal view of the law and recited early traditions. At each of these stages and teachings, Rabbi might and did change his mind on various points. Thus various recensions of the Mishnah and teachings of Rabbi circulated; different people read and taught Mishnah differently. In addition, there existed alternative collections of Tannaitic sayings, even after Rabbi's Mishnah, which were not necessarily consistent with the Mishnah. Since the Mishnah contained different sources, it did not always have the same relationship with these different collections; the relationship in any one place depended on the particular sources that the editors of the Mishnah and of the other collections had chosen to use in their respective collections.

Within the academy of Rabbi was found an additional, supplementary corpus. Further, the corpus of R. Ḥiyya, generally complemented the Mishnah of Rabbi, with portions paralleling it and offering to it explanations, additions, as well as different traditions of the material and new laws. The corpus of R. Hoshaiah, on the other hand, although paralleling the Mishnah, also included explanations often reflecting alternative constructions of the disputes in Mishnah collections older than or of the same time as that of Rabbi. Reciters of the *Beraitot*, who felt their version of the law authentic, and later

---

[20] *ITM*, p. 92, and *TK*, I p. 173. Compare the case on *ITM*, p. 21, concerning M. B.M. 5 : 1, where Epstein seems oblivious to the possibility that the variation in the Mishnah reading and its law can be due to a changed economic conditions — the rising inflation — which is implicit in the two variants. See, however, p. 22 fn. 6.

[21] See esp. *ibid.*, pp. 17-8.

copyists and scribes of the Talmud text corrupted our text of the Mishnah.

The second section of the *ITM* examines the status of the Mishnah among the first two generations of Amoraim, the fellows and students of Rav and R. Yoḥanan. These rabbis formed a transition period between the later Tannaim and the Amoraim, between variant language (ḥilufē lašon) of Mishnayot and between emendations. The rabbis involved here include: Rav, Samuel, Yoḥanan, Resh Laqish, Eleazar, Yosi b. Ḥanina, Huna, Judah, and Zeʿiri. Epstein individually examines each of them as to a) his date and associates; b) the nature of his sources of Tannaitic material, especially Mishnah; and his teachers. He indicates whether the Amora had direct or indirect information from Rabbi or his immediate students or his contemporaries, or from other Tannaim; and finally, c) his relationship to the Mishnah and the Mishnah-text. Epstein examines to what degree the Amora accepted the Mishnah's authority or practiced freedom therefrom. How did he harmonize contradictory sources with the Mishnah and inner-Mishnaic contradictions, or deal with other Mishnah difficulties?

Epstein's analysis shows that Amoraim had access to Tannaitic traditions and Rabbi's material, either themselves directly or through their own teachers. Since the Mishnah-text was reliable, they did not have to emend the Mishnah. Further, they rejected the Mishnah — to lesser and greater degrees — because of a textual difficulty or preference for another non-Mishnah text or tradition. In their independence from the Mishnah, they taught the Mishnah-law either in their own corpus or merely as a separate law, in accord with their own view of the authentic and authoritative law.[22]

Of note are the following observations: Yoḥanan initiated a new form of Mishnah interpretation, the splitting of the Mishnah into parts, into teachings of two different Tannaim. He thus called attention to the presence of different sources in the Mishnah. He also recognized the presence of contradictory reasoning used in different statements of the same Tanna. Judah recited the Mishnah and worked it over *halakhically* in order to expound the law.

Epstein's third section, called "emendations," (*hagahot*), deals with the second "half" of the Amoraic period in Babylonia and Palestine. The rabbis of this period no longer have first-hand knowledge of

---

[22] *Ibid.*, pp. 205, 179, 245, See below, pp. 30-32.

Rabbi's teachings; their link is now at least once removed. As the Mishnah-text is less accurately preserved, its readings are no longer so reliable, which accounts for the greater freedom in reading the Mishnah-text with a greatly increased number of actual emendations. Epstein here examines the particular people involved, with the same questions and method as in the previous chapter. In Chapters Four and Five, Epstein covers this same period by examining questions the Talmud asked concerning the Mishnah and the Mishnah experts, both characteristic features of this period.

This period can be divided into two or, more correctly, three subdivisions. The first consists of the Amoraim before Joseph: Ḥisda, Naḥman b. Jacob, Sheshet, and Rabbah b. Naḥmani—all in Babylonia. These had, once or twice removed, knowledge of Rabbi's teachings. They know other Tannaitic sources and collections, notably Ḥisda, Sheshet, and especially Naḥman b. Jacob. Along with the old methods of Mishnah study, they used new methods. Thus Ḥisda not only isolated the Mishnah into different sources, but he also recognized the presence of *lapsus linguae*. The Amoraim have not yet accepted the superiority of the Mishnah's authority; they still feel free to reject the Mishnah law, and prefer that of a *baraita*. Many Mishnah comments do not yet fully emend the Mishnah, but present explanations and *halakhic* rejections of the Mishnah.[23] Sheshet's willingness to rearrange the names and opinions in a Mishnah dispute with less restraint than his predecessors (*'epokh*) represents the growing freedom.[24]

The second stage in this period comes with R. Joseph—whom Epstein separately studies in Chapter Five—an expert in Mishnah-text and sources, and his students Abaye and Rava. They originated and first used many of the terms of Mishna-text criticism, including "the relation is defective" (*ḥasorē meḥasrāʾ*), "transpose" (*'epokh*), "say" (*'emaʾ*), and "recite" (*tenī*). Many of the anonymous usages of these terms come from their academy. Abaye showed particular interest in the Mishnah-text, explanations, and inferences, and especially adapted the above terms, giving them wide circulation. He did not show unrestrained freedom from the Mishnah. He attempts to harmonize *beraitot* that contradict the Mishnah, by giving a forced interpretation to the Mishnah. As a last resort he will admit that they disagree. Rava

---

[23] *ITM*, p. 353.
[24] *Ibid.*

was very meticulous with the Mishnah-text, taking fewer freedoms with it than Abaye. He wanted, in particular, a smooth text and, therefore, used the eliptical rule of *ḥasorē meḥasrā'*, significantly not used by Abaye. Papa and Zevid continue the work and methods of this stage. Ashi and Ravina represent the third stage of this period. They had little to say concerning the Mishnah. The former only offers one—later to be rejected—comment, which according to Epstein is an explanation. The latter offers several explanations but no emendations.

The process in Palestine parallels that of Babylonia. Epstein examines two Palestinians: R. Yonah, who showed freedom from the Mishnah in rejecting it, but did not emend it; and R. Manah, who offered some emendations and various Mishnah comments. By the end of this period, the Mishnah is accepted as the Law Code, the final authority, with its text basically worked out. Concomitantly, the rabbis no longer centered their discussion around the Mishnah, but around the supra-Mishnaic comments.

The fourth chapter analyzes the doubts and questions concerning the reading and meaning of the Mishnah, queries which greatly increased from the third Amoraic generation on. The most common type of question opened with "it was asked of him" (*'ebayeh lahu*). Epstein argues and demonstrates that we must distinguish between questions of explanations and questions inquiring about actual readings of the variants and the language. The latter often affect the meanings, which can in fact be the unstated reason for the question. These questions may be based upon: 1) a *baraita* with a different reading; 2) dialectal differences in pronunciation; and 3) known Tannaitic disputes. Increased distance from direct traditions of Tannaitic sources and Rabbi's school created the need for systematic experts in the Mishnah-text and its sources, the subject of the fifth chapter. These experts, called *baalé Mishnah*, involved themselves systematically in the research of the Mishnah sources, checked its readings, compared them, and even gave notations on the correct reading. Naḥman b. Isaac and Judah, in Palestine, particularly stand out in giving these notations.

While the rabbis accepted the Mishnah, they knew other traditions and *beraitot*. Therefore, the experts also attempted to harmonize the different sources with the Mishnah (R. Judah). They held the early Amoraic statements in such respect that they also had to harmonize them with the Mishnah. Thus, once one ceased to uncover new material, one had to decide both how to relate to the given material, the alternative traditions and explanations of the Mishnah, and how to remember the correct reading and interpretation. Some scholars, including Naḥman b. Isaac and Mar Zuṭra, attempted, on the other hand, to prove that particular alternative readings both have a valid basis. They used the phrase "one who teaches x is not mistaken" (*man detenī x lo mištabeš*).

As Epstein had previously argued that the third Amoraic generation marked the rise in emendations of the Mishnah, he exhaustively collects, in the sixth chapter, the various types, with their specific terms, whether offered anonymously or by an identified person. He argues that these emendations were traditional, authoritative, and already known in Palestine.[25] He notes, as well, that the rabbis emended *beraitot* with and without these terms. By comparing all the usages of the respective terms and their appearances in the BT sections with their PT parallels, Epstein demonstrates the particular meaning of these terms and their equivalents. He pays special attention to show their emendational or explanatory usage, or both, whatever be the case. The PT uses four terms for emendation: "thus we learn" (*kēynī matnītīn*), "there is not here—but" (*lēt kan—'el'a*), "not here" (*'en kan*), and "there is not here" (*lēt kān*), Epstein examines in depth the first of these. He finds that this term dates relatively late, while the "last editors of the Talmud" later superimposed it on earlier examples of the process, which had lacked, naturally, the introductory term. Significantly, of the 96 usages (plus 1 without the opening phrase), 62 (+1) are explanations or quotes of a Mishnah or of a *baraita*.

Epstein discusses five of the BT terms that he lists[26] —"recite" (*tenī*), "say" (*'em'a*), "thus it is written" (*hakhi qatanī*), "thus it is said" (*hakhi qa'mar*), "this is not a Mishnah" (*'ena mišnah*), "remove from here" (*samē mēkan*), "transpose" (*'ēpokh*), "thus we learn" (*kēn matnitan*), and "join and teach" (*kerokh vatani*). Epstein thus demonstrates marked interest in the Mishnah and its text, with the rabbis' paying great attention to the proper reading of the Mishnah itself, no longer just teaching a different corpus of their own. The increased distance from Tannaitic traditions resulted in a less reliable Mishnah-text and an increased number of emendations.

Chapter Seven studies the eliptical rule of *ḥasuré meḥasra*, the queries concerning a Mishnaic lacuna. Only the BT uses this term,

---

[25] *Ibid.*, p. 44.
[26] Compare the list on p. 439 with that of p. 509.

which occurs from the time of Rava on. The questions concern either a reading brought into question by a seemingly contradictory source or an unsmoothness in the Mishnah, which indicates a missing link. The latter includes a cited case in the Mishnah-text that apparently contradicts the law of the very Mishnah, or a dangling unconnected law in the Mishnah. Though the PT lacks this term, its teachers are familiar with this phenomena. According to Epstein, most of these Talmudic remarks are not emendations, but explanations and quotations of the Mishnah. He finds unacceptable, however, the BT's usual solution of either delineating a separate situation for the clause of the Mishnah or introducing into the text a new and later concept or a Babylonian exegesis. This is not to say that lacunae do not exist. They do. In fact, some are purposely present. In addition, where there is not a lacuna, the roughness of the Mishnah can also be explained.

Excluding the cases where the problem is imagined, lacunae are due to the editor of the Mishnah and the nature of his method. The roughness comes from the differences in the several sources that were put together in forming the Mishnah. The lacunae reflect two Tannaitic views not formed into a smooth unit. Alternatively, Rabbi used a source and either changed the language of the *Ur*-Mishnah, and the wording and style became, thereby, difficult, or he changed the order, leaving the language; or he deleted items from the original text; or he took the Mishnah from a different matrix, where its references had been clear. In addition, Rabbi may have intended the awkward construction to indicate that the second view is a dissenting view.[27] This chapter thus not only demonstrates one way in which the rabbis related to the Mishnah, but also shows the necessity to understand the editing process of the Mishnah itself and the problems of its language and reading. Otherwise, false canons for establishing a correct reading may be used.

The eighth chapter investigates the preservation and use of the Mishnah in the Babylonian and Palestinian academies. For the rabbis studied and quoted the Mishnah through professional memory-banks, the reciters, the oral transmitters of the Mishnah, *tanna* in Aramaic, *šonēh* in Hebrew, and *deuterotēs* in Greek. In reciting the Mishnah-text, the Tannaim did the following:

a) Circumscribed and modified its language, changing unclean language or language offensive to the master or students.

---

[27] *Ibid.*, pp. 606, 605, and 598.

b) Participated in discussions, answering questions or queries. These, though, were not the 'normal' reciters, for most were considered "empty heads" by the Babylonians (in contrast to the Palestinians, who held the reciters in high esteem).

c) Emended the Mishnah they were quoting at the directive of the Amora, often to make it conform to a certain view of the law.

d) Quoted Mishnayot that contradicted the Mishnah.

e) Recited accompanying *beraitot*, especially in Babylonia where there arose a new type of *beraitot* consisting of a short explanation to the Mishnah and a declaration of the law.

As is to be expected, Epstein examines the terms that the Talmud uses in the quotation of these texts: "teaches" (*tāne*), which precedes the main text; and "teaches" (*matni*), which introduces the explanation of the text. The reciters often recited these explanatory additions along with the Mishnah as a unit, and, at times, they have been introduced into our Mishnah-text. We find extant the following: explanations of works, verse parallels and Biblical proof, and law declarations. As with other institutions, Epstein traces the references and nature of the Tanna into Geonic times, demonstrating its continued existence. Epstein argues that there existed a written Mishnah text throughout the rabbinic period, but that study was oral, and only if something was forgotten was the written text consulted.[28]

Considering the nature of the reciters, even if they had all started out with the same text, it is not surprising that variants arose. Different reciters recited the Mishnah differently. Since each academy and scholar had his own "walking book," each would have different texts. Thus clear differences and variants existed in Mishnah readings between Babylonia and Palestine, and within Babylonia itself, from academy to academy—a fact reflected in the variation in Mishnah references within the BT from one tractate to another. Thus the professional reciters provided the Mishnah readings on the basis of memory, and not of the written text. Some reciters knew by heart explanations to the Mishnah; many, however, remained oblivious of the Mishnah's meaning. Variants existed due to the presence of different reciters in different academies.

In the ninth chapter, Epstein collects and categorizes by term early rabbinic quotations and references to texts found in the Mishnah, to

---

[28] Compare S. Lieberman, *Hellenism in Jewish Palestine* (New York, 1950), pp. 83-99; and Y. Kutscher, "Leshon Ḥazal", *Sefer Ḥanokh Yalon* (Jerusalem, 1963), pp. 246, 249.

see where they are present and to determine the type of quotation. The sources he deals with include the following: The Mishnah itself, for quotations of an earlier *Ur*-Mishnah by a later strata; the Legal Midrashim;[29] Seder Eliahu Rabbah;[30] the *Yelamdenu* Midrashim; the Geonic and post-Geonic literature. He examines, in addition, quotations in the BT and the PT. Several of his important observations are as follows: The Amoraim did not all know the Mishnah perfectly, nor were they familiar with all six orders. This was the job of the reciters. Some scholars, though, also served as reciters. Second, the Talmuds attribute precedence and greater authority to the Mishnah over the *beraitot*. In the quotations themselves, one finds the Mishnah at times shortened, paraphrased, expanded to include explanations, and its order of things changed.

The next chapter examines the terms that introduce quotations. Epstein finds that most of the terms do not uniquely serve to refer to the Mishnah, but serve to introduce quotations from *beraitot* and, occasionally, statements. The sharp distinction associated later with some of these terms—e.g. "we learn" (*tenan*) for the Mishnah and "it was taught" (*tania*) for a *baraita*—originates in post-Talmudic times, superimposed by later "correctors" on the texts. The numbers that missed their eye and hand convincingly testify, along with the manuscript evidence, to the original situation. The reason for the original situation and the later "change" is clear: *Beraitot* along with Mishnayot were considered Mishnayot until the Mishnah of Rabbi became accepted as *the* Mishnah and of supreme authority.[31]

The concluding eight chapters deal with the written text of the Mishnah in its various witnesses and forms. In an early period, the rabbis divided the Mishnah into chapters and *halakhot*, divisions already mentioned in the BT and the PT. Later arrangers of the Talmud, in order to facilitate study and understanding, included a lemma (*pisqa*) of the Mishnah before its respective gemara. The internal lemmas are "early", dating from the time of the last editors of the Talmud. These are: "Our rabbis learnt" (*teno rabbanan*); "We learn" (*tenan*); in the PT particularly—"Recite" (*tani*), "in that it is recited" (*mideqatane*), and "it is recited" (*qatane*); and in the BT

---

[29] See now E. Z. Melamed, *The Relationship Between the Halakhic Midrashim and the Mishnah and Tosefta* (Jerusalem, 1967), (Hebrew).

[30] This work, however, is now dated later. See M. Zucker, *Rav Sadya Gaon's Translation of the Torah* (New York, 1959), pp. 205-06.

[31] *ITM*, pp. 776, 778.

particularly—"They learnt" (*tano*), and "the master said". These readings of the Mishnah are thus not necessarily the Mishnah-text that the Amoraim had.[32]

Later lemmas found in all manuscripts and before the Geonim also date from late Saboraic times.[33] Here short lemmas, with or without an introductory notation (*matna* or *pisqa*) and some partially inserted lemmas were placed in their respective locale. After the Mishnayot entered the Talmud text, scribes removed many of the lemmas. In the BT scribes first indicated Mishnayot in their place, in the margin or on the side of the page, and later hands entered them into the text itself. They are thus not originally part of the Talmud. Thus one can not consider the Mishnah of the BT "the Babylonian Mishnah" nor the one automatically used in Talmudic times. One can rely on the Mishnayot of the PT even less than on those of the BT. Epstein demonstrates that the scribe of the Leiden manuscript added the Mishnah at the beginning of each chapter.[34] The text he used consisted of an Italian text, similar to that of the Parma Mishnah manuscript. Thus it is not a pure Palestinian Mishnah-text. In most of the PT, there are found Mishnayot in the respective places, indicated by a "*halakha x*" and the beginning of the Mishnah passage. At some places, the Mishnah has been inserted without indication. Of note, a scribe added the introductory terms (*matn̄* and *pis̄*) in the PT on the basis of the BT. The lemmas in the PT are quite corrupt, full of many mistakes, often placed in the wrong spot.

In the twelfth chapter Epstein collects the additions and supplements to the Mishnah, for the Mishnah had parts added to the original text. These include: (1) emendations, comments and explanations that reciters had fit into the Mishnah; (2) complete laws and Tannaitic disputes, taken from *beraitot* and Tosefta material taught in conjunction with the Mishnah and from Amoraic and Talmudic statements. Some texts indicate the additional nature of this material. And (3) additions and supplements at the end of tractates, taken either from *beraitot*—to finish on a "good" tone, or from Tosefta—to complete the Mishnah with these laws.

---

[32] *Ibid.*, p. 900-06, See p. 909.

[33] *Ibid.*, p. 916.

[34] The importance of Epstein's conclusion is increased by Lieberman's finding that the Venice first edition of the PT is based solely on the Leiden manuscript, and not on three manuscripts as is claimed in its colophon. See S. Lieberman "Yerushalmi Horayot", *Jubilee Volume for H. Albeck* (Jerusalem, 1963), pp. 283-305.

Epstein then examines the divisions of the Mishnah, attempting to determine their antiquity and rationale. All these divisions, into six orders, 63 Babylonian and 60 Palestinian tractates, chapters, and individual Mishnayot come from Talmudic times. The sequence of the orders (*sedarim*) varied according to study needs, while that of the tractates remained relatively set—based on the number of chapters. These divisions reflect the existence of an edited corpus as a distinct volume.

Epstein evaluates together common variants in the Mishnah-text. He exhaustively collects and categories these variants, including for example: The presence or absence of "even" (*'af*); the use of "and thus" (*vekhen*) to join two laws; the conjunctive, disjunctive, and explicative usages of "and" (W); and variants in the names of Tannaim, e.g., Eliezer and Eleazar. Epstein's careful examination warns us not to evaluate an isolated variant without first comparing its usage throughout the manuscripts and texts. Similarly, one must look at orthographic variations, for example the exchange of letters and pronunciation of *b*— and *p*—, as part of a whole and not as an isolated phenomenon. One must consider both the type of variation and its place. Dialectal usages, real mistakes, and manuscript peculiarities, among other factors, cause these variations. Of note, one can find old grammatical forms in manuscripts, which have been distorted by scribes and copyists to the more normal forms.

None of the post-Talmudic Mishnah texts preserves a pure Babylonian or Palestinian tradition. They have all been doctored on the bases of the BT and the PT. The several remnants of a Palestinian type and spelling are hardly pure. The printed editions, too, have been corrupted. The Mishnah-text in the first edition of Maimonides' commentary, Naples 1492, is the intermediary text between Palestinian and Babylonian recensions.[35] Scribes and copy editors gradually further doctored subsequent texts on the basis of the BT, so that we find that by the time of the Justinian, 1546/7, edition, the Mishnah becomes almost totally harmonized with the BT. In the final chapter, Epstein identifies and describes the work of the copy editors of the printed texts.

iv

I shall now examine several of Epstein's main points.
Many terms and references which ostensibly emend the Mishnah in

[35] *ITM*, p. 1282.

actuality do not: they only refer to teaching the law in a separate Mishnah corpus or as a separate law, according to the individual's personal view of the law. Epstein shows a marked tendency so to interpret texts, particularly those from early Amoraic times. Epstein emphasizes this interpretation in connection with the following cases—the first dealing with Rav and the second with Yoḥanan.

M. ʿEruv. 1 : 1 has the following discussion in the PT ʿEruv. 1 : 1, 18d, and a slightly different and shortened parallel in the BT ʿEruv. 2b:

> If the alley entry ... If the entry is wider than ten cubits it must be made narrower; yet if it has the shape of a doorway, even though it is wider than ten cubits, it need not be made narrower.
>
> Ḥananiah b. Shilimyʿ used to teach [texts with explanations][36] to Ḥiyya the son of Rav. Rav looked out the window. He said to him, "It is not here" (*lēt kan*) [the clause "yet if it has the shape ... narrower" is not to be read here]. The other said to him, "And was it not taught here [in the text]?"
>
> He answered him, "Teach it, and proclaim that it is not here."
>
> R. Judah taught to Ḥiyya b. Rav before Rav, "It need not be made narrower."
>
> He said to him, "Teach (*'tnayyeh*), 'it need be made narrower.'"

Epstein reads the BT passage in the light of the PT. It means that Rav does not emend the Mishnah text, for he teaches the Mishnah as it is, he only rejects its legal position. Epstein relies on this interpretation to fix some of the usages of "it is not here" (*let kan*) and "recite" (*tenī*): they do not emend the Mishnah but reject its legal position.[37] Epstein's method follows his pattern of first calling attention to a case where there is inner Talmudic evidence and then demonstrating the viability of his interpretation in other cases where there is no such evidence.

Yoḥanan too does not emend the Mishnah; he teaches his view as a separate law. The important passage is y. Shev. 1 : 1, 33a:

> R. Qeruspi[38] said in the name of R. Yoḥanan: "Rabban Gamaliel and his court permitted the prohibition of the first two chapters [Shev. 1 : 1 and 2 : 1] ...."
>
> Let them then uproot them from the Mishnah?
>
> R. Qeruspi said in the name of R. Yoḥanan, "For [the contingency] if they want to retract, they can retract."

---

[36] See *YK*, p. 226.

[37] Epstein notes the difference in the names of the student, R. Judah, but does not try to account for it, *ITM*, p. 205. See p. 179.

[38] There are several readings of this name. See Albeck, *Introduction, op.cit.*, p. 263; and Jastrow, S. V., *Krispa*, p. 1421a.

Epstein paraphrases this text, emphasizing the point he wants to draw out: "Even though they had permitted the two chapters, they did not tamper with the Mishnah-text—whether because of the reason attributed to Yoḥanan or because of another reason suggested there by R. Yonah ...." On this basis one must understand all the "emendations" of Yoḥanan: they do not uproot the Mishnah-reading, they only arrange it consistently with views alternative and contradictory to the Mishnah, on the basis of parallel contradictory sources.[39]

Although Epstein's analyses in these cases are clear and convincing, he fails to provide criteria for the use of his interpretation. When should we interpret texts along these lines and when not? Where should we see emendation and where a teaching of a separate law or corpus?[40] One quite limited criterion would consist in looking for consistency in an individual Amora: If there is proof of a "separate teaching" or of an emendation-usage, then try to read all his statements in that light.

Another point emphasized by Epstein is that the greater the distance from Talmudic times and sources from the Mishnah itself, the less reliable became the Mishnah text. Amoraim, therefore, took greater liberties with it, including actual emendations. This proposition assumes that early Amoraic Mishnah comments are generally not actual emendations, and that the third generation marks a rise in emendations. This Epstein has quite adequately proved. Nevertheless, the mere repetition of the *historical interpretation* in several places and in several forms[41] does not prove it; nowhere does Epstein demonstrate the *causal relationship*. Even though it is reasonable, however, it should not commit us to the assumption that this is the only or the basic factor at work. For could not a second factor have also greatly contributed to the rise of emendations—the changed role of the Mishnah?

With the spread and authoritative acceptance of the Mishnah, did other collections become less known? Could it be that statements of earlier Amoraim had been based on other Mishnayot and collections, now no longer extant or fully circulating? Could there have now arisen

---

[39] *ITM*, p. 245.

[40] Above we saw, in fact, that Epstein himself interprets one "recite" (*teni*) usage as an actual emendation, in a text where there are grounds, at least, for considering it a separate teaching.

[41] *ITM*, p. 353. See p. 404.

the feeling that everything had to be consistent with the Mishnah—with the presumption that earlier authorities must have felt likewise—and this produced the appearance of more conflicts with the Mishnah? Thus early Amoraic statements did indeed contradict the Mishnah. They had been based on other recensions or other collections before the Mishnah had been accepted as *the* authority. But with the diminished availability of other collections and the supremacy of the Mishnah, later generations did not realize the sources of the early Amoraic statements. They, therefore, felt a pressing need to make these statements consistent with the Mishnah.

Thirdly, Epstein argues that there were Palestinian and Babylonian recensions of the Mishnah, initially from the time the Mishnah came to Babylonia and later in the second and third Amoraic generations. But concerning the former period, Epstein himself says the later editions arrived and circulated in Babylonia, and the Mishnah-texts were corrected thereby.[12] Thus the distinction in the later generations[13] can not stem from the original different editions. For the later distinctions Epstein offers several proofs:

(1) Babylonian-Palestinian travelers. As recorded in the Talmud, transient Babylonian scholars when in Palestine asked questions concerning the Mishnah, and the Palestinians corrected their texts. In addition, Babylonians asked these travelers, on their return to Babylonia, concerning Mishnah readings.

(2) References to "our" *vis-à-vis* "your" division of the Mishnah into chapters.

(3) Presupposed Mishnah differences in pericopae when we compare the BT and the PT and the Mishnah of the BT and of the PT.[14]

Even if Epstein's analyses in each one of the pericopae are correct, they along with the other two "proofs" still do not prove his point. For he has only shown that concerning the particular Mishnah in question some Palestinians had one reading or Babylonians had another, and not what was to be found in other Babylonian and Palestinian academies. Nor does Epstein prove that any of these variations reflects totally separate versions of the Mishnah corpus and should not be considered just variations of an individual Mishnah.

---

[12] *Ibid.*, pp. 11, 706, 1271, and esp. 22.
[13] *Ibid.*, p. 706.
[14] *Ibid.*, pp. 706-20.

Furthermore, Epstein's sharp distinction would be vitiated by a second category of differences that he himself describes. This consists of the category of differences and variants in the Mishnah within the BT, from one tractate to another.[45] His remarks thus indicate that there existed within Babylonia no single corpus, for different academies had different readings and traditions. Significantly, in one of the very examples that Epstein cites[46] the PT agrees with one of the readings of the BT. How could one speak of a strict separation between Babylonian and Palestinian readings? Perhaps we should speak of academy x's reading *vis-à-vis* that of academy y, and the readings moved and circulated. Indeed, considering the nature of the reciters and their movement, it is difficult to imagine a totally isolated, continued existence of a separate recension.[47]

A fourth, and very significant, point is that the "last editors of the Talmud" anachronistically superimpose not only "late" terms into the mouth of people who lived prior to the coinage of the term, but that they also superimpose their understanding of a term into the cases. The latter phenomenon, Epstein demonstrates occurred with the method of *muḥlepet hašitah* of R. Yoḥanan, which originally was a *question concerning reverse logic*. Later, however, the BT editors understood this question as a *statement reversing* the Mishnah clauses because the reasoning of one of the Tannaim conflicts with his views elsewhere. Epstein cites the PT sources which clearly indicate the original meaning, particularly one passage which explicitly contrasts Yoḥanan's query with a transposing of the Mishnah clause.[48] The former phenomenon—that of superimposing later terms anachronistically—occurred with the terms of Mishnah-text criticism that Joseph, Abaye, and Rava developed.[49]

In these observations, Epstein shows some of his most astute understanding of the nature of the Talmud. For this is the beginning of the awareness that one can not automatically accept the historicity of a statement; the Talmud does not necessarily report and record the exact words of a person. Where we find two different accounts of the same statement, logically both cannot be correct. Long ago scholars

---

[15] *Ibid.*, pp. 720-22.
[16] *Ibid.*, p. 722.
[17] See *ibid.*, p. 691.
[18] *Ibid.*, p. 248, see pp. 245-62, esp. 245-46, 248-49, 251 fn. 3, and 262. He nowhere explains who are the "last editors of the BT," See Goldenberg, *op. cit.*, p. 78.
[19] See above, pp. 23-24. See *ITM*, pp. 251, 262, 279-80, 598 fn. 3, and 613.

recognized the need for literary and historical criticism. Here, however, Epstein demonstrates that even when only one version of a statement exists, it need not be historically accurate, for it comes to us through the translation of the document's editors.

V

Thus Epstein has shown us the "journey" of the Mishnah, its role, its circulation, and the nature of its various witnesses. Does the *ITM* also prepare us for a "critical" edition of the Mishnah? Or does it prove the impossibility of producing such an edition? Ostensibly, it is true, Epstein undertook the work as an introduction to a Mishnah edition which was planned, though as of today still unfinished.[50] The real answer, though, can only come after we further refine and delineate the problem. One must first choose criteria and canons of Mishnah-knowledge and quotations applicable for each representation of the Mishnah—for each edition, manuscript, early rabbinic authority, and Gaon, and for each parallel outside text, taking into consideration the nature of that text—from whose academy does it derive, whether it be R. 'Aqiba, Ishmael, or another? Similarly, one must develop such canons for each Amora and reciter-Tanna. Only after considering all this data may one use any of the data. Only when taking into account all these possibilities may one presume to know the Mishnah that any particular Amora or Tanna may have used.

Thus Epstein succeeds in setting before us our task. He gives many examples of textual analyses of individual Mishnayot, demonstrating the process of sources, variants, corrections, etc. We have noticed, however, that he fails to provide criteria and limitations for the applicability of his interpretative methods. Do these analyses yet present us, even inductively, with canons of editing the Mishnah text? Perhaps not, for a mere "critical text" of the Mishnah would level the dialectics of the Talmud. Further, Epstein's conclusions as to the original reading of particular Mishnayot have been occasionally criticized by subsequent scholars, who claim he is wrong in various places, emphasizing to us the difficulty of any determination.

What is possible is a collection of all the data in groupings of manuscripts, printed texts, quotes, lemmas, etc., with a text at the top,

---

[50] See Melamed's introduction to the second edition of the *ITM*, and the author's preface, Hebrew, p. 7.

a non-eclectic text, based on as pure a manuscript as possible.[51] The Mishnah, for example, needed for understanding Tosefta may not be the one for the BT (in a particular place) or for the Sifre Zuṭṭa. One must, therefore, collate the material to determine what each text and manuscript thereof represented as the Mishnah. Similarly, we must determine what each academy and Amora had as a Mishnah. With later periods, the correlation is less difficult, yet even here it has been done only to a very limited degree.[52] If one may further suggest an aide to the study of the Mishnah-text, we need non-literary canons for evaluating variants and recensions. These canons would deal with, for example, content, historical reference, and linguistic knowledge. Then one can start the task of producing an edition of the Mishnah.

vi

This study has examined Epstein's unique achievement in his *ITM*. He has delineated the scholarly process for Mishnah study. We have seen that he deals with a phenomenon as a whole, investigating fully all the evidence, exhaustively treating the material with highly developed philological and literary analysis. What is crucial is not just that he is quite informative concerning all aspects of the problem, but that he realized its immensity. Consequently subsequent scholars can no longer blindly accept any single Mishnah-text as *the* Mishnah text; they must examine all the data and possibilities as Epstein did. He has thus set the stage for further scholarly work by defining the questions and approaches of study. The particular tasks for post-Epstein scholars, therefore, include developing criteria for using Epstein's methods and interpretations; refining his views and interpretations; suggesting interpretations—literary and historical—for phenomena that he merely describes; generalizing and testing hypotheses; offering new hypotheses that may differ from those of Epstein; and finally, producing a critical edition of the Mishnah. Thus Epstein has given scholars a means and a guide to handle the many variants and parallels of the Mishnah and a challenge to study the Mishnah in its many dimensions.

---

[51] On the superiority of the Kaufmann manuscript, see Kutscher, *op. cit.*, pp. 252 f. and S. Friedman, "The 'Law of Increasing Members' in Mishnaic Hebrew", *Lešonenu*, 35 (1971), pp. 117, 127-29.

[52] See S. Lieberman, *Tosefet Rishonim* (Jerusalem, 1938), II, pp. 69, 36, 51, for an example of Tosefta correlation and its implications, explicitly spelled out in Halivni, *Meqorot*, pp. 496-500.

CHAPTER THREE

JACOB N. EPSTEIN ON THE FORMATION OF THE MISHNAH

BARUCH MICAH BOKSER

i

The following pages deal with J. N. Epstein's other works on the Mishnah. Foremost is his *Introduction to Tannaitic Literature*, a volume in three parts: "Introduction to the Mishnah and Tosefta,"[53] "Introductions to Mishnah Tractates,"[54] and "Introduction to the Halakhic Midrashim."[55] It also contains an appended lecture, "Variant Language and Variant Sources."[56] Our interest lies in the first two sections, excluding the Tosefta portion. This volume consists of Epstein's class notes, left when he died. E. Z. Melamed edited the manuscript and published it in 1957. Melamed informs us that the first part, the general introduction, consists of Epstein's lectures, which Epstein had written out in detail. Accordingly, this part of the volume is rather completely worked out. The introductions to the various tractates, on the other hand, are not so complete. Here Epstein used his materials in seminars, for which he wrote out just a detailed outline, relying on his memory to fill in the details.

The reader soon recognizes the incomplete nature of the volume, especially in comparison to the *Introduction to the Text of the Mishnah*. Epstein, however, did arrange the material with the hope and plan of eventually publishing it.[57] He had originally written the material at different times, as he had taught it. In addition, he subsequently went through the material several times, making corrections, though not wholesale revisions.[58] Perhaps this drawn-out

---

[53] *Introduction to Tannaitic Literature* (Hebrew: *Mevo'ot leSifrut HaTanna'im* (Jerusalem, 1957) pp. 9-262.
[54] *Ibid.*, pp. 263-494.
[55] *Ibid.*, pp. 495-746.
[56] *Ibid.*, pp. 234-240.
[57] *Ibid.*, p. 7.
[58] The "Introduction to the Mishnah" had six cycles, five of which are dated, from 1931-46. Of the individual introductions, Melamid indicates that Epstein first arranged

37

composition of the manuscript over many years accounts for the lack of references to scholarly works after the 1920's.[59] The nature of the formation of the volume also helps explain the presence of various inconsistencies and repetitions within the material. Saul Lieberman has pointed out, in addition, that Epstein's original manuscript includes notes that Epstein had made for himself, to indicate matters that he should further investigate.[60] Accordingly, the reader must carefully check Epstein's references.

The "Introduction to the Mishnah Tractates" covers 18 tractates. In each, the author first investigates the development of certain basic laws or institutions dealt with in the tractates, tracing them from the Bible down through rabbinic literature, and paying close attention to evidence from Aramaic papyri, Apocrypha and Pseudepigrapha, Septuagint, Philo, Josephus, and New Testament. Then he uses literary and source criticism to uncover the structure and sources of the tractate, its relation to Tosefta and its sources, and to Halakhic Midrashim. Several sections also contain philological notes on the Mishnah text. In the "Introduction to the Mishnah," he applies his literary and source investigations to the problem of the Mishnah's formation, to uncover the various remnants and strata of earlier *mishnayot* Epstein believes are embedded within the Mishnah, and to discern the role of the Mishnah's editor in editing the Mishnah. He thus makes use of material he had worked through in the several introductions.[61]

Epstein had revealed to the general scholarly world the nature of his critical interests in the Mishnah through articles in *MGWJ*, *Tarbiz*, and in several Jubilee volumes. These publications consisted of either

---

Kelim, as he taught it in 1926-28, and the other tractates in the following years; only three are dated. In addition, he reedited several of these introductions. See pp. 8, 267, and 459. The text itself indicates that Epstein corrected the material. Thus on p. 280 he added a comment in 1950. The appended nature of this very comment, however, proves he did not make a wholesale revision. This is reflected, as well, in the presence in the manuscript of sections crossed out or marked with a question mark. Melamed printed these last two types of sections in small print or in brackets.

[59] Thus Albeck should not be overly surprised that Epstein did not take account of his *Studies in Baraita and Tosefta* (Jerusalem, 1944). See H. Albeck, *Introduction to the Mishnah* (Jerusalem, 1967³), p. 275. If Epstein had included later works, we should have expected him, for example, while comparing Mishnah and Tosefta Shabbat, pp. 284-85, to have mentioned Boaz Cohen, *Mishnah and Tosefta Shabbat* (New York, 1935).

[60] *Siphré Zutta* (New York, 1968), pp. 135-36.

[61] Where Epstein has incorporated this material in the "Introduction to the Mishnah," Melamed has deleted and summarized these parts in the "Introduction to the Mishnah Tractates."

philological notes[62] or examples of the application of his source criticism.[63] In addition, in an important published lecture, "Talmudic Study and its Needs," given in 1925, he stated the central points of his views on the text and sources of the Mishnah.[64] Many of these findings he later published in his *Introduction to the Text of the Mishnah*, and appear in the *Introduction to Tannaitic Literature*.

I shall first present Epstein's approach and thesis concerning the formation of the Mishnah. Then I shall analyze his method, presenting several examples, and finally, review and evaluate his main points and his historical conclusions on the editing of the Mishnah.

ii

Epstein did not concern himself with speculating on the pre-Mishnaic period; he confined his interest to the Mishnah itself. Epstein's own words, in the preface, provide a good statement of his approach.

> This introduction deals with the text of the Mishnah and the history of its sources, remnants of early *mishnayot* that have been preserved [ŠNŚRDW] in it, through the Mishnayot of R. ʿAqiba's students embedded in it, and until the Mishnah of Rabbi and its arrangement [SYDRH]. That is, therefore, the history of the books [SPRY] of the Mishnah, from its earliest stages until the last arrangement of the Mishnah.
>
> For our Mishnah, the Mishnah of Rabbi, was not the first Mishnah collection: Several collections of *mishnayot* preceded it. Though they were similar in some basic laws, they differed in development and in details, explanations, and qualifications (and these are the very bases of the disputes). They differed, as well, in their arrangement and order.
>
> One reciter ... joined different and unrelated items on the basis of external signs [e.g. lists of five items, laws of a certain sage, motif] ....

---

[62] "Zur Babylonisch-Aramäischen Lexikographie," *Festschrift Adolf Schwartz*, ed. S. Krauss (Berlin and Vienna, 1917), pp. 317-27; *MGWJ* 63 (1919), pp. 15-19; "On the Terms of Naziriteship," *Magnes Anniversity Book*, ed. Y. Baer, et al., (Jerusalem, 1938), pp. 10-16; "Mishnaic and Babylonian Aramaic," *Lešonenu* 15 (1947), pp. 103-07.

[63] *MGWJ* 78 (1934), pp. 97-103, 255-56; "He Who Taught This, Has Not Taught This," *Tarbiz*, 7 (1936), pp. 143-58, 245; "The Sages Say," *Studies in Memory of Asher Gulak and Samuel Klien*, ed. J. N. Epstein (Jerusalem, 1942), pp. 252-261; "Addenda to 'The Sages Say,'" *Tarbiz* 14 (1942) pp. 75-76; "Addenda to 'The Sages Say,'" *Tarbiz* 15 (1943), p. 64: "On the Mishnah of R. Judah," *Tarbiz* 15 (1943), pp. 1-13; "Mishnah Kelim Chapter 24," *Ginzberg Jubilee Volume*, ed. S. Lieberman, et. al. (New York, 1946), Hebrew Section, pp. 65-74.

[64] "HaMadaʿ HaTalmudi Veṣorkhav", *Proceedings of the Academy of Jewish Studies*, 2 (Jerusalem, 1935), pp. 5-22. (Henceforth HaMadaʿ).

> A second recited a collection of laws that belongs together: laws of the Sabbath ....
>
> These collections varied, understandably, also in language and style according to their time and place [of composition]. ... At times the same word even had different meanings in different collections.
>
> Remnants of these early and Ur-collections were preserved [NŚRDW] in our Mishnah, whether as complete collections, or as parts and fragments of those collections ....[65]

According to Epstein, at some point some one collected the early traditions of the rabbis. Subsequent generations added to these collections their traditions of the earlier periods as well as of their own teachers. Several individuals did this in every generation. R. ʿAqiba made the first attempt at synthesizing and ordering this material. His students taught their own version of ʿAqiba's Mishnah, thus producing several recensions. Finally, Rabbi tried to mediate among the different traditions and recensions and present one coherent text. Epstein thus pictures successive Mishnah-collections that culminated in Rabbi's Mishnah. Accordingly, one desiring to understand the Mishnah and the original meaning of its clauses and to appreciate what Rabbi did must isolate its contents in their original form, tracing them to earlier collections. One can do this because each corpus had distinctive elements, in terms of content and literary and linguistic features.

The unraveling of the Mishnah involves several steps. One must first use the tools of lower criticism to determine the text's correct reading. Epstein carefully demonstrates in his *ITM* the necessary procedures. Next, one uses internal literary analyses to discern different sources. One looks for inner inconsistencies and contradictions in content and language, repetitions, and illogical order and place of the laws as signs that each text or part of a text originated in a different source. Then one distinguishes between a Mishnah's basic fabric and later glosses. The latter supplement or complement the former. Looking at several *Mishnayot* one after the next facilitates recognition of the basic fabric. Then one uses source criticism. He must collect all versions of a *Mishnah*, foremost those in Tannaitic sources, *Halakhic* Midrashim, Talmudic *Beraitot*, and especially Tosefta. Secondarily, one may rely on later midrashic and Amoraic material, especially comments of early Amoraim. One next compares the different versions, looking to discern differences in formulation, context, order and author. Tosefta may cite in the name of a particular teacher a text which anonymously

[65] *ITL*, p. 13.

appears in the Mishnah. This might then enable one to identify the author of the Mishnah's clause.[66] Alternatively, three versions might exist, then one must attempt to explain what caused the differences. The texts may represent one original and two later recensions, three different recensions of a non-extant fourth text, or three independent texts based on separate early traditions. In addition, even when one finds only two versions, one must consider all these possibilities. Attestation provides an important tool in dating layers of a text. If a person refers to a certain clause or tradition, one may safely assume that it already existed in that formulation in his time. Source criticism thus provides the key to the structure and meaning of the Mishnah.[67]

The picture of the formation of the Mishnah should emerge once one compares and tries to relate the various versions of the Mishnah-texts. Epstein's method, however, assumes the historical conclusions, first, that collections before Rabbi's existed, and second, that the Mishnah's editor used them in forming the Mishnah. Only then one realizes the importance of the quest for sources. Epstein's work thus has an important historical dimension: to see historically what part of the Mishnah existed at what time. In addition, once one has realized the first goal of discovering the Mishnah's formation, then he can adequately answer the general historical questions concerning the editing of the Mishnah.

iii

A good example of Epstein's method consists of his argument that early collections of Mishnayot existed in Temple times. Some of these have left remnants embedded in the Mishnah. Epstein cites parallel sources, attestations, as well as the more 'traditional' external evidence. He uses the external sources—extra rabbinic and rabbinic—to make a *prima facie* case that such collections existed. His citations from IV Ezra, Epiphanius, Hieronymous, and Amoraic texts, however, at most refer to collections of early traditions and laws—but whether or not they were even associated with Pharisees or early Tannaim like ʿAqiba is never shown. The existence of such collections is not the issue.[68] The

---

[66] See *HaMadaʿ*, p. 21.
[67] *ITL*, pp. 234-40; 459, fn *.
[68] See Strack, *Introduction to the Talmud and Midrash* (Philadelphia, 1931), pp. 10-12, esp. 11-12; R. Marcus, *Law in the Apocrypha* (New York, 1927), pp. 70-114, esp. pp. 70-74, 114. The Ben Sira 44 : 4 reference is no longer doubtful, Marcus p. 73, for

issue consists in the existence of a proto-Mishnah or a corpus of Mishnah-like laws before the Mishnah of Rabbi.

While Epstein's external proofs are insufficient, his internal ones are cogent. The primary text he analyzes is the following:

> [The laws of] Release from vows hover in the air and have nothing upon which to rely; the laws [HLKWT] of the Sabbath, Festival-offerings, and Sacrilege are as mountains hanging by a hair, for [teaching of] Scripture [thereon] is scanty and the laws many; the [laws of] cases concerning Property and the Temple Service, and laws about what is Clean and Unclean and the Forbidden Degrees have that upon which to rely, and it is they that are the essentials of the Torah.
>
> (M. Ḥag. 1 : 8)

> A. [Laws of] Temple Service, what is Clean and Unclean, and the Forbidden Degrees.
> B. Add to them [laws of] Valuation [of persons or animals dedicated to the sanctuary]; Dedications [using the term ḤRM]; Sanctified Property [to the Temple]; and Second Tithe.
> C. They have many scriptural verses, exegesis, and laws, and that upon which to rely.
> D. Abba Yosi b. Ḥanan says, "These eight subjects of Torah are the essential laws."[69]
>
> (Tos. Ḥag. 1 : 9; Lieberman ed. 379 : 59.
> = Tos. 'Eruv. 8 : 24; Lieberman ed. 138 : 71)

According to Epstein, (A)-(D) is a unit. Abba Yosi (D), referring to eight subjects, has summarized and counted the items of (A) and (B). Therefore, (D) must postdate (A) and (B). (B) in turn adds onto and therefore postdates (A). Thus (D) comes two stages after (A). Epstein posits one generation — at least — for each stage. Therefore, since (A) is the Tosefta's quote of the Mishnah, (D) comes two generations after the Mishnah. Alternatively, the Mishnah comes at least two generations before Abba Yosi, (D), who is known to have lived in Temple times.[70] These texts, in addition, use the word *halakhot* (HLKWT) to refer to the different type of laws. According to Epstein,

---

the Masada text is clear, Y. Yadin, *The Ben Sira Scroll from Masada* (Jerusalem, 1965), p. 36; S. Lieberman, *Hellenism in Jewish Palestine* (New York, 1950), pp. 83-84; C. Rabin, *The Zadokite Document* (Oxford, 1958²) pp. x-xi, 44-77.

[69] See Lieberman, *Tosefta Kifshuṭah* (New York, 1962), III, pp. 469-470; and "How Much Greek in Jewish Palestine?" *Biblical and Other Studies*, ed. A. Altmann (Cambridge, 1963), pp. 131-32.

[70] *ITL*, pp. 18-19, 46-49. Epstein refers to Tos. Men. 13 : 21, 533 : 34. See Lieberman, *Tosefet Rishonim* (Jerusalem, 1938), II, p. 265; and J. Neusner, *The Rabbinic Traditions About the Pharisees Before 70* (Leiden, 1971), I, p. 417.

halakhot is a collective term for a collection of laws dealing with the several named subjects; he then goes on to identify these different *halakhot* with topics found in the Mishnah. Since the "collections" that M. Ḥag. 1 : 8 refers to must predate the Mishnah itself by at least one generation, they must date, Epstein concludes, no later than the time of Herod. Epstein then cites attestations by R. Eliezer and R. Joshua, to indicate that M. Ḥag. 1 : 8 had already received its present formulation in early times.[71] In addition, he points out attestations to several *halakhot*-collections embedded within the Mishnah. These include references by R. Ishmael and R. Yoḥanan b. Zakkai to *halakhot* of Property and the presupposition by M. Yoma 1 : 3 of *halakhot* of Temple-Service.[72]

While this example enables us to see Epstein's method, it itself proves only Epstein's first point—that *halakhot*-collections of various types existed in an early time. In addition, the Mishnah contains material and topics of the same nature as that of these collections. But he has not proven that these Mishnah elements are *the halakhot*-collections. Nor has he proven that R. Ishmael and the others attest to these *very* collections and not others of similar content. Thus he has yet to prove that the Mishnah contains actual remnants of the *halakhot*-collections. His arguments for that proposition we shall examine below.

As an example of Epstein's source criticism, let us look at one aspect of his discussion concerning the activity of the Mishnah's editor. He cites the following text to demonstrate that when Rabbi, the Mishnah's editor, doubted whether a dispute dated back to early times or was more recent and was only based upon an early dispute, he taught it in the name of the last disputants; then it appeared as a new dispute:[73]

> R. Eliezer says, "On a Festival-day next to the Sabbath, whether before it or after it, a man may prepare two 'eruvs . . . ."
> And the Sages say, "He prepares an 'eruv for one direction or it is no 'eruv at all . . . ."   (M. 'Eruv. 3 : 6)

---

[71] Tos. Ḥag. 1 : 9, Lieberman ed. 379 : 58 = Tos. 'Eruv. 1 : 23, Lieberman ed. 138 : 70 contains a glossed comment by Joshua; y. Ḥag. 1 : 8, 76c, and b. Ḥag. 10a contain a Baraita in which Eliezer and Joshua dispute a point of the Mishnah.

[72] M. Ket. 13 : 1-9. See J. Neusner, *Development of a Legend* (Leiden, 1970), pp. 47-48, 195-96; M.B.Q. 1 : 1-3. To support the historicity of Yoma 1 : 3, he refers to Josephus, Ant. 18.1, 13.

[73] *ITL*, pp. 204, 189-91.

> R. Judah says, "If at the New Year a man feared that [the month] might be intercalated, he may prepare two 'eruvs ...."
> But the Sages did not agree with him.
>
> (M. 'Eruv. 3 : 7)
>
> Moreover, R. Judah says, "A man may make a condition about a basket [of first fruits] on a first Festival-day, ..."
> But the Sages did not agree with him.
>
> (M. 'Eruv. 3 : 8)
>
> The Sages admit to R. Eliezer concerning the two festival days of the New Year that a man may make an 'eruv one day for the North and one for the South, ...
> And R. Yosi forbids. ...
>
> (Tos. 'Eruv. 4 : 2; Lieberman ed. 104 : 13)
>
> A man who has a basket of [first] fruits that are not prepared [as far as Terumot and Tithes], today may say, "If it is a Festival-day my words are not valid, and if not [a Festival-day] let there be called there its Terumot and Tithes," and he sets it down. On the morrow he says, "If it is a Festival-day my words are not valid, and if not, let there be called there its Terumot and Tithes," and he may eat it.
> And R. Yosi forbids.
>
> (Tos. 'Eruv. 4 : 3; Lieberman, ed. 105 : 17)

Mishnah 'Eruv. 3 : 6 presents a dispute between Eliezer and the Sages. The Tosefta does not record an argument concerning the formulation of their dispute. It does, though, include one concerning the issues of M. 'Eruv. 3 : 7 and 8. According to the Tosefta, the Sages agree with R. Eliezer in those cases, 4 : 2 and 3; the Mishnah teaches this view in the name of R. Judah. R. Yosi, in the last clauses of Tos. 4 : 2 and 3, disputes this, and he is represented in M. 3 : 7 and 8 as the Sages.[74] Judah and Yosi had argued over the construction of the dispute between Eliezer and the Sages. Accordingly Rabbi recorded the dispute on the basis of this supra-dispute. Thus M. 3 : 7 and 8 are the Mishnah of R. Judah on the basis of R. Eliezer. Epstein has thus broken down the Mishnah into its component elements with the help of parallel sources. Considering that Yosi and Judah lived only one generation before Rabbi, Epstein seems to be quite justified in not considering that someone else in the interim had transformed the dispute and recited it as a Mishnah, from which Rabbi would have taken the already transformed dispute.

---

[74] See Lieberman, *TK*, III, pp. 365-66.

iv

Since the Mishnah is the culmination of a process of Mishnah-*formation*, Epstein tries systematically to discover the antecedent Mishnayot. He starts with the early period, which presents the first strata of the Mishnah. After analyzing the M. Ḥag. 1 : 8 passage that we have already examined, he turns to internal mishnaic references to the 'first' or 'early' Mishnah, the MŠNH R'ŠWNH. Whether because of the dearth of evidence or some other reason, this section contains one of Epstein's weakest arguments. Several times, the Mishnah and Tosefta call a text or a clause a MŠNH R'ŠWNH, contrasting it with a later Mishnah, for example that of R. ʿAqiba or of the Sages. Epstein argues that these references are not merely to individual early laws, but to an arrangement of such laws in a collection.[75] He bases his argument on the contrast that the texts make: "Since the Mishnah of R. ʿAqiba is a collection, so is its counterpart." Similarly, if the text states "R. ʿAqiba added" to the MŠNH R'ŠWNH, it presumes that R. ʿAqiba added to a fixed corpus.[76] One wonders, however, why does Epstein not claim that the MŠNH R'ŠWNH had all the qualities of R. ʿAqiba's Mishnah? On the contrary, Epstein feels ʿAqiba's Mishnah differed from all those that preceeded.[77] Accordingly, the contrast cannot conclusively prove anything.

It is precisely such weak links in Epstein's argument, though, that demonstrate the importance of his source-analysis. For he clearly does show the presence of strings of early laws embedded within the Mishnah. He examines 15 individual tractates, and demonstrates how considerable parts of their structure are based on early *mishnayot*.[78] He is able to date these portions by attestation, content, language, references, and by identifying their author. Earlier scholars had examined some aspects of several of these tractates, but Epstein goes his own way. Thus Tamid, first carefully examined by Louis Ginzberg,[79] in its present form cannot be considered an early Mishnah. For later

---

[75] See above, pp. 15-16, where we saw that MŠNH R'ŠWNH may, at times, not even actually refer to an "early mishnah."

[76] *ITL*, p. 23.

[77] See *ibid.*, p. 71.

[78] Of the 18 tractates that Epstein examines individually in the second section, 9 are not of these 15. There he also points to some early laws.

[79] L. Ginzberg, "The Mishnah Tamid," *Journal of Jewish Lore and Philosophy*, I, 1, 2, 3, 4, (1919) pp. 33ff. See *The Formation of the Babylonian Talmud*, pp. 107-14. Epstein deals with this in *ITL*, pp. 27-31, and esp. *HaMadaʿ*, pp. 12-14.

Tannaim, especially Rabbi, worked it over and it is part of the Mishnah of Rabbi. It is, however, based on an early Mishnah. We must notice that it is a sign of Epstein's sophistication that he distinguishes between the corpus or work that sources refer to and the present work that bears the same name.[80] Many scholars have equated the two.

Let us look at Epstein's treatment of one individual tractate, M. Hagigah. We have already seen that he claims M. Hag. 1 : 8 must go back to two generations before the Temple's destruction, and the collections to which it refers to one generation earlier.[81] It mentions "Hagigah," Festival-offerings, as one of these very collections, and therefore, Epstein argues, a collection of Hagigah laws, *halakhot*, must date from Herod's time. By examining each Mishnah, Epstein demonstrates the presence of an early core. This basic fabric does not mention 'late' Tannaim; its last reference consists of Yohanan b. Gudgada (2 : 7), a Temple gate keeper from the end of the Temple period. Since the Mishnah refers to him without the title "Rabbi" — a title by which he is called elsewhere,[82] — the author of this mishnah must be his contemporary.

M. Hag. 1 : 7 refers to R. Simeon b. Yohai and R. Simeon b. Menasiah. But someone added this pericope to the Mishnah from Tos. Hag. 1 : 7-8, as a midrashic addition not pertinent to the section. Epstein backs up this claim with the observation that Simeon b. Menasiah, a younger contemporary of Rabbi, is nowhere else mentioned in the Mishnah. Furthermore, the Simeon b. Yohai reference includes the father's name, Yohai, a practice that indicates that it originates on an Ishmaelite text. For throughout 'Aqiban-based sources, particularly the Mishnah, he is only called "R. Simeon."[83]

M. Hag. 2 : 1, the ban on teaching *merkavah* mysticism, also dates from a relatively early time, for a story about R. Yohanan b. Zakkai refers to it,[84] — a weak proof.

M. Hag. 2 : 2 contains the laying on hands dispute of the early pairs. It must date from the time of the last pair, Hillel and Shammai; it is thus also supposed to be early. If more recent scholarship would

---

[80] See, for example, *ITL*, pp. 86, 87, 127, 132, 290, 299, 401, 456, and, 458.
[81] See above, pp. 41-43. On M. Hag. *ITL*, pp. 46-52, 373.
[82] Sifré *Qorah*, 116, Horowitz ed., p. 132.
[83] See *Thesaurus Mishnae* (Jerusalem, 1960), IV, 1791c-1793a. Concerning the R. Simeon b. Yohai reference in M. Avot 6 : 8, see *ITL*, p. 233: Ch. 6 is an addition to the Mishnah.
[84] Tos. Hag. 2 : 1, Lieberman ed. p. 380 : 5. See the parallels cited there.

conclude that this is a revised chain, it would not substantially weaken Epstein's argument, for he continually points to early cores that later generations worked over.[85] Nevertheless, this remains an inadequate proof. For Epstein has only provided the earliest possible date for the formulation of this clause and not its latest. Someone may have formulated this clause at a relatively late date. In a similar manner, Epstein examines each *mishnah*, uncovering the early form, and concludes that M. Ḥagigah consists of two early cores: 1 : 1 - 2 : 4—laws of the Temple-offerings, *hilkhot ḥagigah*; and 2 : 5 - 3 : 8 (the end)—laws of cleanliness of the Holy, *hilkhot ṭaharat haqodesh*. Thus while one may have certain reservations concerning several of Epstein's particular analyses, one yet can clearly see what he has done in attempting to isolate a string of early *mishnayot*. When one can demonstrate their existence, the evidence becomes strong that there exists a core of an early Mishnah. But Epstein's demonstrations are inconclusive.

Epstein argues that the next generation continued this process, and they served as intermediaries between the early Mishnayot and that of R. ʿAqiba. He points out that the descriptions of R. Joshua's activities fit a teacher and reciter of *mishnayot*, characteristic of ʿAqiba's students. Epstein confirms this description by isolating remnants of his Mishnah, including practically the whole tractate of Qinim, "Bird Offerings." This last attribution has been corroborated by Lieberman's studies.[86] Epstein makes a similar study of R. Eliezer's teachings to uncover the remnants of his corpus.[87]

Epstein feels that ʿAqiba marks the first major turning point in the Mishnah, starting a new mishnaic period. He accepts the Amoraic tradition that ʿAqiba edited a Mishnah of a special type and supports this attribution by internal Mishnaic evidence. ʿAqiba not only taught many new laws, he also checked, corrected, and emended old traditions, even on the basic of logic. He was the first to leave his imprint on the Mishnah.[88] Paradoxically, one has difficulty detecting the remnants of ʿAqiba's Mishnah. Meir accepted and used it as the structural basis of his Mishnah, which in turn became the basis of

---

[85] See Neusner, *Pharisees, op. cit.*, I, pp. 12-13, 22-23.
[86] *ITL*, pp. 59-64. S. Lieberman, *Hellenism, op. cit.*, 94-96; "How Much Greek," *loc. cit.*, pp. 131-132; "Response to the Introduction by Professor Alexander Marx," *The Jewish Expression*, ed. J. Goldin (New York, 1970), pp. 119-22.
[87] *ITL*, pp. 65-70.
[88] *Ibid.*, p. 71.

Rabbi's Mishnah, so that it has been almost totally submerged within the Mishnah.

An important element of Epstein's argument is that ʿAqiba arranged an actual collection, and did not merely teach individual traditions and laws. His evidence includes:

> (1) References to the "mishnah of R. ʿAqiba," four times by R. Yosi, and once by R. Eleazar b. Simeon.
> (2) A statement by his student, R. Simeon, to his own students: "My sons, learn my canons [MYDWTY], for my canons are choice ones from the choice canons of R. ʿAqiba" (b. Giṭ. 67a).
> (3) A statement by R. Yona that ʿAqiba "arranged *midrash* (= *midrash halakhah*), *halakhot* (= *mishnayot*), and *haggadot*" (y. Sheq. 5 : 1, 48c).
> (4) A statement by Epiphanius that one of the four Mishnayot, *deuterōseis*, that contain the traditions of the elders is called after R. ʿAqiba.[89]
> (5) The use of the verb ŠWNH, "to recite", with reference to ʿAqiba. Epstein holds this term is exclusively used for teaching material as part of a corpus.[90]

By themselves these proofs are hardly adequate. Statement number two need not apply to a corpus; the term "canons" [MYDWT] surely fits teachings in general. Statement number three is late. *Aggadah* attributes the authorship of the Mishnah and *mishnayot* to various people. By what standard shall we accept one statement over another? PT, immediately following Yona's statement, in fact, emends his remarks. In addition, as pointed out above, numbers three and four need not refer to a "proto"-Mishnah.[91] Number five provides the weakest proof. For we find usages of this verb, ŠWNH, that refer to reciting individual verses of the Bible and to individual laws.[92]

On the other hand, the texts that Epstein collects to describe ʿAqiba's activities would support the thesis that ʿAqiba arranged some type of collection. Besides the famous ARN 18 passage describing how ʿAqiba collected, separated, and arranged the teachings and traditions, Epstein does cite several Tannaitic sources. They include:

> When R. ʿAqiba was arranging [MSDR] laws [HLKWT] for the students, he said, "Whoever has heard a reason [reasonable argument] against his fellow student, let him come forward and tell it."
> (Tos. Zev. 1 : 5, Zuckermandel ed. 676 : 33)

---

[89] *Ibid.*, pp. 17, 72. Epiphanius, *Haeres*, 33 : 9, 15 : 2.
[90] See *ITL*, p. 60.
[91] pp. 41-42.
[92] See Sifré Dt. 4, Finkelstein ed. p. 13, and Mekhilta *Beshalaḥ* 2, Horowitz ed. p. 161. See Halivni, *Meqorot*, p. 671, and Lieberman *TK*, II, p. 202.

Tosefta reports how several students came forward, and their traditions are recorded.[93] The Mishnah and Tosefta illustrate 'Aqiba's work, how he rejected and qualified laws and added new material.[94] Epstein points out, in addition, that one can uncover 'Aqiba's Mishnah in the recensions of his students. His students repeated his Mishnah in their own way, teaching it in their own characteristic fashion. In fact this enables us to understand the construction of the Mishnah and its parallel sources and versions. For example, Judah teaches a statement of 'Aqiba as disputing the House of Shammai, while Yosi teaches that it follows the view of the House of Hillel, and Meir teaches it anonymously, and it thereby became embedded anonymously in the Mishnah.[95] The existence of an archetype also accounts for the Mishnah's parallel structure and format, differing only in particulars and in the legal decision.[96] Epstein finally buttresses his argument by applying his literary and source criticism to demonstrate the presence and identification of strings of 'Aqiban *mishnayot*. He shows, as well, how later generations worked over these *mishnayot*.[97]

Epstein similarly analyzes the Tannaim of the next generation. He isolates the teachings and Mishnayot of 'Aqiba's students, Meir, Judah, Yosi, Simeon, and Eleazar, and their contemporaries, Abba Saul, Simeon b. Gamaliel, and Nathan.[98] He then examines Rabbi's four older contemporaries, some of whose teachings are anonymously fixed in the Mishnah.

Epstein paints his picture of the editing of the Mishnah on the basis of his analyses. He has isolated several strata of early teachings of law, of *mishnayot*—some individual and others strung together—upon which later generations appended their own remarks. These the reciters recited along with the original core. A student adopted the corpus of his teacher and taught his laws anonymously: Meir, that of 'Aqiba; Judah, those of Eliezer and Tarfon; and Yosi, that of Yohanan b. Nuri.[99] Later generations thereby worked over the earlier core.

Epstein then turns to Rabbi, the Mishnah's editor and describes his

---

[93] Tos. Zev. 1 : 4-6; 676 : 29 - 677 : 1. See Lieberman, *Hellenism*, p. 91.
[94] See M. Kil. 1 : 3; Tos. Kil. 1 : 2; Tos. Maksh. 2 : 9; M. Oh. 16 : 1; M. Pes. 9 : 6; M. Nid. 6 : 11; Tos. Nid. 6 : 5-6; Tos. Zab. 1 : 4-6.
[95] *ITL*, pp. 74-75.
[96] *Ibid.*, p. 116.
[97] *Ibid.*, p. 87.
[98] *Ibid.*, pp. 96-171.
[99] *Ibid.*, pp. 186-87.

activities. He based his work on the Mishnah that R. Jacob b. Qursi recited in the court of R. Simeon b. Gamaliel. But he did not just add a new layer. Through his internal analysis, Epstein shows that Rabbi sought out the views of his predecessors.[100] He cites texts that demonstrate Rabbi added to the Mishnah laws he had heard from his teachers.[101] He deleted from the "official" Mishnah items that others had recited, and which were hinted to elsewhere.[102] He joined together conflicting sources of two different Tannaim in order to add some point; he joined together sources that he felt expounded the same view. He emended the Mishnah or its statement of law to conform to his own view or to another's view which he accepted as authoritative.[103] He commented upon a Mishnah text, indicating that it represented a minority view.[104] In addition, he taught his own view of the law, even though disputed by the Sages. Occasionally, he commented upon those who disputed him. Thus:

> [Ears of] corn bending over onto [ears of heterogeneous] corn, or vegetable [leaves] onto [leaves of a heterogeneous] vegetable ...
> All this is permitted, except in the case of the Greek gourd.
> Rabbi[105] said: "[Except] also in the case of the cucumber or Egyptian beans: but I recognize their dictum as more acceptable than mine."
>
> (M. Kil. 2 : 11. Trans. J. Israelstam,
> *The Babylonian Talmud*, ed. Epstein, pp. 99-100)

Rabbi, in addition, taught anonymously his own view of the construction of a previous dispute.[106] At times, he adjudicated a dispute, by declaring that one view applies in some situations, and the other view in other situations. Alternatively, he declared that one view is correct in all cases. The following is an important example:

> A. If a drop of milk fell on a piece of meat, and it is sufficient to impart a flavor into that piece, it [the meat] is forbidden. If the pot was stirred, then it is forbidden only if [the drop of milk] is sufficient to impart a flavor into [all that was in] the pot.
>
> (M. Ḥul. 8 : 3)

---

[100] Tos. Zev. 2 : 17.

[101] *ITL*, pp. 204, 190. See M. Yeb. 8 : 6; Tos. Yeb. 10 : 2, Lieberman ed. 31 : 18; b. Yeb. 84a. See Lieberman, *TK*, VI, p. 94. His slightly different explanation of this text still supports the conclusion on how Rabbi added this clause.

[102] *ITL*, pp. 191-92, 204, 220.

[103] See esp. *ibid.*, p. 217.

[104] *Ibid.*, p. 193. See b. Ket. 93a.

[105] See *ITL*, p. 193, fn. 35: following all the manuscripts this is the correct reading of the name.

[106] *ITL*, pp. 192-193.

> B. A drop of milk that fell on a piece of meat: R. Judah says, "If it is sufficient to impart a flavor into that piece." And the Sages say, "Into [all that was in] the pot."
> Rabbi said, "The words of R. Judah are acceptable when one neither stirred nor covered [the pot], and the words of the Sages when one stirred or covered [the pot]."
> (Tos. Ḥul. 8 : 6, Zuckermandel ed. 509 : 27)

Rabbi adjudicated the dispute between Judah and the Sages, and as we see in the Mishnah, (A), he recited the law on the basis of his adjudication.[107]

Thus Rabbi played an active role in editing the Mishnah. But Epstein demonstrates, by collecting and evaluating later additions, that the Mishnah was not sealed until the time of Rabbi's sons. For it contains several anonymous *mishnayot* that they had taught.[108] We also find an addition by Rabbi's grandson as well as later additions made from *beraitot* and Amoraic sources.[109]

V

Once Epstein has a complete picture of the Mishnah's formation, he elicits from the material answers to questions that scholars have asked concerning the Mishnah's editing. It is important to see his formulation of these questions, for, as we will see, they influence the type of answers he offers.

> How did Rabbi use the Mishnayot of R. Meir, of R. Judah, of R. Yosi, of R. Simeon, and of R. Eleazar?
> There are three problems: 1) How did he transmit [MSR] the Mishnayot that preceded him, did he change the Mishnayot according to his own view (Dünner) or did he not change anything (Albeck)? 2) Does the Mishnah contain legal decisions (Bassfreund) or not (Albeck)? 3) Who arranged the last arrangement [SYDWR] of our Mishnah?[110]

Epstein answers a decided yes to the first question; he continually points out that Rabbi altered the sources he used. We particularly saw this in the example of Rabbi's adjudicating a dispute between Judah and the Sages. He changed the sources in order to teach the law on

---

[107] *Ibid.*, p. 210. See pp. 194-95, 199, 205-11, esp. 208-11.
[108] *Ibid.*, pp. 227-29. See Lieberman, *TK*, II, 483.
[109] *ITL*, pp. 229-32, *ITM*, p. 950.
[110] *ITL*, pp. 188-89. For bibliographical references for Dünner and Bassfreund, see Strack, *op. cit.*, p. 139.

the basis of his adjudication. In a separate section Epstein recapitulates, as well, the various proofs.[111]

Epstein's analysis, however, raises certain questions. Must the only choice consist of whether the editor did or did not change the sources? Epstein has demonstrated that Rabbi made changes. He has also demonstrated, at various times, that the editor did not change his source, but preserved its language, even causing inconsistencies and rough language within one Mishnah.[112] One should notice, in addition, that the rules which Epstein has uncovered, in Rabbi's treatment of his sources, are descriptive of his procedure; they are not a body of normative principles with which Rabbi approached his work.[113] Perhaps we may only discover Rabbi's relation to his sources by determining what type of sources in what situations would Rabbi feel free to change and what type of change would he then undertake. Perhaps it also depended on where Rabbi intended to use these sources in the Mishnah. Thus we must no longer be tied to a "yes" or "no" answer; we must look for a "when" and "where".[114]

Epstein believes that Rabbi intended the Mishnah as a legal code. His proofs for this position are intertwined with his view that Rabbi altered his sources. In order to counter the opposing view and to explicitly make this clear, Epstein cites the following:[115]

(1) The plain sense meaning of several Amoraic statements, including one by R. Yoḥanan, that Rabbi taught particular laws of R. Meir or R. Simeon or R. Eleazar b. Simeon "in the language of the Sages [BLŠWN ḤKMYM = "the Sages say"] or like it."[116] This phenomenon parallels the Tannaitic testimony of Rabbi's adjudications. Epstein cites several texts to prove that the referent "Rabbi" must be Rabbi Judah the Patriarch.

(2) Internal proof: Rabbi's activity in reconstructing a dispute in the Mishnah—known from other sources—such that instead of naming

---

[111] *TL*, pp. 205-21; 212-24; 225-26. See also 127, 128, 130, 132, 134, 138, 150, 299, 335, 340, 353, 354, 366, 378, 380, 393, 402, 404, 416, 428, 438, 449, 450, 455, 458, 460-62, 466. Albeck, *Introduction, op. cit.*, p. 274, should, therefore, not complain that Epstein only states his conclusions without giving his reasons!

[112] See above pp. 16-18, 26; *ITL*, pp. 234-40; *ITM*, pp. 1-2, 595-672.

[113] Rabbi's reformulation of the doubtful construction of early disputes may provide the only exception.

[114] See, for example, the attempts by Halivni, *Meqorot*, pp. 246; 318, fn. 10; 344; 402-03; 457; 542; and 570, fn. 6.

[115] Albeck has claimed, *Introduction*, pp. 274-83, that Epstein misconstrued his view. Nevertheless, Epstein's arguments stand against Albeck's own presentation of his views.

[116] b. Ḥul. 85a; y. Soṭ. 3 : 6, 19b.

both disputants, he names only one, while recording the second view anonymously or as "the Sages." Similarly, Rabbi ascribed views of an individual to the "many," and he represented in two parts what was originally a unitary Mishnah, one portion he attributed to its author, and the other, with which he obviously agreed, he cited anonymously.

(3) The legal comment that M. Toh. 9 : 1 records:

> A. Olives—from what time do they become susceptible to uncleanness?
> After they exude the moisture that comes out of them when they are in the vat, but not the moisture that comes out of them when they are yet in the store-basket, so the words of the House of Shammai.
> R. Simeon says, "The prescribed time for the exuded moisture is three days."
> The House of Hillel says, "From the moment that three stick together."
> Rabban Gamaliel says, "From the moment that their preparation is finished."
> B. And the Sages say like his words [KDBRYW].

Clause (B) is surely a statement of law.

(4) Amoraim identify anonymous views so that they should not be bound by the otherwise anonymous Mishnah—a fact that presupposes its legal authority.[117]

Albeck's objection to this last "proof", while missing the point, underlines a reality that Epstein himself failed sufficiently to express. Albeck asks, if Rabbi reformulated his sources anonymously to make authoritative law, how could the Amoraim dare to attempt to identify the anonymous positions and thereby subvert Rabbi's work?[118] The answers is that *that* is precisely what happened. Rabbi intended the Mishnah to be authoritative, and therefore taught some views anonymously. But early Amoraim rejected Rabbi's purpose. They asserted their autonomy to rely on any Tannaitic source or tradition, even those contradicting the Mishnah. They therefore tried to identify the anonymous parts of the Mishnah, to see if they represent individual or collective views. The real historical question is, Why did Rabbi feel he could authoritatively expound the law, and why did early Amoraim reject the authoritative role of Rabbi's Mishnah?[119] In addition, one wonders whether Epstein and other scholars have

[117] *ITL*, pp. 275-78.
[118] Albeck, *Introduction, op. cit.*, p. 106.
[119] Epstein makes quite clear in his *ITM* the changed role of the Mishnah among the Amoraim, from its initial lack of authoritative acceptance to its eventual acceptance. See above pp. 22-24, 32-33.

incorrectly limited the alternatives to "a code" or "not a code." Are there no other possibilities? And if indeed Rabbi intended the Mishnah as a code, for whom did he so intend it? Furthermore, what did a "code" mean in the second and third centuries?

Epstein's remarks in a related area are also problematic. To make explicitly clear that Rabbi edited the Mishnah, Epstein collects together the several proofs. These include the presence of anonymous *mishnayot* that follow Rabbi's view of the law or of an earlier dispute and the presence of identifiable traditions that Rabbi taught anonymously on the Mishnah. The use of such proofs, we should realize, would be rejected by those who hold that Rabbi never altered his sources, and that Rabbi's sources already contained these anonymous formulations. Others have examined the latter position and have pointed out the circular reasoning involved. We should prefer Epstein's interpretation as far as it adopts the plain sense of the several Amoraic observations that 'Rabbi taught Mishnah anonymously.' We have seen several of Epstein's examples that demonstrate how Rabbi quite changed his sources. Intertwined with Epstein's view is his conception that Rabbi intended the Mishnah as a legal code, and he naturally arranged the material according to his conception of the law. In light of this conclusion, Epstein has to argue that Rabbi's authorship of the Mishnah is not inconsistent with "anti-Rabbi *mishnayot*" in the Mishnah. These consist of *mishnayot* based on another sage's Mishnah, which disputes the view of Rabbi.[120] Epstein's explanation follows his conception of the method of a Mishnah's editor, and in particular Rabbi: an editor taught the opinion of a sage and commented on it, whether in the Mishnah or in an external source. As the *baraita* puts it, "Rabbi taught it, but does not hold its view" (b. 'Eruv. 38b). While this explanation is consistent with the preponderance of evidence and perhaps presupposes fewer assumptions than the alternative point of view, it remains self-serving. Alternatively, one wonders whether one can attribute the presence of these "anti-Rabbi *mishnayot*" to the manner in which Rabbi had access to earlier sources. For Rabbi's Tanna recited the Mishnah and he corrected it.[121] If for some reason, the reciter had included these teachings, perhaps he could not remove them from that "edition." Second, the presence of unsmooth readings in the Mishnah text,

---

[120] *ITL*, pp. 200-01.
[121] See *ibid.*, pp. 182, 211, esp. 212; *ITM*, pp. 13-22, esp. 21-22; Lieberman, *Hellenism, op. cit.,* pp. 87-88, 97.

Epstein himself has demonstrated, is often due to Rabbi's method. His particular use of different sources resulted in rough readings of the Mishnah, with a single *mishnah* containing two different views.[122]

Epstein accomplished the first really internal historical study of the Mishnah and its formation. He explicitly admits he is not the first to use source criticism.[123] But he applied it systematically, to one Mishnah after the next. The reader of the present volume can well judge to what degree he refined and developed this method. Through his source criticism and literary analysis he went beyond earlier scholars by claiming to show actual pieces of various strata of the Mishnah, and reconstructed the process of the Mishnah's formation. Nevertheless, doubts remain concerning several of his points. These include specific issues such as the existence in overall collections of the pre-ʿAqiban topical strings of *mishnayot* and laws, as well as more general points, such as the necessity to choose between two alternatives in a historical interpretation. We have specifically raised the last query concerning Rabbi's changing of sources and his intending the Mishnah as a legal code.

Epstein has been rightly called "the father of the study of careful Talmudic scholarship."[124] In his *Introduction to the Text of the Mishnah* he demonstrated what one may *call* the Mishnah and the procedures necessary in order to define it. In the *Introduction to Tannaitic Literature* he drew attention to the full significance of sources in the Mishnah's composition. He thus laid the foundation for the modern study of the Mishnah. The task of the present study of the Mishnah therefore is to realize the fullest dimensions what Epstein started.

---

[122] See *ITM*, pp. 595-672, and above, pp. 16-18, 26.
[123] *ITL*, p. 459, fn. 2; *HaMadaʿ*, pp. 8-9.
[124] Lieberman, *Siphre Zutta, op. cit.*, p. 135.

PART II

THE BEGINNING OF CRITICAL STUDY

CHAPTER FOUR

THE PIONEER: ZECHARIAS FRANKEL

JOEL GEREBOFF

i

Rabbi Zecharias Frankel was born on September 30, 1801, in Prague and died in Breslau on February 13, 1875. His parents possessed rabbinical lineage. His father was a member of the Spira family, exiled from Vienna in 1670, and his mother was a Fischel, one of the distinguished families of Prague Talmudists. Frankel married Rachel Meyer and had no children. He received his rabbinical training under Rabbi Bezalel Ronsperg, and in 1825 entered the University of Budapest, graduating in 1831. In 1832, as district rabbi of Leitmeritz, he assumed a pulpit in Teplitz where he introduced the use of a boys choir, an organ and sermons in German. In 1836 Frankel became rabbi of Dresden, a position officially confirmed by the government of Saxony, where he remained until his appointment as director of the Jüdische Theologische Seminar in Breslau. Offered the position of Chief Rabbi of Berlin, he refused when the Prussian government would not recognize the appointment.

Frankel is known as the founder of "positive-historical Judaism," a movement which assumed a position between the neo-Orthodox and the Reform. During the Hamburg Prayerbook dispute, he infuriated the Orthodox by advocating the right to change prayers and to pray in the vernacular, and angered the Reform by stating that changes should not be made arbitrarily. Frankel broke all his ties with the Reform movement at the Frankfurt Rabbinical Conference.

Frankel devoted his literary activities to three matters. In 1840 he wrote, *Die Eidesleistung der Juden in talmudischer und historischer Bezeichnung*, and in 1846 *Der gerichtliche Beweis nach mosäisch-talmudischen Rechte*. Written for political reasons, these works argued that a Jew's oath can be trusted and led to a reformation of the Prussian government's attitude toward Jewish oaths. The second area of Frankel's literary endeavors was his effort to demonstrate the antiquity of Jewish Law. This was done in *Vorstudien zu der*

Septuaginta, and in *Über den Einfluss der palästinischen Exegese auf die alexandrinische Hermeneutik*. He was the first Jewish scholar of the nineteenth century to work with the Septuagint. His final literary works were his studies on the formation of Talmudic literature. This exposition is found in *Darkhé HaMishnah, Mevo HaYerushalmi, Grundlinien des mosäisch-talmudischen Eherechts*, and his unfinished *magnum opus*, a new edition of the Palestinian Talmud. The majority of Frankel's other writings appear in the *Zeitschrift für die Religiosen Interessen des Judenthums*, and in the *Monatsschrift für die Geschichte und Wissenschaft des Judenthums*, both of which he edited.[1]

ii

Frankel's opinions on the Mishnah appear in *Darkhé HaMishnah*, and in several articles in the *Monatsschrift*.[2] In order to present Frankel's theory, I will list the topics in an outline which reveals his scientific, systematic method. Frankel was the first scholar to compose a "scientific" introduction to the Mishnah, and his work undoubtedly served as the foundation for future endeavors;[3] therefore, the outline may serve as a basis for comparison between Frankel and later works. I will show that the debate following the publication of the work did not do justice to Frankel's presentation, since it centered only about his theological views. His removal of the Mishnah from the theological realm is the only lasting value of the book.

    I. Content
        A. Definition of Mishnah: nature of the material
        B. Definition of *halakhah*
            1. *Halakhah* as explanation to the Torah
            2. Abstract *halakhah*: purpose, methodology
        C. Reasons for the change in the nature of the *halakhah*
        D. *Halakhah leMosheh miSinai*
        E. Personalities and institutions
            1. Men of the Great Assembly
            2. Sanhedrin
            3. Pairs
            4. *Hokhmé haHalakhah* (Sages of the Law)

---

[1] An extensive biography of Frankel appeared in the *MGWJ* 45, 1901, pp. 193-352. Included in this is a complete bibliography of his writings. Rabbi Saul Rabinowitz, *HaRav Zekhariah Frankel*, (Warsaw, 1898) wrote a complete biography. Rabinowitz, a Conservative, shows his prejudice throughout the book.

[2] The bibliography lists all related works.

[3] Jacob Brüll and Albeck among others.

II. Form
    A. History of the formation of the Mishnah
        1. Personalities
        2. Written or oral traditions?
    B. Textual Criticism
    C. Order in the formation of the Mishnah
    D. Literary principles (KLLYM) employed in the formation of the Mishnah

Frankel's work thus may be divided into two areas. In his introduction he notes that the previous works on the Mishnah did not successfully deal with the generations of the rabbis or with the organization (SDR) of the Mishnah. Frankel tried to answer these questions. The section on the content of the Mishnah was devoted to prove the antiquity of the oral law. By reviewing different personalities and institutions, Frankel wanted to show that the substance of the Mishnah's oral law originated at a very early period. The section on form presents Frankel's contention that the Mishnah (in its final form) was organized and edited by Rabbi Judah the Patriarch (henceforth: Rabbi) using scientific principles. By citing examples, which he never explains, Frankel asserts that the development of the Mishnah was a conservative process. Nothing from the past was changed; those of later generations worked systematically to build on what they had received.

iii

"Mishnah [for Frankel] is synonymous with *halakhah*, when *halakhah* specifically refers to a brief law without stating its reasoning or providing a text. The *halakhah* serves as a guide for Jewish life (the way to walk)."[4] While the Mishnah also contains *taqqanot* and *gezerot*, Frankel largely concerns himself with the *halakhah*. Within the *halakhah*, Frankel finds two methods. The earliest stratum of *halakhah* served as an explanation to the Torah (PRŠ) which clarified the intention of the Torah when the text was not immediately comprehensible: "For they (the Scribes—*Soferim*) explained the commandments and joined their explanation to the Torah. In doing this they explained the commandments for the purpose of practical law. This is the crux of the oral law."[5] Examples of this method are

---

[4] Zecharias Frankel, *Darkhé HaMishnah* p. 7 n. 8 states that, based on M. Ned. 4.3; b. Ber. 47b; and b. Qid. 49a, the Mishnah refers to a law given without a text.
[5] *Ibid.*, p. 5.

M. Neg. 12 : 5-7; M. Soṭ. 8 : 1, 2; and M.M.S. 5 : 7. This method was later replaced by the formulation of abstract law, "law which came by itself to explain an issue ('NYN) of the Torah, without attaching the law to the text [of Scriptures]."[6] The first method relied upon the order of the Torah; the newer material was arranged topically. This facilitated the learning of the law, for all the laws concerning a subject were now organized together. The laws were not formulated arbitrarily but rather were deduced from hermeneutical principles (MDWT): "Even more than their attaching the law to the text, they (the sages) derived and widened the law by the light of their reasoning, and this is the essential part of the abstract law. In order that the truth would not be lacking, they set up rules and they called them MDWT according to which the exegesis was guided."[7] Frankel thus equates the early law of the *Soferim* with that of the later Pharisees.

Although it is undoubtedly true that some form of extra-Scriptural law must have existed always, Frankel offers no evidence that would warrant equating the law of the *Soferim* with the Mishnaic law. Perhaps this demonstrably old law was merely the common law of the land. Moreover, the examples Frankel gives as "old law" come from a much later period. M. Soṭ. 8 : 1, is dated by Y. N. Epstein to the Roman-Jewish War,[8] as it even contains the Latin word QLGSYN. But Frankel throughout assumes that the Mishnaic law originated at the return of Ezra. In his historical analysis, those who returned and formed the Second Commonwealth differed from the members of the First Commonwealth: "For in distinction to those from previous times [First Commonwealth] who desired to be like all the nations which surrounded them, those who returned from the exile and those coming after them had turned their hearts to seek God and to draw from the spring of the Torah."[9] Since these returnees were so dedicated to the Torah, an explanation for the incomprehensible portions of the Torah had to be devised: This was the *halakhah*.

Frankel argues that the first method of *halakhah*, the exegetical, was changed for three reasons.[10] The law by virtue of its dispersion throughout the Torah became confused, requiring acute memory to learn it. Frankel also argues that, when Alexander came to Jerusalem,

[6] *Ibid.*, p. 6.
[7] *Ibid.*, p. 18.
[8] Y. N. Epstein, *Mavo leNusaḥ haMishnah*, p. 43.
[9] Frankel, *op. cit.*, p. 2.
[10] *Ibid.*, p. 6.

as he did in all countries he conquered, he changed the leadership. Aware of the lack of evidence for this claim, Frankel asserts that Josephus purposely neglected this incident in order not to anger the Romans. After the troubles had subsided, a new body, the Sanhedrin, composed of the *Zeqenim* or Elders, was instituted and "also the manner of learning was changed in order to mark a distinction between the Men of the Great Assembly and those that followed."[11]

Frankel's arguments for the antiquity of the law rely on faulty history, circular reasoning, and inner contradictions. Frankel claims that there was an early law. Aware that the Mishnah contains none of this old law, he argues that the old *halakhah* was mostly forgotten and confused. Some of this law however, was transmitted as *halakhah leMosheh miSinai*, which for Frankel means "self-evident or old law"[12] or in the name of the sages. But this argument is circular, for it asserts that there was an old law, and then accounts for the lack of evidence about it. Second, we have no evidence that this law, even if it existed, was the same as Mishnaic law. Third, Frankel contradicts himself, for, as we shall see (p. 71 n. 36) in principle 14 for the Mishnah's organization, he states that the term *sages* always refers to contemporaries of the Tannaim. Moreover, he is not clear who were the ZQNYM and who were the ḤKMYM Here he says the sages came later, and there he says the names are synonymous.[13] He depicts the Men of the Great Assembly as a modern Parliament which voted upon the exegetical *halakhah*. Then he tells us that this method of *halakhah* was replaced for three reasons, as noted. He asserts that Alexander must have changed the leadership when he came to Jerusalem. Moreover, he gives the reason, that out of respect for the past, the members of the Sanhedrin consciously decided to change the law. But Frankel has already stated that the law was changed because of the difficulty in remembering it. The argument that national political upheavals also affected the educational institutions is again used by Frankel in his claim that the breakdown of the Sanhedrin occurred when Herod killed its leaders.[14] This event, according to Frankel, caused the law to be cited in an individual's name and not in the "harmonious voice of the sages."

[11] *Ibid.*, p. 6.
[12] *Ibid.*, p. 20.
[13] *Ibid.*, pp. 10, 12, 42.
[14] *Ibid.*, p. 45.

Frankel offers several other proofs for the antiquity of the Mishnaic law. As stated, he claimed that *halakhah leMosheh miSinai* referred to an "old law or to a self evident law." The latter assertion is supported by the analysis of Rabbenu Asher (Toledo 1250-1327) of M. Yad. 4 : 3, which states that the prohibition against a Moabite partaking of Heave-offering is a "self evident law" (a *halakhah leMosheh miSinai*).[15] He gives no proof for the former assertion. In reviewing the different orders of the Mishnah, Frankel notes that the laws of *Moʻed* are very old because the laws of the holidays were always observed, as is indicated by the *one* Sabbath injunction in Jer. 18 : 21, 22. This claim is as unfounded as his assertion that the laws in *Seder Ṭoharot* are old because it is the largest order, and because I Mac. 1 : 62 shows that the Jews did not use the oil of gentiles. To date a whole order merely on its size and on the fact it contains one law present in another source is not persuasive. Frankel offers no definitive proof for an early dating for Mishnaic law. Frankel's positive contribution is his placing the origin and the development of the *halakhah* within the historical framework. By stating that the Men of the Great Assembly voted on what was to be the *halakhah*, and by claiming that this law was deduced by humanly-determined hermeneutical principles he removed the *halakhah* from the theological realm.

iv

Frankel next describes the institutions and personalities which contributed to the development of the law. His comments may be divided into a description of, first, the historical situation and, second, the legal concerns of the different personalities. In general, Frankel views the people as "devoted servants of God." Simeon the Righteous' comment in M. Avot 1 : 1, to "raise up many students" indicates, for Frankel, that everyone was interested in the Torah.[16] "There was unity throughout the land and the Sages served as the leadership." This situation however changed, when the Maccabees came to power. The Sanhedrin lost its political power, which was transferred to the *Bet Din* of the Hasmoneans, but still maintained its "religious" authority. The Pairs then arose to lead the Sanhedrin and served as its *Nasi* and *Av Bet Din*.[17] Again, Frankel offers no proof for these assertions. The

---

[15] During the debate, Rabbenu Asher's statement was one of the focal points.
[16] Frankel, *op. cit.*, p. 3.
[17] *Ibid.*, pp. 14, 43.

history of the Great Assembly and the Sanhedrin is, even today, not very clear. His attribution of changes in the method of expounding the law to the transition in the nation's leadership is unproven, and his description of the harmony within the country is naive. Frankel would have us believe that the Sanhedrin peacefully gave up its political power and reached accord with the Maccabees. This picture of "peace in the land" and widespread acceptance of the religious and political authority of the rabbis is taken for granted by Frankel for the entire period of the Tannaim. He states that Yoḥanan b. Zakkai received from Rabban Simeon b. Gamaliel (who was engaged in the war in Jerusalem) the authority to issue ordinances for the entire nation.[18] Recent scholarship has shown that Yoḥanan b. Zakkai was not a very important figure in his own day.[19] Moreover, in discussing the place of learning following the destruction in 70 A.D., Frankel states, that everybody studied in his own *Bet Midrash*, while at times, all came together to the Sanhedrin of the *Nasi*, for which (again) there is no evidence. Frankel thus would lead one to believe that everyone in this period of the Tannaim was a good Pharisee. His history is an attempt to show that the whole Jewish people observed the entire Mishnaic law, a point he takes for granted throughout. Modern scholarship has rendered this claim untenable.[20]

Frankel next offers a detailed description of the contributions of the different personalities to the content of the law. Those who lived before the time of Hillel and Shammai were known as the "makers of ordinances" (MTQNY HTQNWT). From this group we have both *halakhot* and *taqqanot*. The *halakhot*, as noted, were transmitted in the name of the sages or as *halakhah leMosheh miSinai*. The *taqqanot* were given in the name of the *Nasi*. The first set of *taqqanot* was those of Ezra (b. B.Q. 82a; y. Meg. 4 : 1). The *taqqanot* of the other sages who lived before Hillel are cited by Frankel and compiled in a list. So we are left with unfounded statements on the origins of the Mishnaic law and a compilation of the *taqqanot* of those who came before Hillel.

One-third of Frankel's entire book is comprised by his section on the "Sages of the Law," the six generations of the Tannaim, in which he intends "to demonstrate the areas of interest and the methodology of the individual sages." He states that he wants to aid "in the

---

[18] *Ibid.*, 15, 66.
[19] See Jacob Neusner, *Development of a Legend*, pp. 297-301.
[20] See E. E. Urbach, *Ḥazal*, pp. 470-6.

understanding of the development of the manner of the early investigation into the law which started from a very small spring and spread into a great river."[21] While Frankel says he gives a history of the law, all he actually provides is his card file. He merely collects the laws in the name of a given rabbi, then states that Rabbi x appears in tractate A and tractate B. This catalogue of sayings in no way shows *development* of the law. The only comment that implies a development of the law is his statement that the later generations of the Tannaim (particularly the fourth) discussed and reworked the material of the earlier generations, which is a valuable, if commonplace, observation. Frankel also attempts to clarify the methodology of the individual rabbis by placing the laws into categories. For example, the Houses' disputes concerned three issues; literal interpretation of the text, definition of the extent of prohibitions, and giving reasons for law.[22] Frankel divides the person's sayings into legal, biographical, historical, and moral-theological dicta, and cites the disputants and the teachers of the individual rabbis, which "aids resolving textual problems."

As we review Frankel's work on the content of the law, we find little critical analysis. His history is a combination of verbatim accounts of Scripture and Talmudical sources, an uncritical chronology based on *Seder 'Olam* and *Iggeret Rabbi Sherira Gaon,* circular reasoning, and arguments from silence. Second Commonwealth law *is* Pharisaic law. His work on the *history* of the law is no more than a collection of rabbis' sayings.

v

Frankel next turns to the formation of the Mishnah. His underlying premise, following the opinion in the *Gemara* (b. Yev. 30a; b. Shev. 4a) is that a "Mishnah does not move from its place." By this Frankel means that once a Mishnah-pericope had assumed a definite place within a chapter of the Mishnah, the pericope was not removed from that place. So it was a process of accretion of new materials to existing, older ones. The later organizer merely built around the earlier Mishnah. Three authorities organized the Mishnah, 'Aqiba, Meir, and Judah the Prince. The Mishnah was to serve as a law code, as numerous Amoraic sayings indicate.

[21] Frankel, *op. cit.*, p. 28.
[22] *Ibid.*, p. 47.

Frankel begins by noting, "The details of law increased to the thousands and the tens of thousands, and only those with very diligent memories could succeed in learning. What would be the purpose of learning the law, if the number of legal sayings increased and the pupils of each master only taught their pupils what they had heard from their masters."[23] Then "God awoke the hearts of the great Sages and clothed them in the spirit of knowledge and understanding to find an order to the *halakhot* and to collect those spread out to the ends of the Torah to the place where they belonged."[24] 'Aqiba was the first to be so inspired. His role as an editor is supported by b. San. 86a, which states that "R. Meir organized the Mishnah according to ('LYB' D) Rabbi 'Aqiba" and by Rabbi Yosi's statements (M. Kel. 30 : 4), "Fortunate is Kelim that it began with [the laws of] uncleanness and concluded with [the laws of] cleanness." Both of these proofs are somewhat problematic. Does 'LYB' prove that 'Aqiba had organized a Mishnah? Why does Yosi's statement at the end of Kelim necessarily imply that 'Aqiba was its organizer? Could Kelim not have been finished by some other rabbi? Frankel also states that 'Aqiba organized the material of the very old laws, the MŠNH R'ŠWNH (the first Mishnah), the disputes of the Houses, and possibly some of the Eliezer and Joshua material.[25] Frankel, however, gives no clue as to exactly what 'Aqiba did. Did 'Aqiba write the material, or did he merely organize pre-existing pericopae? Did early Yavnean masters produce already-organized materials? What were 'Aqiba's principles of organization? Are we to assume he used the same forty-five principles that Frankel then assigns to Rabbi? What criteria did Frankel use for dating a law to 'Aqiba? Which of the Houses disputes did 'Aqiba organize? Frankel is unclear about 'Aqiba's role. He states that, if we are to assume that MŠNT 'QYB'refers to an organized Mishnah, then would not MŠNH R'ŠWNH also refer to organized material?[26]

Rabbi Meir's role, according to Frankel, was to add, to the previous material, the new material from 'Aqiba's generation. If a Mishnah is cited as concluded (STM) by R. Meir, then this is one upon which everyone in the time of Meir had agreed, and it is Meir's work, not Rabbi's. Meir's role is attested to by the statement in b. San. 86b:

[23] *Ibid.*, p. 220.
[24] *Ibid.*, p. 220.
[25] *Ibid.*, p. 221.
[26] *Ibid.*, p. 221.

"R. Meir concluded the Mishnah according to R. 'Aqiba." Frankel again fails to state exactly what Meir did, or how he understands the saying.

Frankel then describes the work of Judah. Judah not only organized material by putting everything in its proper place and concluded (STM) the Mishnah, but he also cited the authoritative decision (PSQ): "With his intelligence, Rabbi compiled the opinions of the earlier Tannaim, and cited the opinion he felt to be correct as that of the first Tanna in a Mishnah, in the name of the sages, or as a concluded decision (STM). After Rabbi had finished his entire work, he went over the Mishnah very critically. If he found something regarding which he had changed his opinion, he still left the old decision and added the new material *"for the Mishnah was already known by the sages."* The purpose of this work was "to lighten the load of looking for the law."[27] As is clear from this description, Rabbi was conservative in his work. Rabbi determined the accepted decision and, as will be seen, Frankel offers principles for this endeavor. But how does a person attempting to formulate a law code allow contradictions to remain in his work? Frankel will also use the idea of Rabbi's conservatism to explain away textual problems. Moreover, he states elsewhere that Rabbi did *not* change the order of the earlier law code, of Meir, because it was familiar to the people. Next he states that Rabbi left his new order unchanged, because the people had already learned it and had forgotten the old code. Last, he states that when he went over his first copy, he left this order unchanged because the people had become accustomed to it. I find this confusing. What is the relationship between Rabbi's first and second codes? More important, why did Rabbi organize the Mishnah? Is it only because, as Frankel writes, the "spirit of God was within him?"[28]

Frankel states, "Rabbi gathered all the laws from the schools of Judah b. Ilai and Meir and also disputes from 'Aqiba's time which Meir had omitted. He also added some disputes of the Houses and possibly some old laws that both 'Aqiba and Meir had left out. We have some evidence that Rabbi changed some of Meir's opinions."[29] Frankel fails to consider why the earlier material was left out of Meir's and 'Aqiba's *Mishnayot*. Why did a law *now* appear which had earlier been omitted, or possibly, in the meantime, forgotten? Was some

---

[27] *Ibid.*, p. 224-7; *MGWJ* 11, 1862, pp. 272-4.
[28] *Ibid.*, p. 226.
[29] *Ibid.*, p. 227.

material permanently lost to Rabbi, which only turned up later in the *Gemara* as *beraitot*? Did later generations tamper with the Mishnah? Frankel states that citations such as "the words of Judah" or "Rabbi says" are late additions, from the sixth generation of the Tannaim. The addition of the views of the sixth generation of Tannaim accounts for laws *concluded* (STM) contrary to Judah's opinion. Frankel allows for some changes in the Mishnah following the time of Judah; he says these are minor. He also notes changes in the Palestinian Talmud on the basis of the Babylonian Talmud. Could these changes have extended to the Mishnah itself? This leads to the question, Was there ever an "original" Mishnah? And if there was, how wide was its initial acceptance?

vi

Frankel emphatically states, "There is surely no doubt that all the members of the generation did not agree with Rabbi's style (ŚGNWN]."[30] Several passages from the *Gemara* are cited to substantiate this assertion. Frankel, however, believes the Amoraim used Rabbi's Mishnah. But these two claims are inconsistent. If Frankel admits that Rabbi's Mishnah was not universally accepted, then how can he claim that the Mishnah used by all Amoraim was Rabbi's? Similarly, he argues the text was written, for "how could all the future work of the Amoraim have succeeded if they did not originally have a written text?"[31] But, then how could there ever have been an oral tradition? Rashi's comment on b. Shab. 138a, "In order that they shall see and read,"[32] indicates, for Frankel, that the Mishnah was *written*. But nothing in these arguments must of necessity date the written text to Rabbi's authorship. Errors could have occurred in later written versions. Frankel offers two justifications for textual errors. The *oral* tradition which existed even *after* the publication of the Mishnah, gave rise to additions to the text. If this is admitted, then what is the limit of these changes? Second, Frankel asserts Rabbi did not write the Mishnah with great care, for the essential part of the tradition remained oral. If Rabbi intended to order a law code, to avoid confusion of the law, how could he have written it so carelessly?

[30] *Ibid.*, p. 228.
[31] *Ibid.*, p. 229.
[32] These comments are not part of the original text but were added in the supplement published in 1867.

vii

By using available texts,³³ Frankel attempted to establish the correct readings for the *Mishnayot* in *Zera'im*. He relied upon the Mishnah text, the Mishnah as it appears in both Talmuds, and also upon the explanations of Rashi, Maimonides, Samson b. Abraham (Sens, ?-1226), and Isaac b. Jacob Alfassi (Alkalai, 1013-1103). Much of Frankel's work appears in the *Monatsschrift*.³⁴ Frankel only cites the differences between the versions and rarely makes corrections. The criteria for the corrections are: the Galileans use of brief language (LŠN' QLYL'), their writing ML' (using vowel letters) while the Babylonians wrote ḤSR (lacking vowel letters), and the different pronunciations between the two countries, such as the Galilean pronunciation of B like W and P like B or W. Frankel, however, realized that future work required a better text for the Palestinian Talmud.

viii

By showing the internal order and the logical sequence of the tractates, Frankel attempts to demonstrate the logical construction of the Mishnah. He contends that the tractates already had their names and their order in Rabbi's Mishnah.³⁵ He gives Amoraic citations to support this claim. Following Sherira's reasoning, he argues that the order of the tractates may be explained in two ways. The first is to demonstrate the logical order between the tractates. The laws in the tractates of Zera'im descend from the commonly observed everyday laws of *Berakhot* to the less frequently observed laws of Ḥallah and 'Orlah. The second way is to give "reasons" for the order; Ta'anit is next to Rosh Hashanah because Ta'anit begins with the law of asking for rain, which in the opinion of some Tannaim is said on Rosh Hashanah. Frankel criticizes Maimonides for employing the latter method. But Frankel also uses it when he states that 'Avodah Zarah is placed next to Sanhedrin because the laws of 'Avodah Zarah appear in Sanhedrin. Many other laws appear in Sanhedrin. Above all, even if the tractates follow a logical order, why must it be Rabbi's?

---

³³ Frankel, *op. cit.*, p. 235 n. 5, 6. Frankel never states what manuscripts he is using.

³⁴ Articles on textual criticism may be found in *MGWJ*, 7, 1858, pp. 419-30; 10, 1861 pp. 431, 2; 12, 1863, pp. 71, 2; 310-12; 13, 1864 pp. 71, 2, 395-7.

³⁵ Frankel, *op. cit.*, p. 270 lists citations from the *Gemara* referring to Kelim, 'Uqṣin, 'Orlah, Terumah, Tamid, Yoma', B.Q., B.M., R.H., Ket., Ned., Nazir, Soṭah, Mak., Shev.

THE PIONEER: ZECHARIAS FRANKEL

Frankel also presents "forty-five principles,"[36] used by Rabbi in organizing the Mishnah. These principles attempt to account for every literary trait of the Mishnah, both the normal and the deviant. Is the placing of the term ZH HKLL (this is the rule) at the beginning, in the middle, or at the end of a Mishnah a rule, or is it simply a matter of choice? For Frankel it is a rule. The principles may be divided into three general categories: twelve principles for citing the accepted law, six principles for relating general categories to particular details (KLL WPRṬ), nine principles for relating the individual laws to one another. There are also brief discussions about linguistic considerations, authenticity of sayings, and strata within the tradition. Underlying the forty-five principles are his first three principles: (1) the

---

[36] The forty five "principles" are:
  1. The Mishnah is brief law,
  2. Mishnah gives the law to explain the commandments.
  3. Mishnah was composed at different times, Rabbi found organized material.
  4. Mishnah citations are given without names of Rabbis (STM).
  5. If the STM has a disputant, the STM is called the Tanna QM'.
  6. Sometimes the Mishnah contains a Tanna QM' and sages; sometimes Tanna Qamma and individual Rabbi and the Sages; sometimes an individual, the sages and then an individual.
  7. Sometimes there is a STM and then a dispute and sometimes it is the other way around.
  8. Two contradictory STMYM (decided laws)—one early, one late.
  9. A STM in a person's name in one place and without a person's name in another.
  10. A Mishnah may appear which is not needed; it may appear in brief in one place and at length in another.
  11. A saying may be given in an individual's name with no Tanna Qamma or STM given along with it.
  12. Sometimes there are two disputants and neither is the Tanna Qamma.
  13. If a law appears in the name of an individual, and elsewhere in the name of the sages, or in the name of a later Rabbi, it was changed to indicate it is the authoritative decision.
  14. The term "Sages" generally refers to contemporaries of the disputant who appears in the Mishnah.
  15. A saying may refer to something which does not appear in the Mishnah.
  16. A STM may be followed by a story (Ma'aseh) which contradicts it.
  17. The organizer may cite the words of a sage as he said them or he may paraphrase them.
  18. When (the words) are quoted in direct discourse, then they usually are what was originally said.
  19. Sometimes the topic may be given and then the dispute, and sometimes a complete saying of a Tanna and then the differing opinion.
  20. Two sayings may be combined which obviously are from different periods.
  21. A gloss may be from a later generation.
  22. A saying and then a dispute about how it was said, and sometimes the later dispute may be in the form of the original dispute.

Mishnah contains *brief* citations of law, (2) the Mishnah consists of law and not *Aggadah*, (3) the Mishnah was composed in an historical framework. Later generations built upon what they had received without ever removing (or moving) anything. Through the use of these principles, Frankel attempts to define Rabbi's role as an organizer and as a law-giver and to show the logical construction of the Mishnah.

Frankel's principles suffer from two unproven assumptions: the antiquity of the law, and Rabbi's knowledge of all the Mishnaic material including the Tosefta. Both these assumptions are asserted without proof. He argues that a law, because of its antiquity, is never removed from its original place. He also states that, if a law is out of

23. Another sage may interrupt a previous discussion in between the topic of discussion and the disputing sages.
24. Debate in the Mishnah, especially from earlier generations.
25. Sometimes a detailed proof may appear to refute a claim.
26. A story may be cited to accentuate some aspect of a law.
27. The terms 'MRW or B'MT 'MRW (they said or they truly said) indicate that the law is old.
28. A short saying may be cited as a general principle for many particular details. This may be given in the form of a number.
29. General categories are used for combining the material.
30. Use of KL (all) to cite all the details of a law.
31. Particular details lacking a general category may be introduced by the word 'LW (these are).
32. The use of the most inclusive or exclusive detail.
33. Comparison of laws to bring out similarities and differences.
34. Details are cited in ascending or descending order.
35. Parts of the law may be cited before the details.
36. All the details may be cited as an index and then dealt with individually.
37. A law which is not part of a tractate may appear as an introduction to the tractate.
38. More general laws are cited first in a tractate.
39. Unrelated laws may appear in a tractate because they bear some linguistic similarity.
40. Laws may appear together because they were taught on the same day, to point to some general idea, there is some relation in some detail, or there is some legal connection.
41. A law may appear in a tractate because it is in some way close (QRWB) to the laws of that tractate.
42. A law may be cited in two tractates because, it either belongs in both or because it has some minor relation to one of the tractates.
43. The Mishnah is in clean, brief language, and if it is overly brief, it may be an early law.
44. The tractate is named after the major issue discussed in it.
45. The tractates and the chapters are organized in a pleasing manner according to logic, and one can see in them the hand of a craftsman. If one discerns the strata he will understand the Mishnah.

place, it is from an "earlier tradition." If, however, the later materials were built around the earlier traditions, how could the earlier law *ever* be out of place? Second, Frankel assumes Rabbi knew all the Mishnaic material. Principle fifteen states, "If something is referred to in the Mishnah and is not cited, but does appear in the Tosefta, Rabbi knew this and omitted the reference from the Mishnah, in order to maintain the Mishnah's brevity." Differences in parallel traditions pose no problem for Frankel, as Rabbi knew all the versions of the text. Frankel contradicts this assertion, for he states that Amoraim did make changes in the text. Moreover, are the principles inclusive enough? And are they mutually contradictory? These principles do not account for any of the smaller elements of the Mishnah. What principles were used for wording the laws? Was Rabbi a mere organizer of material, or did he also compose? Could Rabbi have simultaneously observed *all* the contradictory principles?

Frankel makes several valid observations. Mnemonic patterns certainly were used for composing the material. Certain formulae, such as ZH HKLL (this is the rule), 'LW (these are), KL/ḤWṢ MYN (all/except), KL/WYŠ (all/and there are), 'YN BYN (no difference between ...) were employed. A small corpus such as a law with a few details, or laws given in the same form, or all the sayings of a Rabbi, may appear as a unit within the Mishnah—a good point. Later generations (principles 5, 6, 21, 22, 23) glossed earlier material. His last principle states, "The second volume of this work will delineate the separate strata of the Mishnah. If one understands the strata of the early and the late *Mishnayot* he will have found the key to unlock the Mishnah."[37] Frankel notes a development in the Mishnah. But is it possible to attribute its final form to one man?

Summary: For Frankel, Rabbi was the organizer and the law giver. He compiled the Mishnah in its final form, employing a systematic approach. The Mishnah was a work of art; everything was "necessary" and in its place. All these claims are merely asserted. Frankel gives citations from Mishnaic and Amoraic sources, never demonstrating how the citations prove his contentions. Frankel applied his theory of positive-historical Judaism, which depicted Jewish Life as a process combining the lasting values from the past with human intelligence, in order to face the present and the future, to the formation of the Mishnah. The Mishnah was a product of human intelligence and

[37] Frankel, *op. cit.*, p. 321.

divine inspiration. Using their intelligence, later generations took what they had received from the past and added to it. Nothing was ever removed. Frankel's work has little lasting value. He was, however, the first to analyze the Mishnah critically and historically, and this is his importance.

ix

Frankel's work initially had a tremendous impact. Upon its publication, two camps arose: Samson Raphael Hirsch headed the opposition of the traditionalists, while Shlomo Rappoport led the defenders of Frankel. The arguments appeared in several pamphlets, in the 1861 edition of the *Allgemeine Zeitung für die Wissenschaft des Judenthums* and in S.R. Hirsch's journal *Yeshurun*.[38] The discussion centered about three points: the origin of the *halakhah*, divine or in the Great Assembly? The origin of the MDWT (hermeneutical principles)—divine or human? The meaning of *halakhah leMosheh miSinai*, a divine or very old or self-evident law? The traditionalists argued that Frankel had ascribed all three to human origin. They cited the Talmud and Maimonides as proof for their assertions to the contrary. The traditionalists also claimed that Frankel had not ascribed enough of the law to its Mosaic origin. Second, Frankel had relied upon the Palestinian Talmud while "the explanation of the Babylonian Talmud did not appear."[39] Personal attacks were levelled against both Frankel and his Seminary. Auerbach referred to Frankel as "Haḥakham min Hamizraḥ" (the Sage from the East). Klein, however, reiterates that he does not want to malign Frankel, but only desires further clarification. Even Rappoport demanded clarification of Frankel's theological stands.

In his response[40] Frankel merely stated, "People should read the book without presuppositions. It is a book on the development of the *halakhah* and the Mishnah, and not on theology. Attacks should be made against the book and not against its author or his Seminary." He did not reply to the issues, and probably could not have entered a

[38] A complete history and chronology of the debate may be found in Rabinowitz's biography. The major works of the debate were: Benjamin Auerbach, *haṢofé 'al Darkhé haMishnah*, Shlomo Klein, *Meppiné Qeshet*, and *Ha'emet WeHashalom 'Ehavu*, and Shlomo Rappoport, *Divré Shalom Ve'Emet*, and Samson Hirsch's articles in *Yeshurun*.

[39] Benjamin Auerbach, *haṢofé 'al Darkhé haMishnah*, p. 54.

[40] *MGWJ* 10, 1861, pp. 159-60.

fruitful debate with people whose presuppositions were so different from his own.

Klein also states, "There have arisen in the land a new group of people who do not trust in the truth of faith, but have followed the desires of their hearts. They have vented their disgusting spirit upon the Torah, which they have not accepted as Mosaic and now will do the same to the Talmud."[41] Frankel's work could now serve as a new weapon for the Reform movement. The traditionalists criticized only Frankel's theological beliefs but never dealt with his historical, literary analysis. Their criticism was warranted, for the true innovation of Frankel's work was the claim that the Mishnah was not divine but was the product of human creation.

[11] Shlomo Klein, *Meppiné Qeshet*, p. 14.

CHAPTER FIVE

JACOB BRÜLL: THE MISHNAH AS A LAW-CODE

GARY G. PORTON

i

Jacob Brüll was born in Neu-Raussnitz, Moravia in 1812. After attending the *yeshivot* of Bonyhad, Presburg, and Budapest, he served as assistant rabbi of Neu-Raussnitz and then as chief rabbi of Kojetein. Brüll died in Kojetein in 1896. Besides contributing articles to Lowe's *Ben Ḥananya* and Weiss's *Bet Talmud*, Brüll authored three scholarly works. In 1852 he published *Forschungen über Targumim und Midraschim*. 1864 saw the publication of his *Die Mnemonik des Talmud*, and in 1876 he issued the first volume of his *Mavo haMishnah*. The second appeared in 1885.[42] His *Mavo haMishnah* has now been reprinted in the State of Israel.[43]

ii

In the preface to Volume One, Brüll outlines the reason he wrote the *Mavo haMishnah* and his method of research:

> These many years I set my heart to expound and to explain [perhaps an allusion to Eccl. 9:1] the work of the Mishnah in order to know [its] essence (HWMR), [its] form, and the purpose of its structure (TKLYT BNYNH). Without this [knowledge] it is useless to rise early and to stay up late to study the Torah of the Lord. Without this [knowledge] one cannot find the entrance to come to the Holiness within. Thus, only on this path, which the sages of the *gemara* [used] and which those who came after them, the Great Ones of the early generations (R'ŠWNYM) and those who followed them broadened, is the light of truth given to us [through which we can] understand the words of the Torah and do according to all that is written in it. When I labored ... to investigate

---

[42] Isidore Singer, "Jakob Brüll" in I. Singer (ed.), *Jewish Encyclopedia* (New York, 1902), III, p. 402.

[43] Maqor, Jerusalem, 1970. Since this reprint is merely a copy of the original, the reader must be careful of numerous printing errors. For example, the B and K, the Z and W, and the R and D are often confused. Also, RBY often occurs without the Y. In several instances letters are printed upside down and final letters occur in the beginning or the middle of words.

their opinions and [when] ... I gathered them into a book with notes and additions ..., I saw ... that the beginning of the matter was to know the masters (BʻLY) of the work of the Mishnah, the method of their learning, and the tools with which they built it. While examining and investigating this matter, there came into my hands the book DRKY MŚNH by ... Z. Frankel, in which were mentioned the Tanna'im who were spoken of as the basis of understanding the Mishnah. I said [to myself] I shall walk according to the work which is before me [an allusion to Gen. 33 : 14] in this matter. [Therefore] I set for myself the task of speaking about our Rabbis, the R'SY TWRH who are mentioned in the Mishnah....

Brüll undertook his study of the Mishnah to facilitate his fulfillment of the *halakhah*, for "without this [knowledge of the essence, structure, and purpose of the Mishnah] it is useless to rise early and to stay up late to study the Torah of the Lord." Through this knowledge "one can understand the words of the Torah and do according to all that is written in it."[44] His method of study was that used by the "sages of the *gemara* and ... those who came after them, the Great Ones of the early generation... and those who followed them." In other words, all the material related to a given mishnah, whether rabbinic, Geonic, or medieval, was brought forth to explain the mishnah. If the sources did not agree, it was the interpreter's task to solve the contradiction. With Frankel's book as his example, Brüll began his study with a discussion of the sages mentioned in the Mishnah.

Volume One begins with a brief description of the "power-structure" of Israel during the biblical period: the priests were in charge of worship (ʻBWDH), the kings were responsible for the welfare of the country (ṬWBT HMDYNY), and the prophets, elders, and scribes had charge of teaching the law (TWRH). While the classes of individuals performing any of these three tasks—worship, Torah, and the welfare of the country—might change, the "power-structure" was always divided into these three parts. The sources Brüll used for his comments about the biblical period are the same as those he used for the rabbinic era, with the exception of the Bible. In traditional fashion he accepts the Mishnah, the midrashim, the Geonic literature, and the medieval commentaries all as valid historical sources for the biblical and rabbinic eras. For this reason, Volume One is merely a collection of material found in the documents from the second to the nineteenth century. There is no attempt to challenge the sources or to question their contents. While Brüll's book is an admirable collec-

---

[44] Jacob Brüll, *Mavo haMishnah* (Frankfurt-am-Main, 1876), I, pp. 1-3.

tion of traditional sources, it is an unsatisfactory historical account.

iii

Volume Two of the *Mavo* is subtitled *Concerning Rabbi's Method in [His] Collecting of the Mishnahs (HMŠNYWT)*. The book opens with a discussion of the word MŠNH. Brüll notes that the biblical meaning of the word is two or double,[45] for example, Gen. 43 : 12, Deut. 15 : 18 and so on. Brüll discusses several interpretations of the phrase MŠNH TWRH found in Deut. 17 : 18. In b. Sanh. 21b the sages suggest that Deut. 17 : 18 means "he [Moses] wrote for himself two *torot*; one went forth with him, and one he placed in his *geniza*."[46] Others suggest that the name MŠNH TWRH is derived from Deut. 6 : 7, *And you shall teach them diligently unto your children.* "The Torah is called MŠNH because it is incumbent not only to study its commandments but also to teach them to your children."[47] This two-fold responsibility gives rise to the use of MŠNH. Brüll continues:

> And there are those who say that ... Deuteronomy was called MŠNH TWRH because it is said about it that [in it] Moses explained the Torah (see Maimonides), for in this book are not only those commandments which were not mentioned in the first books [of the Bible], but also those commandments which *are* in the earlier books are more fully explained and expounded in this book.[48]

In b. 'Eruv. 22a the name MŠNH is applied to the Oral Torah (TWRH ŠB'L PH) which Moses taught to Israel "because it is the explanation of the Written Torah (TWRH ŠBKTB)." Finally the term MŠNH was applied to all the explanations of the Written Torah which originated (ḤDŠ) through the Oral Torah.[49]

Brüll, like Frankel, believes that the Scribes taught their laws in conjunction with biblical verses, that is, they engaged in *midrash*. The Tannaitic Midrashim indicate that some of the early Tannaim adopted the method of the Scribes. Most of the early Tannaim, however, did not follow the example of their predecessors; rather, these Tannaim taught their laws without connecting them to biblical passages. Brüll claims that the style of the Mishnah and the name applied to these

---

[15] Jacob Brüll, *Mavo haMishnah* (Frankfurt-am-Main, 1885), II, p. 1.
[16] *Ibid.*
[17] *Ibid.*
[18] *Ibid.*
[19] *Ibid.*

sages support his conclusions. These rabbis were not called Scribes, that is, expounders of a written book; they were called Masters (BʿLY) of the Mishnah, or Tannaim.[50] B. Qidd. 49a-b states that the name MŠNH was applied to those teachings which were taught in separation from the biblical verses.[51]

Brüll remarks that "in all books, the essence (ḤWMR) of the mishnahs (HMŠNYWT) is called the Oral Torah."[52] This term is proper for 1) those explanations of the Written Torah which the Lord said to Moses face to face, and 2) those laws which have no connection with a specific scriptural passage and which are called "laws given to Moses from Sinai (HLKH LMŠH MSYNY)." Brüll claims that there are only a few laws which have no biblical basis. These are correctly designated as part of the Oral Torah, because the Lord told them to Moses face to face on Mount Sinai; hence, they are called HLKH LMŠH MSYNY.[53] On the other hand, there are many passages in the Bible which cannot be understood without divine aid. These are: 1) legal passages in which the Torah speaks in general terms (HLŠWN HKLL), for example, Lev. 23 : 40: *And you shall take on the first day the fruit of goodly trees...*; 2) passages written in sealed language (BLŠWN STWM), for example, Ex. 13 : 9: *And it shall be for a sign upon your hand...*; and 3) passages which contradict (HSWTR) each other:[54]

> In all these cases there is no doubt that with special intent the Lord commanded Moses to write the Torah in this language and He told him the explanations and clarifications.[55]

Teachings and laws which originated among the Scribes and Tannaim are also called Oral Torah. Brüll notes that some have suggested that this name is appropriate because none of these teachings was written down. Brüll rejects this view. Others have claimed that all the teachings which arose after the death of Moses are part of the Oral Torah, because the Lord told *all* of them to Moses on Sinai; Brüll disagrees:

> The correctness of the name Oral Torah is not because the Holy One, blessed be He, told them to Moses face to face as the explanations of the

[50] *Ibid.*, p. 2.
[51] *Ibid.*
[52] *Ibid.*
[53] *Ibid.*, p. 3.
[54] *Ibid.*
[55] *Ibid.*

Written Torah, and also not because it was prohibited to write them in a book; rather, it is [correct] as the general and common name for all matters ('NYNY) of the Torah which are not explained in the Written Torah....[56]

The Oral Torah, which is the essence (ḤWMR) of the Mishnah, includes:

(1) The explanations of the Written Torah which the Lord told Moses.... (2) Those few laws which do not have a peg or a connection to a verse of the Bible and which are called HLKH LMŠH MSYNY.... (3) The laws that originated (NTḤDŠW) during the time of the prophets and ... [those] from the days of Ezra onward which are called 'The Words of the Scribes (DBRY SWPRYM),' for they limit (HGBYLW) and establish (YSDW) the explanations which the Holy One, blessed be He, told Moses concerning the commandment in a particular verse. [The name Oral Torah also applies to] laws that originated in a place which had no traditional explanation (MQBWL)... [and] all [the laws] that originated through reason (SBRH), through exegesis (DRŠH), through an ordinance (TQNH), or through a decree (GZYRH) in order to make a fence and a hedge for the words of the Torah. (4) And those words of the Tannaim which they established (QYMW) and which they received as the words of the Scribes as laws which were not to be transgressed. They made these the prototypes (L'BWT) for their work to produce (LHWLYD) through them new laws. [The name Oral Torah also applies to] what they [the Tannaim] originated in the matters (B'NYNY) of Torah through agreement and through debate....[57]

While accepting the traditional belief that the Oral Torah includes material which the Lord spoke to Moses on Mount Sinai, Brüll is able to move beyond this traditional conception of the Oral Law. He realizes that the Oral Law contains material which the Lord did not tell Moses. He also believes that the Oral Torah could have been written down. While Frankel believed that much of Rabbi's Mishnah had originated at the time of the Great Assembly,[58] Brüll makes no such assertion. For Brüll, the Mishnah contains statements which originated with the Tannaim; even those rabbis who lived after R. Meir finished his edition of the Mishnah made important contributions to the Oral Law.[59] Astutely, Brüll describes the Oral Torah as "the general and common name for all matters of the Torah which are not explained in the Written Torah."

[56] *Ibid.*, pp. 5-6.
[57] *Ibid.*, p. 6.
[58] See the discussion of DRKY MŠNH, above, pp. 59 ff.
[59] See below, p. 82.

iv

Although the first Tannaim did not generally teach their laws in conjunction with a biblical verse, they did organize their teachings according to the biblical commandments. Brüll suggests that each Tannaitic law was arranged under the proper negative or positive commandment stated in the Bible. For example,[60] a teaching which dealt with theft might be placed under the heading of Ex. 20:13, *Thou shalt not steal.* However, the Torah discusses the specifics of this commandment in many places; for example, Ex. 21:22 treats the theft of an ox or a sheep which the thief killed. For this reason not all the laws on theft would be arranged in one place; each law dealing with a particular aspect of theft would be arranged under its appropriate biblical passage.[61] This explains the tradition which states that six hundred Orders (SDRYM) existed from the time of the Men of the Great Assembly until the time of Hillel. With some mental gymnastics, Brüll claims that these six hundred (or, in another version, seven hundred) Orders corresponded to the six hundred thirteen negative and positive commandments.[62]

This same *aggadah* states that Hillel reduced the number of Orders of the Mishnah from six hundred to six. Brüll concludes that Hillel collected all the laws on one matter ('NYN) into one place. In other words, Hillel gathered all the laws which dealt with theft into one Order. Thus Hillel "increased the content of each book but decreased the number of Orders."[63] Among the laws which Hillel gathered, there were many which needed correction from mistakes (ŠYBWŠYM) or in language. Hillel tested and corrected these laws before he placed them into his Mishnah.

Hillel's Mishnah contained short statements which were primarily explanations of the written Torah.[64] After Hillel finished his work, debates began to arise between his students and those of Shammai. Different explanations of earlier laws as well as varying opinions about new laws were expressed. As the content of the laws daily increased, so did the explanations. Each rabbi in his own style taught his students the interpretations of the laws. In time the essence and form of Hillel's Mishnah was lost. R. 'Aqiba began to order a new collection, but the

[60] These examples of laws dealing with theft are the present writer's, not Brüll's.
[61] Brüll, *Mavo haMishnah*, II, pp. 7-8.
[62] *Ibid.*, p. 8.
[63] *Ibid.*, p. 9.
[64] *Ibid.*

upheavals of the Bar Kokhba war prevented him from completing the task. R. Meir continued R. ʿAqiba's project. R. Meir did not finish the work, for "the opinions of all the Tannaim were not there, especially those who lived after R. Meir made his collection...."[65] R. Judah the Patriarch finished the work and was the the final editor of the Mishnah.

Brüll's description of the Mishnah's formation by Hillel, R. ʿAqiba, R. Meir, and Rabbi is "standard." The proofs he brings forth are the same texts which have been used from the Geonim to Albeck (!). Brüll's suggestion that the laws before Hillel were arranged according to the six hundred thirteen positive and negative commandments is pure fantasy. There is absolutely no proof to support this theory. In fact, we have no evidence on the basis of which we can discuss the Mishnah of *Hillel*: the *aggadic* traditions have never been proved.

V

Brüll states that there is no doubt the collectors of mishnahs before the time of Rabbi edited and ordered the material, collected into one place those laws which were related to one another, divided them into orders, divided the orders into tractates, and divided the tractates into chapters.[66] The *gemara* indicates that tractates Negaʿim, Ohalot, ʿUqṣin and Ṭoharot were known to the Tannaim who lived before the time of R. Judah.[67] Besides these collections, Rabbi had before him "all the matters of the law which are before us in the *beraitot*, Tosefta, Mekhilta, Sifré, and Sifra."[68] He also gathered all the laws which were "spread among the mouths of the *talmidim*."[69] Rabbi collected all this material,

> and tested the truth of their content and also the traditional form (NWSḤʾWT) and he ordered them as they are before us with the advice and agreement of the Great Ones of the Torah who stood in his days.[70]

When Judah knew the exact language of the person who originated a particular statement, he quoted the sage's exact words. If Rabbi only

---

[65] *Ibid.*, p. 10.
[66] *Ibid.*, p. 13.
[67] *Ibid.*
[68] *Ibid.*, pp. 54-55.
[69] *Ibid.*, p. 13.
[70] *Ibid.*, p. 10.

knew the content of the saying, he recorded it in short and smooth (ṢḤ) language.[71]

Rabbi was more than a scissors-and-past editor. He examined the material before him and placed in his Mishnah only those statements which conformed to his view of the law. He combined statements, divided statements, and even omitted material. He did not feel compelled to merely collect all the statements he had before him. Rabbi wanted to create a law code, not a random collection of Tannaitic statements. Brüll states:

> The first Tannaim spoke the laws in short phrases (BLŠWN QṢRH) and primarily in general terms (LRWB DRK KLL) and in special language (BLŠWN MYWḤD). The Tannaim who came after them debated the matter[s discussed by the earlier Tannaim] and explained and clarified their words.... The Tannaim placed the explanations of the words of the earlier sages [alongside the original statement] in the Mishnah.... Also, the later Tannaim taught the mishnahs in different ways ('WPNYM) to their students.... [Therefore] there was a need to broaden and to add into the short and anonymous laws these explanations. Because of this there were different [forms of the same] mishnahs. And after Rabbi tested and examined all this and found this [state of affairs] ... was bringing everything to confusion and error ..., he ... [began] to collect his mishnahs, and he did this great work with the help of the Great Ones of the Torah who stood in his days.... What was found good with their advice and agreement ... he collected [and placed in his Mishnah]. Sometimes he cut and placed by itself in the Tosefta or in a *baraita* the explanation which was connected to the mishnah.... Sometimes he added new views or a dissenting opinion (ḤWLQ) which was before him [in] anonymous [form]. Sometimes he omitted ... whole mishnahs because their content was heard from another mishnah or he submerged them into [another] of his mishnahs....[72]

Brüll makes it clear that Rabbi did more than collect material; Judah was an editor in the modern sense of the word. Along this line, Brüll makes an extremely astute statement with regard to the Tannaitic debates we find in the Mishnah:

> Tannaitic debates [in the Mishnah] are of different types. [Some are] face to face, which originated when they [the sages] studied together and argued with one another, and each one spoke his own opinion and his own reasons; or one Tanna originated this law and recited it in the school-house and other Tannaim disagreed with him.... [A face-to-face

[71] *Ibid.*
[72] *Ibid.*, p. 103.

debate] could also originate when the *talmidim* recited their opinion before their rabbi and there was a debate. Sometimes the debates were not face-to-face. For example, in one school-house this law was said, and in another school-house the opposite was said and the words [recited in the first school-house] were not known in the other, or a law (which originated in one school-house) was heard [in another] and the members of [the second] school-house disagreed with it. There were also different statements among the *talmidim*. Some said one thing in the name of one Tanna and the others said the opposite in the name of another Tanna. [Neither of the last two instances were face-to-face debates because the original Tannaim did not confront each other]. When Rabbi collected and ordered the mishnahs, he first collected all the laws which were in the early collections of mishnahs and also the opinions which were spread among the *talmidim*, and he arranged the Tannaitic debates together, this one near the other, as if all of them were face-to-face [debates], even if they were from different times....[73]

Thus Rabbi created many of the Tannaitic "debates" through his arrangement of the material.

Rabbi did not have a free hand to change all of the material. Many times Brüll explains a mishnah by saying that Rabbi wrote it in this way "because it was spread among the *talmidim*."[74] In other words, the mishnah was too well known for Rabbi to change. For example, Brüll notes that in three places we find the phrase "the law follows his words (HLKH KDBRYW): M. Pe'ah 3 : 6, M. Shevi'it 9 : 5, and M. Yevamot 4 : 3. Brüll remarks that this phrase does not mean that Rabbi decided the law according to this Tanna:

> In these instances Rabbi brought after this Tanna the dissenting view (HWLQ), which means that the opinion of Rabbi was opposed to that of the first Tanna. And as it is seen, the phrase HLKH KDBRYW was before Rabbi in the collections of the mishnahs which he had before him from the early orderers, and it was also spread in the mouths of the *talmidim*....[75]

Related to this principle is the rule that "a mishnah does not move from its place" (HMŠNH L' ZZH MMQWMH). Like the above, this rule served as a check on Rabbi's creativity. For example, if Rabbi wanted to add material to a mishnah, he added it in the middle; he did not change the beginning or the end because "the mishnah does not move from its place."[76]

[73] *Ibid.*, p. 69.
[74] BPY TLMYDYM or NTPŠTH BPY TLMYDYM
[75] Brüll, *Mavo haMishnah*, II, pp. 69-70.
[76] *Ibid.*, p. 14.

Rashi believed that the Mishnah was not written in the days of Rabbi. As later generations began to decrease in ability, the Mishnah was set to writing. Maimonides stated that in every generation the prophets and the R'Š 'B BYT DYN wrote for themselves what had originated in their days and what the sages of the previous generations had taught. However, the actual teaching and transmission of the laws were oral. From these statements Brüll concludes that Rabbi could have had a written version of the Mishnah; this written Mishnah, however, was only for his private use. When Rabbi taught his mishnahs, he did so orally.[77]

Much of what Brüll has said is unacceptable. Brüll's claim that Rabbi had all of the Tannaitic material which we have today is untenable. Brüll's theory that Tosefta and *beraitot* contain statements which Rabbi did not want to put in his Mishnah is also unproven. However, Brüll's assertion that many of the Tannaitic "debates" found in the Mishnah were created by an editor or collector is acceptable. Brüll's claim that R. Judah was editor who created these "debates" is unproven.

vi

The larger part of the second volume of Brüll's *Mavo haMishnah* is a discussion of the various types of mishnahs. Chapter titles include (1) [The] anonymous mishnah; (2) Anonymous [passages] on one subject which occur in one mishnah and which contradict each other; (3) Two anonymous mishnahs in two places which contradict each other; (4) Anonymous laws on different matters in one mishnah which contradict each other; (5) The anonymous [passage] and a debate about it in the mishnah; (6) An anonymous mishnah followed by a debate or a debate followed by an anonymous [passage] in a mishnah or a debate in a mishnah and an anonymous [passage] in a *baraita*; (7) Different debates on an anonymous [passage] in a mishnah (8) The manner ('WPN) and order (SDR) of Tannaitic debates in the Mishnah; (9) HLKH MPWRŠT LMḤLWQT HTN'YM in the Mishnah; (10) Words of one mishnah from different periods; (11) Two or more different matters in one mishnah and they relate to one law; (12) A law in a mishnah which is not needed; (13) Laws which follow KLL WPRṬ in the Mishnah; (14) PRṬY of laws according to type (MNYN) and to the word 'LW; (15) The order of PRṬY of the laws in the

---

[77] *Ibid.*, pp. 10-13.

mishnahs; (16) Omissions in the mishnahs; (17) Different corrections in the mishnahs.

Brüll's basic goal is to explain which statements in the Mishnah are the correct legal opinion; this is especially true in his discussions of the anonymous mishnahs. Brüll's analysis of the anonymous mishnahs rests on the assumption that Rabbi intended to produce a law code. He states that there are "many laws in the mishnahs without the name of the one who said them also without dissent (ḤWLQ), and these are called STM MŠNH."[78] These mishnahs may contain old and traditional laws (YŠNWT WMQWBLWT) or laws which the Tannaim originated.[79] These mishnahs may reflect the opinion of the individual (YḤYD) or the many (RBYM). A STM MŠNH usually appears without a dissenting view (ḤWLQ), because Rabbi wanted to emphasize the correctness of its statement of the law and to render null and void (BṬYLH WMBWṬLH) any contrary opinions. Brüll states:

> When Rabbi collected the mishnahs, without doubt he put his eye and heart to all the mishnahs that were gathered and ordered by the early R'ŠY TWRH and especially the mishnahs which R. Meir arranged and collected.... [Rabbi] also collected all the laws which were not there [in the early collections] but were spread among the *talmidim*.... [He] also [collected] the opinions of the individuals concerning laws which were before him [in] anonymous [form] and which were collected after the time of R. Meir.... After he had tested and examined all of them with the Great Ones of the Torah and with his students who stood in the days when he collected the mishnahs, he took those anonymous [passages] which were traditionally accepted (MQWBLWT) or agreed upon by all, as his mishnahs....[80]

In general the anonymous mishnahs agree with R. Judah's legal opinion. Those anonymous passages which Rabbi did not take "as his mishnahs" were not necessarily excluded from the Mishnah. If a passage differed only slightly from the one accepted by Rabbi, the former could be included in the Mishnah. Only if a statement was directly contrary to the anonymous passage accepted by Rabbi was the former completely dropped from the Mishnah.[81]

Brüll notes that in many places we find two anonymous laws in one mishnah which contradict each other. In these instances the *gemara*

---

[78] *Ibid.*, p. 34.
[79] *Ibid.*
[80] *Ibid.*
[81] *Ibid.*

usually states "whoever taught that [first statement] did not teach that [contrary statement] (MY ŠSNH ZW L' ŠNH ZW). The reason that Rabbi included both of these statements was that they were common opinions, and he could not omit one.[82] In these mishnahs, there is no clear statement of the law.[83]

If there are two anonymous mishnahs in two places which contradict each other, the law follows the last anonymous passage. For example, if an anonymous law which appears in M. Sanhedrin is contradicted by a statement in M. Niddah, the law follows the version in M. Niddah "because Toharot is after Neziqin":[84]

> ... At first [Rabbi] reasoned according to the first Tanna and decided (STM) according to his view. After this, he returned and reasoned according to the Second Tanna and decided (STM) according to his view. For this reason, the last anonymous statement is to be preferred (STM DBTR' 'DYP).[85]

This is true only if the opinions are those of individuals. If one is the statement of the majority (RBYM), the opinion of the majority is the correct statement of the law. Rabbi included the contrary statement of the individual (YHYD) because it was well known,[86] and he could not omit it. Only by using the *gemara*, the rest of the corpus of Tannaitic literature, and the traditional commentators can one determine which is the opinion of the many and which is the statement of the individual.

Many times we find an anonymous opinion and after it we find a debate (MHLWQH). Sometimes we find the debate first and then the anonymous statement. Brüll concludes:

> If Rabbi saw that the anonymous mishnah was the correct statement of the law, he first brought the mishnah which contained the debate and after this the anonymous mishnah, to say that the law is according to the anonymous mishnah. On the other hand, if it was not the opinion of Rabbi to decide (LHKRY') on this law, he first brought the anonymous passage and after that [he brought] the debate to lessen the strength of the anonymous passage and to say that one is not compelled (MWKRH) [to decide] according to the anonymous mishnah. However, he did not completely negate the anonymous statement....[87]

[82] *Ibid.*, pp. 47-49.
[83] *Ibid.*
[84] *Ibid.*, pp. 42-43.
[85] *Ibid.*, p. 43.
[86] See above p. 84 and note 74.
[87] Brüll, *Mavo haMishnah*, II, pp. 51-52.

The legal consequence of the anonymous statement is the important aspect of its form. Because it is essential to know which anonymous statement was said by the YHYD and which was spoken by the RBYM, Brüll is forced to explain most of the anonymous passages through Amoraic, Geonic, and Medieval comments. Rarely does Brüll discuss a mishnah only in terms of itself. A mishnah is significant only as a legal statement. The form, style, and structure of a mishnah are discussed only if they affect the legal consequences of the mishnah.

As the chapter titles indicate, the remainder of Volume Two covers a variety of topics. However, the method and the goal of these discussions are the same as those of his comments on the anonymous mishnahs. The goal of the studies is to enable the reader to determine the correct statement of law. The method of the latter chapters is to study the mishnahs through the Amoraic, Geonic, and Medieval commentators. The chapters are repetitious and have little consequence for anyone not interested in the legal content of the Mishnah. For this reason, we have not discussed every chapter of Volume Two.

vii

Although Brüll entitled his book *Mavo haMishnah*, he was not interested in the Mishnah as a literary or historical document; rather, he focused on the Mishnah as a law code. It is significant that Brüll subtitled Volume Two *Concerning Rabbi's Method in [His] Collecting of the Mishnahs (HMŠNYWT)*; he did not use the collective term *Mishnah*, MŠNH. From their inception, the teachings of the Scribes and the Tannaim had legal overtones. Brüll, following Frankel, states that the mishnahs before the time of Hillel were organized according to the six hundred thirteen biblical commandments; in other words, the teachings were organized through their legal content. Tractates and Orders are arranged according to the logic of their legal statements.

Brüll does not examine the Mishnah in terms of itself. When he discusses a mishnah, as noted, he does so by means of the Amoraic, Geonic, and Medieval commentators. He is not troubled by the fact that these comments were made in a land different from the one where the Mishnah originated, or that many of these comments are centuries removed from the mishnahs they treat. Although Brüll does discuss various types of mishnahs, he does not study them from a literary point of view. The various forms of the mishnahs are important only as they affect the legal content. Forms are not compared and examined; Brüll discusses only content.

As we noted above, Brüll's book is worthless as a history of the Tannaim or of the formation of the Mishnah. Like those before him, and many after him, Brüll believed that the medieval commentators were as valuable a source for the history of the Tannaitic period as were the Mishnah, Tosefta, and the other Tannaitic documents. Brüll's "historical" analyses are no more than a rehearsal of traditional sources. We have no proof that the Scribes primarily taught their laws in conjunction with biblical verses. We have no evidence that before Hillel the mishnahs were organized according to the six hundred thirteen biblical commandments. We do not know whether "Hillel's Mishnah" contained only short statements or that debates originated only after Hillel's death. In fact, we know nothing at all about Hillel's Mishnah; we do not even know that such a document existed. Likewise, we know nothing about the Mishnahs of R. ʿAqiba or R. Meir. There is no proof that Rabbi had before him all the Tannaitic statements which we have today in the Mishnah, much less those contained in the Tosefta, Mekhilta, Sifra, Sifré, and *beraitot.* We do not even know the *exact* relationship of our Mishnah to that of Rabbi.

In spite of his limitations, however, Brüll did make some interesting observations about the Oral Law and the Tannaitic "debates" found in the Mishnah. He realized that not all of the Oral Law dated from the time of Moses. Thus he did not attempt to prove that the laws contained in the Mishnah were from the period of Ezra, the Scribes, or the Men of the Great Assembly. He also indicated that the Oral Law could have been written. Brüll recognized that many of the Tannaitic "debates" found in the Mishnah never took place; they were created by the collector of the sources.

For the modern scholar of the Mishnah, Brüll's *Mavo haMishnah* is of little value. It concentrates on the legal aspect of the Mishnah to the exclusion of all else. What is more basic is that Brüll never confronts the Mishnah; he only approaches it through its commentators.

CHAPTER SIX

HIRSCH MENDEL PINELES:
THE FIRST CRITICAL EXEGETE

JOEL GEREBOFF

Hirsch Mendel Pineles was born on December 21, 1805, in Tsymenitz, Poland. At fifteen his family moved to Brody where Pineles was educated in the Hassidic tradition. After marriage, he pursued studies of German, astronomy, physics, and mathematics. His writings include treatises on the Jewish calendar and astronomy. Pineles was able to devote only his evenings to Jewish matters, since he had to work for a living during the days. In 1855 he moved to Galatz, Rumania, where he died on August 6, 1870.[88]

i

In 1861 Pineles published his most important work, *Darkah shel Torah*, with three purposes in mind: (1) "to justify the oral law and to add support to those opinions of the Scribes which diverged from the written law; (2) to defend the Mishnah against those who give it 'excess' honor, namely the authors of the Talmud who changed the simple meaning of the Mishnah by their unnecessary exegesis, and against the Mishnah's adversaries, who attempted to find defects in it and to downgrade its worth; (3) to explain some difficult sayings of the early Amoraim, and some difficult passages in the Palestinian and Babylonian Talmuds."[89] To accomplish this end, Pineles "searched and found changes in the text that appear in Tosefta, Halakhic Midrashim, and in *beraitot*, which aid in determining the truth and simple explanation."[90] The book is not an "introduction" to the Mishnah, but rather a work of exegesis (PRŠNWT). By showing how Amoraic misunderstanding of Mishnaic passages led to unnecessary

---

[88] *Jewish Encyclopedia* vol. X p. 45 and Leopold Löw, *Gesammelte Schriften*, p. 471-9. Throughout the book, Pineles apologizes that he only studies Torah at night and his work is therefore susceptible to error; see pp. 18, 91.
[89] Hirsch Pineles, *Darkah shel Torah*, inside of frontispiece.
[90] Ibid.

argumentation (*pilpul*), Pineles wanted to uphold the integrity of Rabbi's Mishnah. Problems of understanding the Mishnah do not lie in the Mishnah but rather in the *Gemara*.[91]

His theoretical remarks about the Mishnah may be divided into three categories: (1) the origin and the development of the oral law, (2) the formation of the Mishnah, (3) assumptions concerning the nature of the Mishnah. Pineles' historical theories are of little value; he works totally and unquestioningly within the traditional rabbinic model, which equates legal decisions of the *Soferim* with Mishnaic-Pharisaic law. He views the formation of the Mishnah as a process of accretion, in which nothing is ever lost, except the "secret meanings of the laws" (SWD T'MY HHLKT), forgotten during the Tannaitic period. Pineles' strong aversion to *pilpul* colors much of his work.

The historical part of the work suffers from his unproven assumptions, his artificial construction of historical facts, deductive reasoning, and inner contradictions. Moreover, Pineles evidently does not fully realize the implications of this theories. As an introduction to the Mishnah, the work has little lasting value; it does however, represent the first important effort at critical exegesis of Mishnaic literature. By explaining the Mishnah from within, and not by reference to the *Gemara*'s interpretation, by noting the importance of the form and context of pericopae, and by comparing parallel traditions, especially those of Tosefta, Pineles made a valuable and lasting contribution to the critical study of the Mishnah. He was a pioneer, for as an exegete, he viewed the Mishnah as a literary document.

ii

Underlying Pineles' exegesis are two basic arguments: (1) The Mishnah has form and order which must be considered in order to understand fully the legal meaning of a text. (2) Other Tannaitic material must be consulted (especially Tosefta) to understand the Mishnah correctly. As noted, the Mishnah must be explained from within and not on the basis of the *Gemara* and medieval commentaries. Pineles compares parallel traditions, notes their form

---

[91] See David Weiss Halivni, *Meqorot uMesorot* p. 12; and Jacob Neusner, ed., *Formation of the Babylonian Talmud*, p. 136.

and context, compares similar rulings of a given sage, and explains foreign words in order to ascertain the best reading and interpretation for a passage. Several examples will illustrate his method. These examples show Pineles' methods of discerning the meaning of a passage either by noting (1) its context, (2) the relation between the different parts of the pericope, (3) certain formulae, or (4) by comparison to Tosefta material.

1. The following are explanations by reference to a mishnah's context:

> [If the claimant said,] "Thou hast one hundred *denars* of mine," and the other said "Yea," and on the morrow the first one said to him, "Give it to me," [and the other said,] "I have given it to thee already," he is exempt; but if he said, "I have naught of thine," he is liable.
> [If he said,] "Thou hast one hundred *denars* of mine," and the other said, "Yea," [and the first said,] "Do not give it to me save before witnesses", and on the morrow he said to him, "Give it to me," and the other said, "I have given it to thee already," he is liable, since it was needful that he should give it before witnesses.
> (M. Shav. 6 : 2, trans. Danby, p. 417)

This mishnah does not specify to what the laws of liability and exemption apply. The Amoraim (b. Shav. 41b) interpreted the laws to apply to payment of money. Pineles rejects this argument and identifies the issue as that of taking an oath. He supports this claim by noting that all of chapter six of *Shavuot* deals with laws of taking oaths. He further explains what necessitates the taking of oaths in this particular example.[92] Pineles is very explicit in his description and also quotes passages in their entirety, unlike other Mishnaic critics.

2. In the next example Pineles notes the relationship between the sayings of a given sage to reach an understanding of the text.

> A man may say to a shopkeeper, "Fill me this vessel," but not "With the measure."
> Rabbi Judah says, "If it was a measuring vessel he may not fill it."
> (M. Beṣ. 3 : 8, trans. Danby, p. 185)

---

[92] Pineles, *op. cit.*, p. 144. The foundation of his argument is that if a person makes a partial admission to a claim, it is then assumed he is responsible for the entire claim. In this mishnah, the person who at first says he has the money and the next day says he has repaid the loan does not have to take an oath as he is consistent throughout in his claims (that he received the money) and therefore has made a partial admission and does not have to take an oath. The person who, however, denies on the second day that he received the money has to take an oath for he has contradicted himself.

The context of this mishnah is the restrictions that apply to measuring on the festival day. From this mishnah it would appear that R. Judah prohibits measuring on the holiday with a "measuring vessel." The Amoraim ask (b. Beṣ. 29a), "In mishnah (six) of this chapter R. Judah was lenient and the sages were strict" for in that case it states:

> R. Judah says, "They may take the weight of flesh using a vessel or a hatchet for a weight."
> But the sages say, "They may not use scales at all."
> (M. Beṣ. 3 : 6, trans. Danby, p. 185)

To explain the contradiction between the two statements of R. Judah, the Amoraim differentiated "measuring vessels" which have already been used, from "measuring vessels" which are about to be used. Pineles, however, notes that this distinction in no way solves the problem but further confuses the example. He rather states that there is a consistency throughout this chapter: R. Judah is always more lenient than the sages. In the particular case (mishnah 8) of using a "measuring vessel," Judah's suggestion is to use the vessel but "not to fill it completely." The sages, however, contend the person, as with the scales, cannot use the "measuring vessel" at all.[93] This explanation is problematic for it does not have adequate basis for interpreting "do not fill it" to mean "do not fill it completely" and also constructs the non-existent opinion of the sages. But Pineles seeks a simple explanation, avoids making unneeded distinctions, and is conscious of context.

The next example is an analysis on the basis of the relation between the different elements of a pericope:

> A. A man may lift up his child even though he has a stone in his hand, or a basket even though it contains a stone, and he may move from place to place unclean Heave-offering together with clean [Heave-offering] or common produce...
> B. If a stone lay on the mouth of a jar, the jar may be turned on its side so that the stone falls off. If the jar was among other jars, it may be lifted up and then turned on its side so that the stone falls off. If there were coins on a cushion, the cushion may be shaken so that the coins fall off.
> (M. Shab. 21 : 1, 2, trans. Danby, p. 118)

This mishnah pertains to laws concerning moving objects which are

[93] *Ibid.*, p. 29.

not to be moved (MWQSH) on the Sabbath. The Amoraim, argued (b. Shab. 142b) that B contradicts A. To resolve the difficulty they distinguished cases in which the clean Heave-offering was on the bottom and the unclean Heave-offering was on the top, from cases in which the unclean Heave-offering was on the top and the clean Heave-offering was on the bottom. They further distinguished cases in which the common produce was mixed in with the Heave-offering. Pineles notes the construction of the two *mishnayot* and argues that there is no need for these qualifications (DḤWQYM). A deals with cases when the *place* where the prohibited object rested was needed. In these instances one is permitted to move the object which contained the MWQSH. B, however, deals with cases when the permissible object itself (not its place) was needed. In these instances one is not allowed to remove the permitted object with the prohibited object, but rather must shake the prohibited object from the desired permitted object.[94] The above example demonstrates how Pineles, by noting the relationship between elements of a mishnah, interprets the mishnah without resorting to unneeded distinctions.

3. The following are examples of Pineles' use of formulae to explain difficulties in the Mishnah:

> And it is written, *It is time to work for the Lord; they have made void thy law* (Ps. 119 : 126).
> R. Nathan says, "They have made void thy Law, it is time to work for the Lord."
>
> (M. Ber. 9 : 5, trans. Danby, p. 16)

The Babylonian Talmud's version of this mishnah reads, "R. Nathan says, 'They have made void thy law *because* it was a time to work for the Lord'" (b. Ber. 63a). Rabbah provides a *midrash* on this verse to account for the change. Pineles argues this exegesis is unnecessary and the text should remain as it appears in the Mishnah. R. Nathan reversed the clauses simply to end the chapter on a good note. Pineles cites the conclusion of M. Kelim as support for this phenomenon.

Pineles also notes the importance of abbreviations (R'ŠY ṬBWT) within Talmudic literature. He argues that the Amoraim (b. Ber. 47b) failed to understand that the words "ark" and "Shabbath" in the sayings "nine and the ark may constitute a *minyan*" and "two and the

---

[91] *Ibid.*, p. 25.

Sabbath a *mezuman* [three males who recite together Grace after meals]" are abbreviations. "Ark" means "one who sees but is not seen." (ʾḤD RWʾH WʾYNW NRʾH) while "Sabbath" means "he learns the words of Torah" (ŠWNH DBRY TWRH). "Ark" refers to a person who is sitting next to the room in which people are praying (M. Ber. 7 : 5). "Sabbath" refers to an individual who learns Torah among two people who are eating (b. M.Q. 15a; b. Ta. 16b).[95] Although this explanation may be mere conjecture, it is plausible, for abbreviations are a common feature of Jewish literature.

Certain formulae were used to strengthen a person's sayings. Among these are "May I not see consolation" ((ʾRʾH BNHMH) (Tos. San. 6 : 6, b. Mak. 5b; b. Ḥag. 10b)) and "May I be deprived of my son" (ʾQPḤ ʾT BNY, b. Zev. 13a; b. Shab. 106a).[96]

4. Pineles was the first seriously to use the Tosefta to explain the Mishnah. The following are two examples of this method.

> A. No writ is valid which has a Samaritan as witness excepting a writ of divorce or a writ of emancipation.
> B. The story is told that they once brought a writ of divorce before Rabban Gamaliel at Kefar Othani and its witnesses were Samaritans; and he pronounced it valid.
> (M. Giṭ. 1 : 5, trans. Danby, p. 307)

> R. Judah says, "Even if both witnesses were Samaritans, [the writ of divorce] is valid."
> R. Judah says, "The story is told..."
> (Tos. Giṭ. 1 : 4 ed. Zuckermandel, p. 323, lines 23-5)

Pineles first treats the mishnah independently. The pericope deals with writs signed by a Samaritan. Part A states that a Samaritan can only validate a writ of divorce or of emancipation. All other writs witnessed by (even one) Samaritan are invalid. According to the Amoraim (b. Giṭ. 10a) part B disagrees with A, for B states that even if a writ of divorce is signed by *two* Samaritans, it is still valid. Pineles disagrees and argues that B not only does not contradict A but rather strengthens it. B claims even if the writ had *two* Samaritans as witnesses the writ of divorce is still valid. The reason for this is Samaritans can be trusted in regard to laws of personal relationship

---

[95] *Ibid.*, p. 22.
[96] *Ibid.*, p. 91.

95

(DYNY 'RYWT); therefore, even if both witnesses are Samaritans, the divorce writ is still valid. In regard to monetary matters, however, they cannot be trusted and a writ of this nature signed by even one Samaritan is invalid.[97]

To substantiate his claim Pineles cites the Tosefta passage. R. Judah's statement in the Tosefta clearly indicates there is no disagreement in the pericope. The "story" is added to reinforce the fact that Samaritans may sign writs of divorce and emancipation. The editor wanted to cite the law (B) anonymously. He therefore omitted both Judah's saying ("even if") and the attribution of the story to Judah.[98] Whether or not the interpretation of the development of the passage is correct, Pineles did use Tosefta to seek the meaning of the passage.

The following examples show how Pineles uses Tosefta and a precise understanding of terms to interpret a passage:

> Three times in the year the priests four times during the day lift up their hands at the Morning Prayer, at the Additional Prayer, at the Afternoon Prayer, and at the closing of the gates; namely on the days of fasting, on the M'MDWT, and on the Day of Atonement.
>
> (M. Ta. 4 : 1, trans. Danby, p. 199)

The Amoraim, puzzled by this law, asked, "Do we recite the Additional Prayer on fast days and on M'MDWT (b. Ta. 26b)?" They then amend the text contending that it is incomplete (HSRY MHSR'). Pineles argues there is no difficulty in this passage, for Tosefta states:

> Three times in the year the priests lift up their hands four times during the day, at the Morning Service, at midday, at the Afternoon Service and at the closing of the gates.
>
> (Tos. Ta. 3 : 1 ed. Lieberman, p. 336, lines 1-2)

Tosefta also states:

> What is the difference between an individual fast day and a communal fast day? [On] the communal fast day the priests lift up their hands four times.
>
> (Tos. Ta. 2 : 4 ed. Lieberman, p. 330-1, lines 33-35)

This citation clearly demonstrates that the priests did lift up their hands four times on a communal fast day. Regarding the recitation of the priestly blessing four times on M'MDWT, Pineles argues (as does

---

[97] But compare Weiss Halivni, *op. cit.*, p. 493, n. 2.
[98] *Ibid.*, p. 71.

Lieberman)⁹⁹ that the priests did lift up their hands four times. Following the destruction of the Temple in 70, however, the custom was discontinued, and the Babylonian Amoraim failed to understand the law. The extra prayer of the MʿMDWT was not the full Additional service but rather only six blessings.¹⁰⁰ Lieberman, therefore, accepts as the better version the Tosefta's reading of "mid-day." This example clearly demonstrates how the use of Tosefta aided Pineles in determining a simple understanding of the text.

Despite poor texts and manuscripts and lack of knowledge of modern philological and archaeological discoveries, Pineles made a lasting contribution to Mishnaic studies. Aside from occasional use of traditional excuses, for example, when he explains that a portion of a pericope or an entire mishnah is out of place because "a mishnah does not move from its place,"¹⁰¹ Pineles uses critical techniques to explain problematic passages. Several other criticisms, however, follow from Pineles' work. We shall see that Pineles regards the Mishnah as a law-code. If Tosefta must be employed to reach legal decisions, why should the law code have been limited to the Mishnah? Following Pineles' own reasoning much of the Amoraic misunderstanding of the Mishnah was due to their lack of Toseftan material. Could the Amoraim have lacked also some sections of Rabbi's Mishnah? If many misinterpretations arose on the part of the Amoraim, what does this indicate about Judah's Mishnah? Compared to his contribution, however, these objections are minor.

iii

Pineles notes several stages in the development of the oral law. These periods are the age of the Scribes, the conflict between the Sadducees and the Pharisees, the time of Hillel and the work of ʿAqiba and his students. Within each period a significant change occurred in the nature of the oral law. The simplicity of the oral law and also its "secret meanings" (SWD ṬʿMY HHLKWT) disappeared during the Tannaitic period. The oral law originated as a simple explanation of the Torah and degenerated into an involved exegesis (*pilpul*) often obliterating the meaning of the Torah. The Scribes and the Men of the

---

⁹⁹ Saul Lieberman, *Tosefta Kifshuṭah Moʿed* 5, p. 1101.
¹⁰⁰ Pineles, *op. cit.* p. 41.
¹⁰¹ *Ibid.*, p. 66.

Great Assembly, from the time of Ezra onwards, "explained and defined (HGBYLW) everything that was not clear and defined in the Torah, either by using the tradition from the Prophets, or by their wisdom which they received from Heaven. They also passed ordinances for the benefit of the people according to the needs of the times. By following the intention (KWWNT) of the Torah and its spirit, they (the *Soferim*) changed and instituted new definitions that opposed the accepted opinions of the Torah."[102] Pineles follows the traditional view, by placing the rise of the Oral Law in the period of the Scribes. Before this time the Torah, as given to Moses, was observed; however, because of changes in both the internal and external political and social conditions, changes had to be made in the law. Pineles offers several examples of this new law.

The date for the holiday of *Shavuot* in the Torah is not stated in the standard biblical manner "on the fifteenth day of the month the holiday shall occur." Rather, the Torah writes, "*Shavuot* shall be celebrated seven weeks after the day after the Sabbath" (MMḤRT HŠBT Lev. 23 : 19). In the time of the First Temple *Shavuot* was associated with the bringing of the 'Omer and not with any event of national history. The *Soferim*, however, living in a time "when the majority of the people lived in the diaspora, in Babylonia, and did not come to Jerusalem to bring the 'Omer, changed the significance of *Shavuot* from an agricultural holiday to a national holiday because the spirit of the religion and the history of the people returned to be the primary pillar upon which the life of the people was built. The Scribes, therefore, interpreted the 'day after the Sabbath' to mean the day after the first day of Passover, so that *Shavuot*, which falls on the fiftieth day following the first day of Passover, would coincide with the sixth of Sivan, the traditional day of the giving of the Torah. This change was made to instill in the hearts of the people the essential principle of Revelation and to give remembrance to that miraculous celebration."[103] No sources, however, ascribe this change to the Scribes. The dispute which Pineles cites, concerning the meaning of the 'day after the Sabbath' appears in the Talmud as a discussion from a later period.[104] Thus Pineles uses such evidence as was available to support

---

[102] *Ibid.*, p. 3.
[103] *Ibid.*, pp. 3-4.
[104] The discussion appears in Sifra 'Emor 12 : 1-9 and b. Men. 65b-66a. It is between R. Judah b. Bathyra and R. Yosi.

preconceived conclusions. None of the other examples Pineles offers of scribal law can be dated to the period of the Scribes. He states, "The belief in resurrection after death was suppressed by Moses in order that the Jews would not be corrupted by the similar Egyptian belief, and was only later enunciated by the *Soferim*."[105]

The Scribes never revealed the "secret meaning of the law," for they feared the revelation of these secrets would lead to the public disregard of the laws. When God explained to Solomon why a king should not take many wives and many horses, Solomon rejected the reason and no longer observed the law. Fearing this, "the Scribes wisely hid the details of faith in order that the people would not disagree with the intention of the Torah."[106] This esoteric knowledge of the secret meanings of the law through the course of the Tannaitic period was forgotten. This gave rise to *pilpul*, the practice of which began with the Pharisees: "There was no tension in the land, although the people did not know the reasons for the laws, until a group arose and questioned the basis of these laws. From the generations of Simeon the Righteous and Antigonus of Sokho onwards, they began to set the explanations and the definitions of the Scribes into brief formulations of law. When, however, the Sadducean sect arose and differed from the Pharisees, who followed the virtues (MDWT) of Abraham, and began to question the Pharisees on the basis of the Torah and the Writings, the Pharisees had to find evidence in the Torah for their law. They did this by means of exegesis (DRŠ) and proof-texts ('SMKT'). Even though these explanations did not coincide with the Torah's meaning, they (the Pharisees) insisted that they had received these interpretations from the tradition."[107] Pineles assumes Simeon the Righteous formulated the Scribes' work into brief sayings. Is Simeon's law identical with scribal law? Second, Pineles assumes the Pharisees followed the tradition of Abraham, which implies that Pharisaic law was the common tradition of Israel. He furthermore equates the laws of the *Soferim* with the laws of the Mishnah. No date is even offered for the activities of the Pharisaic party. Abraham was a Scribe and a Pharisee (!).

When the Pharisees realized that exegesis could be employed to

[105] Pineles, *op. cit.* p. 7.
[106] *Ibid.*, p. 8.
[107] *Ibid.*

justify changes in the law, they instructed their students "to explain and receive a reward" (DRŠ WQBL ŚKR). By doing this the Pharisees altered the meaning of the Torah. Later generations, however, forgot that this method had been used to alter the meaning of a law, and this gave rise to unnecessary *pilpul*. In Herod's time many disputes arose in the legal interpretation of the laws.[108] Hillel formulated six hermeneutical principles to facilitate the derivation of law; however, ʿAqiba and Ishmael increased the number of principles to thirteen, which led to further DRŠ and *pilpul*.[109] Pineles attempts to use history to support his argument that *pilpul* was a corruption of the original rabbinic method. The purity of the law was hidden and was only recovered by Rabbi's ordering of the Mishnah. Pineles, however, throughout never adequately defines what "secret meaning" was lost. The examples he gives for loss of this secret meaning are Amoraic.[110] Moreover, if the Mishnah was constructed through a process of accretions, as Pineles argues, then a large portion of the work of the Tannaim would be of little value for they did not know either the purpose of engaging in exegesis to alter the meaning of a law or the "secret meanings of the law." Pineles also contradicts himself by stating "the secret meaning of the law was known to every sage who investigated the roots of the Torah and this is true even in the generation of R. Yoḥanan b. Zakkai."[111] Moreover, Pineles' history of the origin and the development of the oral law offers no insight into the activities of the individual Rabbis, the makeup of the schools and the political and social conditions of the Tannaitic period.

iv

As noted, Pineles claims Simeon the Righteous was the first to use brief sayings to transmit the Sages' opinions. He cites several examples which contain this old law. The Tannaim, to avoid confusing their ideas with those of the Torah, "expanded the language to include new grammatical forms, among which are the changes of HḤL to HTḤYL and HRYʿ to HTRYʿ. A law containing an old form, such as Tamid 1 : 2 (uses HḤL) is obviously an old law. All of Tamid, since it

[108] *Ibid.*, p. 9.
[109] *Ibid.*
[110] *Ibid.* He cites the example of the "stubborn and rebellious son" (Deut. 21 : 18-22) which appears in M. Sanh. 8 : 1 and b. Sanh. 71a.
[111] *Ibid.*

contains this old law, is also early."[112] To ascribe the development of Middle Hebrew to the conscious efforts of the rabbis is quite curious. One can also not date a mishnah solely on the basis of an old verb form it contains. The presence of a biblical form in the Mishnah is not unusual and could have occurred at any time in the Tannaitic period. Moreover, to date a whole tractate on the basis of one law cannot be justified.

"In the time of Shemaʿiah and Abtalion the laws, which through the generations were added to one by one, were set and sealed (LQBWʿH WHTWMH). Hillel established six orders of the Mishnah and divided them into tractates and chapters.[113] His Mishnah, because of his prestige as the Patriarch and his humility, became "the Mishnah of the Great Yeshiva." Pineles offers no proof for these claims.

Pineles is also not clear how the Mishnah developed and was transmitted. "Although the Tannaim continued to expand the law, the Mishnah, that is the corpus (TWPS) which was known to all the students, was not moved from its place. Even though the Sages of later generations did not understand some of the earlier laws, they added their explanations while leaving the form (TBNYT) of the earlier material."[114] The Mishnah was composed through a process of accretions. Nothing was ever lost. Rabbi had all from the time of the *Soferim* onwards.[115] But Pineles also states that despite their teachers' warnings the students made changes in the law.[116]

Four methods were used for ordering the laws: (1) according to the order of the Torah, (2) according to the hermeneutical principles, (3) according to stylistic, or linguistic similarities, (4) according to topics. The last method was preferred by Hillel and those who came after him, ʿAqiba, Meir, and Yosi and his associates.[117] The Mishnah does reflect these tendencies, but are they principles of organization? Who employed the principles? How did the linguistic similarities in the

[112] *Ibid.*, p. 10.
[113] *Ibid.*, p. 9.
[114] *Ibid.*
[115] *Ibid.*, p. 12.
[116] *Ibid.*, p. 11.
[117] *Ibid.*

laws first arise? Were these similarities formulated only at the time of the ordering of the Mishnah? Or were the laws originally written in this manner? Pineles does not place great emphasis on the question of the formation of the Mishnah. His only mention of 'Aqiba's and Meir's *Mishnayot* is in the already cited quotation and in one other brief citation, "Rabbi Judah the Patriarch followed R. Meir's order."[118] "Rabbi is the final orderer of the Mishnah, and his collection is the one we possess today."[119] Rabbi's Mishnah was a law code, for Pineles constantly states, the Mishnah contains "practical law" (*halakhah lema'aseh*).[120]

"Judah organized the Mishnah by explaining and by joining all the earlier Mishnah collections that were gathered by the different organizers of the Mishnah, Judah's work was a synthesis of earlier Mishnah collections. Variations had arisen because, within the course of the seven generations of the Tannaim, the students of the Yeshivot had made changes because of either their study, changes in the environment, or political changes caused by the intrusion of Roman customs; or because of different ideas that were taught outside of the accepted legal corpus. The work was difficult because all the versions were not engraved in stone but were oral. The law remained unwritten because the rabbis did not want to close the laws to further changes and improvements. Rabbi did all this work because the spirit of God was within him."[121] Rabbi's version was accepted because of his prestige as *Rosh Yeshiva* and as *Nasi*, and member of the Patriarchal family and of the house of David, because of his proximity to the Roman authorities.[122] Pineles' insight that the Mishnah is a synthesis is supported by modern criticism.[123] What, however, was the nature of the documents Rabbi combined? What principles of organization did Rabbi employ? What necessitated a law code? All of these questions are not asked.

Pineles contradicts himself concerning the nature of Rabbi's Mishnah and the extent of its contents. "Rabbi gathered the individual pericopae according to the order of the Mishnah of Rabbi Meir and

[118] *Ibid.*
[119] *Ibid.*
[120] *Ibid.*, pp. 18, 64.
[121] *Ibid.*, p. 11.
[122] *Ibid.*, p. 12.
[123] See Y. N. Epstein, above.

set them (QB'N), with the aid of his contemporaries, in the Mishnah. He joined all the material in a logical order, for his desire was to arouse his students to learn the six orders of the Mishnah according to the order he had set and which had been already accepted by many of his generation."[124] From this it would appear that Rabbi's Mishnah had a definite order and form; however, Pineles also writes, "Rabbi's Mishnah was only a collection (YLQWṬ) of *halakhot*. Even though there had already appeared the signs (SYMNY) of order, all the needs of organization had not been met because the Mishnah text was gathered from four different sources."[125] Concerning the content of Rabbi's Mishnah, Pineles writes, "The Tannaim transmitted everything they had received, even those sections which they did not completely understand. Just as the Men of the Great Assembly in their canonizing the Torah, which they had gathered from many different *megillots*, (scrolls), had faithfully transmitted, in its form and purity, all they had heard; likewise all the great Tannaim, until the time of Rabbi, transmitted all they had heard."[126] Pineles, however, also states, "Why should one discredit Rabbi, if in the transmission of the material some of the good and useful *taqqanot* were lost?"[127] Pineles also contends the Tosefta and *beraitot* contain material that for some reason Rabbi had omitted. Could material have been transmitted through sources unknown to Rabbi? According to Pineles, Rabbi's Mishnah was a unified document; however, he also states, "Amoraim wrote *beraitot* and Tosefta material in Mishnaic language, which are extremely difficult to distinguish from Tannaitic material."[128] Pineles advances a theory to uphold the integrity of the Mishnah but does not realize its implications.

Pineles only deals briefly with historical questions. Compared to his exegesis of the text, the search for historical knowledge occupied a secondary role. Despite the theological and legal implications of his theories, Pineles above all saw the Mishnah as a literary document. Throughout his book he stated, "I do not want to disagree with the *halakhah lema'aseh*, for we must treat the Sages with great respect and honor; however, I only want to spread a quiet, soft critical light on that which we have received, in order to find the

[124] Pineles, *op. cit.*, p. 294.
[125] *Ibid.*, p. 293.
[126] *Ibid.*, p. 12.
[127] *Ibid.*, p. 293.
[128] *Ibid.*, p. 13.

truth."[129] It is because of his critical examination of the Mishnah that one of today's great Talmudists has written, "Pineles' book is full of correct interpretations. Everything he has written is with good reasoning and based upon straightforward thinking and deep insight. (N'MR BṬWB ṬʿM MYWSD ʿL ŚKL YŠR WHBNH ʿMWQH)."[130]

[129] *Ibid.*, pp. 19, 64. Geiger and Schorr criticized Pineles for this position. They contended that, if Pineles has shown errors exist in the oral law, then he should admit that these laws no longer have any validity.

[130] David Weiss Halivni, *op. cit.*, p. 12.

PART III

THE HISTORIANS AND THE MISHNAH

CHAPTER SEVEN

THE TALMUDIC HISTORIANS: N. KROCHMAL, H. GRAETZ, I. H. WEISS, AND Z. JAWITZ

WILLIAM SCOTT GREEN

i

The lifetimes of the four historians considered here span 139 years, from the end of the eighteenth century to the beginning of the twentieth. They are labelled as Talmudic historians because their accounts of the history of the Jews rely primarily on the statements of the two Talmuds and other rabbinic literature. Biographical information on Weiss, Graetz, and Jawitz, as well as general introductions to their approaches to history can be found in *The Formation of the Babylonian Talmud*, pp. 3, 6-7, and 11-12. Biographical information on Krochmal is provided below.

It is appropriate, at the outset of this essay, to make some general remarks about the method of history practiced by these scholars as it is revealed in their accounts of the formation and development of the Mishnah. Three characteristics predominate throughout. First, their work is primarily narrative and descriptive, not critical. For the most part, they all accept the sayings of rabbinic literature at face value, describe their contents, and write history by stringing random statements together in various orders. This uncritical approach has serious ramifications in their accounts of the Mishnah, for it means that they rely on statements of non-Mishnaic, and largely non-Tannaitic, material to provide an understanding of the Mishnah itself. Pericopae from Tosefta and other Tannaitic literature are seldom employed to help clarify the Mishnah; heavy reliance, however, is placed on statements of Amoraic masters and medieval commentators. Actual Mishnah passages, while frequently cited or alluded to, are rarely examined, and are usually employed only to provide support of general statements. Because their accounts are superficial and guided by the attempt to reconcile the sometimes conflicting rabbinic statements about the Mishnah, they suffer from incompleteness and confusion. Second, all of them operate within a totally traditional framework. This means that central questions are never asked and that disagreements among the several historians are mainly on issues of detail or questions of personal preference and emphasis. That the law originated with Moses at Sinai and was handed down from generation to generation following the account of M. Avot 1 : 1, and similar traditional statements are assumed throughout. Finally, we should note the strong role of imagination employed in their histories. When evidence is not forthcoming from the sources, it is simply fabricated by each historian and treated as if it were fact. None of these accounts can be taken seriously today, and all are interesting to us mainly as curiosities of an earlier age. This is not to say, however, that valid and interesting observations never appear in these accounts, because they do. Were we to regard these accounts seriously and offer detailed criticisms of every statement, we should be reduced to the practice of the same sort of academic *pilpul* and quibbling about details which characterizes so much of their work. Therefore, the following summaries of their views are selective, and consider only the highlights of their accounts of the Mishnah.

ii

Naḥman Krochmal (1785-1840) was born in Brody, Austria, and received no formal education save for his childhood *yeshivah* training, which lasted only until his marriage at age fourteen. He lived most of his life in rather meagre circumstances, preferring to devote his energies to studies rather than to a profit-making occupation. He read voraciously; mastered German, Latin, and French; studied Syriac and Arabic to improve his knowledge of Hebrew; and was fluent with the intellectual developments of his time. During a lengthy convalescent stay in Lemberg, he attracted a zealous group of disciples whom he taught informally, on the Socratic model. His only published work is his *Moreh Nebukhé HaZeman*, which attempted to explain the philosophy and history of Judaism. His writing on the Mishnah occupies but a few pages of that document.

Krochmal's undaunted intellectual curiosity earned him the enmity of the Ḥassidim, who believed he was possessed by a demon. In the face of their vigorous hostility, however, he

> claimed for himself and his disciples ... the right to study what they thought best and in the way they thought best.... To one of his pupils

who made concessions to the Chassidim and their Zaddikim worship, Krochmal wrote, 'Be firm in this matter unless you wish to earn the contempt of every honest man. One who is afraid of these people, and debases himself before them bears a mean soul that was born to slavery. The man that wishes to rise above the mob, with its confused notions and corrupt morality, must be courageous as a lion in conquering the obstacles that beset his path. Consideration of what people will say, what bigots will whisper, what crafty enemies will scheme—questions such as these can have but one effect,—to darken the intellect and confuse the faculty of judgment.'[1]

Non-scriptural law begins for Krochmal with the scribes, a term which, he says, refers to the teachers who lived between Ezra and Simeon the Righteous, the first of the sages of the Mishnah. The scribes never taught fixed laws in one language, and consequently, few of their teachings were remembered by later generations or recorded in their mishnahs, except in an accidental fashion. For example, we speak of the time of the reading of the *Shema'*, but nowhere in our literature is the obligation to read the *Shema'* discussed. This is because it is based on Scribal teaching.[2] The order of the teachers of the law begins with Simeon ben Honi the second, 280 years before the destruction of the Second Temple. These law teachers fixed the details of many Scribal teachings and formulated them into new rules, stated in brief language for easy memory, in Aramaic, the spoken language of Second Temple times. These rules are called *halakhot*, and were taught orally.[3]

Before the time of Hillel, the teachers of the law had tried to find some connection among the laws in order to teach and study them together. These laws were joined in one of four ways: because of a similarity of content; because of a shared form ('YN BYN ZH LZH 'L' ...); because of the presence of a rule common to both (to be lenient ... to be strict); or by numerical similarities (two which are actually four ...). These connected laws were called a tractate (MSKT) which means a "weaving-together" ('RYGH).[4] Just as Ezra had done for the written commandments, "Hillel made a handle for the Torah and

---

[1] Solomon Schechter, *Studies in Judaism* (New York, 1970) provides a brief biographical account of Krochmal. The quotation is from pp. 327-28. A more detailed biography may be found in *The Writings of Nahman Krochmal*, Simon Rawidowicz, ed. (London, 1961) pp. 17-98 (Arabic numerals).

[2] *Ibid.*, Rawidowicz, p. 195. This and all following notes refer to the Hebrew pagination.

[3] *Ibid.*, p. 204.

[4] *Ibid.*, p. 218.

a foundation for the existence of the laws.... By his hand were founded the six orders of the Mishnah ... and he gave each division a number of tractates, and some of the large tractates were divided into gates (Hebrew: ŠʿRYM; Aramaic: BBWT), and he divided all of them into chapters."[5] Hillel fixed the orders of the chapters within the tractates, but not the order of the tractates themselves. Despite the fact that the transmission of the laws was exclusively oral, the arrangement of the content of the chapters was permanent because entire chapters were taught at one time. The tractates, on the other hand, were taught in different orders by different sages. Rabbi is responsible for the arrangement of the tractates.[6]

Hillel taught all the laws anonymously and recorded no disagreements about them. However, as the tractates were taught in each succeeding generation until Rabbi, "the teachers added to a law which was doubtful or unfinished (BLTY NGMRT) the words of the two sides of a dispute, even when an individual disagreed with the many." This accounts for the existence of such terms as, "The words of all" (DBRY HKL), "The words of the many" (DBRY HMRWBYM), and "The words of the individual" (DBRY HYHYD).[7] The smooth transmission of laws was further disrupted because in three periods of stress or war a large number of laws was forgotten. Some were later accidentally recovered through the concentration of various sages, or through casuistry (*pilpul*). M. Pes. 9:6 is an example of such a forgotten law: "R. Joshua said: I have heard a tradition that a substitute for the Passover offering can be offered, and also, that a substitute for the Passover offering cannot be offered; and I cannot explain it. R. ʿAqiba said: I will explain it..." (trans. Danby, p. 149).[8] Therefore, when Rabbi came to order the Mishnah, he had before him "many orders of mishnah" reflecting both forgotten traditions and the teachings of different sages. Krochmal follows tradition and states that Rabbi used Meir's Mishnah as the basis for his own.[9]

To support his assertion that all Mishnah tractates were completed before Rabbi, Krochmal must demonstrate their antiquity. Below are examples of his method. He argues that tractate *Tamid* is "very early," and provides the following justifications:

[5] *Ibid.*, p. 219.
[6] *Ibid.*
[7] *Ibid.*, p. 220.
[8] *Ibid.*, p. 211.
[9] *Ibid.*, p. 220, p. 229.

(1) Its language is anonymous (with a few exceptions).

(2) Its laws are undisputed within the tractate and their arrangement "is according to the order of the daily sacrifice ('BWDT HTMYD)."

(3) The two disputes containing named traditions (Eliezer ben Jacob, 5 : 2; Judah, 7 : 2) "were added by the one who fixed the tractate to emphasize the opposition between the Temple and the State (HNGWD, MQDŠ WMDYNH)." These two statements deal with internal matters of the ritual of the sacrifice. Krochmal's meaning here is unclear.

(4) Tos. Zev. 6 : 3 records that Simeon, Man of Mispeh taught tractate *Tamid* (MŠNH TMYD). B. Yoma 14b ascribes the order of tractate Yoma to Simeon. M. Peah 2 : 6 places Simeon in the time of Rabban Gamaliel the Elder. Therefore, the *whole* of tractate Tamid predates Rabban Gamaliel.

(5) M. Tamid 3 : 2 includes the name of Matia ben Samuel, "one of the guards who were in the Temple and lived in the time of the wars of the sons of the Hasmoneans, shortly before Hillel."

(6) The first arranger of the laws of the *Tamid* sacrifice was Eleazar ben Diglai, who recounts (in M. Tamid 3 : 8) his own experience of the sacrifice: "R. Eleazar ben Diglai said: My father's house kept goats on the mountain of Machwar and they used to sneeze from the compounding of the incense" (trans. Danby, p. 585).[10]

As for other tractates which post-date Hillel, Krochmal regards the statement of b. Ber. 25a, "'Eduyyot was taught 'on that day,'" as proof that tractate 'Eduyyot was created on the day when Eleazar ben 'Azariah replaced Rabban Gamaliel as *Nasi* at Yavneh. Moreover, b. Yoma 16a says that Eleazar ben Jacob is responsible for tractate Middot, and from the story of the dispute between Meir, Nathan, and Simeon ben Gamaliel in b. Hor. 13a, we can infer that tractate 'Uqsin was created at a very late date.[11] Aside from these Talmudic testimonies, no evidence is brought forth to attest to the creators of various tractates, and therefore, we ascribe most of them to the time preceding Rabbi: "There is only doubt about the collection of the tractates, but concerning their division and their detailed laws, the matter is clear that almost all of them were taught in their language and in the foundation of their form long before Rabbi. A large portion of them is from the days of R. 'Aqiba and another portion from the days of Hillel, and the oldest and shortest, and even they are not in small number, are even before him, until one arrives at the beginning."[12]

[10] *Ibid.*, p. 224.
[11] *Ibid.*, p. 219.
[12] *Ibid.*, p. 220.

Krochmal's account of Hillel's literary activity is wholly fictitious, yet he employs its elements as valid criteria for dating Mishnaic material. He has not demonstrated why anonymous language and the absence of legal disputes are necessary hallmarks of early law collections, but he regards the presence of those characteristics in Tamid as at least partial proof of the early date of the tractate. His reasoning is both arbitrary and circular.

iii

Heinrich Graetz (1817-1891) equates Oral law with Scribal law which he defines as "everything which had been handed down from the fathers."[13] This includes the sayings of the Scribes, the decrees of the Sanhedrin, as well as customs which had taken root in the life of the Jews. None of this material had ever been written down and all was transmitted orally from one generation to the next. Before 'Aqiba only the content of the law was studied; its form was ignored and it had not been arranged in any way. But 'Aqiba arranged the Oral law into groups: laws of the Sabbath and holidays, laws of marriage and divorce, laws of property ownership, laws of personal status, and laws of eating and drinking. Each group of laws was called a tractate (MSKT). If many different laws concerned one issue he arranged them according to number, for example, "There are four principal categories of damage . . . ." (M. B.Q. 1 : 1). 'Aqiba called this collection of laws "Mishnah" and it is now known as the Mishnah of R. 'Aqiba to distinguish it from the Mishnah of Rabbi. It was known to the Church Fathers as the Deuterosis Akibaes and was called Mekhilta by the people. Like earlier materials, this collection was never written down.[14] Graetz lists nine citations from rabbinic literature to prove the veracity of his account of 'Aqiba's activity.[15] The best of them is Tos. Zab. 3 : 1, which states, "When R. 'Aqiba was arranging (SDR) laws for the disciples, he said . . . ." Another proof is Tos. 'Arakh. 3 : 15 in which Yosi describes a dispute between the House of Shammai and the House of Hillel as "the Mishnah of R. 'Aqiba." It

---

[13] Heinrich Graetz, *History of the Jews*, Vol. II (Philadelphia, 1956), p. 162. Aside from an occasional pleasant rendering, The Jewish Publication Society English version of Graetz's history, with its somewhat abbreviated translation and lack of footnotes, is useless for serious study.

[14] Heinrich Graetz, *Divré Yemé Yisra'el*, Vol. II, S. P. Rabinowitz, trans. (Warsaw, 1907), p. 189.

[15] *Ibid.*, p. 190.

seems hardly necessary to point out that examples of this sort cannot substantiate Graetz' elaborate account. Graetz adds that ʿAqiba's Mishnah was called "the *Mishnah Aharonah* of R. ʿAqiba" and that it replaced the *Mishnah Rishonah*.[16] Meir added to ʿAqiba's arrangement and his Mishnah was clearer than ʿAqiba's since it was arranged according to content, not numbers. Since the Talmud states that anonymous Mishnahs are Meir's, Graetz argues that Meir was the first to collect anonymous laws. Meir's collection was not authoritative, however, since each rabbi arranged his own collection of laws in his own house of study.[17]

Rabbi took Meir's revised version of ʿAqiba's Mishnah, examined all sides of every legal issue, and determined practical law.[18] He did not accept all of the decisions of ʿAqiba's Mishnah and in the case of a dispute between one rabbi (YḤYD) and the rest of the sages (RBYM) Rabbi fixed the law according to the many and revised the decision in anonymous language. He refined the organization of the Oral law and is responsible for creating the six orders of the Mishnah. However, Rabbi was not completely successful in his work because the nature and content of the material could not tolerate a topical arrangement, and therefore some Mishnah passages do not seem appropriate to their orders. Moreover, Rabbi was unable to abandon the method of earlier sages to arrange legal material according to the name of the speaker.[19] Rabbi did not intend his Mishnah to be a law book, but rather, to be a private aid to himself, to help him remember the order of the issues he was to teach his students. But, because of his personal authority, his collection soon superceded that of others and became the statement of normative law for the Jews. Rabbi's Mishnah was not written down, since the Mishnahs of earlier teachers were never written down. Moreover, because of the well-known prohibition against written preservation of the law, Rabbi's Mishnah was not written until hundreds of years after its compilation; until that time it existed only in the memories of his students.[20] In his old age, Rabbi changed several of the views he had earlier espoused and so produced a "second edition" of the Mishnah, which served as a basis for the law teachers in the Babylonian academies. However, his son,

[16] *Ibid.*
[17] *Ibid.*, p. 274.
[18] *Ibid.*, p. 296.
[19] *Ibid.*
[20] *Ibid.*, p. 297.

R. Simeon, preferred the version of his father's youth and preserved it, making additions, not corrections.[21]

Rabbi's Mishnah gave Judaism a pronounced legal character for all time and the whole of it rests on one principle:

> That the law given to Moses on Sinai includes not only the commandments of explicitly stated warning, but also traditions which are derived from those explicit rules by the exegetical methods of the sages.

All laws not explicitly mentioned in the Torah are referred to in the Mishnah as the "words of the Scribes" (DBRY SWPRYM) and no distinction is made in the Mishnah between what was said by the sages and the decrees of the Sanhedrin. Both kinds of law are equally binding.[22] The remainder of Graetz's account consists of a description of the content of the Mishnah and need not concern us here. It is sufficient to point out that he provides no clear picture of the development of the Mishnah and no critical examination of the Mishnah itself. His account of ʿAqiba's work far exceeds his supporting evidence and is pure fabrication. His view of Meir's work is no more than a repetition of an Amoraic tradition, and any factual basis for his assertion that Rabbi intended the Mishnah for strictly private use is missing. The notion that the *entire* corpus of non-Scriptural law was arranged orally and accurately preserved for centuries only by memory is fantastic.

iv

The account of I. H. Weiss (1815-1905) is somewhat more comprehensive than that of the others and exhibits more courage and creativity. It suffers, however, from vague statements and internal contradictions.

In Weiss' view Meir was the first to arrange a collection of laws. His Mishnah was clear and orderly and followed the view (ŠTH) of ʿAqiba. Although the Talmud states that anonymous Mishnah statements are from Meir (b. Sanh. 86a), Weiss notes that some anonymous Mishnahs reflect views different from Meir's, and some were apparently taught after his lifetime.[23] Therefore, not all anonymous Mishnah passages are

---

[21] *Ibid.*, pp. 298-9.
[22] *Ibid.*, p. 311.
[23] I. H. Weiss, *Dor, Dor, VeDorshav* (Jerusalem/Tel Aviv, N.D.), p. 135.

his. Weiss asserts that the term "mishnah" refers to anything which the sages taught their students for memorization. Thus, "mishnah" may mean law, *midrash*, or *aggadah* depending on the style and preference of the sage. Since Meir preferred law (HLKH) to *midrash* his Mishnah must have been a collection of anonymous *laws*. Weiss cites chapter 3 of M. Ber. as an example of Meir's Mishnah. Since the chapter is largely anonymous, however, we are left with Weiss' circular reasoning as proof that it is part of Meir's Mishnah. Meir also recorded the disputes of his predecessors, for example, the Houses and Eliezer and Joshua. Weiss' proof for this claim is the assertion that all such disputes follow Meir's view.[24]

The Mishnah was *written* by Rabbi Judah the Patriarch to serve as a comprehensive collection for the students of the sages and to prevent people from forgetting "mishnah" in place of *midrash* and casuistry. After his preparation Rabbi decided that he should collect the views of all the sages "who taught Torah in their houses of study in his time and before him. He went from *yeshivah* to *yeshivah*... and gathered... the various Mishnah collections.... These collections were the foundation stones for the new Mishnah which Rabbi arranged and wrote as a book."[25] From an Amoraic passage in b. B.M. 33b Weiss deduces the second reason for Rabbi's new Mishnah:

> In the generation before Simeon bar Yoḥai the hands of the people weakened from mishnah and all their salvation and pleasure was in talmud and in the casuistry (*pilpul*) of the sages. And R. ʿAqiba had already said, "He who jumps [forward with an answer] is not praised, but rather him who gives a reason," and R. Judah made *midrash* the core of his Mishnah, and because of this the paths were distorted until R. Simeon himself said that there was no longer to be found a clear mishnah and a clear *halakah* in one place. And thus matters continued until the days of Rabbi, and he saw that if this situation were to continue that mishnah would be rejected, and the reward of *talmud* as the greater measure would be at the expense of *mishnah*. Thus, he adjusted (TQN) his Mishnah so that all the issues of the Oral Torah would fit in it together, and thus, compared to the arrangement of the mishnah of the early masters, you certainly have no measure greater than *talmud*. But since Rabbi abridged (SQʿ) most of the [other] Mishnahs, people would always follow the Mishnah in which was more *talmud* than the Talmud.[26]

The terms mishnah, *midrash*, *talmud*, apparently refer to different

[24] *Ibid.*, p. 136.
[25] *Ibid.*, p. 163.
[26] *Ibid.*

teaching methods employed by the sages. *Midrash* means Biblical exegesis, and *talmud* refers to rabbinic debates. The precise meaning of the term "mishnah" is unclear, for in the above statement it has at least three connotations. It refers to anything a sage taught, to law, or to a *collection* of laws. It is therefore difficult to understand exactly what kind of material Weiss thinks Rabbi included in his Mishnah or what teaching method Rabbi hoped to preserve.

His account of what Rabbi actually did is no clearer. He was apparently not responsible either for the six orders of the Mishnah or for the division of the law into tractates, since both of these divisions were known to the early sages (QDMWNYM).[27] Nor is he responsible for the breakdown of the tradition into discrete legal statements, since this too, on the basis of b. Sanh. 48b, is also an early division.[28] Moreover, in arranging his material, Rabbi did not follow the Mishnahs of ʿAqiba and Meir, for, "what R. ʿAqiba and R. Meir did, so did all the sages who taught Torah publicly in the houses of study ... And if we designate R. ʿAqiba and R. Meir as organizers of the Mishnah, so will we designate ... all the sages."[29] It seems then, that Rabbi's activity remained primarily in the realms of determining chapter divisions, making legal decisions, and composing certain sayings, but not in the area of the overall organization of the document itself.

With the consent of the other sages of his day, Rabbi made definitive legal rulings between the statements of anonymous legal teachings.[30] He stated some named traditions in anonymous form,[31] and this accounts for the creation of the *tanna qamma*. He placed the anonymous statements alongside of named traditions, so that a court would be able to use either view as a justification for its decision.[32] From the above, it would seem that Rabbi intended his compilation to be a law code, since the bulk of his efforts was directed at determining the correct law. However, Weiss asserts that Rabbi explicitly did *not* intend his compilation to be authoritative, and he states that what appear to be contradictions in the Mishnah appear so only to those who disagree with this contention: "Anonymous

[27] *Ibid.*, p. 184.
[28] *Ibid.*, p. 185.
[29] *Ibid.*, p. 164.
[30] *Ibid.*
[31] *Ibid.*
[32] *Ibid.*, p. 189.

statements in the Mishnah which disagree with each other do not prove that Rabbi indiscriminately collected all that he had before him, but rather, it is a new proof that from time to time different matters were added to the Mishnah. And perhaps they intentionally left the anonymous contradictory statements, so that if a court saw the words of the anonymous statement, it could depend on it."[33] The picture is extremely confused. Rabbi did not intend to write a law code, and this explains the presence of apparent contradictions. Yet, most of his activity was as a final judge to determine normative legal rulings.

At the beginning of each tractate, Rabbi taught "the fundamental laws which were taught on the issue which was the content of the tractate."[34] These laws are old and were taken from the Mishnah of R. Meir, "and there is no doubt at all that they were taken from there as they were written down and in their original language."[35] Therefore, if a mishnah reads, "Rabbi X says...," the language of the law is the exact language of the speaker. If the speaker is a contemporary of Rabbi, then the superscription is Rabbi's creation. If the speaker precedes Rabbi, then the superscription is part of the original saying. If the pericope is not a quotation, but merely attributes words to a particular sage (Rabbi X permits/forbids..."), the language of the statement is Rabbi's creation. Any explanations or limitations of particular laws are Rabbi's additions to Meir's Mishnah, and not from early collections.[36] Weiss agrees with Graetz that, in his old age, Rabbi produced a new edition of the Mishnah and states that this new edition is the Mishnah of the Palestinian Talmud, because the residents of Palestine could not have ignored a new legal ruling of Rabbi. The version preserved in the Babylonian Talmud is not even Rabbi's original, since it was corrupted and altered by Rav when he brought the Mishnah from Palestine.[37]

The two most interesting observations in Weiss' otherwise foggy account are that the Mishnah is the result of various sources, and that it was written. Indeed, he asserts that the notion that such an enterprise could have taken place only orally is foolish, and adds that rabbinic literature abounds with proofs that individual sages, in all

[33] *Ibid.*
[34] *Ibid.*, p. 189.
[35] *Ibid.*
[36] *Ibid.*
[37] *Ibid.*, p. 190.

THE TALMUDIC HISTORIANS

places and times, wrote down their teachings.[38] However, he does not adduce proofs for any of these.

v

Ze'ev Jawitz's account of the Mishnah is a combination of non-Mishnaic sources and healthy imagination. In his presentation he barely looks at the Mishnah itself. He follows the schema of Sherira throughout, with some help from Y. I. Halevy and medieval commentators. In his view the Oral Law comprises laws not taught in the Torah which, from "the days of Moses to Ezra were arranged and guarded in the hands of the priests, and Levites, and the great ones of each generation. And from the day that Ezra the Scribe established the laws for the protection of the whole people until the days of Simeon the Righteous, the Men of the Great Assembly broadened them, arranged them, divided them into divisions, arranged them according to numbers, taught them to their students in fixed and brief sayings, and ordered them memorized."[39] These sayings constitute the "Old Mishnah" which was authoritative and widely-known during the days of Simeon the Righteous. This law was taught anonymously. The situation changed, however, with the arrival of the Hellenists in Palestine, and because of the unusual stress of those times, people "began to forget, little by little, the details of the rules which the early Scribes has collected anonymously in their early Mishnah."[40] This process of forgetting led to the rise of disagreement about the content of forgotten details of the law and necessitated the introduction of named traditions, so that people would know who was responsible for various teachings.[41]

The method of the early sages was to (1) to make (LKWWN) the tradition (ŠMW'WT) conform to Scripture, (2) to arrange the teaching of that tradition according to the order of the Torah portions and their verses, (3) to translate all of the Bible in a disciplined style (BSGNWN NMRṢ), and (4) to reason from the origin of the tradition to the tradition itself (LHŚKYL ... MMWṢ' DBR 'L DBRY HTWRH HMSWRH). All transmission was, of course, exclusively oral. This method of teaching was in effect through the period of the Second

---

[38] *Ibid.*, p. 193.
[39] Ze'ev Jawitz, *Sefer Toledot Yisrael*, Vol. VI, (Tel Aviv, 1932), p. 211.
[40] *Ibid.*, p. 212.
[41] *Ibid.*, p. 213.

Temple.⁴² However, also during that period some teachers began to teach laws, without connecting them to Scripture, in a very precise language, which permitted no place for error or confusion. The laws are called *halakhot*.⁴³ All the laws which were taught before the time of ʿAqiba are called *Mishnah Rishonah*, and his teachings and those of his students are known as *Mishnah Aharonah*.⁴⁴ The proof for this is a statement by Sherira. ʿAqiba then collected and gathered much of what had come before him, arranged them topically, and combined statements which were similar in either form or content. This statement is substantiated by Rashi.⁴⁵ Thus was the situation until the time of Rabbi.

In his old age Rabbi saw that later generations would have difficulty mastering all the material produced by previous generations: "And he inclined to the word of R. Meir, who says that the essence of Mishnah is law (*halakhah*), and he arose and he gathered all the laws which the sages of Israel had taught in the three generations from the days of Yohanan ben Zakkai onward, and he extracted from them a pure summary (THRT TMSYTN), and he eliminated all the proofs the sages had used to prove their laws [from Sherira], and he added them to the substance of the 'Old Mishnah' which had been handed down by the Men of the Great Assembly, to which had been added the words of the House of Hillel and the House of Shammai, who had given the details of its rules and explained its contradictions; and he put all of them into a single work. In the increase of the Mishnahs, nothing has fallen from the style of the 'Old Mishnah', and he preserved all of it in the essence of its purity, and he placed after it the words of the *Tannaim* who spoke about it, to avoid uprooting the purity of the first ones. But there are mishnahs which Rabbi taught in the style of the first, to clarify some issue long forgotten, to explain contradictory language, or to broaden the authority of a law." The proof for this entire account consists of page citations from Halevy's *Dorot HaRishonim*.⁴⁶

Rabbi left no accepted law out of his Mishnah, which contains the best of the traditions of preceeding masters, and included in it everything taught to Moses at Sinai. He even retained laws which had

---

⁴² *Ibid.*, p. 215.
⁴³ *Ibid.*
⁴⁴ *Ibid.*, p. 218.
⁴⁵ *Ibid.*, p. 220.
⁴⁶ *Ibid.*, p. 221.

been discredited because, "a mishnah does not move from its place."⁴⁷ Tractate ʿEduyyot, which existed from the days of Eleazar ben ʿAzaraiah, was the foundation stone of Rabbi's Mishnah. Laws which Rabbi thought were "very right" (NKWNH M'D) he taught anonymously so that the people would accept them, even if it meant ignoring the name of a certain teacher.⁴⁸ "He arranged the enormity of the law (HMWN HHLKH) which the sages of earlier generations had developed, according to the six chapters of the Old Mishnah, and divided them into tractates, chapters, and laws; and each tractate corresponds to a specific commandment."⁴⁹ Finally, "in order to make the Mishnah the fruit of the received Torah which came to Moses at Sinai, he only collected the words of ordained rabbis" (HMWSMKWT) which explains why the views of Ishmael's students never appear in the Mishnah, despite the fact that Rabbi followed the exegetical methods of their teacher. In the confusion surrounding the Bar Kokhba revolt only ʿAqiba's students had been properly ordained.⁵⁰

vi

All four accounts of the formation of the Mishnah have exhibited the characteristics outlined earlier. They are marked by circular reasoning, failure to examine critically the Mishnah itself, and fabrication. For those reasons we cannot regard them as serious discussions of the Mishnah. The fundamental flaw in each version of the history of the Mishnah is the retention of the traditional method of studying the Mishnah and the transformation of that method into an approach to history. It was noted earlier in this volume that traditional study of the Mishnah is marked by failure to consider the Mishnah separately from the *gemara*. That same process is preserved here. In none of the above accounts is the Mishnah examined in isolation; rather, in each case it is seen through the eyes of the *gemara* and the medieval commentaries. History is thus not seen as the task of careful examination of a document, the isolation of its significant characteristics, and the consideration of reasonable paths of explanation, but rather as an attempt to remain faithful to the statements of tradition. Thus, although each historian writes about the

⁴⁷ *Ibid.*
⁴⁸ *Ibid.*, p. 222.
⁴⁹ *Ibid.*, p. 223.
⁵⁰ *Ibid.*, p. 224.

Mishnah independently and regards it as a separate document, none leaves the sphere of tradition. The framework of inquiry is set, not by the Mishnah itself, but rather by the statements of later authorities about it. All four accounts are more polemical and theological than historical, and their attempt to remain true to the traditional, rabbinic notion of the formation of the Mishnah produces confusion, inconsistencies, and, in some cases, nonsense.

CHAPTER EIGHT

DAVID HOFFMANN'S *THE FIRST MISHNAH*

CHARLES PRIMUS

i

David Hoffmann was born on November 24, 1843 in Verbó, Hungary.[51] He received a traditional Jewish education. His teachers included Rabbi Samuel Sommer of Verbó, Rabbi Moses Schück of St. Georgen, and Abraham Schreiber of Pressburg. Beginning in 1860, Hoffmann studied at a seminary founded by Rabbi Israel Hildesheimer, an advocate of modern Orthodox Judaism. This was approximately the time that an Hungarian Hassidic leader, 'Aqiba Joseph, placed a ban on Hildesheimer, who in 1868 moved from Hungary to Berlin. Hoffmann also pursued secular studies and, in 1863, passed final examinations at Pressburg's Evangelical Gymnasium. Two years later he entered the University of Vienna. At the university he met I. H. Weiss, (later) the author of *Zur Geschichte der jüdischen Tradition* (DWR, DWR, WDWRŠYW). Hoffmann went to Germany in 1866. He taught school for several years in Höchberg in Bavaria. He also attended lectures at several German universities, and, in 1870, received a Ph.D. from the University of Tübingen. His thesis was entitled, *Mar Samuel, Rektor der jüdischen Akademie zu Nehardea in Babylonien* (Leipsic, 1873). The same year he began teaching in Samson Raphael Hirsch's school in Frankfurt-am-Main. Three years later he accepted an invitation to join the faculty of Hildesheimer's newly-founded rabbinical seminary in Berlin. Hoffmann lectured there for forty-eight years. He died in 1921.

Hoffmann's *Die erste Mischna und die Controversen der Tannaim* appeared in 1882. The book has been influential in the study of the Mishnah and has been reprinted recently in Israel. References in this essay are to S. Grünberg's Hebrew translation (Berlin, 1913; reprinted, Jerusalem, 1967/8).

---

[51] Biographical information is taken from L. Ginzberg, "David Hoffmann," *Students, Scholars and Saints*, (Philadelphia, 1958 edition), pp. 252-62; A. Marx, "David Hoffmann," *Essays in Jewish Biography*, (Philadelphia, 1947), pp. 185-222; and I. Singer, "David Hoffmann," *Jewish Encyclopedia*, (New York, 1902), VI : 435.

ii

In *The First Mishnah* Hoffmann states that the content of the Mishnah is part of the Oral Torah (TWRH ŠBʿL PH). It stems from a divine source, most of it deriving from the revelation at Sinai. The Mishnah's literary form, however, is the product of "later" development and properly is the subject of critical study.[52] Hoffmann attributes the first recension of the Mishnah to the disciples of Hillel and Shammai. Subsequent editions, by R. ʿAqiba, by R. Meir, and finally by R. Judah the Patriarch (Rabbi), expanded the Mishnah's contents but substantially preserved its earliest formal structure. Hoffmann claims that he critically investigates the relevant source materials, although he never questions the historicity of Tannaitic and Amoraic statements. Nor does he criticize post-Talmudic, Geonic "history-writing." Instead he announces an original interpretation of old, unexamined evidence.

Hoffmann takes as his problem the identification of the earliest redaction of the Mishnah. His search for redactions prior to the Mishnah attributed to Rabbi recognizes that the extant Mishnah is a composite document. But Hoffmann tries to prove more than that Rabbi's Mishnah contains older sources. In *The First Mishnah* he consistently uses the term *"mishnah"* to refer to collections of *halakhot* rather than to individual laws. This contrasts with the confused terminology in the works of other individuals discussed in this volume. Hoffmann assumes that Rabbi's Mishnah underwent a single, sustained editorial redaction, and he tries to prove that Rabbi used material that had undergone prior editorial redactions. Yet Hoffmann never spells out the implications of a sustained editorial effort. He never asks if the Mishnah, which clearly enough reflects disparate sources, exhibits the characteristics of a product of a sustained editorial process. As will be discussed below, Hoffmann identifies discrete units of material within the document and tries to determine the age and origin of these units. But he does not specify the relations between the units in the extant document. *The First Mishnah* deals with the chronological development of the Mishnah text, the accretion of material through a period of about one-hundred thirty years. Its author presupposes, rather than investigates, the document's nature.

[52] Hoffmann, D., *The First Mishnah*, (Hebrew: S. Grünberg), (Jerusalem, 1967/8), p. 3.

Hoffmann's "critical investigation" proceeds from within the traditional, rabbinic frame of reference. His purpose is to show that "sections from [the earliest, pre-'Aqiban] order of *mishnayot* are preserved in our Mishnah."[53] In his "Introduction" he writes that "Sherira Gaon (10th-century Babylonia) and Shimshon of Chinon (13th-century France) already proved (HWKYHW) ... with many proofs that Rabbi collected the *halakhot* of previous Tannaim."[54] According to the later rabbinic "historians" Rabbi ordered the Mishnah on the model of Meir's Mishnah, which was in turn modeled on 'Aqiba's. Furthermore, Sherira stated that *mishnayot* existed before 'Aqiba's. Like many of the individuals discussed in this volume, Hoffmann assumes such statements constitute an adequate historical basis for further work. He passes over the sources of Sherira and Shimshon's "demonstrations," which are Talmudic statements interpreted literally, regardless of their provenance, to deal with his own personal theory. What, asks Hoffmann, were the pre-'Aqiban *mishnayot* that Sherira mentioned? He does not ask how Sherira knows about them.

Hoffmann's traditional, rabbinic viewpoint presupposes, but never spells out, the significant disparities in early rabbinic literature. Yavnean materials greatly outnumber pre-70 A.D. materials. Similarly, later Tannaitic materials are more plentiful than early Tannaitic materials, and the number of Amoraic sources vastly exceeds the number of Tannaitic sources. Historical knowledge is a function of the possibility for verification on the basis of contemporary documentation. Large quantities of documentation do not ensure the reliability of historical knowledge; but generally they do make possible more extensive procedures of verification. Thus historical knowledge about the later Amoraic period, for which documentation is relatively plentiful, seems more reliable than historical knowledge about earlier periods, for which documentation is meager. From the traditional, rabbinic point of view, however, the issue of the reliability of source material does not emerge. All Mishnaic and Talmudic statements are considered trustworthy, although some statements are more authoritative than other statements. The progressive, quantitative increase in material through the Tannaitic and Amoraic periods leads not to methodological questions, but rather to substantive ques-

---

[53] *Ibid.*, p. 5.
[54] *Ibid.*, p. 4.

tions. This occurs because traditional opinion presupposes the continuity of rabbinic-*halakhic* concerns and procedures, beginning with Moses at Sinai. Thus Hoffmann asks when the Mishnah was first edited and expects to find a specific, satisfactory answer. He presupposes that although thoroughgoing *mishnaic* technique may have been a first-century innovation, nonetheless it represented only an innovation within the larger context of the rabbinic-*halakhic* enterprise. Because Hoffmann knows the nature of the rabbinic-*halakhic* enterprise, he assumes he can interpret the relatively meager quantity of evidence regarding the Mishnah's origins. In his own way Hoffmann is bringing to the evidence standards for verification and interpretation, although these are not historical standards.

iii

Of the critical study of the Mishnah, Hoffmann writes,

> ... the investigation of the circumstances of the time of its composition ('WDWT ZMN HBWRH), at the time that it was established ('L PY H'T SNQB'H) in the form that is in our hands, is not only permitted, but the investigation of the sources (ŠHQYRT MQWRWT) of the traditional teaching (HTWRH HMSWRH) is an obligation for us (HWBH HY' 'LYNW).[55]

Thus Hoffmann advocates a source-critical approach to Mishnaic studies, although he opposed source-critical techniques in Biblical studies. His lifelong opposition to the "Higher Criticism" indicates that he was at least familiar with the best nineteenth-century, critical Biblical scholarship.[56] But to what extent does Hoffmann in *The First Mishnah* follow the procedures of critical scholarship, which include the careful accumulation, criticism, and interpretation of documentary evidence? As discussed above, Hoffmann accepts unhistorical theories about *halakhic* development and asks questions that the evidence, on the face of it, cannot answer. Yet it remains possible to work within an unhistorical, traditional framework, to ask questions that the documentation cannot answer, but still to marshall evidence, principally internal evidence, that can illuminate historical issues. Y. I. Halevy's work illustrates this possibility. But does Hoffmann's?

Hoffmann begins with a discussion of a tenth-century Geonic

---

[55] *Ibid.*, p. 3.
[56] Hoffmann's major attack on "Higher Criticism" was entitled, *The Principal Arguments against the Graf-Wellhausen Hypothesis*, (in German), (Berlin, 1904).

statement that six-hundred orders of Mishnah existed until the days of Hillel and Shammai. He writes that among the Geonim there was agreement that

> until Hillel and Shammai they taught the traditional Torah (HTWRH HMSWRH) by means of the Midrash. The *halakhot* were learned together with the words of the Written Torah from which they derived [the *halakhot*] (HWṢY'WM) and upon which they supported [the *halakhot*] (SMKWM). The portion of Torah (ṢY'WR HTWRH) that they studied in the schools (BBYTY HMDRŠWT), the mishnah in the wider sense (BMWBN HRḤB), was in those days much larger, one-hundred times larger (the number is perhaps exaggerated) than in the later time.[57]

Hoffmann notes that the tenth-century Geonic source that mentions the ancient "six-hundred orders of Mishnah" claims to have seen a "seventh order" in addition to the extant six orders of the Mishnah.[58] Hoffmann also cites Talmudic statements that posit the qualitative decline of rabbinic learning in the years following Hillel and Shammai. He quotes the following *baraita*:

> Our Rabbis taught: From the days of Moses to Rabban Gamaliel, they learned Torah only while standing. When Rabban Gamaliel died, feebleness descended on the world, and they learned Torah while sitting. So we have learned, from the death of Rabban Gamaliel honor of Torah ceased.
>
> (b. Meg. 21a, trans. based on M. Simon, p. 119)

Hoffmann identifies the Gamaliel of the *baraita* as Gamaliel the Elder and alleges that this statement is one of the sources of the Geonic view concerning the radical decline in the number of orders of Mishnah. The Torah's honor was identified with its proliferation. Hoffmann then states that the Geonic *Seder Tannaim* "says more clearly ... that the elders of the school of Shammai and the elders of the school of Hillel established six of the orders of Mishnah."[59] Hoffmann accepts these and other statements. His only criticism is contained in the parenthetical remark about a possible numerical exaggeration cited above. On the basis of this discussion, he concludes

> that with the changes of traditional teaching by means of the establishment of six orders of mishnah, an ordering of the Mishnah that is in our hands also began.[60]

---

[57] *The First Mishnah*, p. 13.
[58] *Ibid.*, p. 14.
[59] *Ibid.*, p. 15.
[60] *Ibid.*

Hoffmann alleges,

> in truth it is possible to prove from many places that are in the Mishnah that is before us, that they were ordered (ŠNSDRW) in their [present] formulation in the time of the Temple and in the days of the greatness (GDWLTN) of Hillel and Shammai's schools (ŠL BTY HMDRŠWT 'ŠR LHLL WŠM'Y).[61]

Here Hoffmann deals with internal evidence. In one instance he cites a passage that mentions King Agrippa.

> [How do they take up First-fruits to Jerusalem?] The flute was played before them until they reached the Temple Mount. When they reached the Temple Mount, even Agrippa the King would take his basket on his shoulder and enter in as far as the Temple Court.
> (M. Bik. 2 : 4, trans., H. Danby, p. 97)

Hoffmann identifies "Agrippa the king" as Agrippa I (ruled 37-44) rather than his son, Agrippa II. The former "was a proper (KŠR) king and certainly (BWD'Y) he fulfilled this commandment."[62] Hoffmann does not further elaborate the differences between the father and the son. He concludes, however, that the appearance of the king's name "sufficiently proves (MWKYH LMDY) that these things [the procedure of bringing first-fruits to the Temple, M. Bik. 3 : 2-6] were ordered (NSDRW) in the time of Agrippa the King."[63] He argues that if the ordering had occurred earlier, the name of another king would have been used. He does not consider other possible interpretations of the material, for instance, a post-70 A.D. ordering of the material.

Having "established" the pre-70 ordering of material in M. Bik. 3 : 2-6, Hoffmann turns to the following opinion attributed to R. Judah in 3 : 6. Hoffmann claims that all the material in the section derives at least from the time of Agrippa. Therefore he must explain the presence of a statement by Judah, a second-century Tanna. The dispute in the Mishnah concerns whether or not waving the first-fruits offering is obligatory.

> A. While the basket was yet on his shoulder a man would recite the passage (Deut. 26 : 3ff.) from "I profess this day unto the Lord thy God," until he reached the end of the passage.
>
> B. R. Judah says: Until he reached the words, "An Aramean ready to

---

[61] *Ibid.*, pp. 15f.
[62] *Ibid.*, p. 16.
[63] *Ibid.*

perish was my father." When he reached the words, "An Aramean..." he took down the basket from his shoulder and held it by the rim. And the priest put his hand beneath it and waved it; and the man then recited the words from, "An Aramean ready to perish..." until he finished the passage.

C. Then he left the basket by the side of the Altar and bowed himself down and went his way.

(M. Bik. 3 : 6; trans. H. Danby, p. 97)

Judah, in B, adds the waving procedure, which is not mentioned in A, an anonymous lemma. Hoffmann states that it is

> very close to certain (YWTR QRWB LWD'Y) that R. Judah and the Sages are divided here only about a text of the First Mishnah ('L NWSH HMŠNH HR'ŠWNH)...[64]

But Hoffmann goes beyond alleging that Judah's statement presupposes a prior redaction of the section. He also claims that Judah's statement represents only a later version of a pre-70 opinion. Thus the entire section, including Judah's opinion, if not the attribution to him, remains intact as a first-century unit of material. Hoffmann refers to external evidence as proof. He writes that

> R. Eliezer b. Jacob, who lived in the days of the Temple, read in his mishnah (GRS BMŠNTW) a text [like that] of R. Judah, according to M. Men. 5 : 6...[65]

He adds that b. Mak. 18b also notes the correspondence between the two opinions. M. Men. 5 : 6, which Hoffmann does not quote, states,

> A. These require waving but not bringing near: the leper's log of oil and his guilt-offering.
> B. Also the first-fruits, according to the words of (KDBRY) R. Eliezer b. Jacob.
> C. And the sacrificial portions of the peace-offering of the individual and the breast and the thigh thereof...
> (M. Men. 5 : 6; trans. H. Danby, p. 498)

Eliezer's opinion, clearly enough inserted into the otherwise anonymous pericope, corresponds to Judah's opinion concerning waving the first-fruits offering, although Hoffmann's interpretation of "according to the words of R. Eliezer" as "R. Eliezer... read in his Mishnah" is misleading. Hoffmann probably presupposes knowledge of a statement in b. Yev. 49b and attributed to a third-generation Tanna, Simeon b. 'Azzai, that a "roll of genealogical records" was

---

[64] *Ibid.*
[65] *Ibid.*

found in Jerusalem and that the roll included the statement, "The MŠNH of R. Eliezer b. Jacob is small in quantity but thoroughly sifted." "MŠNH" here does not necessarily mean anything more than "teaching." Also, although Eliezer was an early Tanna, there is no agreement that he "lived in the days of the Temple."

Hoffmann further alleges that since the dispute derives from the interpretation of a Scriptural verse, "The priest shall take the basket from your hand and set it down in front of the altar..." (Deut. 26:4), therefore "this difficult matter certainly was not hidden from the *midrashim* of the elders (BWD'Y ŠL' N'LM MMDRŠY HZQNYM)."[66] Why was the opinion finally attributed to a later Tanna, rather than to an earlier disputant?

> We meet here the sight (HMR'H) that we find many times in the Oral Torah, that the later Tannaim are disputing again in the disputes of the first [sages], that [the later Tannaim] in the sources are as though standing in the last row.[67]

This final statement itself requires further explanation.[68]

In his use of internal evidence, Hoffmann also treats the Mishnah-Tosefta corpus as a uniform body of materials that allows an argument like the following: Tos. (Yom) Kippurim 2:3 mentions a tablet of gold, the gift of Queen Helena of Adiabene, that was used as part of the Soṭah procedure; M. Soṭah chapters 2 and 3 describe the Soṭah procedures in the Temple but do not mention the golden tablet; therefore the M. Soṭah section was compiled prior to Queen Helena's gift, c. 45 A.D.[69] Similarly, Hoffmann cites the example, already cited by Sherira, found in M. Sanh. 5:2: "Ben Zakkai once tested the evidence even to the inquiring about the stalks of figs." Why didn't the Mishnah read, *Rabban Yoḥanan* ben Zakkai? Because (literally following a *baraita* in b. Sanh. 41a) the incident occurred before Yoḥanan received ordination and the section was redacted soon after the incident.[70]

By multiplying such examples Hoffmann tries to demonstrate the antiquity of the material. But whether or not he is correct with regard to any or all of the specific examples, he does not demonstrate that

---

[66] *Ibid.*
[67] *Ibid.*, p. 17.
[68] Hoffmann devotes a chapter to this problem: "The First Mishnah and the Disputes of the Later Tannaim," *Ibid.*, pp. 41-49.
[69] *Ibid.*, pp. 26f., n. 23.
[70] *Ibid.*, p. 25.

in Second Temple times any discrete unit of material was compiled. He shows no editorial patterns of relationship among the examples he cites. Nor does he demonstrate that any particular pre-70 pericope, or any larger body of pre-70 *mishnaic* material, was compiled with some clear relationship to, or some dependence upon, another pericope or another body of material. Yet Hoffmann's theory specifically is that a substantial amount of *mishnaic* material was compiled and underwent a sustained editorial process in the hands of the disciples of Hillel and Shammai.

The most significant part of Hoffmann's theory relies upon a logical argument rather than upon historical evidence. This is clear in his chapter entitled, "A Critical Investigation of ... M. Avot." Using internal evidence, Hoffmann discovers in M. Avot, in its present form, no less than three reworkings of prior material. He attributes the first reworking and addition of material to the time, and probably the hand, of ʿAqiba. He then concludes that, since ʿAqiba "added" materials to M. Avot, a prior compilation, "an early Mishnah" (MŠNH QDWMH), must have existed. The prior compilation is attributed to the disciples of Hillel and Shammai. Hoffmann tries to buttress the argument by identifying the "additions" of later Tannaim to the "Fathers of R. ʿAqiba"; they appear in the "Fathers of R. Meir" and in the "Fathers of R. Judah the Patriarch."[71] Hoffmann states that Rabbi felt permitted to make extensive additions to the text of M. Avot that reached him, because he "knew" that he would be following the example of ʿAqiba.[72]

On what basis does Hoffmann allege that ʿAqiba added material to a prior, original compilation of M. Avot? Hoffmann argues that internal evidence reflects different editorial hands in M. Avot. He specifies "overt problems" in the text itself that "prove to us that many changes have been worked on the *mishnayot* of M. Avot."[73] He lists the problems in five sections, each a "category for investigation" (ŠBṬ HBQRṬ):

> (1) In the first chapter there is a large [chronological] gap (ḤSRWN) between Hillel and Shammai and Rabban Gamaliel who was appointed after them. Missing (ḤSRYM) here are three generations: Simeon b. Hillel, Rabban Gamaliel the Elder, and Rabban Simeon b. Gamaliel the Elder.

[71] Ibid., pp. 33 et passim.
[72] Ibid., p. 48.
[73] Ibid., p. 30.

(2) The son of Rabban Gamaliel the Elder is called in Mishnah 17 only "Simeon his son," without the title, "Rabbi," ... although immediately afterwards in Mishnah 18 he is cited as Rabban Simeon b. Gamaliel. — If we should follow ('M NBW' LWMR) the opinion of many commentators ... that in *mishnayot* 16-17 R. Gamaliel the Elder and his son Simeon are mentioned, then still more difficult is the absence (HSRWN) of the title "Rabbi" Simeon the son of Rabbi Gamaliel, and the difficulty increases; for by this means two gaps (HSRWNWT) result: first between Hillel and Rabbi Gamaliel the First (HR'SWN), and afterwards there will be a gap (HSR) between Simeon the First and [Simeon] the Second, [namely, the latter's father] Gamaliel the Second, ... grandfather of the editor (M'RYK) of the Mishnah.

(3) After the family of the Patriarchs has been listed through Rabban Gamaliel III, son of the editor of the Mishnah, Hillel is brought again ....

(4) From chapter three and following, all chronological order is lacking, and it is impossible to distinguish any substantive order.

(5) The fifth chapter has no connection or continuity with what precedes it. Generally it is impossible to understand for what reason this chapter was inserted in tractate Avot, since in the majority of its sayings the Tanna who said it is not mentioned.[74]

These "categories for investigation" actually relate to problems of chronology and of literary form. The chronological "problems," as specified in 1 and 2, are questionable. Hoffmann himself identifies the master-disciple chain-of-tradition in M. Avot Chapters 1 and 2. The list begins with Moses, continues through Hillel and Shammai (1 : 12-15), and finally ends with Yoḥanan and his five disciples (2 : 8ff.). Of each disciple it is said that he "received from" his master. Thus "authority" passed from master to disciple until the early decades of the second century A.D. Hoffmann also notes that the sayings attributed to Rabban Gamaliel and to his son Simeon (1 : 16-18), as well as the sayings attributed to Rabbi and to his son Gamaliel (2 : 1-4), represent later additions that, in the present form of M. Avot, interrupt the master-disciple chain-of-tradition list. But no chronological "gap" exists in the list, despite the interruption. M. Avot 2 : 8 states, "Rabban Yoḥanan b. Zakkai received from Hillel and from Shammai." Where then is Hoffmann's chronological "gap"? Hoffmann locates the "gap" in the interpolated material attributed to the Patriarchal family. Rabbinic tradition (b. Shab. 15a) subscribes to the following line of Patriarchal succession: Hillel, Simeon [b. Hillel], Gamaliel I, Simeon b. Gamaliel I, Gamaliel II, Simeon b. Gamaliel II,

[74] *Ibid.*, pp. 29f.

Rabbi, and Gamaliel III. M. Avot 1 : 16-2 : 7 mentions only four of these men after Hillel: Gamaliel (1 : 16), Simeon b. Gamaliel (1 : 17-18), Rabbi (2 : 1), and Gamaliel III (2 : 2-4). This chronological "gap" is significant for Hoffmann, because rabbinic tradition accepts the Patriarchal claim, by reason of descent from Hillel, to the authority previously transmitted from master to disciple. Hoffmann therefore investigates whether "Rabban Gamaliel" (1 : 16) is Gamaliel I or Gamaliel II, asks whether "Simeon his son" (1 : 17) is the same person as "Rabban Simeon b. Gamaliel" (1 : 18), and finally states that whatever answers are given, "gaps" will remain. These "gaps," of course, disappear if M. Avot is read without presupposing the traditional "Hillelite" line of Patriarchal succession. Hoffmann notes that M. Avot 1 : 16-2 : 7 represents a pro-patriarchal interpolation into the master-disciple chain-of-tradition, but he does not elaborate upon questions, such as, Why is the formula "X received from Y" not used in the attributions to Gamaliel and his descendents? What relation does Gamaliel have with Hillel in the M. Avot material? Hoffmann does not deal with these problems, although they are as blatant in the text as the absence of the conventional designations, "the Elder" for "Rabban Gamaliel" and "Rabban" for "Simeon his son."

But what specific role did ʿAqiba play in the successive revisions of M. Avot? Hoffmann lists three sections of material that comprised ʿAqiba's collection.

(1) The Fathers until Hillel and Shammai (1 : 1-15).
(2) R. Yohanan b. Zakkai and his disciples (2 : 8-14).
(3) Sayings connected by the numbers ten, seven, and possibly four (5 : 1-5, 7-10).[75]

Hoffmann alleges that "these three sections of the ancient edition (HMʿRKT HʿTYQH)" are a unit; he finds verification in that only these three sections appear, in the same forms as in Avot, in *The Fathers according to R. Nathan*, which Hoffmann considers a Tosefta to M. Avot. "They are the core to which later editors added different additions."[76] Hoffmann argues that these sections must have been arranged by third-generation Tannaim, because second-generation Tannaim, including R. Eliezer and R. Joshua, are the last "fathers of the tradition (ʾBWT HQBLH)" listed. This would place it "in the time of R. ʿAqiba and it is probable (WQRWB HDBR) that R. ʿAqiba

[75] *Ibid.*, p. 31.
[76] *Ibid.*

himself edited it ('WRKH')."⁷⁷ Adding the first two generations of Tannaim to the "fathers of the tradition" listed in M. Avot 1 : 1-15 brings the number of generations since Ezra to ten.⁷⁸ Hoffmann alleges that ʿAqiba, hopeful that the faithful taskmaster, "who shall pay thee the reward of thy labor" (1 : 14), soon would reverse his people's recent misfortunes, added several statements grouped around the number ten and its significance in events of God's saving power, e.g. the world created with ten words (5 : 1), ten wonders and plagues in Egypt (5 : 4), and ten wonders regarding the Temple (5 : 5). To what were these statements added? To the original list of the eight generations of "fathers of the tradition" (1 : 1-15), to which also were added the first two generations of Tannaim. Hoffmann states that after being martyred, ʿAqiba "was joined to the number of the generations." His eschatological hopes were not fulfilled, but his "ten"-sayings "remained joined with the ten generations of the fathers of the tradition."⁷⁹

Hoffmann thus theorizes beyond his supporting evidence. In M. Avot he has identified only one section of the alleged "early *mishnah*" (MŠNH QDWMH), or the "ancient edition."⁸⁰ He argues that substantial editorial work was done on M. Avot during and after ʿAqiba's time, but whether or not he correctly describes the nature of that work has no bearing on his theory of the early ordering of the Mishnah. He would have to present a great deal more evidence regarding pre-ʿAqiban *mishnah*-collections than merely the list that appears in M. Avot 1 : 1-15. As indicated above, he does not do this. He relies upon an analogy with the work of Rabbi: just as Rabbi "ordered" something new from "prior sources," so too ʿAqiba "ordered" his new creation from "prior sources." In the two cases the "prior sources" were similarly ordered before the new editor reworked and added to them. This form of logical argument works only from within the framework of traditional notions about the continuity of the rabbinic-*halakhic* community.

It thus appears that Hoffmann not only fails to prove his theory; he also misuses the techniques of critical scholarship. He theorizes independently of his evidence, which he unsuccessfully tries to shape to fit the needs of his hypothesis. Yet he seems to be unaware of this

---

⁷⁷ *Ibid.*
⁷⁸ The generations are listed, *Ibid.*, p. 32.
⁷⁹ *Ibid.*
⁸⁰ *Ibid.*, p. 31.

deficiency in method. Having rejected critical scholarship in biblical studies, Hoffmann finds that he must embrace it in the study of the Mishnah because it yields accurate historical knowledge. In *The First Mishnah*, however, Hoffmann, with his traditional, rabbinic viewpoint, fails to demonstrate mastery of critical, historical techniques.

CHAPTER NINE

Y. I. HALEVY

BARUCH MICAH BOKSER

i

Y. I. Halevy was born in Iwenec, near Vilna, Russia in 1847. He studied at the *yeshivot* in Vilna, and then in Volozhin. His life is characterized by communal activities for orthodoxy, polemics against reform and liberal Jewish scholars, business failures and debts, the lack of funds for publishing his works, and continuous travels. He died in Hamburg, 1914. He called his major work *Dorot HaRishonim* [*The Former Generations*]. This multi-volume work appeared in different years and not in a chronological order. He himself only saw three volumes to the press: Volume III, *Saboraic and Geonic Period* (Pressburg, 1897); Volume IIa, *Amoraic Period* (Frankfurt A.M., 1901); and Volume Ic, *Hasmonean-Herodian Era* (Frankfurt A.M., 1906). The posthumously published volumes include: Volume Ie, *Tannaitic Period* (Frankfurt M., 1918); Volume I, *Biblical Era* (Jerusalem, 1939); and Volume Id, *End of the Second Commonwealth* (Bené Braq, 1964). The first four volumes were published in Berlin and Vienna, in 1922-23, and in Jerusalem, in 1967.[81] This paper deals with Halevy's remarks concerning the Mishnah and his contribution to its literary and historical understanding. The relevant material is scattered through Volumes Ic, Id, Ie, and IIa. I shall present his thesis and approach, outline his method and proofs, discuss his main points, and offer an assessment.

ii

Dorot HaRishonim gives the reader the impression of a thorough and learned treatment of the Talmudic data concerning the rabbinic period. Halevy bases his work on the claim that the period's history

---

[81] For biographical and bibliographical information concerning Halevy, see David Goodblatt, "Y. I. Halevy," in *The Formation of the Babylonian Talmud*, ed. Jacob Neusner (Leiden, 1970), pp. 26-28.

must emerge primarily from the Tannaitic and Amoraic legal sources and secondarily from the *aggadic-midrashic* material. This conception constitutes his major criticism of earlier works, especially those of Frankel, Graetz, Krochmal, Rapoport, and I. H. Weiss. Halevy feels they base their treatments on external, post-Talmudic data, and employ the rabbinic material only as proof texts:

> Indeed it is strange that for the Tannaitic and Amoraic period one sees long researches structured around the chronology in the Letter of R. Sherira Gaon [*'Iggeret Rav Sherira Gaon*], using it to provide the foundation, at a time when the two Talmuds, the Babylonian and Palestinian, are open before us. Therefore, for every research one must return to this great source and only after fully clarifying material from it can we pay attention to correct R. Sherira Gaon's account and to explain it therefrom [from the Talmuds], once the road is already open before us.[82]

In addition, Halevy uses non-rabbinic sources, Josephus, Maccabees, Tacitus, Eusebius, and Dio Cassius to fill in the narrative provided by the rabbinic material. He evaluates the former in the light of the latter.

While Halevy's work is primarily historical, it provides considerable information concerning the Mishnah. Indeed, Halevy considers the Mishnah not as a strictly literary document but as a historical one; it provides the source for the rabbinic and oral law which was continually clarified by each successive assembly of scholars (W'D; MTYBTH). Halevy considers the *halakhah* tantamount to "tradition" (QBLH) and uniquely equates that *halakhic* tradition with the Mishnah itself.[83] The Mishnah's core, the *Yesod HaMishnah* (YSWD HMŠNH), was uniformly transmitted; each generation added its clarifications, formulations of explanations, and new applications based on the *Yesod*'s original principles.[84] No rabbi individually differed with the accepted law, nor did anyone, on his own, offer a new law or interpretation.

Halevy traces the *halakhic* and therefore Mishnaic development through three stages, ending in its conclusion, or sealing, (HTYMH) by Rabbi and the scholars in his academy. Other writers had already

---

[82] IIa, pp. 1-2.

[83] Most traditional, medieval through modern, authorities have not made this equation. See Yehiel Jacob Weinberg, "R. Y. I. Halevy's Method and Approach in the Study of the Mishnah," [in Hebrew], in *Memorial Volume for Rabbi Yishaq Isaac Halevy*, ed. Moshe Auerbach (Bné Braq, 1964), p. 123.

[84] Goldberg seems to have the same viewpoint.

pointed out that Rabbi's Mishnah was not the first Mishnah-corpus. Halevy, however, claims that neither ʿAqiba nor Hillel originated the first collection. House of Shammai and Hillel-disputes presuppose an earlier collection which circulated at the time of the Men of the Great Assembly. One cannot consider this corpus distinct from that of *the Mishnah*; it represents the early form of the Mishnah. The material which it records consists of laws based on the written and oral Torah: biblical-based laws, other laws contemporary with the Sinaitic Revelation of the Torah, and later authoritative and collective enactments made from the time of the prophets through the days of the scribes (*Soferim*).

The Men of the Great Assembly received these laws, fixed their language and form, and thereby produced the *Yesod HaMishnah*. The laws were short and to the point, neither abstract nor based on Biblical proof texts. Significantly, Halevy disputes many scholars by claiming that *halakhah* preceded *Midrash* and that the Rabbis later found scriptural support, which they attached to the already established legal traditions.[85]

The Men of the Great Assembly did not, however, work over the explanations; each rabbi was to teach the explanations, uniform in content, according to his own way, and therefore, in a varied language and style. As long as the rabbis had their assembled bodies to clarify and vote on the correct interpretations and new applications of the *Yesod HaMishnah*, permanent differences and disputes were prevented. Internal and external causes, however, shattered the peaceful situation in what Halevy calls the "Intermediate Period." When Jewish Hellenizers, led by the Tobiad Joseph, gained control of the priesthood, troubles came upon the rabbis. From then until Hillel's time the rabbis had peace and quiet for only two short periods—the seven years of Simeon Maccabee and Jonathan, until he supported the Sadducees, and under Queen Salomé. At other times they could not peacefully assemble together; they faced harassment, persecutions, forced emigration.

Since Halevy pictures the Mishnah as a record of rabbinic group activity, he naturally posits that the *Yesod HaMishnah*, the early Mishnah formation, could not have come from the "Intermediate Period," but must predate it. The rabbinic activity thus experienced a decline in the "Intermediate Period." Especially during the later

---

[85] Ic, pp. 607-09.

Hasmonean and Herodian period, the harassment and attendant movement resulted in unsure traditions of the *Yesod HaMishnah's* original explanations; the differences and varied formulations lacked a control and soon yielded explanations different in content. The need thus arose to reconstruct the original explanations. When peaceful and quiet conditions came, the rabbis realized the gravity of the situation, and with the arrival of Hillel, who acted as an "angel of God," they possessed the means to correct it.[86] He established an academy, called the House of Hillel; along with the previously existing academy of Shammai, the House of Shammai, it investigated and purified the several Mishnaic interpretations, attempting to establish the correct one. Halevy calls this activity "clarification" (BYRWR). It consisted of explaining, clarifying, and defining (LGDR; LHGDYR) along with applying the principles of the *Yesod HaMishnah* to new cases. They had their remarks added onto the Mishnah-text itself. No one offered individually creative material and thus the *halakhah*-tradition reigned supreme.

The clarification (*bērur*) itself went through various stages; what Hillel and Shammai and their associates did not finish clarifying, their successors did. The events preceding and attending the Temple's destruction, the Bar Kokhba war, and the Hadrianic persecutions created discontinuity. Successive generations had to reconstruct what their immediate predecessors had said. In addition, where a generation did not agree on an explanation, clarification, or new application, subsequent generations, by vote of their collective bodies, adjudicated between the now limited alternative explanations; they added the adjudications to the Mishnah. The rabbis taught the Mishnah according to its agreed-upon text and explanation; where, however, an adjudication (HKR'H) had not yet occurred, each one taught it according to his respective approach (ŠYṬH).[87] The generation preceding Rabbi, the academy and assembly of scholars under R. Nathan the Babylonian, finished this process, and they provided Rabbi and his fellow rabbis with a finished "document" ready for its sealing (ḤTYMH). Rabbi along with his fellow rabbis provided the conclusion, which consisted of the few necessary explanatory glosses and of adjudication of Yavnean materials. Halevy thus claims that *the Mishnah underwent arrangement during the whole Tannaitic period.*

---

[86] Ic, p. 547.

[87] Thus Halevy, as in his analysis of the *Gemara*, avoids the concept of editing; see, Goodblatt, *op. cit.*, p. 29, and esp. p. 29, fn. 1.

This conception guides his account and provides the structure for his particular theory of the uniform halakhic-Mishnaic development.

iii

Halevy attacks other Jewish scholars for adopting Christian, unsympathetic, scholarly views, like those of E. Schürer, and for projecting their negative views of Jewish law, Temple service, sacrifices, and ritual onto the rabbinic narrative. Their "modernization" distorts the true reality and denies the positive qualities of the life and spirit of the people. On the other hand, Halevy himself projects his conservative conception onto his account.[88] This is not to say that he distorts his evidence to fit a theory; it does, however, give him a preconception according to which he interprets the material.

Halevy's assumption often constitutes the nexus between the analysis and the desired proof; where one disagrees with his assumption or feels he has failed to prove his point convincingly, his analysis often remains stimulating and insightful. Precisely because Halevy had traditional conceptions, he felt free to interpret individual texts autonomously from the later rabbinic tradition. He used Tosefta materials to clarify the Mishnah, Palestinian Talmud to explain the Babylonian. He cites medieval authorities for their readings of Talmudic texts and for their sensitivity to literary and historical problems, but does not blindly follow their explanations. He is quite solicitous of them. He writes, for example,

> And Rabbi Tosfot Yom Tov (Heller), of blessed memory, seemingly sensed this [inconsistency between the beginning and the end of a particular Mishnah], but with the lack of the 'great knowledge,' [an ignorance] which remains until today, that the Mishnah consists of two independent parts—the *Yesod HaMishnah* and the conclusion of the Mishnah in the time of Yavneh and of Rabbi respectively, behold even though he sensed the inner contradiction of the Mishnah, he wanted to account for it in an unreasonable manner, which lacks total possibility.[89]

Halevy does not blame the medieval authorities for failing to realize the literary-historical nature of the Mishnah:

> And we have already commented innumerable times that all this was not part of the work of our early [medieval] rabbis, and they discussed this

---

[88] Ic, pp. 146, 148, 155, 607, and esp. 323; Ie, pp. 144, 213, 262, and esp. 106-07.
[89] Ic, pp. 252, see 261, 262; Ie, pp. 470-71; IIa, p. 81.

only incidentally, being involved in the principles of the *halakhot* and they lacked the time for these types of things, and accordingly the matters remained closed and sealed."

Halevy's conviction thus clearly emerges, that *canons of literary and historical interpretation of the rabbinic literature differ from those of the halakhic-legal interpretation.* Many of his particular insights presage the kind of critical analysis of modern scholars. His importance lies in having pointed out many of the critical phenomena and issues overlooked or over-simplified by others. In the effort, he assembled a large number of sources. He failed, however, systematically to arrange the material, and consistently to treat it critically. For example, at times the Tosefta parallel provides the basis for an interpretation, at others where it contradicts his, he fails to cite it. Alternatively, where a Tannaitic or Amoraic reading supports his theory or interpretation, he does not go out of his way to record the readings in the medieval quotations. In addition, he suprisingly fails to seek manuscript, variant readings of the Mishnah and of the Talmud; Rabbinovicz's *Variae Lectiones* had already appeared.

iv

Halevy argues that a Mishnah existed before that of Rabbi. Rabbinic remarks external to the Mishnah provide a *prima facie* case. As mentioned in Sherira Gaon's letter, the story of Meir's and Nathan's attempt to discredit Simeon b. Gamaliel by asking him questions concerning a tractate 'Uqṣin presupposes an extant Mishnah already divided into tractates."[91] The Amoraic statement that Rabbi produced the Mishnah "all on the basis of R. 'Aqiba" means that Rabbi taught the *Yesod HaMishnah* on the "basis of the reading (GRSH) of R. 'Aqiba's approach.'"[92] Especially insightful is his analysis of the six citations of Joseph's statement explaining a seemingly inconsistent Mishnah. The dictum reads: "It is [authored by] Rabbi, and he took it [arranged it] on the basis of the Tannaim."[93] The Talmud contrasts Joseph's statement with Ḥisda's explanation, that the former part of the text represents the "rabbis" and the second half, Meir. Both explanations assign different authors to the two clauses. They differ,

---

[90] Ie, p. 221. See Ie, pp. 101, 471, 523, 882.
[91] IIa, p. 81; b. Hor. 13b.
[92] IIa, p. 82.
[93] IIa, p. 86.

though, in the implications of who joined the two Tannaitic views, and when this was done. Joseph says Rabbi put one view in the first clause, and a second one in the last clause. Ḥisda claims that the reciters prior to Rabbi had already placed one Tannaitic view in the first clause and the latter in the second; this inconsistent text thus actually derives from an early arrangement.[94] Halevy also refers to the several sources which report that Rabbi had doubts concerning a Mishnah-reading, or he inquired to learn a Mishnah's reasoning.[95] One may have, however, one reservation concerning all these arguments and citations. Halevy assumes that the Mishnah text to which the sources refer is the same as today's extant corpus. This he nowhere proves.

Halevy finds his second proof for the existence of a Mishnah before Rabbi in comments which presuppose extant collections. Thus Yosi ends M. Kel. with the remark: "Blessed art thou, O Kelim, for thou didst enter in in uncleanness, but art gone forth in cleanness" [M. Kel. 30 : 4, trans. Danby, p. 649]. Yosi here refers to some type of completed collection.

Furthermore, Halevy devotes considerable efforts to lay out the strata of the Mishnah. He argues not only that an early Mishnah existed, but that it predated ʿAqiba as well as Hillel and Shammai.[96] The Houses of Shammai and Hillel, the first Tannaitic generation, have the first Tannaitic disputes in the Mishnah. This, however, does not mean that they founded [YSDW] the Mishnah, but rather, that they argued concerning explanations, clarifications, and new applications of a pre-existent corpus—*the* Mishnah.[97] Halevy refers to many texts, for example:

> A. [If] a corpse [lay] in a room to which were many entrances, they are all unclean; if one entrance was opened it [alone] is unclean and the rest are clean.
> B. [If there was] intention to take out [the corpse] through one of them, or through a window which measures four handbreadths square, this affords protection to all other entrances.
> The House of Shammai say: "The intention must have been formed before the corpse was added."
> The House of Hillel say: "[It suffices] even after it was dead."
> C. If an entrance had been blocked up and it was determined to open it—

---

[91] Ic, pp. 86-87.
[92] Ic, pp. 82-3, 86-91, 97, 99.
[96] IIa, p. 92, 93.
[97] Ic, p. 206. According to Halevy, Shammai and Hillel are included in the terms House of Shammai and House of Hillel, respectively.

> The House of Shammai say: "[It affords protection to all other entrances only] after it had been opened as much as four handbreadths square."
> The House of Hillel say: "So soon as they begin [to open it]."
> D. But they agree that if an opening was here made for a first time, the opening must be as much as four handbreadths [before it can afford protection].
>
> (M. Oh. 7 : 3, trans. Danby, p. 659)

In this text (A) presents an early law; (B), an extension of (A), also presents a law that predates the Houses. Then the Houses dispute the applicability of the principle of intention, (B); (C) and (D) are further extensions.[98]

Halevy claims that the first strata, the 'early traditions,' now distributed throughout the Mishnah, originally were put together in a unified form, as the *Yesod HaMishnah*, and the Houses' glosses were later distributed throughout the texts. Halevy however does not prove this claim.[99] While one cannot deny that the Houses' disputes gloss earlier traditions, one cannot readily assent to Halevy's conclusion. He does not consider when the document, the Mishnah, received its literary formulation and redaction. For example, the House dispute-form individually may only date to Yavneh. And even if they go back twenty years earlier, ca. 50 C.E., they still fail to prove that the presupposed laws existed *as a corpus* and in their present form and not as thematic traditions.[100] Even if one agrees that the discursive arrangement of the laws implies the existence of a collection, it tells us nothing concerning its origin. Thus from Halevy's point of view, he fails to prove that the Mishnah's early stratum, *the Yesod HaMishnah*, goes back to the time of the Men of the Great Assembly. His whole argument relies on the assumption that the corpus could not have arisen in the "Intermediate Period" and therefore must predate it. This assumption, in turn, depends on his conception of the Mishnah as a record of the decisions of the assembled rabbis and on his picture of the troubled "Intermediate Period."[101]

Other proofs are just as unsatisfactory. These include:

(1) The Mishnah's language is close to that of Ben Sira; the arranged and fixed character of the Mishnah insured the preservation of its

---

[98] Ic, pp. 206-211, 213. See Neusner, *Pharisees*, II, pp. 296.

[99] Ic, p. 206. See also Ic, p. 216. Compare Neusner, *Pharisees*, II, p. 67.

[100] *Ibid.*, p. 3; volume III, pp. 13-14, 89-93, 99-100.

[101] Ic, pp. 146-202, esp. 199-201. Compare Hugo Mantel, *Studies in the History of the Sanhedrin* (Cambridge, 1965), pp. 51-53.

language. This is true, however, only of some portions of the Geniza manuscripts of Ben Sira. Scholars have offered various explanations for these texts with Mishnaic usages, including that they represent a later recension or a retroversion from Syriac. In light of the same passages without the Mishnaic usages, however, they argue that those with the Mishnaic usages are not the original text. In general Ben Sira's language copies the Biblical Wisdom Literature; its grammar is similar to that of the late Biblical books.[102] Even if one would conclude that the original text contained Mishnaic usages, that would not prove anything concerning the Mishnah. The Mishnah's language fits into its place among the other now extant literature of the first to the third centuries.

(2) The *Yesod HaMishnah*'s form, short and without biblical proof texts, reflects its nature in solely recording "traditions." This proposition, however, is based on an assumption concerning the nature of "tradition" (QBLH), and cannot provide any independent evidence.

(3) The *Yesod HaMishnah* refers to the general basic enactments (TQNWT) which predate the Men of the Great Assembly; the later few enactments concern minor matters. Halevy lists among the "general enactments" many Sabbath laws, including the institution of the *'Eruv* for extending the city's domain 200 cubits for walking, and for connecting adjoining courtyards. If anything, however, these laws argue against dating the *Yesod HaMishnah* to the times of the Men of the Great Assembly. The Book of Jubilees (second century, B.C.E.) includes laws indicating that several of these enactments did not then exist, or, if they existed, were not universally adopted. Jubilees bans carrying on the Sabbath from one house to another, or to a courtyard and traveling a distance. The *'Eruv* for extending a city's limits and connecting adjoining courtyards was not applicable. Accordingly one understands Jubilee's ban on drawing water from a courtyard.[103]

Even if one would agree with Halevy in attributing historical accuracy to Talmudic aggadic dating of laws and events, his argument concerning the *'Eruv* would be faulty. The basis for an early dating,

---

[102] See M.S. Segal, *Sefer Ben Sira Hashalem* (Jerusalem, 1958), pp. 18-22, 62-63, and Alexander A. DiLella, *The Hebrew Text of Sirach* (Hague, 1966), esp. pp. 78-81, 106-150 and the literature cited there.

[103] Jubilees 50:8, 12. See *ITL*, pp. 278-80; H. Albeck, *Mishnah Seder Mo'ed* (Jerusalem-Tel Aviv, 1954), introduction to M. 'Eruv., p. 77. Ic, pp. 204f, 220, 223-24.

besides its presence in the early stratum of the Mishnah, consists of the Talmudic statement that Solomon established the law of *'Eruv* for joining domains. It has been pointed out, however, that one only finds this statement in the BT, in the mouth of Samuel, and not in Palestinian sources. On the contrary, the latter contain the statement of Joshua b. Levi that the *'Eruv* to join domains was enacted for 'ways of peace' (DRKY ŠLWM).[104] Accordingly, one cannot find an uncontestable "tradition" for an early date, and Halevy's own argument remains defective. Halevy shows that Houses' disputes concerning *'Eruv* and other matters present a gloss on early laws. He fails to prove that they represent a corpus dating back to the Men of the Great Assembly. In addition, our criticism concerning this issue reflects the two sides of Halevy's scholarship His weakness lies in his speculation and historical conclusion; his strength lies in his analysis of literary texts.

The role of the Tannaim consisted of explaining (LPRŠ), defining and clarifying (LGDR) the *Yesod HaMishnah*, and applying it to new cases. Halevy offers a developed theory about how Hillel began this process. He came at the propitious moment to help arrange the *Yesod HaMishnah* with its explanations. The Bené Bathyra recognized his greatness, and he established an academy. Shammai maintained his academy lest suspicions arise concerning plots by the rabbis to unify their authority. The Houses of Hillel and Shammai thus contained the scholars of the day and Hillel and Shammai respectively.[105]

Halevy then cites and interprets innumerable pericopae to show that the Houses explain biblically based laws and rabbinic enactments like the *'Eruv*. Most disputes concern remote details of the laws; the above case of uncleanness affords a good example. The Yavneans *explained* the House disputes.[106] Of the many cited examples, the following indicate how he makes use of Tosefta materials:

> [If] a sheaf [lay] near the wall or the stack or the oxen or the implements, and he forgot it—
> The House of Shammai say, "[It is] not [considered a] Forgotten Sheaf."
> And the House of Hillel say, "[It is considered a] Forgotten Sheaf."
> (M. Pe'ah 6 : 2, trans. Danby, p. 16)

[104] PT 'Eruv. 3 : 2; 20d and 7 : 9; 24c. See S. Lieberman, *Hayerushalmi Kiphshuto* (Jerusalem, 1934), pp. 262-63, 336-37; Albeck, *Mo'ed, op. cit.*, pp. 79, 438-39; *ITL*, p. 279, fn. 31.
[105] Ic, pp. 548-62; Ie, p. 190.
[106] Ic, p. 220, concerning M. 'Eruv. 6 : 3, 4. Compare Neusner, *Pharisees*, II, pp. 136, 137. See, also, Ic, pp. 231, 603-05.

> R. 'Ila'i' said, "I asked R. Joshua, 'Concerning what sheaves did the House of Shammai dispute?'
>
> "He said to me, 'By this Torah! Concerning what sheaves? Those near a wall, a stack, oxen, or implements, and he forgot it.'
>
> "And when I came and asked R. Leazar, he said to me, 'They agree concerning these that *Forgetting* does *not* apply.
>
> "Concerning what did they dispute? Concerning the sheaf on which he took hold to bring to town, and he set it by the fence and forgot it.
>
> "'For the House of Shammai say, '*Forgetting* does not apply, because he has made acquisition of it.' And the House of Hillel say, '*Forgetting.*'"
>
> "And when I came and I laid the matters out before R. Leazar b. 'Azariah, he said to me, 'By the Torah. These things were said from Sinai.'"
>
> (Tos. Pe'ah 3 : 2, ed. Lieberman, p. 51, lines 13-19, trans. Neusner, *Pharisees*, II, p. 60)

These two texts exemplify the roles of the Houses and Yavnean masters. The Houses disagreed concerning an aspect of the law of the Forgotten Sheaf. The Yavneans investigated the reports of the House disputes to determine whether they had been correctly transmitted.[107] In elucidating individual pericopae, Halevy demonstrates the importance of isolating the activities of the different generations. The above text raises questions concerning one of Halevy's own arguments. For Tos. gives the impression that the Houses' disputes circulated separately from the Mishnah; accordingly Joshua, Leazar, and Leazar b. 'Azariah, while agreeing on the text of the dispute, disagree on its referent.

The Yavnean generation included survivors from the pre-Destruction days. Some perpetuated and represented the views of the Houses. Others provided important testimony concerning Temple procedures. Halevy dates to the immediate post-70 time several tractates and chapters describing Temple rituals, and practices. The Men of the Great Assembly had not included in the *Yesod HaMishnah* daily and well-known activities. After the Destruction, the rabbis quickly realized the need to preserve the Temple procedures; survivors, therefore, provided a descriptive narrative.

Using his "historical" approach, Halevy tries to place the Mishnah strata and activities into the sequence of events. The Yavneans spent three years clarifying the disputes and making adjudications between them. When the leading rabbis traveled to Rome, the assembly

---

[107] Ic, pp. 563-69. See Neusner, *Pharisees*, II, pp. 57, 61-3. esp. 62.

disbanded (80-81 C.E.); the Eliezer ben Hyrcanus affair spanned 82-83, C.E.; and then the assembled rabbis ended and sealed their adjudications and clarifications at the several-day *on that day* [BW BYWM] session, 84 C.E. They arranged in M. 'Ed. all the remaining Houses' materials, now recorded for completion and clarification. Halevy centers his reconstruction on the import of the section of the leniencies of the House of Shammai and the stringencies of the House of Hillel, M. 'Ed. 4ff. The section presupposes a larger corpus of the 'normal situation,' wherein House of Shammai take the stringent position and the House of Hillel the lenient one. Halevy points out that M. 'Ed. itself only contains a few cases, and the rabbis, therefore, must have previously arranged the larger number; one can find these disputes in other Mishnah tractates.[108] Halevy makes some questionable assumptions. His argument assumes that we have *all* the traditions, and disregards the possibility that the Mishnah's editor used different sources. For it is possible that the editor took the collection of the leniencies of the House of Shammai and the stringencies of the House of Hillel from a source that had also contained, or knew of, stringencies of the House of Shammai and leniencies of the House of Hillel; thus the implication of M. 'Ed. 4 cannot provide the basic proof.

The confusion of 123-143 C.E. provides the backdrop for Halevy's analysis of the Ushan period. The students of 'Aqiba met, the Patriarch was appointed, and Nathan the Babylonian joined the newly assembled scholars. On the basis of his interpretation, Halevy explains the statement in B.M. 89a, "Rabbi and R. Nathan, [are the] end of the Mishnah" (RBY WR' NTN SWP MŠNH). This dictum refers to Rabbi's and Nathan's activities concerning the Mishnah; through them the Mishnah received its final arrangement and conclusion. As the sources attribute the Yavnean activity concerning the Mishnah's style to Joshua, the *Av Bet Din*, so this statement assigns it to Nathan, the *Av Bet Din*. Since the final arrangement and conclusion in the days of Nathan and Rabbi, respectively, were consecutive, the dictum joined the two Tannaim.[109]

Nathan, as *Av Bet Din*, headed Tannaim of his generation in giving the Mishnah its last arrangement. Yet he personally did not provide the source, because the generation's main role consisted of

---

[108] Ie, pp. 228-29.
[109] Ie, p. 819. See pp. 754, 761.

reconstructing and elucidating the preceeding generations' traditions and fixing their form and language. For the upheavals and the movements destroyed the continuity and created doubts concerning earlier statements and events.[110] Accordingly, Nathan, stemming from Babylonia, could not provide information concerning the Yavnean generation. Halevy cites pericopae to show that this generation involved themselves in reconstructions and did not discuss the *Yesod HaMishnah*.[111] While some examples he cites are quite cogent, others are not. Thus he quotes the following text:

> One who sleeps under a bed in the Sukkah has not fulfilled his obligation.
> R. Judah said, "It was our custom to sleep under the bed in the presence of the Elders, and they did not say anything to us."
> R. Simeon said, "(M'ŠH B) Tabi, the slave of Rabban Gamaliel, once slept under the bed, and Rabban Gamaliel said to the Elders, 'You have seen Tabi, my slave, is a learned scholar, and knows that slaves are exempt from [the law of] the Sukkah; and so he sleeps under the bed.' So, incidentally, we learn that if a man slept under a bed he has not fulfilled his duty."
> (M. Suk. 2 : 1, trans. Danby, p. 174)

In this text, Judah and Simeon dispute what the earlier rabbis had done. Using this passage, Halevy claims that even where a source does not cite the case, the Ushan disputants based their position on implications of such memories, learning the "*Yesod* from them."[112] From the practice before the Elders, Judah had learned that a Sukkah must be a permanent dwelling and not a temporary tent; therefore a temporary tent or covering of a bed does not make void the upper permanent covering. M. Suk. 2 : 2 contains this deduced conclusion without the case, the source of Judah's view. Halevy's analysis of these texts, however, reflects his selective citation of sources. He does not pay sufficient attention to Tosefta which cites a different case in connection with the law:

> A Sukkah taller than twenty cubits is unfit.
> R. Judah declares [it] fit.
> R. Judah said, "There was the case (M'ŠH B) of Helene's Sukkah that was taller than twenty cubits, and the Elders would come in and go out from there and none of them said anything [in objection]."
> They said to him, "Because she is a woman, and a woman is not obligated [to dwell] in a Sukkah."

[110] Ie, pp. 822-23, 829.
[111] Ie, pp. 823-28.
[112] Ie, p. 824.

> He said to them, "And did she not have seven sons, students of the scholars, and all dwelt in it [in the Sukkah]?"
>
> (Tos. Suk. 1 : 1, ed. Lieberman, p. 256, lines 1-5)

The issue of the height of the Sukkah is part of the dispute on the nature of the Sukkah, whether it should be a permanent or temporary structure. According to Judah and the case he cites, a Sukkah taller than twenty cubits is not disqualified, since it is a permanent structure.[113] According to Halevy's method one would have to conclude that the incident of Helene's Sukkah provided the source for Judah's view; we would then have two sources, one in Mishnah and one in Tosefta. The objective observer must conclude that the cases need not have served as the basis of the dispute but merely as proofs and precedents.

Halevy's claim that Ushans concerned themselves primarily with reconstructing earlier statements and events is integral to his position. He has to argue that *sof Mishnah* applies to Nathan as the one who presided over the assembly that made the final arrangement and yet contributed little to the discussions; the sources record few of his comments. This analysis reflects Halevy's reading of the Mishnah as a record of historical events and not as a literary document.[114] It also serves to explain the Mishnah's use of "Nathan's Mishnah" without an attribution to Nathan. According to Halevy, Nathan's Mishnah consisted of quotations of the Mishnah-traditions that he had brought with him from Babylonia. The Mishnah's use of these views of Nathan reflects his activity in the assembly and its acceptance of his opinions and interpretations: therefore, it incorporated them into the Mishnah. Accordingly, Rabbi could not remove them, even though he may have disputed their positions. We thus read:

> If a man was married to three wives, and he died and the Ketubah of one was one *mina*, of another 200 [*denars*], and of the other 300 [*denars*], ...
> If he left [only] 200 [*denars*] ....
> If he left 300 ....
>
> (M. Ket. 10 : 4, trans. Danby, p. 260)

Concerning this Mishnah, the Talmud quotes the following *beraita*:

> It was taught [TNY], This is the Mishnah of R. Nathan. Rabbi says, "I

---
[113] See *TK*, IV, pp. 835, 851-52.
[114] Ie, p. 821.

do not accept the words of R. Nathan in these [cases]. But they [the women] divide equally."

(b. Ket. 93a)

Once again, one must object to Halevy's disregard for the literary nature of the Mishnah. His underlying motivation consists of his denial that Nathan had a separate corpus which might have served to present his views. But Lieberman has pointed out that *Sifré Zutta* is a Tannaitic Midrash, originating in Lydda, which does not use Rabbi's Mishnah as a base, but another Mishnah (which itself runs counter to Halevy's theory), uses Nathan's Mishnah anonymously. Would Halevy then claim that Nathan attended the academy of Lydda, and thereby pericopae attributable to him found their way into *Sifré Zutta*? On the contrary, it seems that Nathan did have a corpus—a Babylonian corpus of Tannaitic material which the Babylonian Talmud contrasts with Rabbi's corpus. *Sof Mishnah*, "end of the Mishnah," thus means that they had the last Mishnah collections.[115]

Rabbi and his academy received the arranged Mishnah. They therefore did not have to clarify the *Yesod HaMishnah* or rework materials of previous generations. Their job consisted of "sealing the Mishnah." They made final adjudications, especially of Yavnean and later disputes, presenting individual views as anonymous *Mishnayot* or disputes of a minority versus a majority. In addition, they added short explanatory glosses where matters needed further elucidation.[116] Thus, as we have seen concerning Nathan, Rabbi and his fellow scholars found views in the Mishnah with which they disagreed, but they could not (with few exceptions) delete them from the Mishnah text. They could only tell their students that the particular Mishnah was not authoritative and that it represented a minority view.[117] They did not incorporate their disagreement into the Mishnah text. Halevy cites the following to demonstrate that Rabbi and his fellow scholars could not add a new stratum to the Mishnah but could gloss the existing Mishnah text according to their view:

> Standing corn [that has not been forgotten] saves a sheaf and [other] standing corn [from being deemed forgotten].
> A sheaf saves neither [another] sheaf nor standing corn.

---

[115] S. Lieberman, *Siphre Zutta* (New York, 1968), pp. 89-91. See *ITL*, p. 170. The Halevy passage is on Ie, p. 818.

[116] Ie, pp. 829, 866, 879. See his interesting analysis of M. Sanh. 11:4, Ie, p. 834.

[117] Ie, pp. 870-03.

> What standing corn saves the sheaf? Aught soever that has not been forgotten, even though it was but a single stalk.
>
> (M. Pe'ah 6 : 8, trans. Danby, p. 16)

He then cites the Tosefta:

> Rabban Simeon b. Gamaliel says, "As the standing corn saves a sheaf, so a sheaf saves the standing corn. And it is a matter of logic, Just as standing corn that is to the disadvantage of the house-holder [in that the poor can claim from it gleanings and corner sections, LQT and PY'H], saves a sheaf [from being deemed forgotten], a sheaf that is to the house-holder's advantage [in that the poor can have no claim from it of gleanings and corner sections] all the more so should save the standing corn."
>
> *Rabbi said* to him, "[But is it logical]? What of standing corn that saves the sheaf, which is to the holder's advantage, should it save the standing corn which is to the poor's advantage?"
>
> (Tos. Pe'ah 3 : 6, ed. Lieberman, pp. 52-3, lines 35-39)[118]

According to Halevy, Rabbi and his fellow scholars could not add to the Mishnah the dispute about whether a sheaf saves standing corn or not. In reality, Simeon b. Gamaliel and Rabbi argued about the implication of a *Yesod HaMishnah* which had stated that standing corn saves a sheaf from being deemed forgotten. This *Yesod HaMishnah* is the first part of M. Pe'ah 6 : 8. When the assembled rabbis had adjudicated in the favor of Rabbi, they interpolated his view into the Mishnah; thus our Mishnah reads, "A sheaf saves neither [another] sheaf nor standing corn."[119] But all Tosefta readings, other than the first edition, and the Palestinian Talmud parallel have "And the *rabbis* said to him," and not "And Rabbi said to him."[120] Even then, Halevy might argue that the Mishnah text had already been arranged and the rabbis could not therefore add this new dispute."[121] The principle behind Halevy's insight, that interpolations have entered the Mishnah-text, remains important; Halevy cites other cases for such glosses.

Here, however, a different approach could suggest an alternative interpretation. If the text had read "Rabbi," one could say that Rabbi, as the Mishnah's editor, had merely taught and incorporated his view anonymously. Taking the correct reading as "The Rabbis," one could offer a similar interpretation. Rabbi simply taught and incorporated

---

[118] I have adopted Lieberman's emendation, S. Lieberman, *The Tosefta* (New York, 1955), brief commentary, pp. 52f, and *TK*, I, p. 168.

[119] Ie, p. 868.

[120] *TK*, I, p. 168.

[121] On Rabbi Simeon b. Gamaliel, see, Ie, pp. 769-73, 774, 858.

the Rabbis' view. Significantly, even according to Halevy, in this text the last generations of Tannaim argued over the implication of *Yesod HaMishnah*; he had claimed that they only involved themselves in reconstructing earlier statements and events. This would then argue the Mishnah was not finally arranged in the days of Usha.

According to Halevy, where Rabbi and his assembled rabbis did not indicate their disagreement with an anonymous view already incorporated in the Mishnah before them, one must consider their inaction as an endorsement. Accordingly, later writers, the Amoraim, attributed the earlier reformulations into anonymous views to Rabbi, representing his generation.[122] Where Rabbi differs with his fellow scholars, the Mishnah states "Rabbi says .... The Sages say ...." In these situations, Halevy again relies on his conception of the Mishnah as a document recording group activities. In the last case, one may consider Halevy's interpretation plausible. Nevertheless, elsewhere in the Mishnah, assigning a view to "the Sages" often represents an adjudication by attributing a minority view to the majority. Why can it not serve the same purpose here, and not merely record a vote? Thus Rabbi would be recording in his own name his tradition on the matter, but would also incorporate an alternative view which he considers authoritative.

Having to assign some activities to Rabbi's generation, Halevy attributes to them various additions to the Mishnah text. We have already seen one supposed example in the dispute of Simeon b. Gamaliel and Rabbi/the rabbis. Halevy feels that they also added clarifying glosses. Many of the examples he cites remain problematic, and other factors may account for the presence of the particular clause in question. He quotes, for example, the following Mishnah:

> A woman may lend a sifter, sieve, hand mill or oven to her neighbor that is suspected of transgressing the Seventh Year law, but she may not winnow or grind corn with her.
> The wife of an Associate [ḤBR] may lend a sifter or sieve to the wife of an ʿAm haʾareṣ and may winnow, grind or sift corn with her.
> But when she pours water over the flour she may not draw near to her, since help may not be given to them that commit transgression.
> *All these have been enjoined in the interests of Peace* [DRKY ŠLWM].
> (M. Shev. 5 : 9, trans. Danby, p. 45)

The assembly of scholars under Rabbi added the italicized clause;

---

[122] Ie, pp. 880-81, 883-84; IIa, pp. 112-14.

they wanted to make clear the import of the Mishnah. Halevy fails to quote the rest of the Mishnah passage:

> Gentiles may be helped [when laboring in the fields; they may be given encouragement] in the Seventh Year, but not Israelites.
> Moreover, they may be offered greetings *in the interests of peace.*
> (M. Shev. 5 : 9, trans. based on Danby, p. 45)

If the clause in question was an addition, why did they not add it to the end of the whole passage, or why did they not change the end to account for all the cases? Furthermore, the last section, "Gentiles ... peace," appears in an earlier section of the tractate, M. Shev. 4 : 3. In addition both sections appear together (as in M. Shev. 5 : 9) in M. Git. 5 : 9. There it follows many other *Mishnayot* that declare various laws "in the interests of peace;" the purpose-clause is repeated after each rule. Halevy's interpretation does not fit all the locations: the cases in M. Git. 5 : 8-9 indicate that the repetition of "in the interests of peace" is not necessarily strange. Its presence in the latter half of the Mishnah, "Gentiles ... peace," would argue that it is integral to both clauses. The solution that presents itself to the source critic is clear.

Halevy disregards this type of literary analysis. The Mishnah's editor used a source containing "in the interests of peace"-laws; he incorporated that source into M. Git. In M. Shev. he incorporated the sections relevant to the laws of the Seventh Tear; in the process he included the law, "the wife of an Associate may lend a sifter..." which deals with the case of uncleanness. He had to include this last law, because the purpose clause of both laws — "A woman may lend ... grind corn with her" and "The wife of an Associate ... transgression" only comes at the end of the second law. Thus the clause that Halevy had considered a gloss by Rabbi's generation is not only integral, but without it the present sequence of laws in the Mishnah would not make sense.[123]

In Nathan's generation, each Tanna had expressed his explanation of the Mishnah in his own or in his teacher's style and language; Rabbi's generation, which provided the 'conclusion,' collected the different readings. Halevy quotes the following Mishnah along with its Tosefta to prove his point:

> A big baking oven, —
> if it has a rim, is susceptible to uncleanness.

---

[123] Ic, p. 885. Compare H. Albeck, *Mishnah Seder Zera'im* (Jerusalem-Tel Aviv, 1958), p. 154, on M. Shev. 5 : 9.

R. Judah says, "If it is roofed."
Rabban Gamaliel says, "If it has a border."
> (M. Kel. 8 : 9, trans. Danby, p. 616)

A big baking-oven, behold it is clean [unsusceptible to uncleanness], for it is only made to be used with earth.
R. Meir says in the name of Rabban Gamaliel, "If it has a rim it is susceptible to uncleanness."
R. Judah says in the name of Rabban Gamaliel, "If it is roofed."
R. Yosi says in the name of Rabban Gamaliel, "If it has a border."
And all of them are the same (WKWLN ŠM 'ḤD HN).
> (Tos. Kel. B.K. 6 : 17, ed. Zuckermandel, p. 576, lines 20-23)

Thus according to Halevy, the Tannaitic arrangement of the Mishnah meant elucidating what earlier authorities had said on the early stratum, the *Yesod HaMishnah*, and applying its principles to new cases. By Nathan's time this process was completed. Rabbi and his generation could only add the finishing touches. In the case of the big baking-oven, this meant bringing together the different ways the same tradition had been expressed; they could not, however, choose the "correct" one.[124]

V

Halevy's importance is not only "historical." He offers many important insights. His polemic against the claims that the rabbis invented everything—though dogmatically argued—has had the positive effect of inducing open-minded scholars carefully to examine the data; recent studies have shown the rabbis less as complete innovators, than as choosing, "announcing," and clarifying the correct and valid liturgical formulae, customs, and interpretations of laws that had circulated among the people. Of course, this contradicts Halevy's assertion that the *halakhah* developed uniformly.

Halevy presents, analyzes, and cites many texts and points to particular literary phenomena of the Mishnah. He succeeds in demonstrating the existence of several strata, some of which have different qualities from others. But Halevy adhered to the belief in a uniform *halakhic* development which he equated with the Mishnah itself. Accordingly, he disregards the possibility that the Mishnah is composed of different sources and that different, distinct

---

[124] Ic, p. 844.

Mishnah-collections circulated. In addition, while he presents a good balance to a purely literary conception of the Mishnah's formation — as if one person individually, by himself, composed the Mishnah — he nevertheless exaggerates the "historical" nature of the Mishnah. At times, he offers forced explanations of texts in order to provide the data for what had happened and thereby support his interpretation. He always assumes the Mishnah provides a valid historical record, a proposition only possible given his conviction that each stratum of the Mishnah contains only contemporary or immediately previous statements.

His great contribution lies in aspects of his methodology. He surpasses his predecessors. Earlier historians had offered few thorough analyses of internal evidence. They had relied on extra-Talmudic chronologies and sources, mixed with citations of various Talmudic texts. Where based on Talmudic materials, they often used incomplete data. More often they had joined discrete texts in offering a "fact." Halevy clearly demonstrates the need to interpret sources independently of medieval rabbinic authorities. He appreciates their sensitivity to literary problems and textual readings. He himself did not adequately seek to uncover variant manuscript readings, many of which were available in his day. He shows that one must realize that later Tannaitic interpretations can contaminate an earlier statement. While he would consider such interpolations correct, being taken from "tradition," we cannot share that assumption, and must examine each interpolation individually. Modern students are only now systematically starting to evaluate this material.

CHAPTER TEN

JOACHIM OPPENHEIM

JOEL GEREBOFF

i

Joachim (Ḥayyim) Oppenheim, the son of a Talmudical scholar, Rabbi Bernhard Oppenheim, was born on September 29, 1832 in Eibenschutz, Moravia. At first educated by his father, he later enrolled at the gymnasium in Brünn (1849-53) and then entered the University of Vienna, graduating in 1857. He also studied Talmud under Rabbi Lezar Horowitz. Oppenheim wrote many articles for the journals of his time, but devoted the majority of his career to his duties as Rabbi of Jamnitz (1858) and then of Eibenschutz (1860), a position formerly held by his father. Oppenheim died in Berlin on April 27, 1891.[125]

In writing his "History of the Mishnah"[126] Oppenheim notes:

> In spite of all the investigation and labor to explain the origin of the *mishnayot*, how they were written and then transmitted, who were the first to compose these collections and according to what principles, there still remain several questions to be answered. I have, therefore, decided to devote my time to this precious (YQR) endeavor of defining the different names and terms which are related to this subject and to discover the essence (MHWT) of the Mishnah and to resolve the questions of the 'Old Mishnah' (MŠNH YŠNH), the sources and origins of the Mishnah and the question of the apocryphal (external) *mishnayot* (MŠNYWT ḤYṢWNYWT), their sources and history.[127]

Oppenheim, however, did not answer these questions but rather wrote an apology for the activities of the Tannaim. For Oppenheim,

> The work of the rabbis symbolizes the freedom of learning (ḤYRWT HLYMWD) that existed in Tannaitic times. Beginning with the time of

---

[125] See *JE* Vol. 9, p. 410 and Sokolow *Sefer Zikkaron*, pp. 126-7 for biographical information.

[126] His work originally appeared in *Bet Talmud* 2, 1882, pp. 142-151, 172-179, 237-245, 269-273, 304-315, 343-355. The titles of Oppenheim's other articles appear in the bibliography.

[127] Oppenheim, "History of the Talmud," p. 143.

> Shema'iah and Abtalion, the rabbis did not engage in learning strictly for the purpose of deriving practical law (HLKH LM'SH), but rather they learned for learning's sake. The Mishnah is the eternal testimony to the freedom of learning that was imbedded in the hearts of our great sages. Moreover, how great is the merit (KMH M'LWT TWBWT) that we possess, since our sages expanded the field of inquiry. For the freedom of learning and the Mishnah which was the outcome of this endeavor have been the strength of our people in times of distress and have succeeded in preserving our people in times of persecution.[128]

Oppenheim's historical analysis attempts to justify the praise he has bestowed upon the Tannaim by showing that the activities of the Tannaim and their literary creations, particularly the Mishnah, stand for the value of "free inquiry." The Mishnah is not primarily a code of laws, but it is rather a book for instruction (SPR 'WLPNH) containing all the transactions of the *Bet Midrash*. To support his claims, Oppenheim cites Amoraic, Gaonic, and medieval sources, never questioning their veracity and historicity, which testify to the activities of the Tannaim. In using these late sources, Oppenheim manipulates the material to support his claims. If he finds that a term used in a source is not exactly the one he needs for his argument, he merely cites some other commentary's interpretation of the term, which alters the meaning to suit his purpose, and then states, "Our sages were not always careful and consistent in their use of terminology." Although Oppenheim makes several valid observations in his work, these do not necessarily follow from his evidence; his historical analysis represents no more than rabbinic homiletics. He has to come under consideration because his work is still read and was, indeed, reprinted just now in *Studies and Introductions to the Talmud*, (Jerusalem, 1971: Makor).

ii

In recounting his theories on the rise of the *halakhah*, Oppenheim notes:

> In the time of the rule of the Judges and during the period of the kingdoms of Judea and Israel, the place of Torah declined among the people, for after the death of Moses and the Elders (ZQNYM), when the Jews practiced idolatry and only one person in a city and two in a family observed God's Torah, there was no need for many of the laws that had

---

[128] *Ibid.*, pp. 176, 179.

come from Moses. The people also did not have to work with the Torah in order to extract new laws. Only in the time of Ezra and the Scribes was the Torah again made the foundation of the people, and the nation set its heart to explain the commandments according to the depth of their knowledge. It is no doubt that in the time of the Scribes, the interpretation of the Torah and the learning of *halakhot* went hand in hand and were not separated. When, however, sectarianism broke out, and the people no longer used Hebrew, and because of the pressures of the wars and the edicts of the Greek oppressors, the students decided to protect that which had been transmitted (QBLH), and they began to learn the *halakhah* as an entity separate from the interpretation of the Torah.[129]

The method of scriptural exegesis also underwent a transition during this period:

Even as early as the time of the writing of the book of Chronicles the people engaged in exegesis, for I Chronicles 28:9 states, *Keep and explain (DRS) all the commandments of the Lord your God*. In the time of Shemaʿiah and Abṭalion, however, two threats faced the nation. In reaction to these challenges Shemaʿiah and Abṭalion engaged in the exegesis of the Torah in order to find a basis for all that they had received from the Scribes. The search for a scriptural basis for the laws of the tradition led to engaging in exegesis not solely for the sake of deriving practical law but also for the purpose of learning for learning's sake. It is for this reason that Shemaʿiah and Abṭalion are called 'the great exegetes' (DRŠNYM GDWLYM, b. Pes. 70b). The two challenges that these sages faced were, the rise of the Saducean party, which did not accept the tradition of the Scribes but only kept the literal sense of the Torah, and the threat posed by the Pharisees [!], who after having fled to Alexandria under the threat of Yoḥanan the High Priest, returned to Judea with the allegorical method of interpretation. This method of interpretation sought to find the secret meanings of the Torah (SWDWT WRMZYM), while relegating the fulfillment of the commandments to a secondary position.[130]

Oppenheim's analysis merely recapitulates the "traditional" view concerning the period of the Scribes while adding the unfounded argument that the work of Shemaʿiah and Abṭalion represents the beginning of learning for learning's sake. He also offers no evidence for the claim that the *Pharisees* (!) posed a threat to the 'Great Sages' of the time when they returned from their exile in Alexandria and

---

[129] *Ibid.*, p. 145.
[130] *Ibid.*, p. 147. Oppenheim throughout his work relies upon the equally "critical" history of I. H. Weiss, *Dor Dor Vedorshav*.

began to employ the allegorical method. Who were these other "Great Sages"?

Following the period of Shemaʿiah and Abṭalion, the students began to organize the multitude of sayings and explanations of learning and Torah which had been recited in the *Bet Midrash*. Several sources testify to the existence of these sayings, particularly b. Sanh. 68a, which notes that R. Eliezer learned six hundred *halakhot*; and *Seder Hadorot* 2 : 2, which claims that from the time of Moses, until the time of Bené Bathyra, the sages learned eighteen orders of the Mishnah, which Hillel then organized into the six orders of the Mishnah. Oppenheim notes, "Although these sources may be exaggerated, one should still surmise that the number of *halakhot* taught in the time of the Second Temple was very great."[131] These laws were not gathered into one source, which we still possess, but they appear among the *mishnayot* and *beraitot*.

To account for the lack of the sources, Oppenheim states, that since we know Eliezer had six hundred laws but we do not have these laws today, they were undoubtedly collected into *beraita*-collections which were later lost.[132] We also find the implicit assumption that pre-70 Scribal law is identical with Mishnaic-Pharisaic law. The early sayings were usually short and did not cite either a reason, a scriptural reference, or the name of its author, because in the time prior to the Houses everything was agreed upon unanimously. It was only thirty or forty years prior to the destruction of the Temple that matters changed, and as the number of students of the Houses increased, so too the number of disputes increased. The destruction of the Temple, coupled with the rise of the Christian party, caused serious problems for the Jewish nation; however, the sages responded to these troubles by stressing the value of learning. Learning replaced sacrifice.[133] In opposition to the Christian view that faith was the means to salvation, the rabbis stressed learning as the means to salvation. As to Oppenheim's claim that the Pharisees responded to these crises by stressing the value of learning, he writes, "The sources I cite to support

---

[131] *Ibid.*, p. 174.

[132] *Ibid.*, p. 271, "The *Beraitot* and Their Relation to Our Mishnah," *Kenneset Yisrael* 2, 1887, pp. 92-93. Oppenheim presents a detailed argument based on Sherira's comments on b. Ned. 41a which claims that Rabbi ordered thirteen orders of the Mishnah. Six of these are the Mishnah, while the other seven form the basis of the *beraitot* of R. Ḥiyya and R. Oshaya. In the course of time, however, these seven orders of *beraitot* were lost.

[133] *Ibid.*, p. 177.

these claims are Amoraic, but there is no doubt that these ideas were expressed in the time of the destruction."[134]

Oppenheim next offers his original thesis that the rise of learning for learning's sake, i.e. the freedom of inquiry, was threatened by the activities of Rabban Gamaliel at Yavneh:

> Already in the time of R. Yoḥanan b. Zakkai it was decided that the law should follow the House of Hillel (M. Shab. 1 : 4). This decision was made in order to minimize the threat of violent controversy. Rabban Gamaliel, however, as evidenced by b. B.M. 59b, not only wanted the law to follow the House of Hillel but also desired to eliminate the mention of the sayings of the House of Shammai or of any disputant (ḤWLQ) within the walls of the *Bet Midrash*. The other sages, however, did not agree with Gamaliel, for although Gamaliel truly wanted to eliminate the possibility of dispute among the children of Israel, his action also ended the freedom of learning. Therefore, when Gamaliel wanted to punish R. Joshua for his claiming that the Evening Service is not mandatory but only optional, the sages in the *Bet Midrash* at Yavneh rebelled against Gamaliel, deposed him from his position, and placed R. Eleazar b. 'Azariah in his place. It was on that day that M. Ed. 1 : 3, which called for the citation even of the opinion of an individual, was taught. This secured the right of learning for learning's sake.[135]

Oppenheim never demonstrates that the issue between Gamaliel and the sages concerned the question of the freedom of learning and the ability to cite the divergent opinion, even if it is that of an individual Rabbi. A form critical analysis of the different traditions about the incident reveals that the dispute between Gamaliel and the sages centered upon the right of the Patriarch to control the *Bet Midrash*. The dispute was of a political and not an educational nature.

Oppenheim considers the day that Eleazar became the head of the *Bet Midrash* as the birthday (YWM HWLDT) of the Mishnah, for it was on that day that Eleazar taught, "One should make in his heart compartments, (ḤDRY ḤDRYM) and bring into each compartment the teachings of the House of Hillel and the teachings of the House of Shammai" (b. Ḥag. 3a). From that day onward the sages were allowed to cite every opinion in the *Bet Midrash*, whether it was that of a single sage or of a Tanna who disagreed. Oppenheim fails to reveal how he knows the exact day on which the sages voiced their opinions. He concludes by claiming, "All these sayings, including the disputes of the Houses, were gathered into a Mishnah which was not

---

[134] *Ibid.*
[135] *Ibid.*, pp. 174-5.

to serve as a law code but rather as a book for learning and instruction."[136]

Oppenheim's entire argument rests on unproved claims. First, his notion that the dispute between Gamaliel and the sages concerned the right of free inquiry in education cannot be supported. More important, even if, following the appointment of Eleazar, the sages began to learn for the sake of learning alone, it does not necessarily follow that they included pedagogic material in the Mishnah, for the existence of which Oppenheim offers no evidence.

iii

'Aqiba initiated several new trends in the method of learning. According to the well known (late) tradition b. Git. 67a which appears also (in its expanded form) in ARN 18, "R. 'Aqiba was called a packed warehouse ('WṢR BLWM) because he gathered the different grains into their respective place and made the Torah into heaps and heaps" (ṬB'WT ṬB'WT), which according to Rashi means, 'Aqiba divided the Torah or learning into the different disciplines of Mishnah, Midrash, *Halakhah*, and *Aggadah*. Jonah's saying (y. Sheq. 5 : 1), "R. 'Aqiba founded (HTQYN) Midrash, *Halakhot*, and *Haggadot*," also gives evidence for 'Aqiba's endeavors. Based on this evidence Oppenheim concludes, 'Aqiba made this division in order to facilitate the process of learning, for during this period all these disciplines were taught together, and it was difficult for the students to memorize the material.[137] These comments tell us no more than what we had already known from these late traditions.

Oppenheim several times notes the existence of Mishnah collections prior to the time of 'Aqiba. Statements, such as M. Sanh. 3 : 4, which refer to the *Mishnah Rishonah* show that these early collections existed, recording the transactions of the *Bet Midrash*. The material in these early collections was not always organized in an orderly manner, for although some material was recorded according to linguistic formulae ('YN/BYN) other sayings were recorded together, since they were taught on the same day (BW BYWM).[138] R. Ishmael's statement (y. Yev. 13 : 2), in which he refers to MDWT HḤKMYM,

---

[136] *Ibid.*, p. 176.
[137] *Ibid.*, p. 238.
[138] *Ibid.*, pp. 237, 270.

indicates that the individual rabbis all had their own Mishnah-collections. ʿAqiba, realizing the potential trouble that a lack of order of the material could cause to the transmission of the tradition, decided to organize the material according to topics:[139]

> R. ʿAqiba not only gathered almost all the *halakhot*, even those not commonly known to the members of this generation, but he also widened the method of exegesis by the addition of new *Middot* (RYBWY WMYʿWT). R. ʿAqiba attempted to find a scriptural basis for every law, for in his time the chain of tradition had been broken and some people doubted that several of the laws were really part of the tradition.[140]

ʿAqiba employed three principles in working with the earlier material: (1) searching for the source of a saying; (2) discovering who said the saying; (3) organizing the sayings by internal connections. If some material did not have a good reason, ʿAqiba left it out of his Mishnah, in order to facilitate the learning process. This excluded material was gathered into *beraitot*. Quoting Sherira, Oppenheim contends ʿAqiba did not include in his Mishnah material that was unknown to him [!], particularly those sayings which originated in Babylonia: "In gathering the material, ʿAqiba's purpose was not to write a law-code, but rather a book that could be used for instruction for students in order to learn the opinions of the different sages. ʿAqiba omitted material which lacked a sound scriptural basis in order to prevent students from stumbling over material which did not serve any purpose."[141] It may be the case that ʿAqiba did not organize a Mishnah for the purpose of a law code, but without first demonstrating the existence of ʿAqiba's Mishnah, Oppenheim can hardly venture to describe its nature. Moreover, if ʿAqiba's work was only intended to serve as a book of instruction, why could it not have included laws which lacked a sound basis? Students, through their work, could surely have supplied reasons.

Oppenheim also claims that ʿAqiba created the Tosefta, but it is not the Tosefta that we have, for "our Tosefta comes from a very late period and is based on the combination of a variety of sources."[142] ʿAqiba's Tosefta contained all the extended debates of the Tannaim and also the reasons and scriptural bases for many of the laws which ʿAqiba left out in order to keep the Mishnah text short. This Tosefta

---

[139] *Ibid.*, p. 272.
[140] *Ibid.*, p. 240.
[141] *Ibid.*, p. 273.
[142] Oppenheim, "The *Beraitot* and Their Relation to Our Mishnah," *loc. cit.*, p. 97.

collection is known as the Talmud of the Tannaim. Oppenheim cites a series of sources which refer to either the LYMWD of the Tannaim (b. B.B. 130b) which according to Rashbam's (Samuel b. Meir, 1100-1160) interpretation means the *Talmud of the Tannaim*. y. Ber. 1 : 5 refers to 'LPNH and y. Shab. 1 : 2 to 'WLPN RBY, both of which refer to the Talmud or of the Tosefta of the Tannaim originated by 'Aqiba. 'Aqiba was the first to organize the Tosefta, for b. Sanh. 86a refers to the organization of the Tosefta by R. Nehemiah according to ('LYB' D) R. 'Aqiba. The fact that the above terminology is not consistent poses no problem, "for the Rabbis were not careful in using consistent terms."[143] Oppenheim completes his circular argument: "We no longer possess these documents, but they must have existed, because our traditions attest to their existence."

iv

Oppenheim credits Meir with two tendencies in dealing with the Mishnah. Meir's first innovation was to cite laws anonymously (STM), while his second change was his method of deriving law. Instead of relying upon the principles of 'exclusion and inclusion' 'Aqiba had used, Meir derived laws on the basis of other laws. The first change, that of citing laws anonymously, Meir made:

> Because in the time following R. 'Aqiba' and the fall of Betar, there was no longer any threat that one sage, as in the case of Gamaliel, would attempt to stifle the spirit of free inquiry. When Gamaliel had tried to restrict the freedom of learning, the rabbis reacted by including everything that was said in the *Bet Midrash* in their *mishnayot*; however, this process of total inclusion overburdened the students with learning. In Meir's day, however, the sages realized it was possible to cite some laws without mentioning the names of the sage or without noting the name of the disputant. Meir's guiding principle was 'one should always teach a law in brief language' (b. Pes. 3a).[144]

How does changing a law from the name of an individual to that of an anonymous law alleviate the process of memorizing texts? Could Meir have made this change to an anonymous law (if Meir made it at all) simply to record a decision as the binding law?

Oppenheim himself tends toward this latter conclusion, for he states, "If an anonymous law appears in the text and it is the opinion

---

[143] Oppenheim. "History of the Talmud," pp. 243-5.
[144] *Ibid.*, p. 310.

of an individual, the dispute involving that individual also had to appear, in order that people would not follow the opinion of the anonymous law but rather that of the sages which appears in dispute.[145] This type of reasoning, however, views the Mishnah as a law code. Oppenheim's claim concerning Meir's reason for citing both the anonymous law and the dispute also may not be valid, for it is based on the assumption that Meir knew both formulations of the law, the anonymous and the dispute. Perhaps the dispute and the anonymous law derive from different formulations of traditions. Oppenheim's contention that the Mishnah was both a law code and a textbook is also illogical. If the Mishnah was only a law code, then either the dispute or the anonymous law should have appeared, but not both. If the Mishnah was merely a textbook, then what danger was there in citing the erroneous, anonymous law? Oppenheim's retort is that since the sages had already gathered the laws to form a textbook, they decided they might as well decide the law. If in organizing the law, an anonymous law was left, it was done because that was an old law. In either case, the Mishnah is a poor code and a poor textbook. Oppenheim's contention that Meir made these changes in order to facilitate the process of memorization does not follow from his reasoning. The students now had to remember both the anonymous law and the dispute.

Meir's second change was in the method of the derivation of laws:

> In the time of 'Aqiba some people doubted whether several of the *halakhot* really came from the Scribes and the Elders, because the doubters knew that there were students among the pupils of the Houses who did not learn everything correctly. Because of the pressures of wars other laws had also been lost. For these reasons, 'Aqiba attempted to establish all the laws by means of scriptural exegesis. In Meir's time, however, the controversy over the law had ceased; therefore, Meir decided it was no longer necessary to find a basis in Scripture for every law but rather substituted the method of deriving *halakhot* from principles gained from other *halakhot*.[146]

Oppenheim thus imagines historical conditions for which he has no adequate evidence. Oppenheim likewise finds no problems in discussing the different Mishnah collections, although these collections have been largely lost.

---

[145] *Ibid.*, p. 312. Based on the statement in b. Sanh. 86b "STM Mishnah is from Rabbi Meir," Oppenheim concludes that an anonymous law is from Meir.

[146] *Ibid.*, pp. 308-311.

V

Despite the allegedly successful endeavors of 'Aqiba and Meir, Oppenheim contends Rabbi had to order a Mishnah:

> Already by the time of R. Judah b. Ilai there was great confusion in the law, because every sage had his own *halakhot* which he formulated according to his own understanding. R. Judah said, "Those Tannaim who teach from their own *mishnayot* (MTWK MSNTM) are confusing (MBLYM) the world" (b. Soṭah 27a). In response to this danger and confusion Rabbi Judah the Patriarch realized that the previous *mishnayot* had been organized either as law codes or as textbooks; therefore, none of these collections could serve both purposes. Rabbi, therefore, decided to follow a middle path and organize his Mishnah as a means of uniting all the students of the Torah. His Mishnah included both the transaction of the *Bet Midrash* and also legal decisions.[117]

Oppenheim then offers convincing arguments that the Mishnah of Rabbi (which is our Mishnah) contains material belonging to both a textbook and a law code: "If Rabbi had only wanted to organize a textbook, why would he have cited opinions of individuals as the opinions of the sages? If Rabbi had only wanted to organize a law code, why would he have repeated material or cite contradictory sayings?"[148] Although Oppenheim notes that the literary nature of the Mishnah does not allow for solely either a law code or a textbook, his argument that the Mishnah is a combination of both these methods of presentation rests on the unproven assumption that the Mishnah is a unitary document from the hand of a single editor. Even if Rabbi had edited such a book, it would not have been useable as either a law code or a textbook. The more logical conclusion is that the literary character of the Mishnah points to the lack of a unitary, edited text. Oppenheim's only evidence from Rabbi's work is Yoḥanan's interpretation of b. B.B. 33 a, "A person should always follow the Mishnah more than the *Gemara*." This means in Rabbi's day the Mishnah was improved and became the most appropriate text for study.[149] Oppenheim fails to mention that there is a confusion concerning the interpretation of this saying. It is possible to argue that after Rabbi's work on the Mishnah, the *Gemara* became the text for study.

In ordering the Mishnah Rabbi excluded some material because it

---

[117] *Ibid.*, p. 344.
[148] *Ibid.*
[149] *Ibid.*

either was redundant or lacked a sound basis. Many of these excluded laws appear in *beraitot*; however, as already noted, Oppenheim argues the *beraitot* were lost. Oppenheim also furnishes a list of twenty principles that Rabbi employed in organizing the Mishnah.[150] He

[150] *Ibid.*, p. 345-8. Oppenheim's twenty principles are:
1. Rabbi did not deal in the Mishnah with well known laws, as example Mezuzah or Tefillin. He also did not offer scriptural evidence for well known laws. Old laws were cited with the terminology 'They said' ('MRW) or 'they truly said' (B'MT 'MRW).
2. Rabbi cited laws anonymously, as R. Meir did. He would cite the law of the first part of the Mishnah as the anonymous opinion of an individual, and then cite the opposite opinion in the last part of the Mishnah as an anonymous opinion of the sages. He did this because he no longer agreed with Meir's opinion.
3. Sometimes Rabbi would cite a superfluous Mishnah in one place (MŠNH YTYR') as the opinion of an individual rabbi and then would cite the same Mishnah elsewhere as an anonymous law.
4. In accepting an opinion as the correct view, Rabbi, at times, left out the opposite opinions, even if there were many opposite viewpoints.
5. Even though Rabbi generally cited Meir's opinion anonymously, especially when only an individual sage disagreed with Meir, sometimes Rabbi would cite the opposite opinion first, as an anonymous law except for the addition of the words 'the opinion of Rabbi x', and then cite Meir's opinion.
6. Rabbi would cite an opinion as "the words of Rabbi x," and it would seem that the sages disagreed with the opinion.
7. Rabbi cited the dispute of Ishmael and ʿAqiba alone, even though the Talmud says the sages disagreed with them.
8. Because the rabbis learned in different schools, in ordering the Mishnah, Rabbi sometimes would record the opinion of later Tanna before that of an earlier Tanna.
9. When Rabbi found the source and the reason for a Mishnah, he would cite the Mishnah as it originally appeared and then add the reason and source for the law.
10. Rabbi cited a dispute of Judah and Meir even though Simeon taught Meir's opinion in conjunction with a different law.
11. Rabbi taught the opinion of Judah in relation to a Houses' dispute even though the opinions had been changed (NḤLPH HŠYTH).
12. Rabbi would cite the anonymous opinion of the sages and then the opinion of the disagreeing rabbi and state the sages admit the individual is correct.
13. Rabbi would cite Meir's opinion with or without Meir's name. When it was cited without Meir's name, Rabbi agreed with Meir.
14. Rabbi would cite the opinion of the disagreeing rabbis as that of the sages, even though the disagreeing rabbis did not want to alter the law.
15. Rabbi would explain old laws, or else he would cite merely his explanation of these laws in his Mishnah.
16. If a Mishnah contains the words 'the opinion of Rabbi' and then a disagreeing opinion, we need not assume the Mishnah was added after the time of Rabbi; perhaps Rabbi originally cited his opinion anonymously and later rabbis then added 'the opinion of Rabbi.'
17. There are *mishnayot* in which the first part follows Rabbi's opinion, the middle contains a dispute of the sages and Rabbi, while the conclusion follows the sages' opinion. This is because Rabbi did not completely disagree with the sages.

states, however: "My list does not exhaust the principles employed by Rabbi; it is however adequate to demonstrate the superiority of Rabbi's Mishnah to those of his predecessors."[151] His list amounts to no more than a review of every literary phenomenon of the Mishnah. For example, Rabbi would cite the first part of a Mishnah as an anonymous law following the opinion of an individual, while the latter part of the Mishnah would contain the opposite opinion of the sages, as an anonymous saying. An equally valuable observation is Oppenheim's claim that a Mishnah may first include the words of the disputant with the formula 'the opinion of Rabbi x', and then cite the opinion of Rabbi Meir. Oppenheim concludes his section on Judah by noting that later Amoraim made minor changes in Judah's work in response to changing conditions. These changes were not made in opposition to Judah but rather again reflect the "spirit of free inquiry."[152]

Oppenheim merely recounts the well known opinions of the Amoraim and later sages. His arguments are circular, for they posit the nature of the early Tannaitic works and then argue these works have been lost. One valuable observation is his claim that the literary nature of the Mishnah does not satisfy the criteria for either a textbook or a law-code. If he had begun his work from within the text, as he did in making the last observation, and had not attempted to manipulate his evidence to fit his pre-existing theories, he might have made a contribution to Mishnah-studies.

18. Rabbi used the explanation of old *mishnayot* according to principles.
19. Sometimes Rabbi was satisfied with the language of an old Mishnah.
20. Rabbi changed some of his earlier opinions.

[151] *Ibid.* He suggests for the reader to consult *Sefer Hakelalim* for further principles.
[152] *Ibid.*, pp. 350, 53.

PART IV

LITERARY CRITICS

CHAPTER ELEVEN

J. S. ZURI

WILLIAM SCOTT GREEN

i

Insofar as I have been able to determine, J. S. Zuri (1884-1943) did not produce a comprehensive work on the origins, development, and structure of the Mishnah of Judah the Patriarch. The bulk of his published work is an attempt to elucidate the methodological and philosophical principles of Jewish law, principles which, he hoped, would someday shape the legal system of a Jewish State in Palestine. His studies do, however, pay serious attention to Tannaitic literature, and, although the framework of his research is primarily legal and historical, his method of inquiry leads him to the consideration of essentially literary questions. It is possible, therefore, to cull from his writings enough information to formulate a bare outline of his view of the Mishnah. Zuri analyses the structure and content of legal passages which are part of named traditions and applies his observations about those passages to anonymous legal statements which occur in the Mishnah and elsewhere. This means that he assumes the absolute accuracy of recorded traditions. If a passage cites a legal decision in the name of a certain master, Zuri seems to assume that the content and especially the structure of that passage is the true record not only of *what* the sage said, but also of *how* he said it. If a certain structure is evident in several rulings of one sage, Zuri assumes that anonymous passages exhibiting a similar structure may be reliably attributed to that sage. In his introduction to the Mishnah of R. ʿAqiba, Zuri outlines his approach:

> ...we shall need to examine the different Mishnahs to observe the differences which exist between the Mishnah of one sage and the Mishnah of another sage. We shall surely understand R. ʿAqiba's methods of arrangement and presentation (HṢʿH) of the Mishnah if we pay attention to his expressions and his instructions, which are most varied in his *aggadot*.[1]

J. S. Zuri, *Rabbi ʿAqiba* (Jerusalem, 1925), p. 242 (hereafter cited as *ʿAqiba*). A

Elsewhere he discusses the issues involved in a careful study of the Mishnah itself. He feels that such a study demands

> ... attention to the relationship of the laws (SMYKWT HDYNYM) and to their arrangement and their continuation ... and to the concentration (RKWZ) of all the laws of one topic in one place by a logical connection. And it especially demands special aptitude with reference to the arrangements of the early [passages in a given collection,] and the later [passages which follow them in the same collection], and with reference to a suitable relationship between all its parts, especially the first clause [of a passage] (RYŚ') and the last clause [of the same passage] (SYP'). And likewise, it demands attention to the language and its brevity, which facilitates memorization by the students in their own language.[2]

Zuri's emphasis on the structure of rabbinic passages has much to recommend it, and his awareness of some important issues in the critical study of the Mishnah reveals a concern for method which seems novel in the history of the modern study of that document.

It is therefore unfortunate that he is unable, for several reasons, to employ his own insights successfully. His attachment to traditional assumptions prohibits a critical and objective examination of the Mishnah. Thus, while he identifies different literary styles in the Mishnah itself, he explains them not in terms of different *sources*, but as different redactional procedures employed by Rabbi in his activity as sole editor. Likewise, although he isolates discrete literary elements in 'Aqiba's legal traditions, his zeal in behalf of his own goals leads him to overstatement of evidence and a forced interpretation, in terms of philosophy, of matters of literary style. Finally, his own style of presentation severely diminishes the effect of his results. To be successful, Zuri's method depends almost entirely on statistics. The identification of a certain form in the sayings of a given sage is interesting but essentially meaningless unless it can be demonstrated that the same form is dominant in more than a mere majority of the named traditions of the sage. Zuri never follows through. Rather, his method is to make a general remark about the way a certain sage decided legal issues or about the structure of his legal rulings, and then to list, usually without analysis, a handful of examples which supposedly demonstrate the accuracy of his observation. This means

---

biographical sketch of Zuri can be found in *The Formation of the Babylonian Talmud*, pp. 19-20; a complete list of his writings appears there in the bibliography.

[2] J. S. Zuri, *Toledot HaMishpat HaṢiburi Ha'Ivri* [History of Jewish Social Law] Vol. 1, Book Two: *Tequfat Rabbi Yehudah HaNaśi* (Paris, 1931), pp. 26-27 (hereafter, *Toledot*).

either that the reader has to take his word that his observations are proved; or that he must check each citation separately, find the passage to which Zuri refers, and analyse it himself. To make matters worse, Zuri's citations are frequently imprecise and sometimes are either wrong or so vague as to prohibit identification of the passages he has in mind. The importance of his observations, therefore, depends on the desire of some future scholar to investigate their accuracy. In this essay we shall bypass Zuri's historical and philosophical observations and concentrate on his method of literary analyses as it appears in his account of the Mishnahs of ʿAqiba, Meir, and Rabbi.

ii

In Zuri's view, the term "mishnah" refers to a collection of laws [halakhot]. He argues that the term appears chronologically later than the term "midrash" and probably begins with ʿAqiba. Rabbi selected the term to signify the collection of laws he arranged.[3] "Mishnah" is related to, but different from, halakhah. Halakhah is connected to topics, for example, "the laws of the Sabbath" (hilkhot shabbat) but is not employed together with the term "mishnah." "Mishnah," on the other hand, generally appears with the name of a sage, for example, "the Mishnah of R. ʿAqiba."

> For the basis of mishnah is an arrangement of law (SDWR HHLKH) from one party of sages (MṢD ʾḤD HḤKMYM) in a presentation of teaching suitable for its students (BHṢʿH HMTʾMT LŠNWN BŠBYL TLMYDYW).[4]

Zuri's recognition that the best way to determine the meaning of a term is to explore its use in the relevant literature is noteworthy; however, he needs to examine all occurrences of the term before his analysis can be accepted.

Zuri states that his purpose in examining the structure of ʿAqiba's Mishnah is to prove "that the Mishnah which is in our hands was arranged anew after his time and sealed and set by Rabbi." This is a refreshing observation in light of the tedious efforts of many of Zuri's predecessors to attribute most of the organization of Rabbi's Mishnah to ʿAqiba. Moreover, he argues that from Yoḥanan's statement that

---
[3] Ibid., p. 25.
[4] Ibid., p. 26.

anonymous Mishnahs are Meir's, it is "impossible to know whether R. Meir arranged it [his Mishnah] on the order of [that] of R. ʿAqiba or whether he deviated from it." Thus we shall also be spared the false and forced interpretations which attempt to show that Meir followed ʿAqiba's arrangement of laws. Zuri adds, "Moreover, we know nothing of the form, nature, or style of the Mishnah before R. ʿAqiba."[5]

In Zuri's view, ʿAqiba arranged laws primarily as an aid in remembering them. He infers this from ʿAqiba's exegesis of the expression "to guard the commandments" to mean "remembering the judgments and words of the law."[6] Needless to say, this ascription of motive overstates the supporting evidence. Zuri argues that ʿAqiba tried "to arrange together all the divisions of the judgments (KL HLWQY DYNYM SL HHLKH) and to set their number at their head." He cites the form, "R. ʿAqiba said four things ...," as proof of such an arrangement.[7] However, his examples do not testify to such a form, but rather, to the fact that a later sage said that ʿAqiba would rule by reciting a list of principles or conditions. For example, Tos. Ahilot 14 : 4 reads, in part:

> R. Judah says, "They have three measures," in the name of R. ʿAqiba ....
> (ʾWMR BHN ŠLŠ MDWT MŠWM R ʿQYBʾ).[8]

Other similar examples cited by Zuri are Tos. Neg. 5 : 3 and Tos. Git. 6 : 8. From these examples we could not reach Zuri's conclusion. Even if we were to assume the absolute accuracy and veracity of Judah's statement, it would by no means follow that arranging lists was a hallmark of ʿAqiba's Mishnah. At best, we could assume that Judah remembered three things ʿAqiba had said. Judah's statement, in other words, *may* testify to the *content* of ʿAqiba's ruling, but surely not to its *form*. From the fact that the Sifra, which he ascribes to the school of ʿAqiba,[9] is divided into chapters, while the Mekhilta of R. Ishmael

---

[5] ʿAqiba, p. 242.

[6] Ibid. Zuri cites "the beginning of Sifra Behuqotai." He apparently refers to Parashah 1 : 3 which contains an exegesis of the words "remember" (ZKWR) and "guard" (ŠMWR). The passage is anonymous. Among other examples, he also cites Sifré Deuteronomy 58, in which "and you shall guard" (WŠMRTM) is interpreted to mean "mishnah" (MŠNH). This passage, too, is anonymous. See below, note 9.

[7] Ibid., p. 245.

[8] Ibid.

[9] Ibid., p. 239. Zuri's judgment is based on Yohanan's statement in b. Sanh. 86a that anonymous Sifra passages are Judah's "according to R. ʿAqiba." He produces a handful of examples in which anonymous Sifra passages appear in the Mekhilta of R. Ishmael in ʿAqiba's name. It is not a convincing claim.

is not so divided, Zuri concludes that 'Aqiba arranged his Mishnah into chapters.[10] Likewise, from 'Aqiba's statement in Tos. Zab. 1 : 5, "Not everyone who jumps forward [with a legal judgment] is to be praised, but only him who gives the reason for his words," Zuri concludes that 'Aqiba's Mishnah was characterized by reasons which justify every legal decision.[11] These reasons, Zuri argues, were eliminated by Meir and Rabbi in their Mishnahs,[12] and we cannot know what they were. Both of the above claims defy verification.

Zuri carries his observation about 'Aqiba's lists of principles or conditions one step further and states that 'Aqiba's Mishnah was composed of details (PRṬYM), which is indicated by the rubric "these are they" (W'LW HN). This means that 'Aqiba treated all the conditions of a given case individually and did not frame his legal rulings in the form of general principles. In organizing laws in this fashion 'Aqiba was opposed to Ishmael, who combined "the common paths of all of them [laws] into one abstract subject (NWS' MWPŠṬ)."[13] Zuri presents one "interesting" example of this phenomenon:

> The smallest remnants of earthenware vessels and the bottoms and sides [of broken vessels] that can stand without support [remain susceptible to uncleanness], if, [having, when unbroken, held] as much as a *log*, they can still hold enough [oil] to anoint the little finger of a child; or, if, [having when unbroken, held] from one *log* to one *seah*, they can still hold a quarter-*log*; or if [having, when unbroken, held] from one to two *seahs*, they can still hold a half-*log*; or if, [having, when unbroken, held] from two to three or up to five *seahs*, they can still hold one *log*. So R. Ishmael.
>
> But R. 'Aqiba says, I would not prescribe any measure for [the unbroken] vessels; [but, rather, the rule should be:] The smallest remnants of earthenware vessels and the bottoms and sides [of broken vessels] that can stand without support [are still susceptible to uncleanness], if, after having been as large as small cooking pots, they can still hold [oil] enough to anoint the little finger [of a child]; or if having been as large as Lydda jars, they can still hold a quarter-*log*; or if after having been of a size between Lydda jars and Bethlehem jars, they can still hold a half-*log*; or if after having been of a size between Bethlehem jars and large store-jars, they can still hold one *log*.
>
> (M. Kel. 2 : 2; trans. Danby, p. 606)

Zuri notes that Ishmael applies a fixed measure to all the vessels,

---

[10] *Ibid.*, p. 245.
[11] *Ibid.*
[12] *Ibid.*, p. 246.
[13] *Ibid.*, p. 248.

whereas 'Aqiba judges them in terms of other vessels. He points out that there is no legal difference between the two decisions; the difference is merely one of measurement.[14] This is an example of an 'Aqiban tradition which avoids general statements and prefers to treat matters individually. Unfortunately, it is the only one Zuri adduces. His observation is an interesting one, but, if from among the enormous amount of material attributed to 'Aqiba in rabbinic literature this is the best he can produce, it seems rather pointless. Moreover, he ignores statements of other masters which exhibit a similar form.

Zuri attempts to bolster his claim by noting that it was customary for 'Aqiba to add details to teaching he had received from his teachers.[15] An example of this phenomenon is M. 'Orlah 3 : 7:

> For R. Meir used to say: Whatsoever a man is wont to count [when he sells them] can [when it is forbidden produce] render forbidden [other produce with which they are mixed, so that they all must be burnt.]
> But the sages say: Only six [such] things render forbidden [that with which they are confused] (R. 'Aqiba says: Seven), and these are they: . . . .
> (Trans. Danby, p. 92)

Again we are left with a dubious example. It is unclear to me why Zuri assumes that 'Aqiba's addition of the seventh item is his addition to an earlier teaching and not a disagreement with the tradition here attributed to the sages. Again, Zuri appears to be reading far too much into his evidence. Moreover, this is the first of two examples he adduces to prove that 'Aqiba added details to earlier teachings. These examples by no means exhaust all of Zuri's observations about the form of 'Aqiba's Mishnah, but they suffice to present his method.

Zuri tries to approach rabbinic literature "philosophically" and to identify abstract principles which underlie rabbinic law. Actually, the entire attempt to reconstruct 'Aqiba's Mishnah is doomed from the outset, because it is based on the questionable proposition that 'Aqiba did *in fact* produce an arrangement of laws. Zuri accepts that assumption as fact and tries to demonstrate the characteristics of 'Aqiba's collection. Therefore, even if all of his observations were correct, they would amount to no more than a list of discrete literary phenomena. He has not shown why we must consider them as characteristics of a single collection or document.

[14] *Ibid.*
[15] *Ibid.*

iii

Zuri sees Meir's Mishnah as a collection of laws characterized primarily by abstract general principles which could be applied in diverse cases. He asserts that Meir looked for such abstract principles (KLLYM) in ʿAqiba's Mishnah but did not find them. The general statements of Meir's Mishnah appear in two forms:

a) This and this—their judgment is such (ZH WZH, DYNW KK),

b) Everything which is such-and-such, its judgment is such (KL ŠHWʾ KK WKK, DYNW KK).[16]

Examples are the following:

> Restitution may not be made from Gleanings, the Forgotten Sheaf, *Peah* or ownerless produce, nor yet from the First Tithe from which the Heave-offering has not been taken or Second Tithe or dedicated produce which have not been redeemed; for what is dedicated cannot redeem aught else that is dedicated. So R. Meir.
> But the Sages permit it.
> (M. Ter. 6 : 5, trans. Danby, p. 59)

> ... For R. Meir used to say: If aught is in a condition of presumed uncleanness, it continues in its condition of uncleanness until it is known to thee where there is uncleanness.
> (M. Nid. 9 : 5, trans. Danby, p. 755)

Zuri seems to be on firmer ground here. The examples do indeed exhibit general statements of law attributed to Meir. However, unless we assume that these sayings represent the exact words of Meir, Zuri's point that Meir *himself* taught in this way is unproved. Let us state the issue more directly: If the above observation could be demonstrated for the bulk of Meir's named traditions, we should be in possession of an important fact. However, the implications of the observation remain to be elucidated. We would have to examine the sources of his teachings as well as their attestations by other tradents. At best, Zuri has demonstrated that by 200 A.D., people reported some of Meir's traditions in the form he outlined. When that form came into existence and the tradent or tradents behind it are the topics of another sort of investigation. Because of his assumption that rabbinic tradition preserves the *ipsissima verba* of the rabbis, Zuri is unable to carry his observations further.

---

[16] *Ibid.*, p. 249.

Unfortunately, Zuri's zeal to limit Meir's teaching to general statements of law carries him into the kind of far-fetched argumentation we saw earlier with 'Aqiba. For example, he observes that many statements in the Mishnah cite Meir but do not include any general statement.[17] He explains this in two ways.

First, he argues that some of Meir's statements do not appear in Mishnah but rather in Tosefta, *beraitot*, or the statements of various Amoraic masters. We can appreciate his awareness of the special relationship between Mishnah and Tosefta, but, unfortunately, he produces examples only from a *beraita* or from Amoraic masters.[18]

Alternatively, he argues that Mishnah-statements in Meir's name which contain lists of items or conditions, a feature of 'Aqiba's Mishnah, actually were preceded by general statements of law which have now been lost, or eliminated by Rabbi.[19] Again we confront an unverifiable claim which must be rejected.

Zuri further observes that nowhere are Meir's general statements isolated, but rather, all are accompanied by a list of items or conditions. This would seem to refute his initial observation that Meir taught only general rules. His answer to his own evidence is that since Meir's disciple Simeon ben Eleazar "was accustomed (RGYL) to state general rules only, we may assume that R. Meir learned individual cases from his teachers, especially R. 'Aqiba, and continued to clarify the common paths until he arrived inductively at abstract rules."[20] His observation about Simeon ben Eleazar is supported by only four (unexamined and unquoted) examples. In this instance, he has ignored his own evidence in order to prove a point.

iv

We now turn to Zuri's account of Rabbi's Mishnah. It is important to point out here that Zuri does not treat the Mishnah of Rabbi differently from those of 'Aqiba and Meir. He does not offer an account of the organization of the Mishnah into tractates, nor does he examine the Mishnah internally. Rather, he is interested in explaining how Rabbi made legal rulings. Zuri's proof that Rabbi is responsible for the final redaction of the Mishnah consists of several Amoraic

---

[17] Examples are M. Pe'ah 2 : 1 and M. Nez. 7 : 2.
[18] *'Aqiba*, p. 249.
[19] *Ibid.*
[20] *Ibid.*, p. 250.

examples which contain the phrase, "Rabbi taught" (ŠNH RBY) and one which asks "Who fixed the Mishnah?" and answers, "Rabbi" [MŠNH M'N TQN? RBY).[21] It is unnecessary to point out that such examples are hardly probative.

Zuri's account of Rabbi's activity is marvelously brief and based entirely on statements of two Amoraim:

> Rabbi's first intention in arranging the Mishnah was to effect a concentration (RKWZ) of laws, the need for which was especially sharp in his time because collections of Mishnahs had increased greatly in the time of his teachers, for example, those of R. Meir, and R. Eleazar ben Shammuʿa and R. Yosi and the like.... From these many Mishnahs Rabbi made one Mishnah, and that, it appears, is the intention of the Jerusalem Talmud, at the end of [tractate] Horayot, when it explains the phrase, "One should always run after the Mishnah more than the Talmud," [by saying] "what you say [refers to the time] before Rabbi abridged the many Mishnahs (ŠQʿ RWB MŠNYWT), but since Rabbi abridged the many Mishnahs, always run after the Talmud more than the Mishnah." For, before Rabbi there were orders of Mishnahs of different sages. This fact is indicated by the plural form (LŠWN HRBYM) "mishnahs" (*mishnayot*), which does not refer to an increase in the law which is in the Mishnah, but rather, to an increase in *collections* of Mishnahs, for example, "Great Mishnahs like the Mishnah of R. ʿAqiba and the Mishnah of R. 'Oshaya and the Mishnah of Bar Qappara" (Lamentations Rabbati, 23). And so, Rabbi came and abridged (ŠQʿ) all the Mishnahs of his different masters into his Mishnah, that is to say, he combined them together and made of them one Mishnah.
>
> Rabbi's work, therefore, was the work of concentration (RKWZ), for he concentrated and collected all the opinions of the sages which were in their different Mishnahs into one Mishnah. Of course, for this task alone it would have been sufficient for him to connect (LHSMYK) all the opinions together; but Rabbi did more by bringing different Mishnahs into legal decision[s] (HKRʿH) and anonymous phrase[s] according to one or another Tanna. From the literary, pedagogic concentration, therefore, Rabbi passed to the religious (TWRNY) and legal concentration, in fixing one legislation for all of Israel on the basis of his decisions.[22]

Zuri's reasoning is circular. Since Rabbi is reputed to have edited the Mishnah, and since most Mishnah-passages are either anonymous or contain anonymous sections, Rabbi, therefore, is the authority behind all anonymous passages and they, naturally, reflect his view. Thus internal evidence from the Mishnah itself could not be used to document Rabbi's editorship. That Rabbi is responsible for all

[21] *Ibid.*, p. 255.
[22] *Toledot*, p. 29.

anonymous Mishnah-passages, in Zuri's view, is proved by the Talmudic statement, "Who made the Mishnah anonymous? Rabbi" (M'N STYM MŠNH? RBY).²³

While rewriting the opinions of various sages into anonymous form, Rabbi also made legal decisions:

> Rabbi's anonymous formulations are decisions (HKRʿWT). He does not follow the view of a single Tanna on an issue in every place in which it [the issue] occurs, but rather, he follows the view of different Tannaim in different places.²⁴

This means that Rabbi's activity in the realm of legal decision was essentially one of "compromise."²⁵ In one case he would state an anonymous law according to the view of one sage and in another according to the opposing view of a different sage.

This account of Rabbi's literary activity is no different from Amoraic justification for internal contradictions within the Mishnah itself. Indeed, Zuri cites two such Amoraic statements to support his picture of Rabbi's work:

> R. Joseph says, "The Mishnah is Rabbi's creation, and he decided it according to Tannaim."
>
> (b. Meg. 9b)

> R. Yoḥanan says, "Rabbi accepted the words of so-and-so in this matter and taught them in the language of the sages anonymously and accepted the words of so-and-so in this matter and taught them anonymously in the language of the sages."²⁶
>
> (b. Ḥul. 85a)

Zuri further alleges that "all of his [Rabbi's] ways in the work of legislation... are reflected in his anonymous statements of law by their different styles and presentations." This means that Rabbi followed several different methods of making legal decisions, each reflecting the different circumstances which surrounded the decision itself. Zuri identifies four "styles" of legal ruling:

> a) Rabbi states the law anonymously according to the view of one sage or another, or according to the opinion of the many, but does not exclude the opposing opinion. Example is M. Shab. 2 : 4.
> b) Rabbi states the law anonymously and preserves no other opinion.

---

[23] ʿAqiba, p. 256.
[24] Ibid.
[25] Ibid., p. 257. "Rabbi made legal decisions on the basis of compromise" (PŠRH).
[26] Toledot, p. 30.

c) Rabbi states the opinion of the sages but does not employ the rubric, "The sages say...."

d) Rabbi states the opinion of the sages, making clear that it is theirs by preserving the rubric, "The sages say...."

Of these different "styles," Zuri says,

"And in all these minor differences are reflected all of the developments of the different circumstances of the decision ... and all the events which happened in the council sessions [while the decisions were being made]."[27]

This monolithic approach, which sees the Mishnah as a single unified document representing only one editorial hand, renders meaningless any form-critical examination of Mishnah traditions. After the different forms have been recognized, the task is effectively completed, and no further avenues of useful inquiry remain open.

V

We may credit Zuri with recognizing the importance of literary structure in the study of rabbinic literature. However, his retention of traditional assumptions, his attempt to turn matters of form into issues of philosophy, and his failure to produce *and* examine all relevant materials make his use of literary forms a disappointment.

---

[27] *Ibid.*, p. 31. Zuri proposes to deal at length with the formation of the Mishnah in a special volume. To my knowledge he never produced such a work. I assumed that his ʿArikhat HaMishpat HaʿIvri. Ḥoq Ḥevrat HaShutafut im Torat HaMishpat HaʿIvri Ḥevrat HaShutafut [The Editing of Jewish Laws. Laws of Partnership] (London, 1941) might deal with the Mishnah, but the volume, among other of his works, was unobtainable.

CHAPTER TWELVE

DAVID WEISS HALIVNI ON THE MISHNAH

JOEL GEREBOFF

i

David Weiss Halivni's *Sources and Traditions* represents the best of modern criticism in Talmudic legal-literary studies.[28] Halivni attempts to unravel the sources, the original sayings of the Tannaim and Amoraim, from the forms (or traditions) the sayings took through the process of transmission. Although Halivni's book focuses upon the Amoraic traditions (presently limited to the order of Nashim), it contains comments concerning the Mishnaic portions, the methodological importance of which cannot be exaggerated.

Halivni's basic assumption is as follows: "The transmission of the Talmud was not, and perhaps could not have been verbatim. The text was altered in transmission with the result that many statements in the Talmud have not come down in their original form."[29] The transmission was not a mechanical process, for the Tannaim and Amoraim were only human. In analyzing Halivni's work it is possible to divide his comments concerning the Mishnah into two general categories. The first category contains comments related to the organization of the Mishnah. The second concerns the nature of the Mishnah-texts in the hands of the Amoraim. In both areas, the literary nature of the Mishnah text was affected by the organizers (redactors) and the transmitters of the text. Although Halivni does not develop a detailed theory concerning the formation of the Mishnah, he does make some general comments concerning its organization and subsequent transmission.

The organizer of the Mishnah[30] attempted to order a document which preserved, as best as was possible, the original wording of the

---

[28] *The Formation of the Babylonian Talmud*, ed. Jacob Neusner, pp. 134-73 for a biography and a detailed exposition of Halivni's work on the Talmud.

[29] Halivni, *Meqorot uMesorot*, English Introduction.

[30] Halivni is very hesitant to credit any one individual with the organization of the Mishnah although he does show a strong inclination for accepting Rabbi as a key figure in the development of the Mishnah.

sages, while allowing for a brief and logically ordered text. The organizer of the Mishnah had to shorten material taken from different sections of earlier traditions (QTYM).[31] The organizer preserved the wording of the first Tanna (Tanna Qamma), but would change the wording of the sage who disagreed (ḤWLQ). In joining different sections, or in moving a section of a Mishnah from its original place to a second location, the organizer attempted to preserve the original wording, even if this involved poor syntax or led to misunderstandings. The organizer was not a mere collector of sources, for he also altered sources to follow his own opinion. Because of this process of joining, rearranging, and rewording material, errors arose in the text.

In the transmission of the Mishnah's text, particularly by the Amoraim, further errors occurred. The Amoraim at times lost parts of texts,[32] or added to texts.[33] Most of the changes, however, were unintentional: "Since the Amoraim did not realize they had made changes, they also did not greatly alter the original text, and therefore it is possible for us to reconstruct the original."[34] Other changes occurred, either because Amoraim attempted to harmonize the laws of the Mishnah with the practise of Babylonian Jewry, or because they no longer understood the terminology of the Mishnah.[35] Above all, "The Amoraim in Babylonia possessed not one version of the Mishnah only, but rather many different readings were transmitted to and by the Amoraim." It is only through a careful comparison of parallel traditions and a deep understanding of the meaning of the sages' comments that one can hope to reestablish the sources and the traditions.

ii

Halivni offers four principles that the organizer (MSDR) of the Mishnah used in his work: 1) The organizer, although he preserved the language of the first Tanna in the pericope, did change the wording of the Tanna who disagreed, and formulated his words briefly. 2) The

[31] Halivni, op. cit., Introduction p. 16 n. 24.
[32] Ibid., Introduction p. 8.
[33] Ibid., Introduction p. 15.
[34] Ibid., Introduction p. 14 n. 19.
[35] Ibid., Introduction p. 17 n. 28. As an example for the Babylonians attempt to harmonize the Mishnah with their practice, Halivni cites Pineles' analysis of Ta. 2 : 4.

organizer chose from among the opinions of the Tannaim the one he thought best and eliminated the others. 3) The organizer violated rules of normal syntax in order to transmit his teacher's sayings verbatim. 4) The organizer maintained the original wording, even when he joined together different sources. Beside these principles, Halivni makes other comments concerning terminology, order, and frequent tendencies of the Mishnah.

iii

In the following example Halivni demonstrates how the organizer of the Mishnah shortened the saying of the rabbi who disagreed, which gave rise to a dispute on the part of the Tannaim. The pericope deals with the circumstances under which an appointed guardian of an orphan must take an oath that he has not impaired the property of the orphan:

> If a guardian was appointed by the orphans' father, he must take an oath [that he has not impaired their property]. If he was appointed by the court, he need not take an oath.
> Abba Saul says, "The rule is to the contrary (HLWP HDBRYM)."
> (M. Git. 5 : 4, trans. Danby, p. 313)

Halivni comments, "We can be sure that Abba Saul did not say, 'The rule is to the contrary.'" This is the wording of the redactor. It is a general principle that Rabbi would render briefly the words of the sage who disagreed.[36] The problem, however, is to determine the words of Abba Saul. Since he says 'the rule is to the contrary,' one could conjecture that Abba Saul said, "If a guardian was appointed by the orphans' father, he does not have to take an oath, but if he was appointed by the court he does have to take an oath." But if this is the case, then how does this Mishnah correspond to Abba Saul's comment in Tos. B.B. 8 : 13, in which he says, "Even if ('P) he was appointed by the court, he has to take an oath." From this evidence it would follow that Abba Saul said only this latter statement concerning a court appointee; when the organizer of the Mishnah shortened his comment he meant the rule was opposite *only* in regard to an appointee of the court. The use of the term ('P) clearly indicates that Abba Saul meant that even in the case of the court appointee an oath must be taken, then surely in the case of a person appointed by the

---

[36] *Ibid.*, pp. 569-71, 318 n. 10.

father an oath must be taken. The opinion of Abba Saul, as it appears in Tosefta, does appear in the *Gemara* following this Mishnah but in the name of Taḥalifa b. Maʿarava.

Halivni, in the above example, has shown how the redactor of the Mishnah would shorten the words of a disputant. He has also demonstrated that this can lead to misunderstanding.

iv

In M. Yev. 4 : 7, the rabbis discuss conditions under which a person who is required to enter into Levirate marriage is entitled to the property of his deceased brother. The Mishnah discusses four cases: The brother refused to marry his late brother's wife and submitted to *ḥaliṣah*, he did perform the Levirate marriage; he did the one or the other while the father of the dead brother was alive; he did the one or the other when the father was dead. Halivni contends that the organizer of the Mishnah, in citing Judah's opinion, omitted part of Judah's saying and only cited the part of Judah's opinion he thought important:[37]

> A. If a man submitted to *ḥaliṣah* from his deceased brother's wife, he still counts as one of the brothers in what concerns inheritance. But if the father was still living, the property falls to him.
> B. If he consummated marriage with his deceased brother's wife, he thereby acquires title to the property of his brother.
> R. Judah says, "In either case, if the father was living, the property falls to him."
>
> (M. Yev. 4 : 7, trans. Danby, p. 224)

The *Gemara*, b. Yev. 40a, y. Yev. 4 : 7, interprets the dispute between Judah and the sages as concerning merely the right of the brother to the inheritance while the father was living, even when he consummated the marriage. The sages argue that the brother may acquire the property, while Judah contends that just as in the case of a first-born son who does not inherit while the father is still alive, the brother who consummates the marriage also cannot acquire property if the father is still alive. The Amoraim also infer that in the case in which the father is dead, Judah agrees with the rabbis that the brother may acquire the deceased brother's property if he consummated the marriage.

Halivni, however, notes that in Tosefta Yev. 6 : 3, Judah explicitly

[37] *Ibid.*, pp. 46-7.

states, "If the father is dead, in either case, the brother only counts among the other brothers." This indicates that Judah does not disagree merely in the case in which the father is still alive, but rather does not accept the principle that the brother is entitled to the property. Halivni also argues that the failure of the Mishnah to include this second opinion of Judah does not pose any problems. The organizer of the Mishnah chose from among the opinions of Judah the one he felt worthy of citation, that is, Judah's opinion in the case in which the father was still alive, and omitted Judah's second opinion, in the case in which the father was dead. Halivni further notes that there are two Tannaitic sources in which Judah also admits that the brother who consummates the marriage may inherit, even when the father is alive.

Halivni thus analyzes a disagreement between the sages and an individual rabbi and argues that the redactor of the Mishnah has cited only one of the individual's opinions. He does not, however, consider the possibility that the organizer of the Mishnah was unaware of Judah's saying in the Tosefta.

V

Halivni contends that one of the organizer's principles was to retain the original wording of a saying when he combined it with another saying, even if this led to awkward syntax. The example in Nazir deals with the respective limits of wine and poll that may be consumed by a Nazirite without violating his vows:[38]

> 1. Three things are forbidden to the Nazirite:
> 2. uncleanness, cutting off the hair, and aught that comes from the vine (WHYWṢ' MN HGPN).
> 3. Whatsoever comes from the vine can be included together,
> 4. and he is not culpable unless he eats an olive's bulk of what comes from the grapes. ('NBYM)
> 10. The First Mishnah [taught], "Unless he drinks a quarter-*log* of wine [he is not culpable]."
> 11. R. ʿAqiba says, "Even if he soaks his bread in wine, and there is enough to make up together an olive's bulk, he is culpable."
> (M. Naz. 6 : 1, trans. Danby, p. 287)

Halivni notes that there are several possible interpretations of the dispute of this pericope. It is possible to say that 10 disagrees with 1-4

---
[38] *Ibid.*, pp. 401-3.

concerning the amount of wine that may be taken; 1-4 say an olive's bulk, 10 a quarter-*log*. It is also possible to say there is no dispute in the pericope, for 1-4 state an opinion only concerning 'that which comes from grapes' ('NBYM), while 10 deals with wine. Halivni points out there are problems in either interpretation.

If one wants to say that 1-4 and 10 disagree concerning the amount of wine, then it must be assumed that 10 comes after 1-4. This, however, means that the First Mishnah comes chronologically after the later Mishnah. An even more serious objection can be raised: Why did 1-4 specifically mention that which comes from grapes (4), if it also meant that an olive's bulk of wine is sufficient for defilement? This particular reference to 'that which comes from grapes' may lead one to say that 1-4 deal only with the derivatives of grapes, while 10 pertains to wine, and there is no dispute in the pericope.

An alternative solution is to argue that 11 reflects the opinion of the later Mishnah, 1-4 in regard to wine. Halivni, however, argues the above can not necessarily be inferred, for it is possible 'Aqiba is concerned with the case in which the bread is soaked in wine and not the case in which the person drinks pure wine. This last alternative, however, is close to the truth, as Halivni explains:

M. Naz. 6 : 1	Tos. Nezirot 4 : 1
1. Three things are forbidden for the Nazirite	1. — —
2. uncleanness, cutting off the hair, and aught that comes from the vine	2. — —
3. Whatsoever comes from the vine can be included together [Thus Sifré Nas'o 24, *as an olive's bulk*]	3. and they can be included together as an olive's bulk
4. And he is not culpable unless he ate an olive's bulk of what comes from grapes	4. — —
5. — —	5. Thus (KYWṢ' BHN) wine and vinegar
6. — —	6. How does he measure?
7. — —	7. He brings a glass full of wine
8. — —	8. He brings an olive's bulk and pours the [wine] into it and lets it overflow.
9. — —	9. If he drinks it, he is culpable, if he does not, he is innocent, the words of R. 'Aqiba
10. The first Mishnah [taught], unless he drinks a quarter-*log* of wine.	10. R. Eleazar b. Azariah says, "He is innocent unless he drinks a quarter-*log* of wine."
11. R. 'Aqiba says, "Even if he soaks his bread in wine and there is enough to make up together an olive's bulk, he is culpable."	11. — —

In Tosefta Nezirot 4 : 1, 3 but not 4 is cited as the opinion of ʿAqiba while 10 is the opinion of Eleazar b. ʿAzariah. The organizer of the Mishnah agreed with ʿAqiba in regard to that which comes from the vine, that the limit is an olive's bulk, but in regard to wine the organizer agreed with the First Mishnah or Eleazar (10). In dealing with the passage, however, the organizer wanted to preserve the original language despite the difficulties it might cause. The later Mishnah did not distinguish wine from that which comes from the vine, for both had a limit of an olive's bulk. ʿAqiba's statement, 11, agrees with this claim and states "Even if he soaks his bread in wine, an olive's bulk is sufficient for defilement." The organizer did not completely accept the opinion in No. 3, therefore used Nos. 1, 2, and 3 as his statement concerning "that which comes from the vine," and in order to mention his opinion in regard to that which comes from the grapes, he added No. 4, "and he is not culpable ..." Accepting the opinion of the First Mishnah in regard to wine, he cited it in its entirety. He concluded by adding ʿAqiba's statement, 11, which was for him another example of food which comes from the vine, whose limit is an olive's bulk. ʿAqiba's statement, however, caused a problem, for the "even" in his original statement was used to join his statement to the claim that the limit of wine is also an olive's bulk as in 3. As it appeared in the redacted pericope, however, the "even" was not appropriate from a legal point of view, for, as noted, it could lead to misunderstanding. The organizer agreed with ʿAqiba only in regard to the bread in wine, but not in regard to wine itself. The organizer left the "even", for "in combining sources he was careful to preserve the original language even when this gave rise to syntactical difficulties."

Halivni contends that the pericope reflects the activity of the organizer, who, because of his decision concerning the law and his desire to preserve original readings, was forced to admit awkward constructions, while also formulating his own saying. Halivni's comments concerning the addition of No. 11 to the Mishnah cannot be supported. This saying nowhere appears together with Nos. 3 and 4.

vi

The organizer of the Mishnah would frequently transpose one Mishnah pericope to another Mishnah pericope while still preserving its original language. By removing a saying from its original context, however, the meaning of that saying could be changed. The question discussed in the following pericope concerns the conditions which require a husband to grant a *Ketubah* to his wife when he had either prior knowledge or posterior knowledge of some defect of his wife:[39]

> A. If a woman exercised the right of refusal (HMM'NT), or was within the secondary grade [of kinship to her husband = HSNYH], or was sterile (H'YLWNYT), she may not lay claim to her *Ketubah* ...
> But if at the outset he married her with knowledge that she was sterile, she may lay claim to her *Ketubah*.
> B. If a widow was married to a High Priest, or a divorced woman, or one that had performed *ḥaliṣah* was married to a common priest .....
> these may lay claim to their *Ketubah*.
> (M. Ket. 11 : 6, trans. Danby, p. 261)

In the *baraita* that follows the Mishnah, R. Huna and R. Judah debate the circumstances under which a widow is entitled to her *Ketubah*. R. Huna (b. Ket. 101b) contends, in distinction to a sterile woman whose husband does not know of her sterility prior to the marriage, a widow, who has all the rights of a normal wife, is entitled to her *Ketubah* whether or not prior to the marriage her husband knew that she was a widow. Judah disagrees, arguing that the widow is entitled to her *Ketubah* only when her husband had foreknowledge that she was a widow. The *baraita* concludes that Huna is wrong. Halivni notes that this conclusion does not seem to follow from the construction of the Mishnah, and therefore the *baraita* and the Mishnah are really opposed to one another. If Huna's interpretation is not correct, and the law concerning the widow is identical to the law concerning the sterile woman, why was the case of the widow cited separately?

Halivni offers a proposal which avoids claiming that the Mishnah and *baraita* are in disagreement. He thereby supports Judah's interpretation. In M. Yev. 9 : 3 the example of the widow (B) appears. In that context, the case of a widow is compared to that of a woman within secondary grade of kinship to her husband, and all agree that the woman within secondary grade, even when her husband has foreknowledge of her condition, is not entitled to her *Ketubah*. When the husband, prior to the marriage, knew that his wife was a widow, he must grant her the *Ketubah*. However, Mishnah Yev. does not conclude that when the husband did not have foreknowledge he must grant the *Ketubah*; therefore, Judah's interpretation of Mishnah Ket.

[39] *Ibid.*, pp. 245-8.

is correct, for he states that without foreknowledge the widow is not entitled to the *Ketubah*.

In order to resolve an apparent contradiction between a Mishnah and a *baraita*, Halivni analyzes the construction of the Mishnah and notes that a part of the Mishnah was removed from its original context, and, when placed in a new context, it gave rise to a misinterpretation of the passage. In moving the passage, the redactor did not change the original wording, despite these difficulties.

vii

The organizer of the Mishnah occasionally interpolated material from outside Mishnah-Tosefta. In the particular case of M. Naz. 1 : 2 an interpolation caused the Amoraim to state, "The passage is incomplete (HSWRY MHSR')." By showing that part of the passage in question is clearly an interpolation, Halivni avoids claiming the passage is incomplete. The pericope discusses the differences between a Nazirite like Samson and a lifelong Nazirite.[40]

> A. (If a man said), "I will be an abstainer from grape stones (HRṢNYM) . . . . .," he becomes a Nazirite and is pledged to every rule of the Nazirite-vow.
> [If he said], "I will be like Samson, like the son of Manoah, ...," he becomes a Nazirite the like of Samson.
> B. How does a lifelong Nazirite differ from a Nazirite the like of Samson?
> If the hair of a lifelong Nazirite becomes too heavy, he may lighten it with a razor, and he then brings the three [offerings of] cattle. If he becomes unclean he brings the offering of uncleanness; but as to a Nazirite the like of Samson, if his hair becomes too heavy he does not lighten it, and if he becomes unclean he does not bring the offering for uncleanness.

(M. Naz. 1 : 2, trans. Danby, p. 281)

The Amoraim comment that something is missing in B for the preceeding *mishnayot* deal with the substitute terms by which a man may take the Nazirite vow upon himself. This Mishnah, in asking what is the difference between a lifelong Nazirite and one like Samson, does not provide the substitute utterances as the answer to this question. The Amoraim, however, do not provide any hint as to

---

[40] *Ibid.*, pp. 357-63, See Epstein, *ITM*, p. 612.

what should be inserted to complete the reading. Halivni notes, it is obvious that part B originally was not part of this pericope but was taken from some other source and interpolated.

Y. N. Epstein offers a solution to this problem. The proper place of B as well as the whole of M. Naz. 1 : 2, is following 1 : 4 (as it appears in the Tosefta following 1 : 4) which deals with the other requirements of a lifelong Nazir. Epstein contends that B is a continuation of Judah's opinion in 1 : 4. Halivni, however, finds several difficulties with this explanation. Epstein argues that the order of the Tosefta, which places B after 1 : 4, is correct, and the redactor of the Mishnah, for some reason, moved B to 1 : 2. Halivni challenges this contention: the order of the Mishnah in Nazir 1 is different from that of Tos. Nezirot 1. The order of the Tosefta follows the chronological period involved in the different forms of Nazirite vows; therefore, B should follow 1 : 4. The Mishnah, however, follows a different order, for its sequence is related to the different substitutes for the words used to utter vows. Halivni does not merely refute Epstein on this point but also demonstrates the error in Epstein's argument that B is a continuation of Judah's saying.

M. Naz. 1 : 2 (B)	M. Naz. 1 : 4 = Tos. Nezirot 1:4
If the hair of a lifelong Nazirite becomes too heavy, he may lighten it with a razor and then brings the three [offerings of] cattle. If he becomes unclean, he brings the offering of uncleanness.	........, he becomes a lifelong Nazirite and he must cut his hair every thirty days. Rabbi says, "such a one does not cut his hair every thirty days."

In 1 : 4 the first Tanna is R. Judah; Epstein and Halivni contend Judah stands behind the entire chapter.[41] Judah says a lifelong Nazirite may cut his hair every thirty days. Halivni notes that the first Tanna in part B of Mishnah 2 claims a lifelong Nazirite can only thin his hair when it is overburdening but he cannot cut it. Halivni, therefore, refutes Epstein's view that Mishnah 2 is that of Judah. Halivni also says that the organizer of the Mishnah purposely did not place B of 2 after Mishnah 4 because the term *lifelong Nazirite* is used differently in the two pericopae. He also notes a further error in Epstein's theory. If 2B was the saying of Judah, it would contradict his saying in Tos. Nezirot 1 : 5.

[41] *Ibid.*, p. 361.

M. Naz. 1 : 2 (B)	Tos. Nezirot 1 : 5
But a Nazirite the like of Samson, if his hair becomes heavy, does not lighten it; and if he becomes unclean he does not bring the offering of uncleanness.	R. Judah says, "A Nazirite like Samson can become unclean in the case of a corpse, for even Samson became unclean for the dead."

In Mishnah 2, a Nazir like Samson was prohibited from becoming unclean, while in Tosefta, Judah claims he can become unclean.

Halivni next answers the two additional questions: from where does B of 2 come? Why did the redactor place it in the second Mishnah? Halivni finds a source in Sifré Zutta[42] which states that "a Nazir like Samson is not permitted to become unclean." Halivni concludes his argument by offering a reason for the placing of B in Mishnah 2. A of Mishnah 2 deals with the question of substitutes for the terms Nazir the like of Samson and one who, by his utterance, is pledged to every Nazirite vow. Unless a person stipulates the limitations of his Nazirite vows, it can be assumed that he is a full-fledged Nazirite. To show the difference between the two types of Nazirites, the one like Samson and the lifelong Nazirite, the redactor has taken the passage from Sifré — or a similar source — and has cited it in Mishnah 2.

The Amoraim frequently claim that a Mishnah text is incomplete. Halivni in this example has shown that through a careful analysis of *halakhic* principles and literary structure he can unravel a composite source. After the critic has succeeded in isolating the different elements of a pericope, he can then reconstruct the original meaning of the pericope and avoid claims of incomplete texts.

viii

The redactor's desire to maintain the original wording of the sources which he combined led to unnecessary duplication. The following example discusses the waiting period of a widow before she can remarry:[43]

> So too, other widows may not [again] be betrothed or married until three months have passed, whether they are virgins or not virgins, whether they are divorced or widows, whether they were married or [only] betrothed.
> R. Judah says, "They that had been married may forthwith be

[42] *Sifré Zutta* ed. Horowitz p. 244.
[43] Halivni, *op. cit.*, pp. 49-51.

betrothed, and they that had been [only] betrothed may forthwith be married...."

R. Yosi says, "All women may be betrothed [immediately] excepting the widow, because of her [prescribed] time of mourning."
(M. Yev. 4: 10, trans. Danby, p. 225)

In the *baraita* following the pericope (b. Yev. 42b) Judah equates virgin and betrothed and non-virgin and married. The question then arises why there is a duplication of language. Halivni's solution is that this pericope is made of two distinct arguments. The first Tanna of the original pericope in which Judah's statement occurs would have said, "And so it is with all women, whether married or betrothed." The first Tanna in Yosi's pericope would have said, "And thus it is with all women, whether virgins or non-virgins, whether divorced or widows." The only difference between the two statements was the use of the terms for married and betrothed girls. When the redactor combined the sources, despite the awkward duplication, he maintained the original terminology.

ix

In the following example Halivni demonstrates how the paraphrasing of another source by the organizer of the Mishnah led to a misinterpretation of some of the terms in the source. The example cited refers to the ceremony performed for the *Sotah* (the suspected adulteress):[44]

> And they that wished to behold her (WKL HRWṢH LR'WT) came and beheld her, excepting her bondmen and bondwomen, since with them she feels no shame (ŠLBH GS BHN). And all women are allowed (MTRWT) to behold her, for it is written, *That all women may be taught* (WNWSRW) *not to do after your lewdness.* (Ezek. 23 : 48)
> (M. Soṭ. 1 : 6, trans. Danby, p. 294)

Raba and Abbaye (b. Soṭ. 8b) claim there is a contradiction in the passage. If it says that whosoever wants to look upon her can look upon her, then why must the Mishnah state that all women are permitted to look upon her? There should be no distinction between men and women. Raba therefore concludes, women are obliged to look upon her. The reason women must view the spectacle is that they will learn (WNWSRW) from the example.

[44] *Ibid.*, pp. 438-50, See Epstein, *ITM*, p. 725-6.

Halivni however, questions Raba's interpretation. He argues MTRWT should retain its usual meaning 'they are permitted'. Halivni cites the parallel to this Mishnah in Sifré[45] which states, "Whether men or women, whether relatives or whether strangers, they all may come to see her, for it is written . . . ." This proves it is only optional and not mandatory to view the *Soṭah*. If it were otherwise, the reading in Sifré would mean that men also are obligated to view the ceremony, which would contradict, 'whoever wants to come may come.'

Halivni next disagrees with the Raba's interpretation of WNWSRW. Halivni argues that this whole pericope is a paraphrase of the version which appears in Sifré, and it is necessary to review that passage in its entirety in order to understand our Mishnah. Basing his argument on the comments of R. Yoḥanan b. Beroqah, who throughout the passage in Sifré contends people should not excessively torture the *Soṭah*, Halivni interprets WNWSRW to mean they shall inflict pain (YSWRYM) on the *Soṭah*. Halivni also notes that the Palestinian Talmud (y. Soṭ. 1 : 5) explains WNWSRW, "and they shall punish her (make her suffer)." Halivni, therefore, concludes the Amoraim in Babylonia did not interpret the passage correctly because they did not rely upon the version of Sifré.

Puzzled by the interpretation of certain terms by the Amoraim, and a lack of consonnance between two parallel traditions, Halivni thus concludes that the Mishnah has paraphrased the version of the pericope which appears in Sifré. An alternative conclusion is that the text of the Mishnah is corrupt; but Halivni also discounts Epstein's attempted emendation.

x

Halivni also comments upon the frequent confusion of the names of certain rabbis in the Mishnah and the discretion of the redactor in ordering the pericope of a chapter. For example, the names of Meir and Judah the Patriarch are frequently switched in Mishnaic material. Halivni offers several examples of this phenomenon citing the parallel traditions which verify his claim.[46]

In analyzing the order of the *mishnayot* in the fifth chapter of Yev., Halivni notes that the only two disputes of the chapter appear in its

---

[45] *Sifré Bamidbar*, Chapter 11.
[46] Halivni, *op. cit.*, p. 285 n. 9.

first and last *mishnayot*, while all the other *mishnayot* are anonymous, undisputed laws.⁴⁷ By analyzing the content of the individual pericope, Halivni offers a reconstruction of the proper order of the chapter. He concludes that underlying the redactors' organization of chapter five of Yev. was the desire to preserve the original wording of the individual pericope even if this led to duplication. As in several other cases in *Nashim*, the placement of *mishnayot* also follows a definite plan, in this example, citing disputes only at the termini of the chapter.

xi

Many examples of Halivni's remarks concerning the Mishnah texts before the Amoraim have been noted in *The Formation of the Babylonian Talmud*. He gives several additional examples, demonstrating how the change of a single letter and the lack of part of the source caused Amoraim to make seemingly extraneous comments. In the following Halivni shows that a *sugya* in the Babylonian Talmud refers to the Mishnah version of the Palestinian Talmud and *vice versa*. The problem discussed in the Mishnah concerns the right of a person to make certain vows and then fulfill them:⁴⁸

> A. If a man said to his wife, "Be thou as a mother..."
> B. If a man said to a woman (L'ŠH), "*Qonam*, if I have intercourse with thee," to such applies [the law], *He shall not profane his word* (Num. 30 : 2).
> (M. Ned. 2 : 1, trans. Danby, p. 265)

The Babylonian Amoraim comment, "But he is obligated to have intercourse with her (HŠT'BD LH)." Halivni notes that such a comment would only make sense if the Mishnah read, "If a man says to his wife (L'ŠTW)," which is the reading that appears in the Palestinian Talmud. The discussion in the Palestinian Talmud between Rav and Samuel, however, only makes sense if their text read 'to a woman' as the reading appears in the Babylonian Talmud. The immediate conclusion is that the texts upon which the Amoraim were commenting were the opposite of those which appear in the respective Talmuds.

⁴⁷ *Ibid.*, pp. 55-9.
⁴⁸ *Ibid.*, pp. 279-82.

M. Ned. 2 : 1	b. Ned. 14b	y. Ned. 2 :1	Tanḥuma Matot 1 (p. 157)
1. If a man said to a woman	,, ,,	,, ,, said to his wife	,, ,, said:
2. "Qonam, if I have intercourse with thee"	,, ,, ,, ,,	,, ,, ,, ,,	,, ,, ,, ,,

Halivni chooses an alternative reading which appears in Tanḥuma:[49] "Qonam, if I have intercourse with thee (MŠMŠK)." If this was the original reading, two possible explanations exist for the development of the passage. The first and less acceptable is that the Amoraim added the words 'to his wife' to B because A read "If he said to his wife, 'Be thou as a mother' ..." The Amoraim therefore assumed that B also relates to the man who speaks to his wife. Halivni chooses an alternative solution. At first the Amoraim interpreted MŠMŠK as Rav and Samuel did, to mean 'to a woman'. The later Amoraim, following the first half of the Mishnah A interpreted it to mean 'to his wife.' In the course of time both explanations were included. Through an analysis of the comments of Amoraim, and a comparison of the different readings for the Mishnah, Halivni claims to reconstruct the original reading and the history of a passage.

xii

The following example demonstrates how the change of one letter in a source can produce different interpretations for the text. The example concerns admissible testimony for the case in which a city has been conquered by gentiles and it is possible that the women have been defiled:[50]

> If a city was overcome by a besieging troop, all women therein of priestly stock become ineligible (for marriage with a priest). but if they had witnesses, even a bondman or a bondwoman, these may be believed [in their testimony]. But none (W'YN) may be believed when he testifies of himself.
>
> (M. Ket. 2 : 9, trans. Danby, p. 247)

Papa comments, "But we also do not believe her bondwoman." The Amora disputing with Papa says, "We do believe the bondwoman of the woman of the priestly class but do not believe the woman herself." Halivni explains this dispute by claiming the Amoraim had different

---
[49] *Tanḥuma* Matot, p. 157.
[50] Halivni, *op. cit.*, pp. 166-7.

readings for the text. Papa's text read, "Because none may be believed (Š'YN).' If this is the reading, the last clause of the Mishnah does not determine whose testimony is admissible, but rather *why* the woman cannot testify for herself. The other Amora, however, read (W'YN) 'But none' which meant the Mishnah specified whose testimony was not admissible, the defiled woman herself. Halivni strengthens his argument, by noting the reading he assigns to Papa appears in the Tos. Ket. 3 : 2. Halivni thus shows the change of one letter can alter the meaning of an entire passage; therefore, it is necessary to establish original readings to understand later comments.

xiii

The following example shows an Amoraic explanation of the Mishnah was later interpolated into the Mishnah while also remaining in the *Gemara*, thus appearing to be redundant. The example relates to the limits of vows:[51]

> If a man vowed to have no benefit 'from any sea-farers,' he is permitted to have benefit from land-dwellers. But if 'from any land-dwellers,' he is forbidden to have benefit from sea-farers, since sea-farers are included in the term 'land-dwellers.'
> [By 'sea-farers' is meant] not such as go only from Acre to Haifa, but such as sail afar off.
> (M. Ned. 3 : 6, trans. Danby, p. 267)

The Amoraim in the Palestinian Talmud ask, "And why should a person not be allowed to have benefit from the sea-farer who goes afar off?" The answer given is, "This is the case (HD' 'MRH) because 'sea-farers' are also 'land-dwellers'" (y. Ned. 3 : 6). But Halivni notes this question and answer are redundant, for the Mishnah explicitly states why the person may not benefit from 'land-dwellers.' The term HD' 'MRH, 'this means' cannot be used to refer to something that is explicitly stated, but rather is the term used when something is inferred. Halivni solves the problem by noting certain manuscripts lack the words in the Mishnah, 'since sea-farers ....' The Amora who commented on this passage also lacked them in his text and therefore asked his question. The answer given 'since sea-farers ...' was later interpolated into the text making the original question appear redundant. Using evidence from other manuscripts Halivni thus

---

[51] *Ibid.*, pp. 299-300.

unravels the development of a passage, showing how comments of Amoraim relate to the original reading of the passage.

xiv

Halivni reconstructs the sources before the Amoraim. He demonstrates that very minor changes in the original sources caused the Amoraim to make comments which appear to be unrelated to the Mishnah with which they deal. He also shows how comments of early Amoraim appear inappropriate because of subsequent interpolations. Halivni pays careful attention to the parallel traditions of the Palestinian Talmud and at times shows that the comments of the Babylonian Amoraim relate to the Mishnah now in the Palestinian Talmud, while the remarks of the Palestinian Amoraim relate to what is now the Babylonian.

Halivni's insight into *halakhah*, his knowledge of variant readings found in the different manuscripts and other rabbinic works, and his desire for a simple understanding of the text have enabled him to claim to reconstruct and understand many difficult Talmudic passages. Halivni fails to give an historical explanation for the development of the passages. Why were certain changes made? Why was material omitted? From which circles did certain passages emerge? Who were the redactors of the Mishnah? Was there ever an editor of the Mishnah?

But literary criticism must precede historical analysis and Halivni's work in the former area is the best of modern work in Talmudic studies. His one serious shortcoming—and it is sometimes fatal to his argument—is that he fails to consider alternative solutions to the problems before him or to test several possible methods. He sets out to prove his own points, particularly to apply his own general principles (*shitot*), rather than open-mindedly to explore and test various ways of understanding the data. In this regard he evidently remains within the limits of the traditional frame of mind and cannot be called wholly critical or fundamentally "modern."

CHAPTER THIRTEEN

ABRAHAM WEISS

CHARLES PRIMUS

i

Among recent writings on Talmudic literature the works of the late Abraham Weiss[52] deserve special consideration. He devoted his major efforts to the investigation of the development of the *sugya* in the Babylonian Talmud. His books and articles, published during the last fifty years, consistently exhibit exceptional methodological concern and thoroughness. In this he is virtually unique among the modern scholars of the Mishnah. In his investigations of the *sugya*, Weiss reviews a vast amount of internal evidence. He patiently attends to each detail and nuance in the sources. His conclusions incorporate the results of extensive research, and consequently his books and articles bear up well under close, critical reading.

It is therefore a disappointment to read Weiss's explicit statements regarding the nature and purpose of the Mishnah. They do not accurately reflect his own investigations. Weiss asserts that the Mishnah is a set of lecture-notes, incorporating the source material used by Judah the Patriarch in his public discourse. Weiss claims this theory accounts for many otherwise unsolved problems, e.g. the wide variety of sources reflected in the Mishnah and the complex arrangement of material. His own studies, however, as they touch upon Mishnaic topics, reveal relationships only among discrete units of material within the Mishnah-corpus. He adduces no internal evidence on the use of the Mishnah as a source-book for academic lectures, whether by Rabbi or by any one else. We shall review Weiss's explicit statements regarding the nature and purpose of the Mishnah, give an example of his Mishnaic investigations, and consider the relationship between these statements and the results of the investigations.

---

[52] *The Abraham Weiss Jubilee Volume*, (New York, 1964) includes "A Biographical Sketch," pp. 1-7. See also Shammai Kanter in J. Neusner, ed., *The Formation of the Babylonian Talmud*, (Leiden, 1970), p. 87. Weiss died in 1970.

ii

Weiss ascribes to the Mishnah a unique place in Tannaitic and Amoraic literature:

> The Mishnah is the single Talmudic creation for which there is in our hands a clear tradition (MSWRT BRWRH),[53] that in its present form it came from a certain compositor (MSDR)—from the hand of Rabbi.[54]

In a discussion of the sources used by the creators of the *sugya*, Weiss writes,

> ... Among all the books of Tannaitic literature, only with regard to the Mishnah is it possible to say with complete certainty, that it was before the creators of the Amoraic *sugya* in the same form in which it exists today.... This is different from collections of other Tannaitic sources, in general, and the Tosefta and the Halakhic midrashim that are before us, in particular.[55]

In these passages Weiss asserts that a distinct document called *The Mishnah* existed and was attributed to Rabbi's editorship during the early part of the third century. He asserts that the Mishnah of the third century is identical with the extant Mishnah. His investigations deal primarily with the substantive arrangement of the document itself. He never asks the question, Was the Mishnah ever redacted? Instead he asks, *How* was the Mishnah redacted? From his detailed investigations of selected passages, he concludes,

> ... not only is there a general order (STM SDR) to the Mishnah but there is an order to the point of amazement (SDR 'D LHPLY').[56]

Weiss does not dispute the conventional attribution of editorship to Rabbi, although his theory, affirming the existence of a distinct document in the early part of the third century, does not require attribution of editorship specifically to Rabbi.

Weiss is aware of criticism of the notion that the third-century Mishnah is identical with the extant Mishnah. Most notably, the work of J. N. Epstein questions the existence of the linear transmission of a single Mishnah-text. Weiss, however, rejects the implications of Epstein's work. He asserts that the third-century Amoraim had the Mishnah before them in the same form in which it exists today, and that

---

[53] The meaning of "clear tradition" is discussed below, pp. 204f.
[54] "On the Arrangement of M. Qid.," *Sinai* 48 : 3-4 (1960-61), p. 161.
[55] *Studies in the Literature of the Amoraim*, (New York, 1962), p. 168.
[56] *On the Mishnah*, (Tel Aviv, 1968), p. 132.

all the textual variations that are in the editions and also those in Epstein's *Introduction [to the Text of the Mishnah]* do not change the face of this fact.⁵⁷

Dismissing Epstein so facilely is simply impossible.

Weiss identifies the Mishnah as one of several collections of Tannaitic sources.

> The Mishnah was like a collection that included the material that functioned for Rabbi as the basis for discussion in his lessons (ŠŠYMŠ LRBY YSWD WBSYS LDYWN BŠY'WRYW). Hence in the Mishnah, in ('L) the orders, tractates and chapters before us ... is the source-material of Rabbi's lessons as they were arranged ('L SDRM).⁵⁸

Rabbi also exercised the lecturer's prerogative to use his sources to fit his own purposes:

> Generally he fixed these sources in his Mishnah according to their own language, but not always in the same form of presentation (BHWYTM HHṢTYT). Here he seems to have enlarged them by introducing additional explanations. and there he established something as though it came from different sources and fixed it as though without any agreement with their language (WQB'N KMW ŠHN MBLY LHT'YM 'T LŠWNN)...⁵⁹

Furthermore,

> Naturally, no teacher places in the source-collection of his lectures all the relevant material, or all the different readings in it. Similarly, he does not present only the material sympathetic to his own point of view; on the other hand, it is impossible that he should not sometimes adapt the presentation of material to his own approach.⁶⁰

Also,

> ... it sometimes happens that in connection with one matter he will present a certain source from one edition, and at another time, when considering another matter, he will bring the same source from another edition .... Sometimes he will present material like [his own, but not in his own name], and he will make known his own opinion in the discussion (W'T D'TW HW' YŠMY' BDYWN).

---

⁵⁷ *Amoraim*, p. 168 n. 6.
⁵⁸ *Studies in the Law of the Talmud on Damages*, (New York, 1966), p. 29. The idea first occurs in Brüll.
⁵⁹ *Ibid.*, pp. 29f.
⁶⁰ "Explanations and Notes on Mishnah and on Talmud," *Horeb* 14-15, (1960), p. 129 n. 12. The translation follows M. Feldblum, "Prof. Abraham Weiss—His Approach and Contribution to Talmudic Scholarship," *Jubilee Volume*, p. 61.

Indeed, even when he lectures he presents only material for discussion (RQ ḤWMR LDYWN)...[61]

Weiss's (unsubstantiated) theory, to be sure, solves two problems. First, he explains opinions expressed in the Mishnah that contradict opinions attributed to Rabbi in other collections: Rabbi did not always agree with material that he quoted for the purpose of discussion.[62] And second, he accounts for the substantive disjunction between the chapters of the Mishnah: "The chapter in the Mishnah apparently was from its inception a standard form of a single lesson."[63] The latter argument also explains instances in which "the division of chapters does not fit at all the substantive divisions."[64] Presumably the chapter-divisions reflect the time limits which Rabbi observed for each of his lessons. Of course, these problems exist only if it is assumed that the Mishnah underwent a single, sustained redaction, and that Rabbi was responsible for that redaction.

iii

The previous passages, as well as the following discussion, are the more remarkable in view of Weiss's often expressed thoughts about the nature of Talmudic literature. "Of Amoraic literature, there exists nothing apart from the Talmud itself."[65] Tannaitic literature consists of collections, e.g., Mishnah, Tosefta, Halakhic Midrashim, which include great varieties of materials. Tosefta, for instance, in its present form is a "literary creation":

> From the entire substantive and literary character (MHWTH) of the Tosefta, it appears that in the hands of its creators (B'LYH) there were sources, and sections of sources, from different schools and from different times. They fused these sources into one [document]...[66]

Insofar as possible, the material in Tosefta was fixed to follow the order of material in the Mishnah. But discrepancies occur. Sometimes a discussion in Tosefta contains more material than a parallel discussion in the Mishnah; sometimes a discussion in Tosefta contains

---

[61] *Damages*, p. 30.

[62] For example, see *Court Procedures: Studies in Talmudic Law*, (New York, 1957), p. 4 n. 10 and p. 172.

[63] *The Talmud in its Development*, (New York, 1954), p. 308 n. 81: "After I wrote this I found a similar idea in [I. H. Weiss,] *Dor, Dor veDorshav*, 6th ed., p. 185."

[64] *Ibid.*

[65] *Amoraim*, p. 168.

[66] *Damages*, p. 29.

less material than a parallel discussion in Mishnah; often the details in two apparently related discussions are very different in arrangement and/or in language; sometimes it is difficult to determine if similar discussions in Tosefta and in Mishnah share a common source; sometimes a passage in Tosefta has no parallel at all in Mishnah.[67] In other words, the nature of Tosefta and its relationship to Mishnah continue to be questions for close study and for only hesitant generalization.

Similarly, in a discussion of the sources of the *sugya*, Weiss criticizes the opinion that it is possible

> to infer from the nature of a certain number of the sources of *sugyot* about the nature of the sources of the whole Talmud.... the essence of this viewpoint is the assumption that the Talmud... is a complete, unified, literary [document]; but this assumption is needed first. From an explanation of the *sugyah* material and its analyses, it appears that the Talmud is only a sort of collection that includes certain different *sugyot*; and for each one there is not only its own development and formation-history (WQWRWT HTHWWTH), but also the problem of its sources and the question of its relationship to those sources.[68]

Given his general views concerning Talmudic literature, Weiss's arguments for the uniqueness of the Mishnah require close attention.

iv

Weiss claims that in his studies of the Mishnah he carefully examines his evidence and rigorously tests his conclusions.

> Since neither theory (ŠYṬH) nor general rules have been transmitted to us, and in our hands there is only the order of our Mishnah, it is incumbent upon us to derive as far as it is possible these general rules from the Mishnah that is before us. On the basis of the text of the Mishnah itself it is our task ('LYNW) to explain the ways of its compositor (MSDRH) and his theory in the work of arrangement. When in the Mishnah we come upon a difficulty or a strange phenomenon, we must, of necessity, break the given passage down into its components, both topical and formal... and search for a reason that can explain this phenomenon and resolve the difficulty. When this explanation serves in other difficult places as well ... it becomes a general rule followed by the editor in his arrangement of the material before him and in his placing of earlier sources into his Mishnah.[69]

---

[67] *Ibid.*, pp. 28f. and *Court Procedures*, p. 122.
[68] *Amoraim*, p. 169.
[69] *On the Mishnah*, p. 27. Latter part follows translation in M. Feldblum, *idem.*, p. 56.

We now turn to specific examples of Weiss's method of investigation and argument. Some aspects of Weiss's discussion of the arrangement of the four chapters of M. Qid. will be described here.

Weiss observes that the content of the four chapters of M. Qiddushin (Betrothals) can be divided into three units. The first unit, M. Qid. Chap. One, touches only in the first Mishnah upon the subject of betrothal: "By three means is the woman acquired (NQNYT) ..." (M. Qid. 1:1). The materials in the *mishnayot* in the first part of this unit (1:1-6) deal with acquiring possession of various kinds of property: wives (1), slaves (2-3), cattle, land, and movable property (4-6). A similar formula introduces each of the first five *mishnayot*:

> 1. By three is the woman acquired (NQNYT) ...
> 2. A Hebrew bondman is acquired (NQNH) ...
> 3. A Canaanite bondman is acquired (NQNH) ...
> 4. Large cattle are acquired (NQNYT) ...
> 5. Property for which there is security can be acquired (NQNYT) ...
> And that for which there is no security can be acquired (NQNYT) ...
> (M. Qid. 1:1-5; trans. H. Danby, p. 321)

Weiss claims that this group of *mishnayot* constitutes a document that was already fixed before it was placed at the beginning of M. Qid. He notes that passages in the Mishnah which parallel the first pericope read, "A woman is betrothed (MTQDŠT) ..." (M. ʿEd. 4:7; M. B.M. 4:7), instead of, "A woman is acquired (NYQNYT) ..." Weiss argues that in these contexts the use of the term NYQNYT preceded the use of the term MTQDŠT.[70] The term NYQNYT remained unchanged at the beginning of M. Qid. because an entire section of ancient material, to which the repetition of the term NYQNYT was essential, was quoted. Elsewhere in the Mishnah, however, in contexts dealing solely with the betrothal of women, the term was changed to MTQDŠT.[71] This argument suggests a specific relationship between several passages in different sections. But it does not support the idea that seems to be presupposed, namely, that the entire Mishnah underwent a single, sustained editorial redaction. It suggests the very opposite.

The second part of the first unit of M. Qid. includes material dealing with ritual obligations (7-9) and moral conduct (10). What connection does this material have with what precedes it? Weiss observes that this

---
[70] *Sinai*, p. 163.
[71] *On the Mishnah*, p. 208.

section of material itself also seems to be a distinct document. Yet it has been connected to the preceding section. Weiss cites Tos. Qid. 1 : 10-11, a passage parallel to Mishnah seven (7), and notes that Tosefta reverses the two phrases. The Mishnah reads,

> A. All the obligations of a father towards his son enjoined in the Law are incumbent on men but not on women, ...
> B. The observance of all the positive ordinances that depend on the time of year is incumbent on men but not on women, ...
> (M. Qid. 1 : 7; trans. H. Danby, p.322)

Why does Tosefta reverse B and A? Weiss states,

> The arrangement in Tosefta appears to be from the general to the specific: from a broad category of commandments, "that depend upon the time of the year," to a more restricted group of commandments, of "obligations of a father roward his son." It further appears that the arrangement of Tosefta is the prior one (R'ŠWNY), and Mishnah changed it in order to emphasize further the substantive connection between this source and the section of the acquisitions (PRQ HQNYNYM). For it is not likely that in such a conspicuous point, emphasizing the substantive connection between the sources, the Tosefta would have changed the arrangement in order to put first the broader category.[72]

Weiss does not further elaborate upon the "substantive connection" between the two sections of material, although beyond a shared tendency toward denigrating the female, such a "connection" is not obvious. He writes,

> In the material that is in Mishnah and in Tosefta there is ... something like (KMN) an ordered framework; in Tosefta there is a parallel to our Mishnah, and ... the original connection between the parallels is positive.[73]

Weiss here indicates a close relationship between texts in Mishnah and Tosefta. But he hardly shows the purpose of the arrangement of the materials in the first chapter of M. Qiddushin.

M. Qid. 2 : 1-3 : 11 comprises the second unit of material in the tractate. It deals specifically with matters of betrothal. Weiss distinguishes two different sections of material within this unit. The first, M. Qid. 2: 1-10, concerns questions relating to the act of the "acquisition of betrothal" (KNYN QYDWŠYN). After listing the contents of the section, Weiss notes,

---

[72] *Sinai*, idem. Cf. *On the Mishnah*, pp. 209ff.
[73] *On the Mishnah*, p. 211.

> The essential framework ... is the problem of men who make an acquisition (QNYN), and the money with which it is done. And within this framework it proceeds from subject to subject ...⁷¹

Weiss observes that this section, which focuses upon matters of QNYN, follows the lead of the opening sentence of the tractate, "By three means is the woman acquired ..." (1 :1). That sentence

> serves as a kind of (K'YLW) basis and framework for these *Mishnayot*, and in them there is a kind of (M'YN) *Gemara* for this ancient halakhah.⁷⁵

Weiss thus tries to connect not only all the details within a single unit but also details that appear in different units.

The third unit of material, M. Qid. 3 : 12-4 : 14, comprises questions concerning family genealogy (YḤWS). Weiss notes that, like each of the sections in the first unit of material, the third unit begins with material somewhat degrading to women: "If the betrothal was valid and no transgression befell [by reason of the marriage], the standing of the offspring follows that of the male [parent]" (3 : 12).

Weiss's discussions of M. Qid. suggest several things. Definite arrangements of material exist within discrete units, about the size of a chapter. Evidence suggests that such units of material have been purposefully brought together in M. Qid. Extra-Mishnaic passages, particularly in Tosefta, also stand in some relationship to passages in Mishnah. What Weiss's discussions do not even hint at, however, are the major elements of his theory concerning the formation and purpose of Mishnah. He adduces no evidence that M. Qid. is arranged as a collection of source-materials for Rabbi's lessons. No evidence even suggests that Rabbi edited the material. The editorial tendencies in this tractate remain unclear.

V

The traditional connotations of his terminology frequently obscure Weiss's meaning. For instance, Weiss claims:

> The Mishnah is the single Talmudic creation for which there is in our hands a clear tradition (MSWRT BRWRH), that it came in its present form from the hand of a certain compositor, — from the hand of Rabbi.⁷⁶

---

⁷¹ *Sinai*, p. 164.
⁷⁵ *Ibid.*
⁷⁶ *Ibid.*, p. 161.

What is a "clear tradition"? Does "clear" mean "reliable"? For rabbinic tradition a "clear tradition" certainly constitutes valid testimony. For the purposes of scholarly investigation, however, it does not. But what, in fact, is Weiss's view of the differences between tradition and internal evidence? In "Prof. Abraham Weiss—His Approach and Contribution to Talmudic Scholarship," Meyer S. Feldblum writes:

> Tannaitic discussion relies almost exclusively upon the Torah as its authority, aside from logical argumentations. But the Talmudic *sugya* uses Tannaitic and old Amoraic material to a much greater degree than it utilizes verses of the Torah. Mishnah and *baraita* are for the Amoraim what Torah is for the Tannaim.[77]

I do not know that Abraham Weiss ever made such a gross statement. But given the rabbinic frame of reference, the statement, "Mishnah and *baraita* are for the Amoraim what Torah is for the Tannaim," follows ineluctably from Weiss's investigations, so long as those investigations are couched in rabbinic language.

Similarly, Weiss's general preference for stating only his own position, without reviewing the positions of his contemporaries, calls into question the whole scholarly process. In footnotes Weiss frequently refers to the work of others, including Frankel, I. H. Weiss, Adolf Schwartz, Albeck, Boaz Cohen, and J. N. Epstein. But most often he only notes, "I have a different approach to this whole problem,"[78] or, "I shall speak here also about the *mishnayot* which are spoken of there. But the opinion will be altogether different [!]."[79] Then comes the enigmatic comment, "And let the chooser choose (WHBWḤR YBḤR)."[80]

vi

Why does Weiss offer a theory utterly unsubstantiated by his own investigations? Weiss's position is pure traditionalism. The traditionalist does not really consider the Mishnah as an independent document. Attention focuses on the Babylonian Talmud and the works of Talmudic commentators. The Mishnah is viewed as the source which gave to Talmud its framework of discussion;[81] the

---

[77] M. Feldblum, *idem.*, p. 13.
[78] *On the Mishnah*, p. 61 n. 10.
[79] *Ibid.*, p. 26 n. 1.
[80] *Ibid.* and p. 61 n. 10.
[81] *Amoraim*, p. 168.

Talmudic discussions, however, are of primary importance. Thus, although he does deal with problems in the Mishnah itself, Weiss is more concerned about the relevance of Mishnaic studies to Talmudic studies. Each time he lists the purposes of studying Mishnah, he concludes with a sentence like the following:

> Moreover, the proper explanation of a *Mishnah* makes it possible to gain a clearer recognition of the nature and the formation of a Talmudic *sugya* which later tries to interpret and to explain the *Mishnah*.[82]

Because Mishnaic studies are not considered to be so important as Talmudic studies, wholly unsubstantiated theories about the Mishnah, its origins, purpose, and functions are propounded. Weiss makes no attempt to test his theory. He does not assemble any evidence, internal or external to the document, that the Mishnah ever served as a collection of "source-materials for lessons." He does not ask, Were there "collections of source-materials" for the lessons of any Tanna, or Amora, besides Rabbi? He does not ask, What evidence is there concerning teaching methods and procedures in Tannaitic and Amoraic times? Instead, Abraham Weiss, who used internal evidence to refute conventional rabbinic opinion concerning the redaction of the Babylonian Talmud, allows himself to speculate quite uncritically about Rabbi's "lecture-notes."

[82] *On the Mishnah*, p. 133.

PART V

RECENT ISRAELI CONTRIBUTIONS

CHAPTER FOURTEEN

ḤANOKH ALBECK ON THE MISHNAH

GARY G. PORTON

i

Ḥanokh Albeck[1] has devoted much of his scholarly career to the study of the Mishnah.[2] In 1936 he completed his first major work on the subject, *Untersuchungen über die Redaktion der Mischna*.[3] His second book on the Mishnah and related texts, *Studies in the Baraita and Tosefta and their Relationship to the Talmud* (*Meḥqarim beBaraita veTosefta veYaḥasan laTalmud*)[4] was published in 1944. 1952 saw the first publication of his edition of the Mishnah,[5] and in 1959 Albeck issued his *Introduction to the Mishnah* (*Mavo laMishnah*).[6] In addition to these books, Albeck has published several articles on the subject.[7] The major portion of his earlier theories and discussions is contained in his *Mavo*. In fact, many of the statements in this book are *verbatim* quotations from his earlier works. For this reason, we shall draw our discussion primarily from Albeck's latest volume.

Albeck's *Mavo laMishnah* opens with an interesting, if from a scholarly point of view not significant, discussion of the root ŠNH and the noun MŠNH.[8] Although he devotes a chapter to the study of the development of the oral law, he has no new thoughts on the problem.[9] His section concerning the Tannaim mentioned in the

---

[1] For a biographical sketch of H. Albeck see this writer's chapter in Jacob Neusner (ed.), *The Formation of the Babylonian Talmud*, p. 127.
[2] I have used the term mishnah to denote a paragraph of our printed Mishnah. *Mishnahs* is a translation of MŠNYOT. Mishnah, with a capital "M," denotes a collection of laws, especially that of Judah the Patriarch.
[3] H. Albeck, *Untersuchungen über die Redaktion der Mischna* (Berlin, 1936).
[4] H. Albeck, *Meḥqarim beBaraita veTosefta veYaḥasan laTalmud* (Jerusalem, 1944).
[5] H. Albeck, *Shishah Sidré Mishnah. Seder Qodashim* (Jerusalem, 1956). *Seder Moʻed* (Jerusalem, 1952). *Seder Nashim* (Jerusalem, 1954). *Seder Neziqin* (Jerusalem, 1953). *Seder Toharot* (Jerusalem, 1958). *Seder Zeraʻim* (Jerusalem, 1957).
[6] H. Albeck, *Mavo laMishnah* (Jerusalem, 1959).
[7] For a complete index of Albeck's writings see *Sefer haYovel leRabbi Ḥanokh Albeck* (Jerusalem, 1963), pp. 9-16. Add.: H. Albeck, *Mavo laTalmudim* (Tel Aviv, 1969).
[8] *Mavo laMishnah*, pp. 1-2.
[9] *Ibid.*, pp. 3-39.

209

Mishnah is a standard collection of citations and texts.[10] In his chapter entitled "The Language of the Mishnah," Albeck offers a brief discussion of the differences between Classical Hebrew and Rabbinic Hebrew, of words which first appear in Rabbinic Hebrew, of words which have a different meaning in Rabbinic Hebrew from their meaning in Classical Hebrew, and of foreign words which occur in the Mishnah.[11] A book also contains a section about the sages who wrote commentaries to the Mishnah.[12] These chapters are not germane to the problems discussed in this volume; therefore, they will not be analyzed here. We shall concentrate on Albeck's views about the state of the *mishnahs* before the time of Judah the Patriarch and his opinions concerning the editing and style of Rabbi's Mishnah. It should be stated at the outset that Albeck has no doubts that R. Judah the Patriarch was the *first and only* editor of our Mishnah.

ii

Albeck states that with the Babylonian Exile and the Return to Palestine, an oral tradition (TWRH ŠB'L PH) developed alongside the written Scriptures. This was a natural development because 1) "anything which is written can be explained in many ways..."[13] and 2) the Torah is often vague and unspecific in its discussions of legal matters; therefore it needs some explanatory remarks.[14] We find examples of the oral tradition as early as the prophet Ezekiel as well as in many sections of the Apocrypha, the Pseudepigrapha and the Septuagint.[15] There is no need to enter into a discussion of Albeck's theory about the oral law or the problem of the existence of the oral tradition in general.[16] The important aspect of Albeck's comments is that he concludes that a number of laws existed before the time of the Tannaim. Albeck states:

[10] *Ibid.*, pp. 216-236.
[11] *Ibid.*, pp. 128-215.
[12] *Ibid.*, pp. 237-253.
[13] *Ibid.*, p. 3.
[14] *Ibid.*, p. 4.
[15] *Ibid.*, pp. 3-39 is a discussion of this whole question. Compare Albeck's comments with those of Renée Bloch, "Écriture et tradition dans le judaïsme — Aperçus sur l'origine du Midrash," *Cahiers Sioniens*, VIII, 1954, pp. 1-34 and "Midrash" in *Supplément au Dictionnaire de la Bible*, V, cols. 1263-1280.
[16] For a complete discussion of the problem of the oral law see Jacob Neusner, *The Rabbinic Traditions about the Pharisees before 70* (Leiden: 1971-1972), III, pp. 143-180.

It is clear that there were old laws in the hands of the Tannaim which were transmitted within the Tradition. The Tannaim occupied themselves with these laws as [they occupied themselves] with the written Torah. They joined them to Scripture, explained them, and through rules and through logic [they] extracted from them new laws.[17]

Albeck now asks the important questions:

> These old laws that were in the hands of the Tannaim, were they transmitted in a fixed language and form? Were they fixed in a complete edition and in their proper place according to specific signs, for example, according to the names of the sages who transmitted the laws, or according to expressions which were common to several *mishnahs,* or according to the content [of the laws]... or were they individual laws with no connection between them?[18]

In order to answer these questions, Albeck reviews the theories of R. Saadya Gaon, R. Sherira Gaon, Nahman Krochmal, Zecharias Frankel, David Hoffmann, Heinrich Graetz, and Y.I. HaLevy. Although most of these individuals are discussed elsewhere in this volume, it will be useful to treat some of Albeck's summaries of their views and his comments on their theories in order to understand how Albeck's own theory developed and how his opinions relate to those of earlier scholars.

R. Saadya Gaon stated:

> The fathers began to collect the Mishnah at the end of forty years after (the building) of the Second Temple [and they continued to collect it] for one hundred fifty years after the destruction of the Temple... They collected it for eleven generations: [From] the generation of the men of the Great Assembly... [until] the generation of Our Holy Rabbi (Judah the Patriarch). The reason that compelled them to collect it was that after the prophets had ceased from them and they saw themselves scattered, they feared lest the tradition would be forgotten; therefore, they put their trust in writing... They collected all the opinions that were kept (orally) and wrote them and collected them and called them by the name of Mishnah.[19]

Saadya's theory is no more than a compilation of rabbinic lore.[20] However, Albeck does not point out this fact.

---

[17] *Mavo laMishnah*, p. 63.
[18] *Ibid.*, p. 65.
[19] *Ibid.*, pp. 65-66
[20] We do not object to the use of rabbinic tradition for a source of the history of Judaism in late antiquity. However, the sources must be used critically. Every statement must be analyzed; not everything is to be taken as fact.

In opposition to Saadya, Albeck discusses the opinions of R. Sherira Gaon, upon whom Albeck bases much of his own thinking. Sherira believed that before R. Judah, the Mishnah was not ordered (SDWRH) and that "there was not even one way of expressing the laws (WL' HYH 'PYLW LŠWN 'PYLW LHLKWT)."[21] In fact, none of the sages before Rabbi committed his views to writing.[22] Each taught the laws to his students in his own manner and in his own language. The sages before Judah did not have orders (SDRYM) of the Mishnah, fixed formulae(?) (DBRYM MTWQNYM), or a known Mishnah (?) (MŠNH YDW'H).[23]

Sherira believed that M. Sanh. 5:2 proved that Judah did not change any of the material which he had before him. In this mishnah we find the name "ben Zakkai." The Gemara tells us that this was the name applied to R. Yoḥanan b. Zakkai while he was still a student. Sherira concludes that the event described in this mishnah occurred while Yoḥanan was still a student. Sherira reasons that "already during the time of Hillel and Shammai, they taught M'ŚH WBDQ BN ZK'Y." We know that Judah did not change the material before him, because he did not alter the less familiar "ben Zakkai" to the more common "Yoḥanan ben Zakkai"—so Sherira.[24] B. Horayot 13b tells us that R. Meir and R. Nathan asked R. Simeon b. Gamaliel to teach 'Uqṣin. B. Berakot 28a states that 'Eduyyot was taught during the life-time of R. Eleazer b. 'Azariah. Sherira concludes that these two tractates "were ordered (NSDRW) before [the time of] Rabbi, and he added to them laws that were taught in the days of his father. But with regard to the rest of the tractates of our Mishnah, Rabbi was the first Orderer...."[25]

Albeck accepts three main points of R. Sherira's theory. First, Albeck agrees that 'Eduyyot was one of the first tractates compiled. From this Albeck concludes that one cannot base his theory about the editing and style of our Mishnah solely on an analysis of this tractate[26] Second, he accepts Sherira's view that with the exception of a few orders, R. Judah the Patriarch was the first editor of Mishnah. Third, he wholeheartedly accepts Sherira's statement that Judah

---

[21] *Mavo laMishnah*, p. 66.
[22] *Ibid.*
[23] *Ibid.* By MŠNH YDW'H he may mean a standardized collection.
[24] *Ibid.*, pp. 67-68.
[25] *Ibid.*, p. 68.
[26] *Ibid.* However, as we shall see, Albeck does base much of his theory on his analysis of 'Eduyyot.

did not change any of the material that he had received from his predecessors.

Naḥman Krochmal agreed with Saadya that from the days of the Great Assembly, the sages began to order the laws and to find connections between them so that they could teach them together.[27] The beginning of M. Bava Qamma, which is an example of old *mishnahs*, demonstrates that the early *mishnahs* were brief statements of law.[28] Albeck's criticisms of Krochmal's theory are insightful. Albeck states:

> In truth there is no proof that even the old laws that are in our Mishnah are from the time of the men of the Great Assembly. How much the more is there no proof that [these laws] were ordered and edited at that time![29]

This is a remarkable statement for a scholar with Albeck's background. Krochmal also claimed that foreign phrases in a mishnah indicated that that mishnah was old. To this Albeck replies:

> There is no need to say that Greek words and foreign expressions do not argue for an early period [for the origin of a mishnah] when the land was under Greek rule, for in all times, even after the Destruction [of the Second Temple] the Greek language was spread throughout the land of Israel and it was even used among the [common] people.[30]

Following one rabbinic tradition, Krochmal claims that six hundred laws had grown up between the time of the Great Assembly and Hillel. Hillel collected these six hundred laws and divided them into the six orders of our Mishnah: "Hillel established the six order of the Mishnah and divided them into tractates and chapters, [and he divided the chapters] into laws."[31] In short, Hillel was the first editor of the Mishnah. He claims that the phrase MʿSH WBDQ BN ZKʾY in M. Sanh. 5:2 indicates that this mishnah "was taught in [this] style and in [this] language close to [the time of] Hillel." Krochmal also claims that M. Sheq. 5 was ordered by Hillel. In this chapter, the officials of the Temple are listed by name. According to one explanation in the Palestinian Talmud, these are names of officials who lived at the time of the editor of the chapter. One of the officials has two names: Petaḥiah and Mordecai. According to b. Men. 46b, Petaḥiah lived

---

[27] *Mavo laMishnah*, p. 69.
[28] *Ibid.*
[29] *Ibid.*, p. 72.
[30] *Ibid.*
[31] *Ibid.*, p. 70.

213

during the days of Hyrcannus and Aristobulus, that is close to the time of Hillel. Because Hillel is the most likely sage of that period to have ordered these *mishnahs,* Krochmal suggests that in fact he is their editor.[32]

In response to Krochmal's analysis of M. Sanh. 5:2, Albeck states:

> In truth the word M'SH argues that they fixed the language [of this mishnah] a long time after the event. They called R. Yohanan b. Zakkai by the name 'ben Zakkai' to allude to the time of the incident which occurred while he was still a student.[33]

In other words, the mishnah was *not* ordered while Yohanan was a student, that is, while Hillel was still alive. Concerning Krochmal's discussion of M. Sheq. 5, Albeck notes:

> The officials who were in the Temple and who are named in M. Sheq. 5 did not [live] only in the days of Hillel, for Gabini Karoz who lived during the days of Agrippa (y. Sheq. *loc. cit.* and b. Yoma 20b) is also mentioned there. The opinion of Hoffmann is that this mishnah was ordered at the time of Agrippa. But the truth of the matter is that also the rest of the officials were called by these names in a later period, for these were not names of individuals, but were general names that were given to all who were appointed for specific jobs [mentioned] in the Mishnah.[34]

Although Albeck disagrees with Krochmal, both scholars used the same method. While Albeck suggests that the word M'SH means that the mishnah is later than the event, he offers no proof for this assertion. In any case, even if the mishnah were edited after the death of Hillel, Albeck believes that it still reflects an early statement, as the name "ben Zakkai" indicates. In his discussion of M. Sheq. 5, Krochmal believed that the mishnah could be dated through the names which appear there. Krochmal dates the mishnah through the name Petahiah; Albeck objects to Krochmal's date because of the name Gabini which appears in the chapter. While Krochmal believed that only one Petahiah lived during the rabbinic period, Albeck implies that *one* Gabini was born in that era. Albeck concludes, however, that the mishnah cannot be dated by means of the names which appear in it. On the other hand, Albeck never proves his assertion that the names "were not names of individuals, but were general names that were given to all who were appointed for specific

[32] *Ibid.*
[33] *Ibid.,* p. 72.
[34] *Ibid.*

jobs [mentioned] in the Mishnah." In other words, Albeck does not object to Krochmal's method in general; he only rejects its use in this instance.

Albeck's refutation of Krochmal also applies to Zecharias Frankel's theory that the old laws in the Mishnah were established (NWSDW) during the period of the Great Assembly.[35] However, Frankel's work adds another aspect to our discussion. Frankel argued that R. ʿAqiba was the first editor of the Mishnah. R. Meir continued his work and R. Judah completed it and added traditions which came after Meir's death.[36] Frankel argued that the Avot deRabbi Nathan alludes to ʿAqiba's ordering of the laws:

> He called R. ʿAqiba the sealed treasury. To what may R. ʿAqiba be compared? [He may be compared] to a worker who took his basket and went outside. He found wheat and he placed it in it. He found barley and he placed it in it ... When he entered into his house, he sifted the wheat ... and the barley.... Thus did R. ʿAqiba do, for he made the whole Torah explicit (ṬBʿWT ṬBʿWT).[37]

The famous passage in b. Sanh. 86a also suggests that R. ʿAqiba was the first editor of the Mishnah:

> For R. Yoḥanan said, "Anonymous mishnahs are from R. Meir. Anonymous toseftas are from R. Nehemiah ... And all of these are according to the opinion of (WKWLHW ʾLYBʾ D) R. ʿAqiba."

Albeck says that Frankel believed that

> The intention of 'all of them are according to the opinion of R. ʿAqiba' is that they went in the footsteps of their teacher to order the laws in their proper place. There is no doubt that they heard many old laws from R. ʿAqiba which were transmitted from his hand to their hands. They also added to his orders and created new ones ... And this was the work of R. Meir in the Mishnah and the work of R. Nehemiah in the Tosefta ....[38]

In his refutation of Frankel, Albeck states:

> The intention of this expression [all of these are according to the opinion of R. ʿAqiba] is [to teach] that R. Meir taught the old laws in the style and language in which he had heard them from R. ʿAqiba.... Therefore, there is no mention here of an ordering of the Mishnah by R. ʿAqiba: rather, [the passage speaks of] R. ʿAqiba's fixing the language and tradition (NWSḤ) of the laws.[39]

---

[35] *Ibid.*, p. 73.
[36] *Ibid.*, p. 74.
[37] Quoted in *Mavo laMishnah*, p. 74.
[38] *Ibid.*, p. 74.
[39] *Ibid.*, p. 76.

Albeck is merely quibbling with Frankel's interpretation of the passage. Frankel's claim that the passage refers to a fixed sequence of the laws is no less questionable than Albeck's belief that the passage refers to "R. 'Aqiba's fixing the language and tradition of the laws." Neither man challenges the historical validity of the passage.

As noted above, Albeck's own theories owe a good deal to Sherira. Albeck believes that 'Eduyyot was the first tractate to be ordered:

> 'Eduyyot was ordered first, before they began to order the other tractates. It was not ordered according to content but was ordered according to the name of the sage who transmitted the law. After they began to edit the mishnahs according to the content [of the laws], those who ordered and edited them returned and fixed the laws of 'Eduyyot, that were edited before them, into the other tractates according to the content [of the laws].[10]

According to Albeck, one of the striking features of 'Eduyyot is that it contains laws dealing with many different subjects. The mishnahs were not collected according to the content of the laws; rather, laws of a given sage were placed together. Because Rabbi ordered his Mishnah according to the content of the laws—he collected all the laws on one subject into one tractate or chapter—Rabbi did not order this tractate. Albeck concludes that 'Eduyyot was ordered first, in Yavneh. He bases his opinion on the first Tosefta of 'Eduyyot:

> After the sages entered into the vineyard [at Yavneh], they said: 'In the future a person will seek a word from the words of Torah and he will not find [any] and [he will seek a word] from the words of the Scribes and he will not find [any], for it is said: *Behold the days are coming, says the Lord God, when I will send a famine on the land; not a famine of bread nor a thirst for water, but of hearing the words of the Lord. They shall wander from sea to sea and from north to east; they shall run to and fro to seek a word of the Lord, but shall not find it* (Amos 8:11-12).... Let us begin from Hillel and Shammai (NTHYL MHLL WSM'Y)....'[11]

This Tosefta indicates to Albeck four things. First it makes clear that no ordered tradition existed before Yavneh. For if such a tradition had existed, why were the sages afraid that the "words of Torah" and the "words of the Scribes" would not be available to one who sought them? Second, the phrase NTHYL MHLL WŠM'Y means that the laws were taught according to the sage who transmitted them. Third, this passage also supplies the reason for the first ordering of the

---

[10] *Ibid.*, p. 82.
[11] Quoted in *Mavo laMishnah*, p. 82.

mishnahs. They were collected so that the laws would not be forgotten. Fourth, because this is the first Tosefta in 'Eduyyot, it must be referring to the compilation of that tractate. Therefore, 'Eduyyot was the first tractate ordered. It was ordered according to the names of the sages and the work was done at Yavneh.[42]

There are serious problems with Albeck's reasoning. First, he has failed to realize the complexity of 'Eduyyot. As J.N. Epstein has shown, 'Eduyyot is not a simple collection of laws ordered by the names of their transmitters.[43] Second, even if 'Eduyyot were ordered through different principles from the rest of the tractates —a fact Albeck never *proves*—this does not mean that 'Eduyyot is the *earliest* tractate. Albeck does not engage in a detailed comparison of the mishnahs which occur in 'Eduyyot and in other tractates in order to determine which version is earlier. The most Albeck can really say is that 'Eduyyot appears to be *different* from the other tractates. Third, Albeck has accepted the Tosefta in 'Eduyyot as a historically accurate description of the situation in Yavneh and of the origin of 'Eduyyot.

The remarkable fact about Albeck's analysis of 'Eduyyot is that in spite of his method, part of his conclusion is probably correct. The recent work of Professor Jacob Neusner, especially his *Rabbinic Traditions about the Pharisees before 70*,[44] has demonstrated the extensive creative and literary activity of Yavneh. Through a detailed form-critical analysis and a process of verification[45] Neusner has shown that a number of rabbinic traditions were formed at Yavneh. Albeck claims much more from much less evidence.

iii

Albeck views the Mishnah as a collection of sources. These sources, which Rabbi merely collected and arranged, were composed in Tannaitic school-houses between the time of Yavneh and that of Judah the Patriarch. Albeck believes it is extremely easy to discover the sources from which the Mishnah was composed. The task of discovering the sources is simplified because, according to Albeck, Rabbi 1) did not change any of his sources; and 2) he arranged his

[42] *Ibid.*, pp. 82-83.
[43] Neusner, *Rabbinic Traditions*, II, pp. 324-343.
[44] See note 15.
[45] Neusner, *Rabbinic Traditions*, III, pp. 180-238. Neusner also uses the term attestations.

Mishnah *only* according to the content of the laws. Albeck repeatedly states that Rabbi did not change any of the material which he had received:

> The editor of the Mishnah did not change, did not distort, and did not mutilate the material that was before him; rather, he fixed it in our Mishnah as he found it.[46]

Elsewhere Albeck states:

> Mishnahs entered into our Mishnah as they were transmitted, even though they differed fundamentally in structure from those mishnahs [which were ordered according to content], because neither Rabbi nor those who ordered the Mishnah before him changed the form in which the sages before them had constructed them.[17]

Rabbi ordered his Mishnah *only* through the principle of content:

> All the laws on one subject (NWŚ') were collected into one context ('NYYN). Those which were more closely related were unified into one chapter. And the chapters were woven (N'RGW) through their closeness into one tractate (MSKT) and the tractates were tied together (NTQŠRW) according to their type (SWG) into orders (SDRYM).[48]

As we shall see, Albeck never attempts to prove either of these two assertions; he merely states them as axioms. However, we will review some of Albeck's comments on how to discover sources before we discuss his two basic presuppositions.

Because Rabbi ordered his Mishnah according to *one* principle, any section which is collected according to another principle was formed into a unit *before* the time of Rabbi. 'Eduyyot, which was collected according to the names of the sages, is an example of a whole tractate collected on a principle other than content. M. Rosh Hashanah 4:1-4, the end of M. Ma'aser Sheni, and M. Sotah 9:6 were collected according to the same principle as 'Eduyyot.[49] Albeck also isolates collections that were unified by common phrases. For example, M. Ketuvot 2:2ff contains the phrase "the mouth that prohibited is the mouth that permitted" (HPH Š'SR HW HPH ŠHTYR)[50] and M. Megillah 1:4-11 contains laws which begin with 'YN BYN...L... 'L'.[51] While we agree with Albeck that these and other units were

---

[46] *Mavo laMishnah*, p. 102.
[47] *Ibid.*, p. 91.
[48] *Ibid.*, p. 88.
[49] *Ibid.*
[50] *Ibid.*
[51] *Ibid.*, p. 89.

collected together because of common phrases, we find no proof that this was done *before* the time of Rabbi. They could have been formed into units *before* the time of Rabbi, *by* Rabbi himself, or *after* the time of Rabbi. The fact that Albeck only considers the first possibility does not eliminate the other two.

Albeck also believes that mishnahs that are taught in conjunction with biblical verses were joined to the verse before the time of Rabbi:

> In truth there are in our Mishnah laws ... that are taught as explanations (PYRWŠ) to the Torah like a Midrash, and the Scriptural passages come joined with the explanation and the Midrash ...[52] These mishnahs certainly (WD'Y) come from Tannaitic schools that ordered the laws together with the passages in the Torah.[53]

M. Ma'aser Sheni 5:10 is an example of this type of mishnah:

> At the time of the Afternoon Offering on the last Festival-day they used to make the Avowal. How used a man to make the Avowal? [He said], *I have removed the Hallowed Things out of my house* — that is Second Tithe and the fruits of Fourth-year plantings: *I have given them to the Levite* — that is the Tithe of the Levites; *and also [I have given them]* — that is the Heave-offering and the Heave-offering of Tithe; *to the stranger and the fatherless and widow* — that is the Poorman's Tithe, Gleanings, the Forgotten Sheaf, and *Pe'ah* (Although these do not render the Avowal invalid): *from the house* — that is Dough-offering.[54]

Albeck views this mishnah as a midrash on Deuteronomy 26:13ff.[55] In order for Albeck to prove this was constructed in a school-house before the time of Rabbi, he must demonstrate that Rabbi *never* taught a law in conjunction with a biblical verse. Albeck never proves this claim. He must also consider the possibility that verses were added in order to amplify the laws after Rabbi had completed his text; Albeck never considers this possibility. He must also establish that certain schools taught their laws in conjunction with biblical verses. He never proves it. He only asserts it as fact.

> If Rabbi found in the collections before him a mishnah in which were joined many laws (DYNYM) which were suitable according to content to other tractates, he returned and taught, in general, the whole mishnah in each tractate. The editor did not rend (QR') the mishnah into decrees and

---

[52] *Ibid.*
[53] *Ibid.*, p. 90.
[54] H. Danby (trans.), *The Mishnah* (Oxford, 1933), pp. 81-82.
[55] *Mavo laMishnah*, p. 89.

he did not fix one decree in one tractate and another decree in another; rather he ordered the mishnah in its entirety, as it was taught in the school-house, in two tractates.[56]

M. Ketuvot 7:7 and M. Qiddushin 2:5 exemplify this type of mishnah. Although Albeck did not present the mishnah in the following chart-form, this is what his analysis implies:

> A. If a man betrothed a woman on the condition that she was under no vow and she was found to be under a vow, her betrothal is not valid.
> B. If he married her making no conditions, and she was found to be under a vow, she may be put away without her *Ketuvah*.
> C. [If he betrothed her] on the condition that there were no defects in her, and defects were found in her, her betrothal is not valid.
> D. If he married her making no conditions and defects were found in her, she may be put away without her *Ketuvah* ....[57]

This same mishnah appears in Ketuvot and Qiddushin. Albeck argues that the mishnah contains laws dealing with two different matters. Parts A and C deal with betrothal while B and D are concerned with the *Ketuvah*. If Rabbi had received each section separately, Albeck claims that he would have placed A and C in M. Qiddushin, and B and D in M. Ketuvot. However, since the whole is repeated in two places because some parts of it do not belong according to the principle of content, Rabbi must have received the mishnah as a whole unit. Albeck does not consider the possibility that the mishnah was ordered in a tractate for a reason other than content. For example, M. Qiddushin 2:5-10 all begin with the same phrase (HMQDŠ).

Albeck contends that if one mishnah is taught in two places but in one tractate it contains a section which is lacking in the other tractate, each version is the product of a separate school-house.[58] M. Yevamot 4:3-4 = M. Ketuvot 8:6-7 is an example of this phenomenon. M. Ketuvot 8:6-7 reads:

> A. If a woman awaiting levirate marriage inherited property, the School of Shammai and the School of Hillel agree that she may sell it or give it away and the act will be valid. If she died, what should be done with her *Ketuvah* and the property that comes in and goes out with her? The School of Shammai say: the heirs of her [deceased] husband share with the heirs of her father. But the School of Hillel say: Her property falls [equally] to them [both]; the *Ketuvah* falls to the [deceased] husband's heirs, and the property that comes in and goes out with her falls into the possession of her father's heirs.

[56] *Ibid.*
[57] Danby, p. 255 and pp. 323-324.
[58] *Mavo laMishnah*, p. 103; *Untersuchungen*, pp. 14-16.

B. If his brother left money, land is bought therewith and he has the use of it. [If he left] produce that was already reaped, land is bought therewith, and he has use of it; if unreaped produce, R. Meir says: 'They estimate how much the land is worth with the produce and how much without it, and with the difference land is bought and he has the use of it.' But the sages say: 'The unreaped produce falls to him, and as for the reaped produce, whosoever comes first gets possession: if he came first he gets possession; if she came first, land is bought therewith and he has the use of it.'

C. But if he [the brother-in-law] had consummated marriage with her, she counts as his wife in all respects save that her *Ketuvah* is a charge on her first husband's goods.[59]

M. Yevamot is the same as the above mishnah, except that part B is missing. Albeck contends that we have two versions of the same mishnah. Each was formed in a different school-house and each was included by Rabbi because he ordered everything that he received.

If we have a mishnah in which certain laws were taught in a different language in two tractates, each version is the product of a different school-house.[60] M. Qiddushin 4:6-7 = M. Bikkurim 1:5 is an example. M. Qiddushin 4:6-7 states:

A. The daughter of a male of impaired priestly stock [and so, too, any female descendant] is for ever disqualified for marriage with priestly stock. If an Israelite married a woman of impaired priestly stock, his daughter is qualified for marriage with priestly stock; but if a man of impaired priestly stock married the daughter of an Israelite, his daughter is disqualified for marriage with priestly stock. R. Judah says: 'The daughter of a male proselyte is regarded as a daughter of a male of impaired priestly stock.'

B. R. Eliezer b. Jacob says: 'If an Israelite married a proselyte, his daughter is qualified for marriage with priestly stock, but if a proselyte married a proselyte, his daughter is not so qualified. A proselyte is regarded as of like standing to freed slaves even to ten generations, until such time as his mother is of Israelitish stock.' R. Jose says: 'Even if a proselyte married a proselyte, his daughter is qualified for marriage with priestly stock.'[61]

M. Bikkurim 1:5 reads:

R. Eliezer b. Jacob says: 'A woman that is the offspring of proselytes may not marry into the priestly stock unless her mother was an Israelite: it is

---

[59] Danby, p. 257.
[60] *Mavo laMishnah*, p. 104; *Untersuchungen*, pp. 27-28.
[61] Danby, p. 328.

all one whether [she is the offspring of] proselytes or freed slaves, even to the tenth generation: [her like may not marry into the priestly stock] unless her mother was an Israelite...."[62]

Albeck claims that we have two versions of the same mishnah; each version teaches the same law, but in different language. He concludes that each version was formed in a different school before the time of Rabbi. Even if we do have two versions of the same teaching, why must each be the product of a school-house? Albeck does not consider the possibility of individuals transmitting laws, combining units, and so on. Everything is the work of the schools. He never attempts to prove this assertion.

Albeck offers other examples of "sources". The above, however, should be sufficient to illustrate his presuppositions and method. Albeck's theory rests on two unproven assumptions: (1) Rabbi ordered the material which he received according to *one* principle — the principle of content; (2) Rabbi did not change any of the material which he received. Both principles are merely stated, and both rest on circular reasoning. (1) We know that Rabbi ordered the material *only* according to the content of the laws because any material not collected according to this principle was formed into units *before* Rabbi received them. We know that they were formed into units in Rabbi's sources, because Rabbi ordered his material *only* according to the content of the laws. (2) Rabbi did not change any of the materials he received, because the sources are not changed. We know the sources are not changed, because Rabbi did not change any of the material.

Most of Albeck's assertions are never proved. He posits the existence and function of Tannaitic schools without ever submitting his claim to criticism. As we have tried to show, each of Albeck's examples of sources which Rabbi had before him can have at least one other interpretation. Perhaps Rabbi formed the units. Perhaps individuals after the time of Rabbi collected sources or added to Rabbi's Mishnah. Albeck accepts without question that Rabbi was the only editor of the Mishnah, that he merely collected the material before him, and that the material did not undergo any changes[63] after Rabbi had collected it.

There is little doubt that the Mishnah is a collection of sources. In fact, it might be the best example of edited sources which has survived from the ancient world. However, Albeck has not proved — he merely

---

[62] Danby, p. 94.
[63] Albeck does recognize the possibility of scribal errors. *Mavo laMishnah*, p. 116.

accepted—the fact that Rabbi was the final editor of the Mishnah. He further accepts the idea that the Mishnah is a unified document in the sense that it underwent one final compilation and editing at the hands of Judah the Patriarch. The diversity of the text is a result of Rabbi's sources; it is not the result of subsequent editings, changes, and so on. Once Rabbi's Mishnah was published, it underwent no further changes:

> Immediately after Rabbi had sufficient time to order the collection of mishnahs from the many school-houses and while he had not yet completed his holy work, his Mishnah was spread among the students and was received in every settlement in Israel. And even though many additions were added to it from many school-houses, the first Mishnah did not move in essence (B'YQRH) and in fundamentals (WBYSWDH) from its place.[64]

I am not sure about the meaning of this paragraph. It comes as an explanation of the fact that the Tosefta and *Beraitot* contain laws which are not found in the Mishnah. For this reason I assume that Albeck is saying that after Rabbi's Mishnah was published, no additions to it and no changes in it were made.

iv

Because the Mishnah contains so many contradictions and repetitions, Albeck does not believe that Rabbi meant it to be a code of practical law (HLKH LM'SH):

> The editor did not take upon himself the task of ordering in his Mishnah chapters of laws intended for practice (HLKH LM'SH), for if [this were his goal] he needed to change the laws and to make from the mishnah of an individual a mishnah of the sages, so that the law would be according to them, and also [he needed] to turn the mishnah of the sages into the mishnah of an individual if he and his court did not decide [a case] according to them [the rulings of the sages], or to add words and to change them according to his opinion.... On the contrary, we see that the editor did not take the power to himself to change the mishnah of his predecessors; rather he fixed the mishnahs as he had received them and he even kept the special marks of his sources.[65]

This statement again rests on the unproven assumption that Rabbi did not alter the material he had before him. How can one claim that Rabbi did not change the material unless we know the state of the material he used?

[64] *Mavo laMishnah*, p. 110; *Mehqarim*, p. 182.
[65] *Mavo laMishnah*, pp. 105-106.

In spite of the fact that we often find the statement that the law follows the anonymous mishnah,[66] Albeck states:

> We find many times, that the Amoraim decided [cases] not according to the anonymous mishnah if it were clear (NTBRR) to them that it was the mishnah of an individual. They did not say: 'Because STM Rabbi is like this, behold he and his court are the majority and the law is according to the majority.' Rather, the Amoraim certainly knew ... that Rabbi did not form the mishnah of an individual into an anonymous mishnah in order to decide the law according to it, but he fixed in his Mishnah anonymous mishnahs, whether they were [the opinion] of an individual or [the opinion] of the majority, because they were taught in this [anonymous] style in the sources which he had before him. And we find that in general he did not intend to have the law decided according to them [the anonymous mishnahs].[67]

As we noted, this view is contrary to the opinion of the early Amoraim. Most of the evidence indicates that the Mishnah was treated as authoritative, as a law code; and that rulings were decided according to the anonymous mishnahs.

Albeck concludes that like ʿEduyyot, the prototypical Mishnah (ʾB MŠNH), the rest of the tractates were compiled because Rabbi feared that the law would be forgotten:

> Even in the days of Rabbi a fear existed (QYYM) that because of the different orders 'a clear law and a clear mishnah would not be found in one place ....' Therefore, Rabbi collected, gathered and ordered the Mishnah.[68]

One wonders, if Albeck had concluded that ʿEduyyot was collected as a law code, would he have concluded the same for Rabbi's Mishnah?

v

Albeck never moves outside the tradition. He never challenges the belief that Rabbi was the final editor of the Mishnah. Therefore he must assume that all the difficulties in our Mishnah are a result of the sources Rabbi used. While he is correct that the Mishnah is a compilation of sources, his method of isolating and analyzing the sources is faulty. It rests on two unproven assumptions. In fact most of Albeck's conclusions are unproven, or at least are open to various interpretations not considered by Albeck. While Albeck reached some acceptable conclusions, he did so in spite of his method.

[66] For example, see C. Y. Kosovsky, *Thesaurus Talmudis* (Jerusalem).
[67] *Mavo laMishnah*, p. 106.
[68] *Ibid.*

CHAPTER FIFTEEN

ABRAHAM GOLDBERG

WILLIAM SCOTT GREEN

Professor Abraham Goldberg was born in Pittsburgh in 1913. In America, he was educated at City College of New York, the University of Pittsburgh, Columbia University, and the Jewish Theological Seminary of America, where he was ordained in 1941.[69] After World War II he went to Palestine and in 1952 received a Ph.D. degree from the Hebrew University, where he is now Associate Professor in the Department of Talmud.[70] His major work to date is a critical edition of and commentary on the Mishnah treatise Ohalot. Since its publication in 1955, he has written a number of articles on various topics relating to rabbinic law and literature, several of them on the Mishnah. His Mishnah articles, for the most part, apply the methods employed in *The Mishnah Treatise Ohalot* (Jerusalem, 1955) to other portions of the Mishnah and attempt to prove that what was true for Ohalot is true for the rest of the Mishnah as well.

Goldberg's importance for our problem rests on the fact that he was trained in Israel, as a student of Albeck, and is the one contemporary Israeli scholar to devote a major academic effort to the study of the Mishnah. His method is marked by a rigorous and impartial attempt to establish a critical and reliable text, attention to variant readings and parallels in other rabbinic literature, heavy emphasis on the legal content of various pericopae, but also by lack of attention to evidence external to rabbinic materials, and the unstated and unself-conscious retention of certain traditionalist views of rabbinic literature. These hallmarks will be noted in our analysis of Goldberg's work. It is important to point out that Goldberg's research is still in progress and consequently many of his theoretical remarks about the Mishnah, by his own admission, remain to be carefully justified. Moreover, since he has not produced a systematic and comprehensive work on the Mishnah as a whole, a total theory of the Mishnah, its origins and

[69] *Register of the Jewish Theological Seminary of America, 1970-73*, p. 52.
[70] *Who's Who in Israel*, 1967.

development, has not evolved. For the most part, his articles consist of brief theoretical statements supported by several examples which, neither individually nor together, are evidently intended as definitive proof. Therefore, we must pay special attention to specific and representative examples in order to outline his method.

i

Goldberg sees the Mishnah as the culmination of several generations of rabbinic teaching, the teaching of each generation having been arranged by its successors. He asserts that the organization of the Mishnah as a book did not begin before Yavneh. The first stratum of teaching, which constitutes the core of the Mishnah, is the teaching of the generation of Rabban Yoḥanan ben Zakkai as arranged by Rabban Gamaliel and his contemporaries. Explanations of, and additions to, the first stratum were made by Eliezer and Joshua, and consolidated as an additional stratum to that teaching by ʿAqiba in his Mishnah. The teachings of ʿAqiba and his contemporaries were added to his Mishnah principally by Simeon ben Gamaliel. The teaching of ʿAqiba's students, which concentrated primarily on the understanding and interpretation of their teacher's words, was added by Judah the Patriarch to the "official Mishnah" and constitutes the final stratum in the Mishnah. Practically *none* of the teachings of Rabbi and his contemporaries is included in the Mishnah; they are found instead in a parallel collection, the Tosefta, arranged by R. Ḥiyya and augmented by R. Oshaya. The presence in Tosefta of so much material dating from the time of Rabbi means that, as a collection, it is chronologically later than the Mishnah. However, Goldberg maintains that Tosefta also contains "strata of teaching of generations preceeding that of Rabbi which did not merit inclusion (SL' ZKW LHYKLL) within the official Mishnah,"[71] most notably, the stratum of the teachings of ʿAqiba's students.[72] The single difference between a stratum in the Mishnah and its chronological parallel in the Tosefta is that "the first is, as it were, more 'official,' in that it is included within the principal collection of Tannaitic teaching."[73]

The reason for the failure of certain teachings to find their way into

---

[71] "Tosefta to Tractate Tamid," *Benjamin De Vries Memorial Volume* (Jerusalem, 1968) pp. 18-42, pp. 18-19.

[72] *Ibid.*, p. 40.

[73] *Ibid.*, p. 19.

the Mishnah is not that the arrangers of the Mishnah over several generations did not know them: "One certainly cannot say that the arrangers of the Mishnah in the various generations after Yavneh to Judah the Patriarch did not know at all any of the immense material of the teaching of R. ʿAqiba and the teaching of his students taught before us only in the Tosefta. It would be strange to suppose that only R. Ḥiyya knew this teaching, and not Rabban Simeon ben Gamaliel, and not Judah the Patriarch."[74] Rather, Goldberg argues, the failure of some materials to appear in the Mishnah depends on the rules for the arrangement of the Mishnah which the editors set for themselves and the special form of each tractate of the Mishnah itself.[75] We shall discuss the former later on. As for the latter, Goldberg tells us that certain Mishnah-tractates are composed of early strata of legal material, principally those which contain much historical description. Other tractates are composed primarily of later strata. Most of the commentary on the early strata is found within the Mishnah itself; although, as we saw, some also appears in Tosefta. Commentary on the later strata, on the other hand, generally appears external to the Mishnah, in Tosefta. The relationship of one stratum to its predecessor is constant, regardless of the collection in which it appears; nor does the method of teaching differ from one stratum to the next. The later stratum is a commentary on, or continuation of, the earlier one. This means that Mishnah-tractates whose external commentaries are relatively small consist of material which is basically early, perhaps in the time up to ʿAqiba's Mishnah. Mishnah tractates with large external commentaries consist primarily of later material.[76] In Goldberg's view, "It is even possible to say that for every Mishnah tractate there are two 'tosafot' — one tosefta which was made an integral part of the Mishnah and another tosefta which remained outside it."[77]

Admittedly, Goldberg has thus far only briefly outlined his theory; yet, even at this stage it is appropriate to note the following observations. It does not give an account of *beraitot* which have no parallels in Mishnah or Tosefta. It does not define the notion of "official Mishnah" nor state its relationship to an "unofficial Mishnah." It presupposes a uniform development of Jewish law in which all members of each generation knew *all* the teaching of their

[74] *Ibid.*, p. 40.
[75] *Ibid.*, p. 40.
[76] *Ibid.*, pp. 40-41.
[77] *Ibid.*, p. 19.

predecessors. Consequently a common background of legal knowledge shapes the framework of later teachings. Only in this way is it possible to account for the strata-system Goldberg envisions. Although he does not try to prove that his schema of strata is applicable to all of Mishnah and Tosefta, Goldberg does attempt to demonstrate such a strata system in a few situations. His method of determining the chronological relationship between passages is crucial, for if such a determination cannot be strongly maintained, then neither can the existence of the strata.

Below is a synoptic table which lists all of the passages considered by Goldberg in one example. Note that in column IV he is only concerned with the order of the limbs of the sacrifice, and not with the pericope as a whole.

I.	II.	III.	IVa.
M. Tamid 3:1	M. Yoma 2:3	Tos. Yoma 1:13 (ed. Lieberman, p. 225, lines 64-71)	M. Tamid 4:3
A. The officer said to them, 'Come and cast lots,'	A. —	A. ,, ,, ,, ,, ,, ,,	
B. — —	B. The second drawing	B. —	
C. who slaughters, who tosses blood who cleans the inner Altar who cleans the Candlestick, who brings up the limbs to the Ramp,	C. ,, ,, ,, ,, ,, ,, and ,, ,, ,, ,, ,, ,,	C. ,, ,, ,, ,, ,, ,, ,, ,, ,, ,,	
D. the head and the foot, and the two forelegs the rump and the foot the breast and the neck and the two flanks the inwards and the fine flour	D. ,, ,, ,, ,, ,, ,, ,, ,, and ,, ,, ,, ,,	D. ,, ,, ,, ,, ,, ,, ,, ,, ,, ,, ,, ,,	1. head and foot 2. two forelegs 2. rump and foot 4. breast and neck 5. two flanks 6. the inwards 7. fine flour

and the Baken Cakes and the wine	„ „ „ „	„ „ „ „	8. Baken Cakes 9. wine
E. —	E. —	E. these (ʾYLW) are words of Simeon, man of Mispeh	
			IVb.
F. —	F. —	F. R. Yosah says; The head and the foot and the two forelegs the breast and the neck and the two flanks the rump and the foot	M. Tamid 4:2-3 head forelegs foot breast neck left flank right flank rump left foot
G. —	G. Said Ben ʿAzzai before R. ʿAqiba in the name of R. Joshua: it was sacrificed according to the way of its walking.	G. „ „ „ „ „ „ „ „	
H. —	H. —	H. the head and the foot the breast and the throat the two forelegs the two flanks the rump and the foot.	
I. they cast lots, he who won, won	I. —	I. —	
J. —	J. Thirteen priests won it	J. Thirteen won it.	

Of passages I and II Goldberg writes the following: "The Mishnah of Tamid is brought here in Yoma in a combination of explanations and comments, and that is generally Tosefta's way relative to quotations from the Mishnah. Our Mishnah in Yoma notes for us, first of all, that

229

the drawing mentioned there in Tamid is already the second drawing. Secondly, our Mishnah in Yoma summarizes for us the number of victors in this drawing, something not done in Tamid. Finally, the Mishnah in Yoma adds the divergent teaching which Ben ʿAzzai transmits in the name of R. Joshua. These are the things which are frequently found in completions of Tosefta to the Mishnah in all places. Our Mishnah in Yoma, therefore, is a *'tosefta'* to Tamid."[78]

Tos. Yoma 1:13 (column III above), supplies, in Goldberg's view, the third stratum. He comments: "This completion of Tos. Yoma to M. Yoma (which is itself a completion to Tamid) comes to teach several things. It brings the language of the Mishnah, not as it is taught in Yoma, but rather, as it appears in its first source in Tamid, and this is to signify that our Mishnah in Yoma is essentially only a quotation from Tamid."[79] The reasoning behind this conclusion seems to be as follows: Tos. Yoma 1:13 is a comment on M. Yoma 2:3 because of its location in the parallel Tosefta tractate. But the fact that it quotes M. Tamid 3:1 and not M. Yoma 2:3 shows that the *source* of M. Yoma 2:3 is M. Tamid 3:1. Goldberg continues, "Secondly, it tells us that R. Simeon of Mispeh, is the anonymous Tanna of M. Tamid here. Third, Tosefta explains to us here the words 'according to the way of its walking,' — the words of Ben Azzai brought in M. Yoma without explanation. And finally, Tosefta brings in a third opinion, that of R. Yosi, on the order of bringing the limbs up to the Ramp."[80]

Goldberg goes on to point out that the order of the bringing up of the limbs to the sacrifice recounted in M. Tamid 3:1 and M. Yoma 2:3 is identical to that stated in M. Tamid 4:3, which, he asserts without explanation, "seems to be the first and original view."[81] The second view is found in Tos. Yoma 1:13 in the explanation of "the way of its walking" of Ben ʿAzzai. The third view occurs in the divergent view of R. Yosi in Tos. Yoma 1:13, which, Goldberg says, "is in agreement with the order of the slaughter of the animal as described in M. Tamid 4:2-3."[82]

---

[78] *Ibid.*, pp. 23-24. The example is on pp. 23-26. On page 24 Goldberg cites Tos. Yoma 5 : 13. It should read Tos. Yoma 1 : 13.
[79] *Ibid.*, p. 24.
[80] *Ibid.*
[81] *Ibid.*
[82] The chart reveals that M. Tamid 4 : 2-3 differs from the order of R. Yosi in Tos. Yoma 1 : 13. Goldberg notes this and says, "Aside from this, that the cutting of the forelegs precedes the cutting of the right foot in M. Tamid v : 2-3 the order of the Mishnah with reference to the slaughter of the animal is the order of the bringing up

The operative rule here seems to be that any passage which adds to, or complements, the legal content of another passage constitutes a later stratum. Legal *content*, therefore, forms the basis for chronological judgment. The weak point in this kind of approach lies in the narrowness of its scope. Even if we accept all of Goldberg's legal observations, without his theoretical framework the evidence cannot sustain his conclusions. We have before us three interrelated passages for which Goldberg has specified certain legal relationships. However, it is one thing to specify the legal relationships and quite another to prove the existence of three *successive* chronological levels of teaching. For this kind of result, one would need to consider certain historical controls, such as named traditions of later tradents; literary evidence and relationships, the precise form and wording of the passages and their relationships to each other; and the overall trend of the literature itself to add details in all cases rather than delete them. The last of the above three elements would require careful documentation. Moreover, we may observe that, if we stand outside of Goldberg's presuppositions, the cases before us seem susceptible to other reasonable explanations. The results of legal investigation alone cannot constitute probative evidence for historical conclusions.

Let us examine another example.

I. M. Tamid 5:2	II. M. Yoma 2:4
A. He said to them	A. — —
B. — —	B. The third lot —
C. 'Those who are new to the incense, Come and cast lots.'	C. „ „
D. — —	D. And the fourth lot —
E. 'The new and the old, come and cast lots to decide who shall bring up the limbs from the Ramp to the Altar.'	E. „ „
F. R.Eliezer B. Jacob says: He who brings up the limbs to the Ramp, he takes them up on the Altar.	F. — —

---

of the limbs which R. Yosi teaches...." (p. 25). *Nearly* identical, in this case, is equivalent to identical.

Goldberg comments here: "Our Mishnah in Yoma adds an explanation to Tamid that the drawing for the incense is the third drawing, and that the bringing up of the limbs from the Ramp to the Altar is the fourth drawing. It does not mention the divergent opinion of R. Eliezer b. Jacob because it does not bother to return to an explicit dispute in Tamid when it has nothing to add to it."[83] This example makes it possible to argue that for the sake of legal amplification and completeness later tradents would reduce a relatively smooth and independently comprehensible passage to a form which makes little sense out of the context of its Mishnah chapter or when taught separately from the passage on which it comments. Moreover, it opens the question of the precise criteria of chronological judgment. In the previous example, the divergent view of Ben ʿAzzai (M. Yoma 2:3) was viewed as an addition to the teaching of M. Tamid 3:1 and used as a justification for placing M. Yoma in a later stratum of teaching. The same was true of the teaching of R. Yosi in Tos. Yoma 1:13 in its relation to M. Yoma 2:3. Yet here, the addition of R. Eliezer b. Jacob is not judged to be a factor. Why does the addition of the number of the drawing constitute a proof for the relative lateness of M. Yoma 2 : 4, and should the addition of the divergent view of R. Eliezer b. Jacob not do the same for M. Tamid 3 : 2? The precise criteria for chronological judgment are nowhere stated. The entire line of reasoning here seems to me circular. Viewed from within the perspective of uniform legal development, the above examples cannot help but demonstrate its existence. The point is, if one approaches the same materials without the above presuppositions, or with no presuppositions at all, they are susceptible to reasonable, alternative explanations. As long as they are, Goldberg's results are not compelling.[84]

ii

We now turn to Goldberg's discussion of Rabbi's role in shaping the Mishnah. He follows Albeck's conclusion that in his organization of

---

[83] *Ibid.*, pp. 27-28.

[84] Goldberg, in part, bases his judgment on the antiquity of Tamid on the conclusions of Louis Ginzberg in "The Mishnah Tamid," *Journal of Jewish Lore and Philosophy*, 1919, pp. 33 f. For a critique of Ginzberg's approach see Herman J. Blumberg, "Saul Lieberman on the Talmud of Caesarea and Louis Ginzberg on Mishnah Tamid," *The Formation of the Babylonian Talmud*, J. Neusner, ed. (Leiden, 1970) pp. 107-114.

the Mishnah, Rabbi intended only to collect, without alteration of either form or content, the different legal teachings of the various houses of study. This means that the Mishnah is a collection of laws, but not a law book intended to provide definitive rulings for specific cases. Goldberg takes his teacher's conclusions one step beyond and argues that Rabbi had a specific purpose in his organization of the Mishnah, which was primarily pedagogic. When Rabbi, "collected, chose, and combined law with law, he never forgot, even for a moment, to teach (without making legal rulings) the best of all that was before him, so that little would contain much and so that the student would study broadly and with ease."[85] The Mishnah, then, was a textbook of various legal rulings, and in arranging it, Rabbi employed all the methods available to a good teacher.

Goldberg discerns six principles of organization used by Rabbi:

(1) According to subject.
(2) According to the ease of explanation (not to introduce tangential issues which were apt to burden the understanding of the issue being discussed).
(3) According to the wealth or multiplication of views and the completeness of explanation (Rabbi tries to include in a chapter or tractate all the viewpoints of the students of 'Aqiba—each viewpoint is placed in a location most suitable to the fullness of explanation and presentation, which prevents the concentration of the viewpoint of any one of 'Aqiba's students in any one place).
(4) According to a linguistic connection, i.e, words or names which resemble each other.
(5) According to sources—therefore the division of Mishnah-chapters is according to issues.
(6) According to insight, novellae, which are inside the legal teaching itself (the law which contains a novella or whose view says more, is chosen, especially in the case of a dispute).[86]

At the outset, we may note that, if viewed from outside Goldberg's presuppositions, the above rules of organization could provide a useful framework for form-critical studies of the Mishnah. Might not the arrangement of different sections of the Mishnah according to different organizational schemes reflect different sources for those sections, rather than the work of one man? We should point out that Goldberg nowhere asserts that all six rules were simultaneously

---

[85] "The Method of Judah the Patriarch in the Arrangement of the Mishnah," *Tarbiz* 28, 1958-59, pp. 260-269. p. 264.
[86] *Ibid.*

brought to bear in any one place, but rather, that throughout the Mishnah, Rabbi employed one or another of them to arrange the material before him. He has not yet demonstrated the ways in which all these rules function in the Mishnah. He has, however, provided us with a few examples, of which we shall examine one which demonstrates rule two, and another which demonstrates rule three.

Goldberg states that M. Git. 1:1 and M. Git. 2:1 show how Rabbi organized his materials according to the ease of explanation.

> If a man brought a bill of divorce from beyond the sea, he must say, 'It was written in my presence, and it was signed in my presence...'
> M. Git. 1:1 (trans. Danby, p. 307)

> If a man brought a bill of divorce from beyond the sea and said, 'It was written in my presence but it was not signed in my presence,' or, 'It was signed in my presence but it was not written in my presence,' or 'The whole of it was written in my presence and a half was signed in my presence,' or, 'A half was written in my presence and the whole was signed in my presence,' it is not valid.
> M. Git. 2:1 (trans. Danby, p. 308)

Goldberg points out that b. Git. 15a notices that M. Git. 2:1 seems superfluous, but nonetheless finds a reason for the presence of both in the Mishnah. He then states that it is difficult to understand why Rabbi simply did not teach M. Git. 2:1 first, thereby rendering M. Git. 1:1 completely superfluous. He says, "From here [the fact that 1:1 precedes 2:1] we see that many times Rabbi duplicated teachings in our Mishnah for educational and pedagogic reasons. His way is to teach first the simple rule and only afterwards to return to the issue to expand it and to include more complicated details."[87]

It is difficult to understand how the explanation that Rabbi went from the simple to the more complex does more, in this case, than simply turn a statement of fact into a reason. M. Git. 1:1 is manifestly less detailed than M. Git. 2:1. Therefore, to assert that Rabbi arranged the Mishnah in some places from the simple to the complex is merely to describe an observed phenomenon; it really does not explain anything. Moreover, we must ask, what is it that Rabbi intended to teach in M. Git. 2:1? What did he want the users of his textbook to learn? Goldberg tells us that Rabbi wanted to give a "good presentation"[88] of the various legal rulings when he arranged the

---

[87] Ibid., p. 266.
[88] *The Mishnah Treatise Ohalot* (Jerusalem, 1955), Introduction, p. 16.

Mishnah. That may be the case, but it is hard to see how one gets from good presentation to carefully arranged textbook. This notion needs careful refinement. Moreover, evidence external to the rabbinic tradition to show that such textbooks were common in the third century would help strengthen this claim. Evidence of this sort is nowhere present in Goldberg's study.

We now turn to a consideration of rule three in Goldberg's list of the organizational principles of the Mishnah. This rule states that Rabbi organized some teachings in the Mishnah according to the wealth of viewpoints. What he means here is that Rabbi intentionally arranged legal rulings so as to include, whether openly or clandestinely, all the viewpoints of 'Aqiba's students about their teacher's rulings. This notion is based on the assumption that everything 'Aqiba's students said was based on his teaching and that their disagreements were within the "broad framework of that teaching" and principally concerned its interpretation.[89] This means that no matter which teaching of which of 'Aqiba's students Rabbi chose to include in the Mishnah, he ordered essentially the teaching of 'Aqiba himself.[90] This assumption is crucial to Goldberg's understanding of the Mishnah, and in order to muster evidence for it, he must identify the teachers of anonymous legal rulings to show that the rulings indeed were the views of 'Aqiba's students. A large portion of his published work has been devoted to his task of identification, because, in Goldberg's view, it is only after identifications of anonymous Tannaim have been made that the Mishnah can be properly understood on its own terms. Just as the failure to maintain a sufficient rationale for the chronological relationship between passages will leave the notion of a strata-system unsupported, so will the failure to provide adequate criteria for the identification of the teachers of anonymous legal rulings render rule three inoperative.

In the following lengthy example, through the use of parallel texts and legal rulings, Goldberg attempts to reconstruct the views (*šitot*) of five of 'Aqiba's students on the issues of the Heave-offering involved in M. Ter. 1:4,8, and 9 and to offer an explanation for the appearance of these versions in the Mishnah. We shall not consider the entire example, but just enough of it to demonstrate Goldberg's method. The following synoptic table lists the full versions of four of the passages

---

[89] "And All are According to R. 'Aqiba," *Tarbiz* 38, 1968-69, pp. 231-254; p. 231.
[90] *Ibid.*, p. 234.

Goldberg considers; however, it does not follow his order of presentation, but rather that of Tos. Ter. 3 : 14. For the sake of convenience, I have divided the Tosefta pericope into two parts, each with its own set of sub-headings, and reversed the order of M. Ter. 1:4 and 1:8 so that they coincide with Tosefta.[91]

M. Ter. 1:8	Tos. Ter. 3 : 14 [Pt. I] (ed. Lieberman, p. 119, lines 50-54)
A. They do not give Heave-offering for oil instead of for pressed olives, nor for wine instead of trodden grapes	A. „ „
B. And if he gave Heave-offering, his Heave-offering is Heave-offering and he will return and give Heave-offering. (TRWMTW TRWMH WYHZWR WYTRM)	B. „ „ it is (TRWMH WYHZWR WYTRWM)
C. The first renders subject to Heave-offering and they are culpable on account of it for the law of the [Added] Fifth.	C. „ „
D. —	D. And it is necessary to take out Heave-offerings and tithes for them.

M. Ter. 1 : 4	Y. Ter. 1 : 8 (40d)[92]	Tos. Ter. 3 : 14 (Pt. II)
1. They do not give Heave-offering for olives instead of for oil nor for grapes instead of for wine.	1. „ „	1. (E) —
2. And if they gave Heave-offering,	2. And if he gave Heave-offering,	2. (F) —
3. —	3. his Heave-offering is Heave-offering and he need not give Heave-offering — the words of R. Meir	3. (G) —
4. —	4. R. Yosi says:	4. (H) —

---

[91] See Saul Lieberman, *Tosefta Kifshutah* (New York, 1955) pp. 331-332.

[92] This reading is not found in printed versions of the Jerusalem Talmud. Lieberman cites it from *Melekhet Shelomo* and accepts it, arguing that the versions in the printed editions were revised to coincide with M. 'Ed. 5 : 2. Goldberg apparently accepts Lieberman's preference since he cites Lieberman's comment on the *baraita*, but not the *Melekhet Shelomo*.

5. The House of Shammai say: The Heave-offering of the grapes and olives is in them. The House of Hillel say: Their Heave-offering is not Heave-offering	5. ,, ,,	5. (I) —
6. —	6. —	6. (J) R. Yosa says: The House of Shammai say: They give Heave-offering. The House of Hillel say: They do not give Heave-offering.
7. —	7. They all agree (HKL) that if he gave Heave-offering, he need *not* give[93] Heave-offering a second time. (S'NW ṢRYK LTRWM ŠNYYH)	7. (K) They agree that if he gave Heave-offering, he must give Heave-offering a second time. (ṢṢRYK LTRWM ŠNYYH)

Goldberg excludes, without explanation, part 7("They all agree ...") from his quotation of Y. Ter. 1:8 *baraita*. He compares this version to M. Ter. 1:4 and concludes that "the anonymous teaching of Mishnah 4 is ... the Mishnah of R. Yosi."[94] To maintain that Rabbi knew that the House-dispute of M. Ter. 1:4 was R. Yosi's teaching, Goldberg must account for its anonymity in the Mishnah. Two possibilities present themselves. Either Rabbi had before him two versions of the same teaching, one named, the other anonymous, and he chose the anonymous version; or, there was a corpus of Yosi-teachings which circulated in anonymous form. However, Goldberg does not deal with this question.

He cites parts 6 and 7 of Tos. Ter. 3:14 as a unit, argues that part 7 refers to the House of Hillel, and states on that basis that M. Ter. 1:8 is the teaching of R. Yosi according to the House of Hillel.[95] If we accept this reading of the passage, it is correct that the view of the House of Hillel coincides with that of M. Ter. 1:8. However, Goldberg fails to note that the linguistic structures of the two passages are very different (TRWMTW TRWMH WYḤZWR WYTRM vs. ṢṢRYK LTRWM ŠNYYH); nor does he include, in his quotation from Tosefta, parts A-C, which repeat *verbatim* the teaching of M. Ter. 1:8. If we

---

[93] In Lieberman's view, this should read, "They all agree that if he gave Heave-offering, he must give Heave-offering a second time (LYTRWM ŠNYYH.)," making it identical with part 7 of Tos. Ter. 3:14 above.

[94] *Tarbiẓ* 38, p. 237.

[95] *Ibid*.

compare the full versions of both passages and follow Goldberg's chronological reasoning, the attribution of M. Ter. 1:8 to R. Yosi becomes highly doubtful, because the Toseftan version bears all the marks of a later stratum. It repeats the legal ruling of the Mishnah and adds the detail about taking out Heave-offerings and tithes (part D) as well as R. Yosa's version of the House-dispute. It could not alone provide sufficient justification for a firm identification of the teacher of the anonymous Mishnah law. So even if we accept all of Goldberg's claims here, his attribution of M. Ter. 1:8 to R. Yosi seems difficult to maintain.

A more comprehensive analysis of the above three pericopae is provided by Saul Lieberman. He argues that Y. Ter. 1:8 is an alternate tradition (*masoret aheret*) to parts 6-7 of Tos. Ter. 3 : 14.[96] Goldberg notes Lieberman's claim and disagrees, saying, "...from the place of the [Toseftan] *baraita* in the order (*siddur*) of the Tosefta, it seems that it is based not on our mishnah [M. Ter. 1:4] but rather on M. [Ter. 1:] 8...."[97] This argument presupposes that the Mishnah and Tosefta are unified documents possessing *exactly* parallel structures, an assumption which requires careful and extensive documentation. Lieberman then states that part 7 ("They agree...") of Tos. Ter. 3:14 does not refer to R. Yosa's House-dispute, but rather to M. Ter. 1 : 4, which *followed* M. Ter. 1:8 in the Mishnah collection before the Tosefta.[98] M. Ter. 1:4 does not appear in Tosefta (as does M. Ter. 1:8 above it) because the Tosefta "taught here the rule of the Mishnah (*din haMishnah*) and therefore skipped over it" and attached it to the House-dispute of R. Yosa (part 6).[99] Lieberman's analysis seems preferable because it takes into account the complete versions of all three pericopae, the literary relationships between them, and the fluid nature of the compilations themselves, as well as legal issues. As we have noted throughout, Goldberg is preoccupied with legal questions, often to the exclusion of other elements of the literature.

In Tos. Ter. 3:16 Goldberg believes he has found the divergent views of two other of 'Aqiba's students to the teaching of M. Ter. 1 : 9.

---

[96] *Tosefta Kifshutah*, p. 331.
[97] *Tarbiz, op. cit.*, p. 237.
[98] *Tosefta Kifshutah*, p. 332, note 54.
[99] *Ibid.* Lieberman also suggests the possibility that a scribe dropped the Mishnah passage here, which is commonplace when Mishnah passages occur in Tosefta.

M. Ter. 1:9
   They give Heave-offering for oil instead of for dried olives and for wine instead of for grapes which are to be made into raisins.

Tos. Ter. 3:16
   A. He who gives Heave-offering for grapes which are for the market which are to be made into raisins, figs which are to be made into dried figs, pomegranates which are to be made into dried pomegranates; it is Heave-offering and he need not give Heave-offering a second time.
   B. R. Eliezer ('LY'ZR) says: The House of Shammai say: One need not give Heave-offering a second time. And the House of Hillel say: He must give Heave-offering a second time.
   (ed. Lieberman, p. 120, lines 61-64)

Goldberg states that the anonymous teaching of M. Ter. 1:9 is, as in M. Ter. 1:4 and 8, also the teaching of R. Yosi according to the House of Hillel.[100] But he brings no evidence to support this claim. He sees in part B of Tos. Ter. 3:16 the teaching, not of R. Eliezer, but rather of R. Eleazar. He states in a footnote, "In all the versions of the Tosefta, the reading here is R. Eliezer ('LY'ZR). But I have no doubt that before us is the divergent opinion of another of 'Aqiba's students, and therefore, one may read Eleazar ('L'ZR).[101] It is possible that this observation is correct, and we shall not dispute it here. It is sufficient to point out that without more justification for his decision to read Eleazar instead of Eliezer, there is no reason to accept this attribution.

In part A of Tos. Ter. 3:16, Goldberg sees the teaching of R. Judah. The reason is that "usually ... he is very close to the teaching of R. Eleazar, who, according to most, is more strict than R. Judah."[102] So, we have moved from assertion, to assumption, to fact. The attributions in this last case do not survive careful scrutiny. Conclusive identification of the teachers of anonymous legal rulings is simply impossible if one concentrates solely on the legal content of the passages. This approach, which bypasses literary and historical aspects of the literature, is able to provide only part of the evidence required for the kinds of results Goldberg envisions.

Goldberg then attempts to reconstruct the views of Eleazar and Judah on the issues of M. Ter. 1:4 and 8. "If in the case of one who gives Heave-offering for oil instead of for dried olives, R. Eleazar teaches according to the House of Hillel, 'He must give Heave-offering

---
[100] *Tarbiz, op. cit.* p. 238.
[101] *Ibid.,* note 10.
[102] *Ibid.,* p. 239.

a second time,' one may assume that in the case of one who gives Heave-offering for oil instead of for crushed olives, which is, *a fortiori*, one degree more strict (BMDRGH 'ḤT YWTR LḤWMR')... R. Eleazar will say that according to the House of Hillel his Heave-offering is not valid, and according to the House of Shammai, it is Heave-offering and he will return and give Heave-offering. And, in the case of one who gives Heave-offering for olives instead of oil, a law which is yet one degree more strict, R. Eleazar will say that his Heave-offering is not valid at all, even for the House of Shammai; that is to say, on this point there is no disagreement between the House of Shammai and the House of Hillel."[103] Using this style of Talmudic reasoning, Goldberg reconstructs House-dispute versions on the *three* mishnahs in M. Terumot for five of 'Aqiba's students. Even if we accept these purely theoretical reconstructions as correct, it is hard to know what it all means.

After he has made the reconstructions, Goldberg asks why Rabbi set (STM) the three Mishnah-passages according to the teaching of R. Yosi. The answer is "in Rabbi's way of arranging, not the entire framework of the teaching, but rather only its central points, from which it is possible to arrive with greater ease at the rest of the teaching. The art in Rabbi's organization is that he places in a minimal formulation (NYSWḤ) of teaching a lesson of maximum meanings. In the framework of our problem, (SWGY'), one finds three different laws in three different situations, according to the House of Hillel, only in the teaching of R. Yosi: in giving Heave-offering for olives instead of oil, the Heave-offering is not Heave-offering; for oil instead of pressed olives, it is Heave-offering and he returns and gives Heave-offering; and for oil instead of olives which are to be eaten, he gives Heave-offering at the outset. And so, by mentioning the dispute of the House of Hillel and the House of Shammai on giving Heave-offering for olives instead of for oil, it is already possible to arrive with ease at the completion of the view (ŠYṬṬ) of the House of Shammai in mishnahs 8 and 9 from R. Yosi's teaching of the words of the House of Hillel alone. Thus, Rabbi brings before us the more variegated view, the more detailed view, the more central view, from which the path to the rest of the teaching is cleared."[104]

The only element of this answer which has any basis in fact is that

---

[103] *Ibid.*
[104] *Ibid.*, pp. 245-246.

House-disputes on the *issues* of M. Ter 1:8 and 9 do not appear in the Mishnah. The conclusion that these two passages are the teaching of R. Yosi according to the House of Hillel is based, in the one case, on partial evidence, and, in the other, on none at all. That Rabbi himself arranged these teachings is the assumption of tradition, not the result of investigation. To say that these House-disputes do not appear in the Mishnah because Rabbi limited himself to the minimal formulation of teachings is speculative, turns the fact of the absence of the House-disputes into a reason for their absence, and does not explain anything. Moreover, it seems to go against Goldberg's assertion that the Mishnah was intended to be a textbook and not a law-code. If Rabbi wanted to teach the views of the House of Shammai on mishnahs 8 and 9, he presumably knew the Houses argued these issues because he had records of such House-disputes before him. If so, it is difficult to understand why, if he wanted to teach them, he deliberately obscured them.

iii

If we review the above examples, we can see the presence of all the characteristics of this method outlined at the beginning of this essay. The emphasis of the research falls entirely on the legal content of the passages. The uniformity of the texts themselves and the development of the tradition are presupposed, never explicitly stated or defended. These presuppositions determine the conclusions and obviate the need for careful consideration and refutation of alternate explanations. This kind of approach is well-suited for the kind of legal studies found in both the *Gemara* and the commentaries, but it is inadequate when applied to the kinds of historical questions which form the framework of Goldberg's research. The fundamental weakness of Goldberg's approach is a failure fully to come to grips with his own supposition that the Mishnah was not intended to be a law-code, but rather a pedagogic collection of legal traditions. As mentioned, Goldberg produces a number of examples. Unfortunately, they do not seem to be able to bear the burden of their own conclusions.

CHAPTER SIXTEEN

BENJAMIN DEVRIES

CHARLES PRIMUS

i

Benjamin DeVries was born in the Netherlands in 1905.[105] In Amsterdam he attended a boys' school, the curriculum of which included classical humanist studies as well as Hebrew and Talmud. At age fourteen he published his first Hebrew article. In 1924 DeVries matriculated at the University of Amsterdam, where he trained in Semitic philology and Islamic history; he received a Litt. Cand. in 1928. Three years later he received rabbinical ordination. Long active in Zionist youth programs, DeVries emigrated to Palestine in 1934. In 1938 the University of Leiden granted him a Litt. Doctorandus. At the age of fifty DeVries entered academic life. In Amsterdam he had taught in Jewish parochial schools, and in Palestine he had served as a principal and then as a superintendent in the religious school system. In 1955 he was appointed lecturer in Talmud at the newly founded University of Tel Aviv. The following year he accepted a similar position at Bar Ilan University. In 1960 the University of Leiden granted him a Ph. D.; his thesis was on the formation of the *Halakhah*. Three years later DeVries was appointed professor of Talmud by both the University of Tel Aviv and Bar Ilan University. He died in December 1966 while on sabbatical in the Netherlands. During his sixty years DeVries published hundreds of articles about education, Jewish religion and folklore, and *Halakhah*.

ii

DeVries is a transitional figure in the modern study of the Mishnah. Unlike many of the individuals discussed in this volume, DeVries received formal training in western European universities. He took two advanced degrees from the University of Leiden; presumably therefore he was familiar with the nature of university scholarship. When

---

[105] Biographical details are taken from "Professor Benjamin DeVries," *Benjamin DeVries Memorial Volume*, ed. E. Z. Melammed, (Tel Aviv, 1968), pp. 5f.

discussing studies concerning mishnaic development, he frequently objects to unscholarly procedures. For instance, in a review of H. Albeck's *Introduction to the Mishnah*, DeVries criticizes "the lack of historical grasp" and

> the ⟨l⟩ack of the modern and scientific instruments of thought and expression, which might elevate an introducti⟨on to⟩ the M⟨i⟩shna⟨h⟩ from the formal point of view ... up to the level of ⟨stu⟩di⟨es⟩ ⟨a⟩s c⟨o⟩mposed for other branches of s⟨c⟩holarly investigation.[106]

DeVries writes that Al⟨bec⟩k's argument proceeds "alm⟨o⟩st ⟨i⟩n a total void." It lacks regard for the "errors, logical fa⟨ults⟩' and incon⟨s⟩istencies" that necessarily inhibit "literary-historical sc⟨hol⟩arship ..."[107] DeVries also observes that the polemical tone and purpose of Albeck's *Introduction* improperly intrudes into the study.

To what extent does DeVries' own work meet the standards of academic scholarship? Despite his university training, DeVries does not critically examine the evidence. He does not ask, What are the sources? What do they mean? Instead he presupposes the validity of the conventional rabbinic view of the Mishnah's formation. Thus he invariably accepts the historicity of Tannaitic and Amoraic assertions. He sometimes questions information added by later rabbinic authorities, but he never steps outside their historical framework. Consequently, in describing *halakhic* development he becomes involved in unevidenced historical speculation. We first shall describe the nature and methodology of DeVries' *halakhic* investigations, then briefly sketch his three-stage theory of post-biblical *halakhic* development, and finally examine his use of evidence.

iii

DeVries published more than twenty-five scholarly articles and book reviews relating to the Mishnah's formation. These articles are divided into three categories:

> (A) Inquiries into the development, or original form, of specific rabbinic concepts, and ideas; e.g. "Development of the [Exegetical] Principles 'General and Specific' and 'General and Specific and General'[108] and "The Dispute" (HMḤLWQT).[109]

[106] B. DeVries, "H. Albeck, *Introduction to the Mishnah*," *Journal of Jewish Studies*, X :3-4 (1959), p. 178.
[107] *Ibid.*
[108] B. DeVries, *Studies in the Literature of the Talmud*, (Heb.) (Jerusalem, 1968), pp. 161-4.
[109] *Ibid.*, pp. 172-8.

(B) Comparisons of Mishnah and Tosefta texts with emphasis on identifying prior sources; e.g. "Mishnah and Tosefta Makkot"[110] and "Toward the Original Form of Several *Halakhot*."[111]

(C) Two long efforts at historical synthesis, "Halakhah" in the *Encyclopedia Hebraica*[112] and "The Formation of the Mishnah" in *A General Introduction to Talmudic Literature*.[113]

Each of these articles proceeds out of the context of DeVries' broader concern for *halakhic* development. He writes that the *halakhah* is "the principal content" of Talmudic literature, of which the Mishnah is one part.[114]

In the review of Albeck, cited above, DeVries elaborates some of his presuppositions. He contrasts two ways of approaching the Mishnah. The first, which he attributes to Albeck, treats "the Mishnah as a book." The second focuses on "the contents of the Mishnah in general."[115] The former is primarily concerned with literary form and the latter with legal content. DeVries cautions that "form and content presuppose each other," and that the two ways of approaching the Mishnah cannot be disentangled. However, he states, "the aims of an Introduction may be either of the two."[116] DeVries chose the second way of approaching the Mishnah. That way confronts problems concerning "the chain of *halakhic* transmission," e.g. dating extra-biblical laws, establishing early forms of halakhot, and distinguishing the relationship of *midrash* to *halakhah*.[117] It leads to a history of *halakhic* development:

> ... Primary concern must be with the *prolegomena* to the Oral Law which has been embodied above all in the Mishnah where it has crystallised out; i.e. ... [it] must present an account of the development of the *halakhah* up to the close of the age of the Mishnah, which obviously constitutes the corresponding landmark.[118]

DeVries thus equates rabbinic *halakhah* with the Oral Torah (TWRH ŠBʿL PH) and postulates an historical development that culminates in the Mishnah.

---

[110] *Ibid.*, pp. 102-8.
[111] *Tarbiz*, (1965), 35: 369-87.
[112] (1960 edition) 14 : 498-529. For the history of pre-Mishnah development, see pp. 512-521.
[113] (Tel Aviv, 1966), pp. 1-63.
[114] *Ibid.*, p. 6.
[115] "Albeck," *idem.*, p. 173.
[116] *Ibid.*
[117] *Ibid.*, p. 174.
[118] *Ibid.*, p. 173.

DeVries recognizes the paucity of extant evidence relating to the state of the *halakhah* prior to the Mishnah's formulation. But he sees this primarily as a hindrance to the full recovery of ancient forms of *halakhot*. He does not consider other possible interpretations of the lack of evidence, for instance, that Pharisaic traditions during the Second Commonwealth had more limited existence and functions than rabbinic traditions had in later periods. He thus considers the formation of the Mishnah as one part of a continuing halakhic process that can be traced back to Biblical times.

DeVries' argument presupposes that different "strata" are reflected in the Mishnah. He uses "literary-historical" procedures to distinguish one stratum from another. He claims to identify "fragments" from halakhic *collections* prior to the Mishnah. By comparing these "fragments" with contemporary materials, which he finds chiefly in Tosefta but also in non-rabbinic sources, DeVries pieces together his history of *mishnaic* development. He assumes that *halakhic* traditions were transmitted through master-disciple relationships, and he then claims that the purposes of pre-*Mishnaic halakhic* collections related to rabbinic instruction. He does not distinguish between pre-70 Pharisaic traditions and post-70 rabbinic traditions. He states that in the Second Commonwealth groups other than the Pharisees, for instance, the priests, had their own collections of *halakhot*.[119] Yet he never specifies the limits of Pharisaic jurisdiction in Jewish life in Palestine.

It now becomes necessary to ask, (1) Does DeVries properly use "literary-historical" procedures to identify pre-Mishnaic *halakhic* collections? (2) Does he establish that men who functioned like post-70 rabbis guided all post-biblical *halakhic* development?

iv

DeVries describes three phases of post-biblical development prior to the "crystallisation"[120] of *Halakhah* in the Mishnah. We shall briefly sketch his entire theory and then examine his evidence for each stage. The first stage begins with the "Period of Ezra" and extends through, and possibly beyond, the "Hasmonean Period." DeVries refers to this phase as the "*Midrashic* Period," because in this era *midrashic* technique functioned as the main vehicle of *halakhic* development.

[119] "Halakhah," *idem.*
[120] "Albeck," *idem.*

Other terms referring to this phase are "Period of the Scribes" and "The Anonymous Period."

The second phase of development begins with a shift away from *midrashic* technique as the principle *halakhic* effort. Abstract *halakhot*, i.e. legal formulations divorced from scriptural references, become the primary *halakhic* unit. *Midrashic* efforts had derived *halakhot* from Biblical verses. *Midrashic* collections had been organized according to the order in which those verses appear in Scripture. DeVries follows conventional rabbinic opinion in alleging that the multiplication of *halakhot* gradually necessitated new, more convenient organization of material. New methods of compilation included grouping *halakhot* that begin with the same number, or contain the same legal formula, e.g. "there is no difference between ... and ... except ..." ('YN BYN ... W- ... 'L' ...). The purpose of these collections was to facilitate the teaching of the Oral Torah. Each collection was called a *mishnah* and reflected the traditions and views of its compiler.

The third phase of development begins at Yavneh with R. 'Aqiba's *mishnah*. 'Aqiba was the first consistently to separate material by rules of logic rather than by external matters of form. In the collections they individually compiled, 'Aqiba's disciples revised texts and legal interpretations. But they all followed the structure of their master's *mishnah*. Rabbi's Mishnah represents the last, and greatest, recension of 'Aqiba's work.

v

The first phase of DeVries' three-stage theory of post-biblical *halakhic* history does not pertain directly to the formation of the Mishnah. However, DeVries' comments illustrate the limitations of his investigation. He notes that the paucity of evidence precludes knowledge about this era. He cites Ephraim Urbach[121] and Yeḥezkel Kaufmann[122] on the lack of historicity of the title, "Period of the Scribes." No evidence indicates the existence of any "school"[123] or group of individuals in the period following Ezra who claimed the title

---

[121] E. E. Urbach, "The Homily as the Basis of the *Halakhah* and the Problem of the Scribes," *Tarbiz*, (1957/8) 27 : 2, 3; cited in B. Devries, "*Halakhah*," *idem.*, 514.

[122] Y. Kaufmann, "Was there a 'Period of the Scribes' ?", *History of Israelite Religion*, (Heb.), (Tel Aviv, 1956), Vol. VIII, 181-5, cited in B. DeVries, "*Halakhah*," *idem*.

[123] Y. Kaufmann, *op. cit.*, p. 484.

"scribe." Kaufmann also notes that in Talmudic tradition (MSWRT TLMWDYT) the term "scribe" refers to men in every historical era. Kaufmann cites both Talmudic tradition and New Testament passages for the use of "scribe" as synonymous with "sage" (ḤKM) with reference to Tannaim.[124] DeVries himself claims that the Mishnah preserves *halakhot* from the "Midrashic Period," but such *halakhot* appear anonymously. They lack formal attributions characteristic of post-Mishnaic rabbinic literature, e.g. " 'Ulla said in the name of R. Yohanan."[125]

Despite these *caveats*, DeVries does make the following historical assertions:

> (1) "Teachers of the people" existed as early as Ezra.
> (2) These teachers used *midrashic* technique to deal with the Oral Torah.
> (3) Collections of *midrashim* existed at an early time.
> (4) Collections of abstract *halakhot* gradually developed.
> (5) Two new communal institutions, the synagogue and the school (BYT MDRŠ), emerged as "the Torah passes from the private to the public domain."[126]

DeVries makes assertion (1) although he admits no evidence exists that any group or individuals claimed the title "scribe". To corroborate (1) and (2) he cites verses in Psalms, Ezra, Nehemiah and Chronicles that relate to the "Period of Ezra." He specifically cites passages in which the terms MBYN and MŚQYL are used synonymously with the term ŚWPR and are contrasted with the term TLMYD, meaning student. His more pertinent examples include, "They cast lots for their duties, small and great, MBYN and ('M) TLMYD" (I Chron. 25:8) and "Jonathan, David's uncle, was a counselor, being a man of understanding ('YŠ MBYN) and a SWPR" (I Chron. 27:32).[127] These examples require neither that MBYN mean teacher nor even that the term refer to men who functioned as teachers. Nonetheless, DeVries alleges that "learned-men-scribes" (MBYNYM SWPRYM) did exist. Furthermore, he quotes Ezra 7:10 to indicate what they taught:

> So Ezra had set his heart to study (LDRWŠ) the Torah of the Lord, and to do it, and to teach his statutes and ordinances in Israel.

Even if DeVries is correct and "learned-men-scribes" did exist, he still

---

[124] *Ibid.*, p. 483, nn. 70-81.
[125] B. DeVries, "Halakhah", *idem.*
[126] *Ibid.*, 513.
[127] "Formation", *idem.* p. 8.

has not demonstrated (2), that their teaching corresponds to the Oral Torah expounded by Tannaim and Amoraim after 70 A.D. The two correspond only from a traditional, rabbinic point of view.

DeVries cites Tannaitic and later rabbinic statements to corroborate (2), (3), and (4). His use of Tannaitic sources will be discussed below (p. 252 ff.) Here we will examine his use of an Amoraic tradition. DeVries states,

> The Palestinean Amora R. Abbahu in y. Sheq. 6:1 thinks, it appears, that already in the Period of the Scribes abstract *halakhot* were formulated according to associative connections, for thus he interprets the verse II Chron. 2:55: "It is written, 'The families of the scribes (SWPRYM) that dwelt in Jabez.' Why does Scripture say SWPRYM except that they prepared the Torah according to numbers (ŠʿŠW ʾT HTWRH SPWRWT SPWRWT), Five kinds may not give heave-offering' [M. Ter. 1:1], 'Five kinds are liable to dough-offering' [M. Hal. 1:1]. 'Fifteen women render their co-wives exempt' [M. Yev. 1:1]..."[128]

DeVries notes with approval Lauterbach's remark that Abbahu interprets a Scriptural verse. The Amora neither transmits an "historical tradition" (MSWRT HYSTWRYT) nor expresses an opinion concerning the "Period of the Scribes." However, DeVries adds,

> But it is clear that [Abbahu] would not have interpreted this way (KK) if he had not seen (HYH RWʾH) also in the Period of the Scribes an ordering effort like this (PʿWLH SDRNYT KZʾT) and seen in it the beginning of the foundation of the Mishnah (RʾSYT YSWD HMŠNH). *And if there is not here an historical tradition, there are here supports for that view* (HRY SMWKYN LHŠQPH YŠ KʾN).[129] [Italics added.]

DeVries seems to imply several things in these passages:

(A) Abbahu's statement does not constitute adequate historical evidence for events prior to his lifetime; and (B) Abbahu's statement constitutes proper evidence concerning his historical views; but (C) Abbahu's historical views constitute proper evidence for events prior to his lifetime. Furthermore, DeVries also implies that the existence of "an historical tradition" would constitute proper evidence regarding events long prior to Abbahu's lifetime. But DeVries does not explain what that "historical tradition" is. If he means a tradition that focuses on historical events rather than on Scriptural exegesis, then he fails to escape the logical gap between (A) + (B) and (C). Such a tradition must be dated, and its reliability regarding prior events must be questioned.

---

[128] *Ibid.*, p. 13.
[129] *Ibid.*

However, if "an historical tradition" is one that attributes statements to properly qualified sources, then DeVries should more clearly specify the limited usefulness of Abbahu's statement.

Finally, scholars generally agree that the synagogue and the school did emerge during the "Anonymous Period" (5). But DeVries offers no evidence to relate the emergence of these institutions to the development of the specifically rabbinic *halakhah.*

DeVries appears to rely upon a "common-sense" understanding of *halakhic* development in lieu of evidence. Thus he dismisses Halevy's theory of the basic formulation of the Mishnah in the time of the Men of the Great Assembly because it "contradicts all historical understanding" (MTNGDT LKL HTPYSH HHYSTWRYT).[130] That is, Halevy does not properly appreciate "that the study of Torah 'for learning and for practicing' was at first connected with reciting the Torah and explaining it and translating it."[131] Apparently according to "common sense," the refinement of the recitation, explanation, and translation required much time and delayed the desire for collections of material not organized according to Scripture.

vii

DeVries asserts that in the second phase of post-biblical *halakhic* development, individual sages compiled *mishnayot* (MŠNYWT). We shall now examine his evidence for three arguments:

> (1) Abstract *halakhic* formulations existed in Second Temple times.
> (2) Collections of such *halakhot* (MŠNH QDWMH ŚDWRH) existed in late Second Temple times.
> (3) Sages at Yavneh compiled their own *mishnayot.*

De Vries demonstrates (1) by referring to formulations in the Mishnah attributed to early masters. He cites M. ʿEd. 8:4 as one example:

> R. Yosi b. Yoʿezer of Ṣeredah *testified* (HʿYD) *concerning* (ʿL) (1) the *ʾAyil-* locust (QMṢʾ) is clean (DKY), and (2) *that the liquids* in the Temple shambles are clean (DKYYN), and (3) that he who touches a corpse becomes unclean (YQRB LMYTʾ MSTʾB). And they called him "Yosah the Permitter" (WQRWN LYH YWSH ŠRYYʾ).
> (M. ʿEd. 8:4; trans. J. Neusner,
> *Rabbinic Traditions,* I:64
> only words in italics are in Hebrew)

[130] *Ibid.*
[131] *Ibid.*

DeVries notes that the formula HʿYD and the appearance of the *mishnah* in this particular section of M. ʿEduyyot established for it "a foothold in a very late time."[132] DeVries means that the pericope's *terminus ante quem* is long after the lifetime of Yosi b. Yoʿezer, because in its present form it appears in ʿEduyyot, to him a Yavnean document. He notes that the use of Aramaic in the pericope suggests, but does not prove, its antiquity. He claims only that the core of the *mishnah* dates to the second century B.C. He identifies the core as the row of "associated" terms, *clean/clean/unclean;* this formulation follows "the style of the ancient essence and the condensed and associative style of the ancient *halakhot*" (HHLKWT HQDWMWT).[133] For this early dating DeVries depends upon the attribution to Yosi. Yet even if DeVries is correct and "the core" of M. ʿEd. 8:4 dates from the second century B.C., he has demonstrated almost nothing about *halakhic* formulations in Second Temple times. He has produced only one, three-word, Aramaic sequence attributed to a person in the second century. No similar evidence exists. For example, he cites Tos Maksh. 3:4 and introduces it as one of the "ancient *halakhot*" transmitted "from approximately the same time as [M. ʿEd. 8:4]".[134]

> Joshua b. Peraḥiah says, "Wheat that comes from Alexandria is [capable of becoming] unclean on account of its bailing machine (ʾNTLYʾ) [which sprinkles water on the wheat]."
> The sages said, "If so, let it be unclean for Joshua b. Peraḥiah and clean for all Israel."
> (Tos. Maksh. 3:4; trans. J. Neusner, *Rabbinic Traditions*, 1:83; ed. Zuckermandel, p. 675, lines 21-3)

What does DeVries mean by "from approximately the same time as [M. ʿEd. 8:4]"? The passage is entirely in Hebrew and exhibits no formal "core" like that of M. ʿEd. 8:4. DeVries can mean only that the saying is attributed to a person who is supposed to have lived in the second century. On the basis of a mere attribution, nothing can be said about the form of the original statement, let alone about its date.

DeVries presents both internal and external evidence to demonstrate that collections (QWBṢY) of abstract *halakhot* existed in late Second Temple times (2). Yet his evidence does not support his conclusion. We shall consider two examples. Chapter five of M. Sheq. lists Temple officers and Temple procedures. DeVries claims that it

---

[132] *Ibid.*, p. 16.
[133] *Ibid.*
[134] *Ibid.*

constitutes a "*mishnah* from a Tanna of that time."[135] To corroborate the authenticity of the material in the list, DeVries cites a reference by Josephus to the name of a Temple officer. The list in M. Sheq, includes the same name. The relevant passages from the two sources follow:

> These are the officers (HMMWNYM) who served in the Temple: Yoḥanan b. Phineas was in charge of the seals ... [ten other officers and their duties] ... the House of Garmu was in charge of the preparation of the Show-bread, the House of Abtina was in charge of the incense, Eleazar was in charge of the hangings, and Phineas was in charge of the vestments.
>
> (M. Sheq. 5:1; trans. Danby, p. 157)

> Furthermore, the treasurer of the temple, by name Phineas, being taken prisoner, disclosed the tunics and girdles worn by the priests, an abundance of purple and scarlet kept for necessary repairs to the veil of the temple, along with a mass of cinnamon and cassia and a multitude of other spices, which they mixed and burnt daily as incense to God...
>
> (Josephus, *Wars*, 3:387-90; trans. Thackery, vol. VI, p. 489)

Josephus identifies Phineas as "treasurer of the temple." The Phineas in M. Sheq. is simply in charge of the vestments. Josephus's Phineas gives "tunics and girdles" to the Romans; but he also gives them other treasures beside vestments. Josephus's account does not "corroborate" the Mishnah. But even if it did, what would be proved? Only that a man named Phineas was a Temple officer in 70 A.D. Furthermore, even if chapter five in M. Sheq. does represent a collection of material from Second Temple times, how does that material relate to rabbinic instruction? It is clear why priests would be interested in lists of Temple officers and Temple procedures. But why would Pharisaic sages have compiled such material? DeVries does not ask this question.

DeVries also states that Tractate Yoma contains fragments of an *halakhic* collection from Second Temple times. He gives several reasons. For instance, "the chapters developed a continuous story,"[136] the instruction of the high priest for his role on the Day of Atonement. However, content does not determine the date of a document. Nor does the fact that a story is told in a continuous sequence indicate the story's date. DeVries does not explicate the form

[135] *Ibid.*, p. 19.
[136] *Ibid.*, p. 20.

or purpose of the alleged collection. Does he mean that such a collection reflects what actually took place? The "fragments" which he cites (1:1,4; 3:2,4; 5:1,3-6)[137] describe Pharisaic masters instructing the high priest. Yet the priests, not the Pharisees, controlled Temple worship and ritual. DeVries does not claim that the "remnants" in Yoma derive from priestly sources. But what then do Pharisaic collections containing fanciful views of Temple practices signify? DeVries does not discuss this problem, because from his (rabbinic) point of view the problem does not exist.

DeVries alleges that masters at Yavneh compiled *mishnayot* (3).[138] He presents inconclusive evidence. He notes that "it is possible" that R. Eliezer b. Hyrcanus had his own "ordered *mishnah*" (MŠNH SDWRH).[139] However, he brings as evidence only the use of the phrase "MŠNT R. Eliezer":

> ... Judah was the son of Ilai, and Ilai was the student of R. Eliezer. Therefore Judah teaches the *mishnah* of R. Eliezer.
> (Tos. Zev. 2:17; ed. Zuckermandel, p. 483, lines 14-5)

But what is the "*mishnah* of R. Eliezer"? Does this saying mean Eliezer composed a *mishnah* like the *mishnah* of 'Aqiba or of Rabbi? Or does it mean simply "teaching of R. Eliezer"? DeVries introduces the statement by noting, "It is known that R. Judah very much loved to quote [Eliezer]."[140] DeVries demonstrates neither that Eliezer had an ordered *halakhic* collection nor that he transmitted it to his disciples. If he had dealt with internal evidence, DeVries might have made a cogent argument for the existence of Mishnah-collections or composites to be attributed to Eliezer. But, unlike Epstein, DeVries does not examine internal evidence.

viii

The final phase of DeVries' three-stage theory of post-biblical halakhic development begins with 'Aqiba's innovations. DeVries alleges,

(1) 'Aqiba introduced logical divisions into halakhic literature.
(2) 'Aqiba's disciples, in their compilations, transmitted the structure of 'Aqiba's *mishnah*.
(3) Rabbi edited the Mishnah.

---

[137] *Ibid.*
[138] *Ibid.*, pp. 26 ff.
[139] *Ibid.*, p. 27.
[140] *Ibid.*

DeVries claims (1) by stating, "There is almost general agreement (M'YN HSKMH KLLYT) about ['Aqiba's] editing work ('L P'WLTW H'RYKTYT)." He demonstrates this by citing "evidence from the period of the Amoraim and from the period of the Tannaim about his ordering work ('DWT MTQWPT H'MWR'YM WMTQWPT HTN'YM 'L P'WLTW HSDRNYT)":[141]

> (A) This is R. 'Aqiba who established (ŠHTQYN) *midrash, halakhot*, and *aggadah*. (y. Sheq. 5:1)

> (B) When R. 'Aqiba ordered *halakhot* for his students (KŠHYH ... MSDR HLKWT LTLMYDYW).
> (Tos. Zab. 1:5; ed. Zuckermandel, p. 676, line 33)

> (C) Rabbi 'Aqiba he called "A well-stocked storehouse." [To what might Rabbi 'Aqiba be likened? To a laborer who took his basket and went forth. When he found wheat, he put some in the basket; when he found barley, he put that in; ... Upon returning home he sorted out the wheat by itself, the barley by itself, ... This is how R. 'Aqiba acted, and he arranged the whole Torah, rings upon rings.
> (ARN, ch. 18, trans. J. Goldin, p. 90)

DeVries afterwards states,

> It appears implied from the foregoing (LK'WRH MŠM' MK'N), that until his days everything (HKL) was still mixed up (M'WRB) and not ordered—just as in truth Albeck thinks—but it appears (KNR'H) that if there were indeed existing collections (SDRYM), *halakhic* and *aggadic midrashim* were mixed together in them.[142]

Thus DeVries admits that the "evidence" yields "implications," not proofs of (1). (C) can be understood only if we have a prior theory of what 'Aqiba actually did. (A) and (C), attributed respectively to Rabbi and to R. Yona, a Palestinean Amora, derive from sources compiled long after 'Aqiba's lifetime. Yet even if we grant that DeVries correctly interprets the implications in these passages, does he therefore correctly identify 'Aqiba's work as a shift in an already long-established *halakhic* enterprise? I think not. The evidence in rabbinic literature overwhelmingly indicates that 'Aqiba did something new. But the nature of what preceded 'Aqiba's innovations is not at all clear. Why does DeVries stress 'Aqiba's role within an already developed *halakhic* tradition? Because DeVries himself

---
[111] *Ibid.*, p. 29.
[112] "Formation", *idem.* p. 30.

remains within the framework established by rabbinic literature.

DeVries alleges that Tosefta and Mishnah contain "fragments" from the *mishnayot* of ʿAqiba's disciples (2). According to this theory, these *mishnayot* were structured like ʿAqiba's. He lists the disciples as R. Meir, R. Judah, R. Simeon, R. Eleazar, Abba Saul, R. Nathan, and R. Simeon b. Gamaliel.[143] Only Amoraic attributions and unexamined Tosefta statements are adduced as evidence. Furthermore, he notes in some cases the "disciple" transmitted significant information from sources other than ʿAqiba. For instance, R. Țarfon, frequently cited material designated "formerly" (BR'ŠWNH) as preferable to ʿAqiba's innovations.[144] DeVries also admits little information exists indicating ʿAqiba's relationship to Nathan, Abba Saul, and Simeon b. Gamaliel. Why then does he list all these men as "disciples" of ʿAqiba? Probably because, in his theory, he postulates the specific result of ʿAqiba's innovations. ʿAqiba allegedly laid the basis for all later rabbinic thinking. From the rabbinic point of view, no one after him could ignore his work. Therefore, all later individuals could be counted as ʿAqiba's disciples. In any case, what effect does this sweeping assertion have regarding the formation of the Mishnah? It only indicates that the Mishnah's editor had many sources from which to choose. As much could be learned from examining the document itself.

DeVries attributes editorship of the Mishnah to Rabbi (3). He notes *prima facie* evidence locates the redaction of the Mishnah in Rabbi's lifetime. Relatively few references to Rabbi and to other men in his and later generations appear in the Mishnah, in contrast to numerous references to men in former generations. Also Rabbi's name and the names of his contemporaries appear considerably more frequently in *beraita* literature. DeVries further notes that early Amoraic traditions unanimously assign editorship to Rabbi.[145] The rest of DeVries' discussion of Rabbi's editorship proceeds within the rabbinic frame of reference. He examines Mishnah passages and compares them with Toseftan statements to determine Rabbi's editorial procedures.[146] He quotes Sherira Gaon's statement that "the whole world saw the beauty of our Mishnah's structure and language,"[147] and then he lists five

---

[143] *Ibid.*, pp. 39 f.
[144] *Ibid.*, p. 43.
[145] *Ibid.*, p. 50.
[146] *Ibid.*, p. 52.
[147] *Ibid.*, p. 55.

editing principles that distinguish Rabbi's Mishnah from Tosefta.[148] DeVries also asks why the Mishnah contains opinions that Rabbi opposed. He answers that Rabbi intended the Mishnah not to be merely "a book of positive law but rather a collection (QWBṢ) that wants [intends] (ŠRWŠH) to give a summary of the whole tradition."[149] These are familiar contortions. They result from the discrepancy between the literary problems of the Mishnah and the traditional attribution of editorship to Judah the Patriarch. The document itself reflects several different, and unreconciled, editorial concerns. Yet if it underwent a final, sustained redaction, why were these obviously different editorial tendencies not obliterated? Does the Mishnah reveal a sustained editorial process, such as is assigned to Rabbi? Can the evidence actually prove or disprove Rabbi's editorship? DeVries does not step out of the traditional rabbinic framework to ask these questions.

ix

It is essential to DeVries' thesis to prove, first, that collections of *halakhot* existed prior to the Mishnah, and second, that such collections were transmitted from generation to generation. He proves neither. He makes inadequate use of "literary-historical" techniques, and he uncritically accepts statements in his "historical" documents. He recognizes these faults in the work of others, but he does not overcome them in his own work. He advocates modern scholarly standards, but he retains the traditional rabbinic frame of reference of Frankel and Sherira Gaon. He seems much like David Hoffman — a transitional figure.

---

[148] "1. The Mishnah contains much less *midrash halakhah* than does Tosefta.

"2. The portion of *Aggadah* is smaller than in Tosefta. The arranger of the Mishnah placed in his composition (QBL LTWK HBWRW) neither *aggadic midrashim* nor many *aggadic* or ethical sayings (MRBYT M'MRY H'GDH WHMWSR].

"3. When there exist two versions of the same *halakhah* in the Mishnah and in Tosefta (or another *baraita* mentioned in the Talmud), the version in the Mishnah is always shorter; and even if we assume that it was not Rabbi who shortened it, but that he found two versions in front of him, in any case he chose the shorter version.

"4. Many examples, explanations and definitions are found in Tosefta that are not in the Mishnah, and it is difficult to say that they were not known to the arranger of the Mishnah (ŠL' HYW LPNY MSDR HMŠNH).

"5. Many stories that come to strengthen the *halakhah* or from which the *halakhah* was created (HRBH M'ŚYM HB'YM LḤZQ 'T HHLKH 'W ŠMHM NWSRH HHLKH), are not mentioned in the Mishnah but are found in Tosefta; and even historical stories are always mentioned more concisely than in the Tosefta." *Ibid.*

[149] *Ibid.*, p. 54.

BIBLIOGRAPHY

— —, "Entstehung und ursprünglicher Inhalt des Tractates Abot," *Jahrbücher für jüdische Geschichte und Literatur* 7, 1885, pp. 1-17. Avot different from rest of Mishnah. Mishnah a product of the Pharisees. Bases of tradition which traces tradition back to Moses. Placed next to Sanhedrin because it validates the authority of the Sanhedrin. Gives analysis of formation of the text. Recounts the history according to Abot 1-2. Redaction initially began in time of Eleazar b. ʿAzariah. Finished in the time of R. Gamaliel 3rd.

— —, — —, *Kerem Ḥemed*, 4, 1839, pp. 204-239. Studies and notes on *Seder Tannaim and Amoraim*; Principles, order and chronology (especially of Rabbi).

— —, — —, *Kerem Ḥemed* 5, 1841, pp. 170-197. M. ʿEd.; esp. M. ʿEd. 1:5,6.

— —, — —, *Kerem Ḥemed* 7, 1843, pp. 157-205. On Rabbi's writing of the Mishnah, pp. 157-158. Rav brought Mishnah text to Babylonia, pp. 158-160. Recensions of Mishnah. Lost Recension. Post-Rabbi additions to the Mishnah, pp. 160-167. Soṭah, pp. 204-205.

— —, — —, "Recensionen: *Einleitung in den Talmud* von Hermann L. Strack;" *Jahrbücher für jüdische Geschichte und Literatur* 9, 1889, pp. 153-4. A handbook.

— —, "Recensionen: *Erste Mischna und die Controversen der Tannaim. Ein Beitrag zur Einleitung in die Mischna* von Dr. D. Hoffmann," *Jahrbücher für jüdische Geschichte und Literatur* 7, 1885, pp. 96-99. Views Mishnah as an historical-literary creation.

Adler, Lipman, "Mishnah Avot," (Hebrew) *Bet Talmud* 4, 1884, p. 173. Mishnah Avot 1:3.

Albeck, Ḥ. *Introduction to the Mishnah [Mavo LaMishnah]* (Hebrew) (Jerusalem, 1959).

— —, *Introduction to the Talmuds* (Hebrew) (Tel-Aviv, 1969).

— —, "On Commentaries of the Six Orders of the Mishnah," (Hebrew) *Sinai* 45, 1960, pp. 204-212.

— —, "Readings of the Mishnah of the Amoraim," (Hebrew), *Chajes Memorial Volume* (Vienna, 1933), pp. 1-28.

— —, *Shishah Sidré Mishnah. Seder Qodashin* (Jerusalem, 1956). *Seder Moʿed* (1952). *Seder Nashim* (1954). *Seder Neziqin* (1953). *Seder Toharot* (1958). *Seder Zeraʿim* (1957).

— —, *Studies on Beraita and Tosefta and their Relationship to the Talmud (Meḥqarim baBeraita veTosefta veYaḥasan laTalmud)* (Hebrew) (Jerusalem, 1944).

— —, *Untersuchungen über die Redaktion der Mischna* (Berlin, 1936).

Allony, Nehemiah. "A Section of Mishnah with Palestinian Punctuation" (QṬʿ MŠNH ʿM NYQWD ʾRṢ-YSRʾLY), *Hanokh Albeck Jubilee Volume (SPR HYWBL LRBY ḤNWK ʾLBQ)* (Jerusalem, 1963), pp. 30-40. MSS. from sixth to tenth century; includes M. B.B. 4:8-5:11 and M. Sanh. 6:4-7:4.

Auerbach, Benjamin, *The One who looks upon Darkhé HaMishnah* (HaṢofé ʿal *Darkhé HaMishnah*) (Frankfurt, 1861). Worried about effect of Frankel's book on the Reform movement. Criticizes Frankel for using the Palestinian Talmud. Argues that all the versions of any story in the Talmud are true because there are different episodes.

BIBLIOGRAPHY

Baniel, Jacob, "Clarification of the Mishnah" (Hebrew), *Sinai* 20, 1945, pp. 153-54. Explains M. Ḥul. 5:1-2.

Bassfreund, J., "Zur Redaktion der Mischna," *MGWJ* 51, 1907, pp. 291-322, 429-444, 590-608, 678-706. A combination of Frankel and Brüll.

Bieberfeld, Shraga, "Form of the Mishnah in its Essence" (ṢWRT HMŠNH BYSWDH), *Halevy Memorial Volume,* (Bné-Braq, 1964), pp. 210-213. Follows Halevy's theories.

Blau, Ludwig, "Tosefta, Mischna et Baraita," *REJ* 67, 1914, pp. 1-23. An excellent critical review pointing out the errors of Zuckermandel's theories. Notes that Amoraim in Babylonia may have made changes, but most appear in *beraitot.* PT also contains many *beraitot*, which points to changes for the times. History knows nothing of the full scale redaction of Tosefta to form the Mishnah by the Amoraim in Babylonia. When did this redaction occur? Zuckermandel offers no answer. Even in the redacted Mishnah there remained many cases in opposition to Babylonian practice. Why? Terminology is not Babylonian. There are Palestinian tractates which lack *Gemara.* What *evidence* is there for the elimination of material in Tosefta to make it appear as a supplement to the Mishnah? The Palestinian Talmud is largely based on Mishnah and not Tosefta. Blau examines specific texts, compares the parallel sources, notes earlier and later versions in order to show that the Tosefta is not the original Mishnah. Amoraim in both Palestine and Babylonia used the Mishnah and may have made only minor changes in the text.

Bleichrode, Avraham Y., "Rambam's Commentary on the Mishnah (M. San. chaps. 6-7) in the Arabic Original with a Critical Hebrew Translation and Notes" (PRWŠ HMŠNH LHRMBM (MSKT SNHDRYN PRQ 6-7) BMQWRW H'RBY 'M TRGWM 'BRY MTQWN WH'RWT), *Kook Memorial Volume,* (Jerusalem, 1937), Vol. III, pp. 3-43.

Bloch, Renée, "Écriture et Tradition dans le judaisme—Aperçus sur l'origine du Midrash," *Cahiers Sioniens* 8, 1954, pp. 1-34.

——, "Midrash," *Supplément au Dictionnaire de la Bible* 5, cols. 1263-1280.

Brüll, Nehemia, "Begriff und Ursprung der Tosefta," *Jubelschrift zum... L. Zunz,* (Berlin, 1884), pp. 92-110.

——, "The Dispute between the Pharisees and the Sadducees concerning the Red Heifer," (Hebrew) *Bet Talmud* 1, 1881, pp. 240-5, 270-8.

——, "Explanation of M. Meg. 4:10," (Hebrew) *Bet Talmud* 2, 1882, pp. 46-8.

——, "Explanation of M. Shab. 16:1; M. 'Arak. 9:4," (Hebrew) *Bet Talmud* 4, 1884, pp. 74-5.

Brüll, Jacob, *Introduction to the Mishnah (Mavo haMishnah)* (Hebrew) (Frankfurt-am-Main, 1876), Vols. I-II. (Reprint - Maqor: Jerusalem, 1971).

Büchler, Adolf, "An Interpretation of M. Shab. 23:5, 'They may make ready all that is needed for the dead, and anoint it and wash it,'" (PYRWŠ HMŠNH ŠBT 23:5, 'WŚYN KL ṢWRKY HMT SKYN WMDYḤYM 'WTW), *Samuel Krauss Jubilee Volume* (Jerusalem, 1936), pp. 36-54. Burial practices.

Chayes, Z. H., *The Student's Guide through the Talmud* (London, 1952).

Cohen, Boaz, *Mishnah and Tosefta Shabbat* (New York, 1935). Includes an introduction to the formation of the Mishnah. Cohen states that Rabbi intended the Mishnah to be "a guide to practice" (p. 17). Following Brüll, Hoffmann, and Halevy, Cohen deals with such questions as, what was the nature of Mishnah-collections in the time of the Second Temple? What roles did 'Aqiba and Meir play in the development of the Mishnah? How did Rabbi arrange the Mishnah?

BIBLIOGRAPHY

Cohen, David, "Man in the Mishnah" ('DM BMŠNH), *Herzog Memorial Volume*, (Jerusalem, 1962), pp. 534-544. Use of the term 'DM in *Seder Mo'ed*.

Cohn, T., "Aufeinanderfolge der Mischnaordnungen," *Jüdische Zeitschrift für Wissenschaft und Leben* 4, 1886, pp. 126-140.

Derenbourg, J., "Les sections et les traités de la Mischnah," *REJ* 3, 1881, pp. 205-210.

DeVries, Benjamin, Review of *The Mishnah Treatise Ohalot*, (Hebrew) *Tarbiz* 25, 1955-56, pp. 237-242.

——, *A General Introduction to Talmudic Literature (MBW' KLLY LSPRWT HTLMWDYT)* (Hebrew) (Tel Aviv, 1966). Includes a discussion of the historical development of Mishnaic literature.

——, *Introduction to the Talmud and the Halakhah* (Hebrew) *(MBW' LTLMWD WLHLKH)* (Tel Aviv, 1965). Includes a history of the development of the literature.

——, "Mishnah and Tosefta: Bava Meṣi'a'" (Hebrew), *Tarbiz* 20, 1920-21, pp. 79-83.

——, "The Mishnah and Tosefta of Makkot" (Hebrew), *Tarbiz* 26, 1956-57, pp. 225-261.

——, "The Mishnah and Tosefta of Tractate Me'ilah" (Hebrew), *Tarbiz* 29, 1959-60, pp. 229-49.

——, *Studies in the Development of the Talmudic Halakhah (TWLDWT HHLKH HTLMWDYT)* (Hebrew) (Tel-Aviv, 1962). Discussions regarding the development of halakhic concepts, e.g., positive and negative commandments, and the relationship between Tannaitic and Amoraic materials.

——, *Studies in the Literature of the Talmud (MHQRYM BSPRWT HTLMWD)* (Hebrew) (Jerusalem, 1968). Collected essays relating to specific exegetical and historical problems in Tannaitic and Amoraic literature.

Dobschütz, L., "Fränkel's *Einleitung in die Mischna*," *MGWJ* 45, 1901, pp. 262-78. Summarizes the major points and the reaction to its publication. Frankel had a tremendous influence on the historical work that followed him.

Dünner, J. H., "R. Juda Hanasi's Antheil an unserer Mischnah," *MGWJ* 21,1872, pp. 161-178, 218-235.

——, "Veranlassung, Zweck, und Entwickelung der halakhischen und halakhisch-exegetischen Sammlungen," etc. *MGWJ* 1871, pp. 137ff., 313ff., 363ff., 416ff., 449ff.

Epstein, Y. N., "Addenda to 'The Sages say,'" (Hebrew) *Tarbiz* 14, 1942, pp. 75-76.

——, "Addenda to 'The Sages say,'" (Hebrew) *Tarbiz* 15, 1943, p. 64.

——, "An Arabic Translation of Mishnayot" (TRGWM 'RBY ŠL MŠNYWT), *Alexander Marx Jubilee Volume* (New York, 1950), pp. 23-48. M. 'Ed. 5:6; M. Kel. 5:6-6:1, 7:1-5, 27:1-7, 28:2-6.

——, *Commentaries of R. Judah b. Natan to Ketuvot* (Hebrew) (Vienna and Jerusalem, 1933).

——, *Commentary of the Geonim on Seder Ṭoharot* (German introduction) (Berlin, 1915; Hebrew ed., introduction, and text: Berlin, 1921-1924).

——, "HaMada' HaTalmudi Vaṣorkhav," (Hebrew) *Proceedings of the Academy of Jewish Studies* 2 (Jerusalem, 1935), pp. 5-22.

——, "He who Taught This Has Not Taught This," (Hebrew) *Tarbiz* 7, 1936, pp. 143-58; 245.

——, *Introductions to Tannaitic Literature* (Hebrew) (Jerusalem, 1957).

——, *Introduction to the Text of the Mishnah* (Hebrew) (Jerusalem, 1948; 1964²).

——, "M. Kelim 24," (Hebrew), *Louis Ginzberg Jubilee Volume*, ed. S. Lieberman et al. (N.Y., 1946), pp. 67-74.

— —, "Mishnaic and Babylonian Aramaic," (Hebrew) *Lešonenu* 15, 1947, pp. 103-07.
— —, "On the Mishnah of R. Judah" (Hebrew), *Tarbiz* 15, 1943-44, pp. 1-13.
— —, "On Terms of the Naziriteship," *Magnes Anniversary Book*, ed. Baer, et al. (Jerusalem, 1938), pp. 10-16.
— —, " 'The Sages Said' ('MRW ḤKMYM), *Studies in Memory of Asher Gulak and Samuel Klien* (Hebrew) (Jerusalem, 1942), pp. 252-261. Variations in the use of the formula 'MRW ḤKMYM.
— —, "Ziqin und Ruḥot," *MGWJ* 63, 1919, pp. 15-19.
— —, "Zur Babylonisch-Aramäischen Lexikographie," *Festschrift Adolf Schwartz*, ed. S. Kraus (Berlin and Vienna, 1919), pp. 317-27.
Falk, M., "The meaning of Tos. Ber. 6:25," (Hebrew) *Bet Talmud* 1, 1881, p. 83.
Falk, Zeev, "From the Mishnah of the Pious Ones" (MMŠNT ḤSYDYM), *Benjamin DeVries Memorial Volume* (Hebrew) (Jerusalem, 1968), pp. 62-69. Attributes passages in Mishnah and Tosefta to the "ancient pious ones" and dates the passages to Hasmonean times and earlier.
Feldblum, Meyer S., "Professor Abraham Weiss: His Approach and Contribution to Talmudic Scholarship," *The Abraham Weiss Jubilee Volume* (New York, 1965), English, pp. 7-80; Hebrew, pp. 13-72.
Feunn, Samuel, "Explanation of Several Mishnayot," (Hebrew) *Kenesset Yisra'el* 2, 1887, pp. 2-27. On the basis of the interpretations of medieval commentaries.
Finkelstein, Louis, "The Antiquity of M. Sheq. 1:5," *Benjamin DeVries Memorial Volume* (Jerusalem, 1968), pp. 43-61. Differences regarding Jews and gentiles.
Francus, Israel, "On the Explanation of Several Mishnahs" (Hebrew), *Sinai* 66, 1969-70, pp. 292-302. Explains M. Ket. 1:3,6,7.
Fränkel, Zecharias, "Anzeigen *Darkhé HaMishnah*," *MGWJ* 8, 1859, pp. 276-82. Review of his own book.
— —, *Darkhé HaMishnah* (Leipzig, 1859).
— —, "Erklärung die Schrift, *Hodogetica in die Mischna* Betreffend," *MGWJ* 10, 1861, pp. 159-60.
— —, Geist der Palästinensischen und Babylonischen Hagada," *MGWJ* 2, 1853, pp. 388-98. Mekhilta has some early halakhic material, which was left out of the Mishnah.
— —, "Lapidarstil der talmudischen Historik," *MGWJ* 2, 1853, pp. 203-22, 402-21. Contains the same material as appears in *Darkhé HaMishnah* concerning the period of the scribes and the Pharisees.
— —, "Nachwort des Herausgebers," *MGWJ* 17, 1868, pp. 181-2. Use of the term 'M KN in the Mishnah. Notes additions to the text after the time of Rabbi. There is a development in the text.
— —, "Die Redaction der Mischna schriftlich," *MGWJ* 11, 1862, pp. 272-4. Whether Mishnah was oral or written — different views. Redaction points to a written text. Aim of redactors is to lighten the process of looking for the law. If it was not written, how would the redactor support his opinion? Errors point to a written text.
— —, "Traditionelle Erklärung der Mischna und des Talmuds," *MGWJ* 11, 1862, pp. 274-5. Talmud was originally arranged in mnemonic patterns. There was an oral tradition or commentary on the written text. Rabbi wrote the law in a short form because an oral commentary existed from the time of Meir's Mishnah onwards.
— —, "Wissenschaftliche Aufsätze zum Tractat Abot," *MGWJ* 7, 1858, pp. 419-30. Analysis of the order and formation of M. Avot. It is the history of the early period.

QBL means to receive the *leadership* of the Sanhedrin. Important for both history and ethics. Chapter 5 probably redacted by R. Nathan, since its form is different from the other chapters. Rabbi had a plan in organizing the tractate.

— —, "Zum Mischnatext," *MGWJ* 12, 1863, pp. 71-2. Shows difference in versions of M. Tamid 3:8 and y. Suk. 5:3. Also comments upon the order of tractates of *Zeraʿim* and *Toharot*.

— —, "Zur Kritik des Mischnatextes," *MGWJ* 12, 1863, pp. 310-2. Argues for written character of Rabbi's Mishnah based on M. Ber. 7:3, change of word ŠKY to ŠNY in Talmud. Also studies M. M.S. 2:3 and its parallel in the Talmud. Palestinian version changed on the basis of Tosefta.

— —, "Zur Kritik des Mischnatextes," *MGWJ* 13, 1864, pp. 71-2. Most errors in versions caused by copyists. Re M. Pe'ah 1:6 of Palestinian Talmud. M. Ma. 1:1, M. Ber. 8:7, M. Ket. 1:1 show how changes were made on the basis of late additions.

— —, "Zur Kritik des Mischnatextes," *MGWJ* 13, 1864, pp. 395-7. M. Demai 1:1, M. Abot 2:10. Analysis of the texts based on the Palestinian Talmud and ARN.

— —, "Zur Textkritik der Mischna," *MGWJ* 10, 1861, pp. 431-2. Comparative study of texts.

Friedman, Shamma, "The 'Law of Increasing Members' in Mishnaic Hebrew," (Hebrew) *Lešonenu* 35, 1971, pp. 117-129.

Friedman, Simeon, "M. B.Q. 2:1,4," (Hebrew) *Bet Talmud* 3, 1883, pp. 331-2.

— —, "M. B.Q. 4:1," (Hebrew) *Bet Talmud* 3, 1883, pp. 376-7.

Gandz, Solomon, "Kritische Studien über das Verhältnis der Mišna zu den anderen tannaitischen Quellen," *Festschrift Adolf Schwarz* (Vienna, 1917), pp. 247-57.

Geiger, Abraham, "The Conflict between the Pharisees and the Saducees," (Hebrew) *Hehalus* 6, 1861, pp. 13-30. The Pharisees come from the time of Ezra. They were innovators on the law and issued *taqqanot* in order to adjust the law to their times. The Mishnah contains only the Pharisees' traditions. Rabbi in organizing the Mishnah had to work with many different versions. In Babylonia the Mishnah was modified for the conditions in that country. Continual modification by the BT on the PT and *vice versa*. Many textual corruptions. The Tosefta is badly corrupted and the Mishnah we have is not that of Rabbi. Many changes made in the law so that it would be easier for people to observe the law. Implies the same sort of changes should now be made in the law. A polemical article.

— —, "Einiges über Plan und Anordnung der Mischna," *Wissenschaftliche Zeitschrift für jüdische Theologie* 2, 1836, pp. 474-92.

— —, "Male (ZKWR) as Defined in Mishnah . . .," (Hebrew) *Kerem Hemed* 9, 1856, pp. 19-26.

— —, — —, *Kerem Hemed* 5, 1841, 99-104. M. Sot. 9:5.

Gelbhaus, S., *R. Jehuda Hanasi und die Redaction der Mischna* (Vienna, 1876).

Gilat, Y., "Understanding the Mishnah" (Hebrew), *Sinai* 43, 1958, pp. 401-18. Explains M. Ber. 1:1-2.

Ginzberg, Louis, "The Mishnah Tamid," *Journal of Jewish Lore and Philosophy* I, 1,2,3,4, 1919, pp. 33ff. See *Formation of the Babylonian Talmud*, pp. 107-114.

— —, "On the Relationship between the Mishnah and the Mekhilta," *Studies in Memory of Moses Schorr, 1874-1941* (New York, 1944), pp. 57-95. Many passages compared and chronological relationships considered.

— —, "Zur Entstehungsgeschichte der Mischnah," *Festschrift zum . . . David Hoffmann* (Berlin, 1914), pp. 311-45. Investigation of the 'YN BYN formula.

BIBLIOGRAPHY

Glatzer, N. N., *Untersuchungen zur Geschichtslehre der Tannaiten* (Berlin, 1933).
Goldberg, Abraham, "And All Are According to R. 'Aqiba" (Hebrew), *Tarbiz* 38, 1968-69, pp. 231-254.
— —, *The Mishnah Treatise Ohalot* (Hebrew) (Jerusalem, 1955).
— —, "The Method of Judah the Patriarch in the Arrangement of the Mishnah" (Hebrew), *Tarbiz* 28, 1958-59, pp. 260-69.
— —, "Tosefta to Tractate Tamid" (Hebrew), in *Benjamin DeVries Memorial Volume* (Jerusalem, 1968), pp. 18-42.
— —, "The Use of the Tosefta and *Beraita* of the School of Samuel by the Babylonian Amora Rava for the Interpretation of the Mishnah" (Hebrew), *Tarbiz* 40, 1970-71, pp. 144-157.
Goldenberg, Samuel L., — —, *Kerem Hemed* 6, 1841, pp. 50-53. M. 'Ed. 1:5.
Graetz, Heinrich, *Divré Yemé Yisra'el, Vol. II* (Hebrew: S. P. Rabinowitz) (Warsaw), 1907).
— —, *History of the Jews* (Philadelphia, 1956) Vol. II.
Gruebert, David, "Explanation of M. Ned. 2:1," (Hebrew) *Bet Talmud* 5, 1885, pp. 362-8.
Guttmann, A., "The Problem of the Anonymous Mishnah," *HUCA* 16, 1941, pp. 137-155.
— —, "Das Problem der Mišnaredaktion aus den Sätzen Rabbis in Mišna und Tosephta synoptisch beleuchtet," *Festschrift zum 75 jährigen Bestehen des jüdisch-theologischen Seminars*, ed. I. Band (Breslau, 1929), pp. 95-130.
— —, *Rabbinic Judaism in the Making: The Halakah from Ezra to Judah I* (Detroit, 1971). Guttman argues (p. 240) that Rabbi's Mishnah was different from those of other sages, "which were works of individual sages, who considered exclusively or predominantly the views and traditions of their own respective schools." Judah's Mishnah was to be "acceptable to the various local academies ... and thus to work toward the unification of Jewish life." On the basis of comparison with the Tosefta, Guttman concludes that "Judah's intention was to create a code of more important laws and to include also some basic traditions and beliefs. For this reason he reduced greatly the contents of his *Vorlagen* by following redactional steps: omission or abbreviation of numerous details such as definitions, exegeses, examples, generalizations, reasons for certain laws, and actual cases, omission of the historical background of a number of *Halakhot*, and a shortening of many background stories or reports. The Mishnah often reduces the number of different opinions uttered in a controversy, and also shortens the retained parts of the controversies, mostly giving just the views, but not the arguments, or, if given, abbreviating the arguments. Most significant are the numerous instances in which the Mishnah omits the entire controversy and gives but one view in anonymous form, or where the Mishnah omits the author or transmitter of a law." On p. 243 he argues, "The best proof that Judah did not intend to make a mere collection of traditions, or to write a personal Mishnah, is the fact that most of Judah's own views are not included in the Mishnah, neither in anonymous form nor explicity. This tells us unequivocally that Judah in redacting the Mishnah accepted the majority view even if it opposed his own."
Hakohen, Shalom, "Correction of Tos. Ber. 6:25," (Hebrew) *Bet Talmud* 1, 1881, p. 53.
Halevy, Abraham, "The Meaning of Tos. Ber. 6:25," (Hebrew) *Bet Talmud* 2, 1882, pp. 62-3.
Halevy, V. I., *Dorot HaRishonim Ic* (Frankfurt A.M., 1906; reprint: Jerusalem, 1967).
— —, *Dorot HaRishonim Id* (Bené Braq, 1964; reprint: Jerusalem, 1967).

― ―, *Dorot HaRishonim Ie* (Frankfurt A.M., 1918; reprint: Jerusalem 1967).
― ―, *Dorot HaRishonim IIa* (Frankfurt A.M., 1901; reprint: Jerusalem, 1967).
Halivni, David Weiss, *Meqorot uMesorot* (Tel Aviv, 1968).
― ―, "Notes on the Mishnah and *beraita*" (Hebrew), *Tarbiz* 27, 1957-58, pp. 17-30.
― ―, "Notes on the Mishnah and *beraita*: Tractate *Ketuvot*" (Hebrew), *Tarbiz* 29, 1959-60, pp. 32-46. Deals with M. Ket. 4:7, 7:2-5, 9:4, 11:5, 12:11.
Heinemann, Joseph, "The Meaning of Some *Mishnayot* in the Order Mo'ed" (Hebrew) *Tarbiz* 29, 1959-60, pp. 21-31. Discusses M. R.H. 1:3 and 4, M. Ta. 2:4, 4:5.
Herford, R. Travers, "Pirke Aboth, Its Purpose and Significance," *Occident and Orient*, ed. B. Schindler (London, 1936), pp. 244-252. M. Avot as *"an epilogue to the Mishnah"* (p. 248).
Hirsch, S. R., *Gesammelte Schriften* (1912), Vol. VI pp. 322-434. Contains the majority of Hirsch's attacks upon Frankel's work.
Hoffmann, David, *Die erste Mischna und die Controversen der Tannaim* (Berlin, 1882; Hebrew: S. Grünberg, Berlin, 1914 and Jerusalem, 1967-8, HMŠNH HR'ŠNH). Attributes the earliest redaction of the Mishnah to the disciples of Hillel and Shammai; subsequent generations of Tannaim added material to that first redacted work.
Ish-Shalom, Meir, "The Meaning of MDL in a Mishnah," (Hebrew) *Bet Talmud* 2, 1882, pp. 151-2. M. Pe'ah 3:3.
Jawitz, Ze'ev, *Sefer Toledot Yisra'el* (Tel Aviv, 1932), Vol. VI.
Karl, Z., "Remarks on Some *Mishnayot* in Bava Qama" (Hebrew) *Tarbiz* 25 1955-56, pp. 21-26. Discusses M. B.Q. 2:6, 8:1, and 10:3.
Kasher, Menahem M., "One Mishnah in Error Divided into Two" (MŠNH 'HT NTHLQH BT'WT LŠTYM), *Essays presented to Chief Rabbi Brodie*, (London, 1966), pp. 195-205. M. Shab. 2:2-3.
Klein, Shelomo, *Mepné Qeshet* (Frankfurt, 1861). Reply to Frankel. Criticizes him for refuting tradition and not understanding *halakhah*. Tone is "respectful" and requests Frankel to correct his "errors".
― ―, *Love Truth and Peace* (Ha'emet vehashalom 'Ehavu) (Frankfurt 1861). Reply to Frankel. Criticizes him for writing in Hebrew. Suggests Frankel should allow only S. R. Hirsch to write about these matters. Asks Frankel to correct his "errors" (divergence from tradition). If he does not, then we should agree he has left the fold.
Kook, Shaul C., "On the Mishnah of the 'Hive'" (LHMŠNH DKWWRT), *Kook Memorial Volume* (Jerusalem, 1945), pp. 253-256. M. Shev. 10:7 and M. 'Uqṣ. 3:10.
― ―, "The Seven Middot of Hillel," *HaSofe LeHokhmat Yisra'el* 13, 1929, pp. 90-1. The seven Middot are old principles. They were announced when Hillel explained to Bené Bethyra the law of Passover's superceding the Sabbath.
Krauss, S. "Études sur la Mischna," *REJ* 67, 1914, pp. 24-39. Krauss attempts to prove that the Mishnah contains traditions dating from the last prophets.
― ―, "Review of Hermann Strack's *Introduction to Talmud and Midrash*," *JQR* O.S. 7, 1895, pp. 33-9. Praises Strack's work, particularly since it is that of a Christian.
― ―, "Tadi Gate" (Š'R HTDY), *Louis Ginzberg Jubilee Volume* (New York, 1945), pp. 391-399. Discussion of the Tadi Gate, which is mentioned only three times: M. Mid. 1:3, 1:9, and 2:3.
Krochmal, N. "Responses" and "Notes," (Hebrew) *Kerem Hemed* 4, 1839, pp. 260-274, 285-286. Response to S. D. Luzzatto, *Ibid.*, 3, 1838, pp. 61-76. Notes on Pharisees and Sadducees.

BIBLIOGRAPHY

— —, *The Writings of Nahman Krochmal*, Simon Rawidowicz, ed. (London, 1961).
Kutscher, Y., "Leshon Hazal," *Sefer Hanokh Yalon* (Jerusalem, 1963), pp. 7-23.
Landsberg, W., "Plan und System in der Aufeinanderfolge der einzelnen Mišnas," *MGWJ* 1873, pp. 208-215.
Lauterbach, J.Z., "Mishnah," *Jewish Encyclopedia* VIII, pp. 609-619.
Lerner, M., "Die ältesten Mishna-Kompositionen," *Magazin für Wissenschaft des Judenthums* 1886, pp. 1-20.
— —, *Torath haMishnah* (Berlin, 1914), Vol. I.
Lieberman, Saul, *Hayerushalmi Kiphshuto* (Jerusalem, 1934).
— —, *Hellenism in Jewish Palestine* (New York, 1950).
— —, "How Much Greek in Jewish Palestine," *Biblical and Other Studies*, ed. A. Altmann (Cambridge, 1963).
— —, "Interpretations in Mishnahs" (Hebrew), *Tarbiz* 40, 1970-71, pp. 9-17. Interprets M. Git. 9:4, M. Sanh. 9:5, M. Miq. 9:6.
— —, "Response to the Introduction by Professor Alexander Marx," *The Jewish Expression*, ed. J. Goldin (New York, 1970), pp. 119-133.
— —, *Siphré Zutta* (New York, 1968).
— —, *Tosefta Kifshutah* (New York, 1955-1967), Vols 1-7.
— —, *Tosefeth Rishonim* (Jerusalem, 1938-1939), Vols 1-4.
— —, "Yerushalmi Horayot," (Hebrew) *Jubilee Volume for H. Albeck*, Jerusalem, 1963. Proves first edition of Y. Hor. is based on Leiden MS.
Lerner, M., "Grundlagen der Mischna," *Festschrift zum... David Hoffmann*, (Berlin, 1914), pp. 346-361.
Lowenstamm, Samuel E., "What is above? What is Beneath? What was Before? And what will be Hereafter? (MH LM'LH WMH LMTH MH LPNYM WMH L'HWR), *Yehezkel Kaufmann Jubilee Volume*, ed. M. Haran (Jerusalem, 1960), pp. 112-121. Argues that M. Hag. 2 : 1 reflects "mystic-philosophical," but not Gnostic, sources.
Luzzatto, S. D., "Houses," (Hebrew) *Kerem Hemed* 3, 1838, pp. 219-223. House of Shammai and House of Hillel.
— —, — —, *Kerem Hemed* 3, 1838, pp. 61-76. Re: Geiger, in Geiger's *Zeitschrift* II, pp. 474-492. Arrangement of the Mishnah. Sequence of tractates according to number of chapters. Rabbi did not write down the Mishnah. M.'Ed. 1:5. Minority view recorded concerning power of Tannas to dispute earlier views and annulling decision of other courts.
— —, — —, *Kerem Hemed* 4, 1839, pp. 145-157. M. 'Ed. 1:5.
— —, "Reply," *Kerem Hemed* 4, 1839, pp. 287-293. Defense of article in *Kerem Hemed* 3, 1838, pp. 61-76, concerning Maimonides; see Krochmal's criticism in *Kerem Hemed* 4, 1839, pp. 260-274.
— —, "Seder Tannaim and Amoraim," (Hebrew) *Kerem Hemed* 4, 1839, pp. 184-204. Text, pp. 184-200. Notes on the chain of tradition, pp. 201-204.
— —, — —, *Kerem Hemed* 3, 1838, pp. 196-199. On ban against writing down Oral Tradition.
Mantel, Hugo, *Studies in the History of the Sanhedrin* (Cambridge, 1965²).
Margoliot, Reuven, *The Foundation and Arrangement of the Mishnah* (Hebrew) (Tel Aviv, 1940). Margoliot's account is uncritical, homiletical, and traditional, and provides no examination of the Mishnah itself. He attributes the arrangement of the Mishnah to Rabbi (p. 26), and argues that Rabbi intentionally left out certain matters,

for example, redemption by the Messiah and laws of Ḥanukkah, to avoid attracting the attention of the Roman government (p. 23). The Mishnah was arranged according to one general principle: the concluding saying in each passage represents the law. Thus he states that the House of Hillel appears after the House of Shammai only in those places where the law follows the House of Hillel (p. 32) [!]. He further states that all anonymous statements in the Mishnah represent the "opinion of the Council" (p. 35).

Marx, Alexander, "Review of Hermann Strack's *Introduction to Talmud and Midrash*," *JQR* n.s. 13, 1922-23. A detailed review of this reference book. Considering that Marx aided Strack in rewriting the later editions of his work, it is no wonder that Marx writes, "There is no one book of such scope." He does criticize Strack for his all-too-brief history and his lack of depth, particularly in regard to his treatment of Yavneh and the work of Rabbi.

Malter, Henry, "A Talmudic Problem and Proposed Solutions," *JQR* 2, 1911-12, pp. 75-98. Reviews Zuckermandel's theory on Tos. and Mishnah. He does not see why anyone should not accept this theory. Argues most scholars oppose Zuckermandel's theory on theological grounds, for this means the oral law is based on a fabricated Mishnah. Malter argues this is no problem, for being a Conservative, Zuckermandel views the changes that the Amoraim made in Tos. to form the Mishnah as changes in adaptation to the times. Pseudepigraphic changes were common for that period. Palestinian Jewry did not have to make any changes, therefore they retained the original Mishnah, i.e., the Tosefta. Later events led to the acceptance of BT and its Mishnah and the insertion of the BT's Mishnah in PT.

Melammed, Ezra Z., *Introduction to the Literature of the Talmud* (Hebrew) (Jerusalem, 1965).

— —, "Lives of the Tannaim and their Sayings in Pirke Avot" (HYY HTN'YM WM'MRYHM BPRQY 'BWT), *Hommage à Abraham* (*Elmaleh*), (Jerusalem, 1959), pp. 49-55. Suggested reasons for the influence of passages in M. Avot relating to various Tannaim.

— —, *The Relationship Between the Halakhic Midrashim and the Mishnah and Tosefta* (Hebrew) (Jerusalem, 1967).

— —, "Tannaitic Controversies concerning the Interpretation and Text of Older *Mishnayot*" (Hebrew), *Tarbiẓ* 21, 1949-50, pp. 137-64.

Mielziner, Ella McKenna Friend, *Moses Mielziner* (New York, 1936). Biography, writings and a complete chronological bibliography, by his daughter-in-law.

Mielziner, Moses, *Introduction to the Talmud* (New York, 1925). Mielziner divides his book into an historical and literary introduction to the Talmud. He has sections on rabbinic hermeneutics, offering examples for each rule and a very useful section on terminology. He notes the use and meaning of terms in Talmudic literature. He, like Strack, wrote for the modern student who is unable to deal with the original language of the Talmud. He considers his work more comprehensive than Strack. He, however, merely reviews everyone else's theories on the history of the Mishnah. His book does contain good bibliography, greatly expanded by Alexander Guttmann, for 1925-1967, in ed. N.Y., 1968: Bloch Publishing Co.

Mirsky, Samuel K., "The Mishnah as viewed by the Amoraim," *The Leo Jung Jubilee Volume*, ed. M. Kasher, N. Lamm, and L. Rosenfeld (New York, 1962) pp. 155-174. Includes a reinterpretation of statement attributed to Yoḥanan: The Halakhah follows an anonymous Mishnah (HLKH KSTM MŠNH).

BIBLIOGRAPHY

— —, "The Place of Tractate Rosh HaShanah in the Order Mo'ed" (Hebrew), *Sinai* 56, 1965, pp. 1-7.
Mittwoch, Eugen, "Some observations on the language of the prayers, the benedictions, and the Mishnah," *Essays in Honour of ... J. H. Hertz*, ed. I. Epstein, E. Levine, and C. Roth (London, 1943), pp. 325-330. Different usages in Biblical Hebrew and in Mishnaic Hebrew.
Neusner, Jacob, *The Rabbinic Traditions about the Pharisees before 70. I. The Masters. II. The Houses. III. Conclusions* (Leiden, 1971).
Onah, Avigdor, "Notes on the New Commentary to the *Six Orders of the Mishnah*," (Hebrew), *Sinai* 41, 1957, pp. 61-63. A review of Albeck's *Six Orders of the Mishnah*.
— —, "Notes on the New Commentary on the *Six Orders of the Mishnah*," (Hebrew), *Sinai* 45, 1960, pp. 181-83. A review of Albeck's *Six Orders of the Mishnah*.
— —, "The Transportation of W and Š in the Mishnah," (Hebrew), *Sinai* 56, 1965, pp. 8-12.
Oppenheim, David, "M. Abot 2:6," (Hebrew) *Yeshurun* 5, 1886, pp. 91-2.
— —, "The Thirteen Middot of R. Ishmael," (Hebrew) *Yeshurun* 6, 1886, pp. 201-5. Notes the different versions of this text and deals with Rashi's explanation. All versions are "original."
Oppenheim, Joachim, "Analysis of Homiletical Midrashim," *He'Assif* 5, 1889, pp. 1-22; 6, 1893, pp. 87-103. *Aggadah* goes hand in hand with *halakhah*. *Aggadah* reflects the spirit of the times, reaches ethical values, and reflects the freedom of learning. Analysis of passages to demonstrate these claims.
— —, "The *Beraitot* and their relation to the Mishnah," (Hebrew) *Kenesset Yisra'el* 2, 1887, pp. 81-98. There were many *baraita*-collections after Rabbi organized the Mishnah. Most of these, however, were lost.
— —, "Correction of Several Tosefta Passages," (Hebrew) *Bet Talmud* 5, 1885, pp. 296-99, 325-9, 354-8.
— —, "A Critical Analysis of the Development of the Halakhot of the Tradition," (Hebrew) *Bet Talmud* 3, 1883, pp. 360-9. Anything but "critical."
— —, "R. Eliezer b. Hyrcanus," (Hebrew) *Bet Talmud* 4, 1884, pp. 311-16, 332-8, 360-6. A summary of the tendencies in Eliezer's work, citing different passages in which his name appears.
— —, "The General Principles (KLLYM) in the Mishnah and Tosefta," (Hebrew) *Kenesset Yisra'el* 1, 1886, pp. 351-78. Reviews the use of the terms KL, KLL, and ZH HKLL.
— —, "History of the Talmud," (Hebrew) *Bet Talmud* 2, 1882, pp. 142-51, 172-79, 234-45, 269-73, 304-15, 343-55.
— —, "Incomplete Texts (HSWRY MHSR')," (Hebrew) *Kenesset Yisra'el* 3, 1888, pp. 303-31. Attempts to show these texts of the Mishnah are not really incomplete. He gives no critical analyses, but only *pilpul* to justify the excellence of the Mishnah text.
— —, "R. Yosi the Galilean," (Hebrew) *Bet Talmud* 5, 1885, pp. 138-45, 172-6. Cites sources in which his name appears.
Paris, Benjamin, "Explanation of M. Naz. 4:5, M. B.M. 4:1," (Hebrew) *HaSofe LeHokhmat Yisra'el* 13, 1929, pp. 212-4. The last Mishnah in Nazir is homiletical.
Pineles, Hirsch Mendel, *Darkah shel Torah* (Vienna, 1861).
Rabinowitz, Saul, *HaRav Zechariah Frankel* (Hebrew) (Warsaw, 1898). Biography of Frankel containing a bibliography. Bias for Conservative Judaism.

Rapoport, S. J., *Words of Peace and Truth* (Hebrew) (Prague, 1861). A half-hearted defense of Frankel. Attempts to show that Frankel is not attacking tradition and that his views are scholarly and accurate. Requests Frankel to make some further "clarifications."

— —, — —, *Kerem Hemed* 7, pp. 157-167.

Ratner, B., "The Mishnah of Levi b. Sisi" (Hebrew) (MŠNTW ŠL LWY BN SYSY), *Harkavy Memorial Volume* (St. Petersburg, 1908), pp. 117-122. Argues that Levi b. Sisi, a younger contemporary of Rabbi, ordered his own Mishnah and subsequently moved from Palestine to Babylonia.

Reggio, Isaac Samuel, — —, *Kerem Hemed* 7, 1843, pp. 113-118. On M. 'Ed. 1:5. 'Plain sense of Mishnah' free from Amoraic explanations.

— —, "Response," *Kerem Hemed* 3, 1838, pp. 77-87. Response to S. D. Luzzatto, in *ibid.*, 3, 1838, pp. 61-76.

— —, "Response," *Kerem Hemed* 4, 1839, pp. 155-159. Response to Luzzatto in *ibid.*, 4, 1839, pp. 145-7.

Rosenthal, Ludwig, *Über den Zusammenhang, die Quellen und die Entstehung der Mischna* (Berlin, 1918), Vols. I-III.

Roth, Cecil, "Historical Implications of the Ethics of the Fathers," *Meyer Waxman Jubilee Volume* (Jerusalem, 1966), pp. 102-112. Historical "sidelights on the circumstance of the time," as reflected in M. Avot, Chapter One.

Sachs, Yehiel Michael, — —, *Kerem Hemed* 7, 1843, p. 269. M. Sot 9:15 "from the death of R. Yohanan b. Zakkai . . ." Wisdom (HKMH) refers to 'hidden matters.'

Sachs, Mordecai Y. L., "From a Mishnah Commentary by R. Natan, Head of a Palestinian Academy," (Hebrew) *Kook Memorial Volume* (Jerusalem, 1945), pp. 171-179. Selections from M. Ber. and M. Shev.

Sachs, Senior, "Gezerah Shavah," (Hebrew) *Kerem Hemed* 9, 1856, p. 136. Use by Tannaim of GZRH ŠWH.

Schachter, M., *The Babylonian and Jerusalem Mishnah Textually Compared* (Hebrew) (Jerusalem, 1959).

Schechter, Solomon, *Studies in Judaism* (Repr.: New York, 1970).

Schmida, Shmuel, "Mishnah and Tosefta, Beginning of 'Eduyyot," (Hebrew) *Benjamin DeVries Memorial Volume* (Jerusalem, 1968), pp. 1-17. Reviews the sources and asks whether the materials in the Mishnah and in the Tosefta are to be considered part of the same unit.

Schorr, Joshua, "Certain *Halakhot* and Customs Deriving from Persian Sources," (Hebrew) *Hehalus* 8, 1869, pp. 39-51.

— —, "Concerning the Torot ('L HaTorot)," (Hebrew) *Hehalus* 7, 1865, pp. 1-74. The history of the ideas of the Bible and the *Gemara*. Many Persian ideas have been included in our tradition. Deals with the lives of several personalities, Rabbi, Shammai, and Eliezer.

— —, *"Darkah Shel Torah,"* (Hebrew) *Hehalus* 7, 1865, pp. 144-57. Review of Pineles. Vehement attack. Continually reiterates the assumption that, since Pineles has shown there are errors in the Talmud, one should no longer observe commandments based on the erroneous texts and interpretations.

— —, "Halakhah LeMosheh MiSinai," (Hebrew) *Hehalus* 5, 1859, pp. 28-59. Originally the term was used in the period before 'Aqiba to refer to old laws. This was done to give the laws greater validity. In 'Aqiba's time, however, when there were many disputes, 'Aqiba began to use *Middot* to derive a Scriptural basis for these laws. He even opposed some of these old ŠM'WT with the laws he derived by *Middot*. Regarding y. Shab. 1:5, Schorr argues Rabbi had to have the signatures of his contemporaries for the law he issued. After Rabbi died, the Amoraim resumed calling old laws *Halakhah LeMosheh MiSinai*, in order to give these laws added authority. Later sages did not understand the use of the term and they thought it meant all of the *halakhah* or oral law comes from Moses; therefore, Jonathan, y. Shab. 1:2, instructs his students to trace a law back to Moses if it is possible. The Amoraim then began to apply this term without knowing its true meaning.

— —, "Personal Hebrew Names," (Hebrew) *Hehalus* 9, 1873, pp. 1-65; 10, 1877, pp. 1-32. Analyzes the meaning and origin of certain Hebrew proper names. Titles and nicknames given to the people on the basis of certain mannerisms, actions, sayings, or beliefs. Names given because of *halakhot* the individuals said and derogatory titles. The influence particularly of Greek names.

— —, "A Subject for its Time (DBR B'TW)," (Hebrew) *Hehalus* 1, 1852, pp. 47-66. Schorr attacks Orthodoxy for not making concessions in *halakhah*. He argues that *halakhah* is no longer valid for two reasons: 1) Just as in the time of the Mishnah and *Gemara* the sages made changes to suit the times, so too changes should now also be made. 2) In studying the *Gemara* it becomes evident that the Amoraim did not understand much of the Mishnah. Rabbi purposely altered material, and we no longer should have to observe laws which are based on these changes and errors.

— —, "Textual Criticism," (Hebrew) *Hehalus* 11, 1880, pp. 51-64. Comments on certain texts in Mishnah, B.T., P.T., Sifra, Sifré, Midrash and Pesiqta. Mostly explanations of certain terminology and the meaning of texts.

Shavtiel, Yishaq, "Yemenite Traditions relating to the Grammar of the Language of the Mishnah," (Hebrew) *M. Yalon Jubilee Volume*, ed. S. Lieberman (Jerusalem, 1963), pp. 338-359. Notes and vocalized text.

Slonimisky, Hayyim, "M. 'Eruv. 2:4," (Hebrew) *He'Assif* 2, 1885, pp. 228-32.

— —, "Review of J. H. Weiss, *Dor Dor VeDorshav*," (Hebrew) *Bet Talmud*, 1, 1881, pp. 253-5.

Sokolow, Nahum, "The Living Hebrew Language in the Foundation of the Mishnah," *Klausner Jubilee Volume* (Tel Aviv, 1937), pp. 109-131. Use of Hebrew for basic expressions that appear in the Mishnah.

Strack, Hermann L., *Introduction to Talmud and Midrash* (New York, 1931). Strack lists the names of all the tractates, their main ideas, and their scriptural bases, rabbis, and bibliography. Strack himself notes that his book is intended for those who cannot understand the Talmud in its original language. The information he gives to these readers is no more than a summary of the views of others.

Tchernowitz, Chaim, "Later Mishnah," (Hebrew) *Studies in Memory of Moses Schorr, 1874-1941* (New York, 1944), pp. 259-263. Discusses the order in which disputants are named in the Mishnah.

— —, "The Pairs and the Temple of Onias," (Hebrew) *Louis Ginzberg Jubilee Volume* (New York, 1945), pp. 223-247. Identifies anti-Alexandrian tracts in rabbinic tradition-chains.

Waldberg, Moses, *Kakh hi Darkah Shel Torah* (Hebrew) (Jassy, 1864). Attempts to criticize Pineles' analysis. Fails to understand Pineles' method. Merely attempts to defend Amoraim despite their errors.

Weinberg, Jechiel J., "Toward the Investigation of the Mishnah," *Samuel K. Mirsky Jubilee Volume*, ed. S. Bernstein and G. A. Churgin (N.Y. 1958), pp. 222-247.

Rejects notion that scholarly study of the Mishnah began only in the twentieth century. Reviews theories of Hoffmann, Halevy, and Albeck; disputes Albeck's criticism of Hoffmann.

— —, "Y. I. Halevy's Path and Theory in the Investigation of the Mishnah," (Hebrew) *Halevy Memorial Volume*, ed. M. Auerbach (Bené-Braq, 1964), pp. 119-130. Critical review of Halevy's theories.

— —, "The Talmudic Exegesis of the Mishnah," (Hebrew) *Isaiah Wolfsberg Jubilee Volume* (Tel Aviv, 1955), pp. 86-105. Reviews Amoraic interpretations of Mishnah and also the opinions of recent writers.

Weiss, Avraham, "History of the Introductions to the Talmud," (Hebrew) *Bet Talmud* 1, 1881, pp. 26-31, 55-60, 85-90, 115-22, 153-9, 181-4. Traces the history of introductions from *Seder Tanna'im we'Amora'im* until the *Introduction to Zera'im* by Maimonides. A good summary of the major points of the different introductions.

— —, "The Meaning of 'D in Rabbinic Literature," (Hebrew) *Bet Talmud* 1, 1881, pp. 16-17.

Weiss, Abraham, *The Babylonian Talmud as a Literary Unit* (HTHWWT HTLMWD BŠLMWTW) (New York, 1943). Includes discussion of Amoraic use of the Mishnah.

— —, *Court Procedures. Studies in Talmudic Law* (SDR HDYWN) (New York, 1957). Includes discussion of literary problems raised, and historical content reflected, in several Mishnah passages.

— —, "Explanations and Notes regarding the Mishnah and the Talmud" (Hebrew) *Horeb* 14-15, 1960, pp. 127-156. M. Ber., 6.

— —, "On the Arrangement of Mishnah Qiddushin" (Hebrew), *Sinai* 48, 1960-61, pp. 161-167.

— —, *On the Mishnah* (Hebrew) (Tel Aviv, 1968). Collected essays relating to literary problems in Mishnaic literature.

— —, *Studies in the Law of the Talmud on Damages* (DYWNYM WBYRWRYM BB Q) (New York, 1966). Commentary on b. B.Q. Includes discussions of Mishnah passages.

— —, *Studies in the Literature of the Amoraim* ('L HYṢYRH HSPRWTYT ŠL H'MWR'YM) (New York, 1962). Includes a discussion of the nature of Tannaitic literature.

— —, *The Talmud in its Development* (LḤQR HTLMWD) (New York, 1954). Includes discussion of sources of the Talmud.

Weiss, I. H., *Dor Dor VeDorshav* [*Zur Geschichte der jüdischen Tradition*] (Wilna, 1904)., Vols. I-V.

Yalon, Ḥanokh, "Gleanings on Mishnaic Hebrew" (Hebrew), *Tarbiz* 37, 1967-68, pp. 133-34.

— —, "Mishnahs and their Pointing" (Hebrew), *Sinai* 48, 1960-61, pp. 89-105. A philological study.

— —, "Versions and Forms of Language in Various Mishnahs" (Hebrew), *Sinai* 48, 1960, pp. 254-260. A philological study.

Yary, Abraham, "Text Changes in Mishnah Pesaḥim" (Hebrew), *Sinai* 43, 1958, pp. 233-249.

Zeitlin, Solomon, "A Note on the Principle of Intention in Tannaitic Literature," *Alexander Marx Jubilee Volume* (New York, 1950), pp. 631-636. Principles followed by the School of Hillel and the School of Shammai in M. Shab. 21:1-3.

Zuckermandel, Moses Samuel, *Tosefta, Mischna und Beraitha in ihrem Verhältnis zu einander* (Frankfurt, 1908-1909). Final two volumes appeared in *Gesammelte Aufsätze* (Frankfurt, 1911, 1913. Vols. I-IV. Tosefta is Judah's original Mishnah. The Mishnah that we have is the Tosefta which was reworked by the Babylonian Amora'im to meet the needs and conditions of that country. The Palestinian Amoraim did not change Tosefta; therefore, the Palestinian Talmud usually agrees with Tosefta and not with Mishnah. If PT does not agree with Tosefta, this is because PT was changed because of BT. The Mishnah which appears before PT was only added in a much later period. It is for this reason that, even though PT is based on Tosefta, Mishnah (or the reworked Tos. by the Babylonian Amoraim) is found before PT's text. A further change occurred in Tos., for since Mishnah did contain material from the original Tos., this material was later removed from Tos., making Tos. appear to be a supplement to the Mishnah. Now both documents must be studied. See s. v. Malter. For a bibliography of Zuckermandel, see Vol. 4, pp. 197-200.

Zuri, J.S., *Rabbi ʿAqiba* (Jerusalem, 1925).

— —, *Toledot HaMishpat HaṢiburi HaʿIvri* [History of Jewish Social Law] *Book Two: Tequfat Rabbi Yehudah HaNasi* (Paris, 1931).

Weis, P. R., *Mishnah Horayoth: Its History and Exposition*, Manchester, England, 1952.

Presents a Hebrew text of *Horayoth* based on the Naples MSS. along with Danby's translation and critical notes explaining the meaning of the text and suggesting the "sources" from which each mishnah was composed. Weiss presents his conclusions in the Introduction. "We have shown that [M.] Hor. 1 : 1-2 is the logical continuation of [M.] Sanh. 11 : 2-4. [M.] Horayoth 1 : 4 relies also on [M.] Sanh. 4 : 2. On the other hand, [M.] Shav. 2 : 4 explains [M.] Horayoth 2 : 4, which shows that the original place of Horayoth had been between Sanhedrin and Shabuoth." He further suggests that the lack of "arrangement and uniformity" in Horayoth can be explained by "the fact that Rabbi incorporated in his Mishnah collections of earlier authorities which had been arranged according to different principles." Page references to Frankel and Danby are cited in support. He also suggests that "the different *mishnayoth* of this tractate go mainly back to R. Judah and R. Simeon."

Weis's commentary is quite thorough and usually considers versions of passages in Horayoth which occur elsewhere in rabbinic literature. However, the framework of the commentary is traditional and the analysis is primarily legal. His explanation of the laws themselves consists mainly of summaries of Talmudic discussions of the different mishnahs. While literary questions are considered, the analysis of the composition of the tractate aims at identifying some basic principles which appear to underlie the various legal rulings. Thus if Meir, Judah, or Simeon elsewhere employ the same basic principle as is identified in Horayoth, this constitutes sufficient basis for attribution to one of them of the pertinent passage of Hor. It is for this reason that Weis so frequently is unable definitively to attribute or identify the "sources" of Horayoth. More often than not we are told that a certain law in Horayoth "emanated" from one sage or another.

INDEX OF BIBLICAL AND TALMUDIC PASSAGES

i. *Biblical References*[1]

Amos 8 : 11-12	216	26 : 3	127	Genesis		
I Chronicles		26 : 4	129	33 : 14		77
25 : 8	247	Ecclesiastes 9 : 1	76	43 : 12		78
27 : 32	247	Exodus		Jeremiah 18 : 21, 22		64
28 : 9	157	13 : 9	79	Leviticus		
II Chronicles 2 : 55	248	20 : 1	2	23 : 19		98
Deuteronomy		20 : 13	81	23 : 40		79
6 : 7	78	21 : 22	81	Numbers 30 : 2		193
15 : 18	78	24 : 12	1	Psalms		
17 : 18	78	Ezekiel 23 : 28	191	85 : 9		2
21 : 18-22	100	Ezra 7 : 10	247	119 : 126		94

ii. *Mishnah*

Avot		Bikkurim		2 : 1		46
Chs. 1, 2	131	1 : 5	221	2 : 2	xii,	46
1 : 1	64, 108	2 : 4	127	2 : 5		47
1 : 14	133	3 : 2-6	127	2 : 8		47
1 : 1-15	132-33	3 : 6	127-28	Hallah		
1 : 12-15	131	'Eduyyot		1 : 1		16
1 : 16	132	Ch. 4	17, 146	1 : 6		248
1 : 16-18	131	1 : 3	159	Hullin 8 : 3		50
1 : 17-18	132	4 : 7	202	Kelim		
2 : 1	132	5 : 2	17, 236n	2 : 2		173
2 : 1-4	131	8 : 4	249-50	8 : 9		153
2 : 2-4	132	'Eruvin		30 : 4	67,	141
2 : 7	132	1 : 1	31	Ketuvot		
2 : 8	131	3 : 6	43-44	2 : 2		218
2 : 8-14	132	3 : 7	44	2 : 9		194
5 : 1-5	132	3 : 8	44	7 : 6		20
5 : 4	133	6 : 3, 4	144n	7 : 7		220
5 : 5	133	Gittin		8 : 6-7		220
5 : 7-10	132	1 : 1	234	10 : 4		148
5 : 21	9	1 : 5	95	11 : 6		187
Bava Meṣi'a' 4 : 7	202	2 : 1	234	13 : 1-9		43n
Bava Qamma 1 : 1	112	5 : 4	182	Kila'im		
Berakhot		5 : 8, 9	152	1 : 3		49n
Ch. 3	115	5 : 9	152	2 : 11		50
7 : 5	95	Hagigah		Ma'aser Sheni		
9 : 5	94	1 : 1-2	47	5 : 7		62
Beṣah		1 : 4	47	5 : 10		219
3 : 6	92	1 : 7	46	Megillah 1 : 4-11		218
3 : 8	92	1 : 8	42-43, 45-46	Menahot 5 : 6		128

[1] Indices were prepared by Mr. Arthur Woodman, Canaan, New Hampshire, on a grant from Brown University. The editor acknowledges with thanks the University's support for this project.

INDEX OF BIBLICAL AND TALMUDIC PASSAGES

Nazir	
1 : 2	188-90
1 : 4	189
6 : 1	184-86
Nedarim	
2 : 1	193-94
3 : 6	195
4 : 3	61n
Negaʿim 12 : 5-7	62
Nezirot 7 : 2	176n
Niddah	
6 : 11	49n
9 : 5	175
ʿOrlah	
3 : 7	174
7 : 3	142
16 : 1	49n
Peʾah	
2 : 1	176n
2 : 6	111
3 : 6	84
6 : 2	144
6 : 8	150
9 : 6	49n, 110
Qiddushin	
1 : 1-6	202
2 : 1-3	203
2 : 1-10	203
2 : 5	220
2 : 5-10	220
2 : 11	203
3 : 1-4	204

3 : 14	204
4 : 6-7	221
Rosh Hashanah 4 : 1-4	218
Sanhedrin	
3 : 4	160
5 : 2	129, 212-14
8 : 1	100
11 : 4	149
Shabbat	
1 : 4	159
2 : 4	178
21 : 1, 2	93
Shavuʿot 6 : 2	92
Sheqalim	
Ch. 5	213-14, 250-51
5 : 1	251
Sheviʿit	
4 : 3	152
5 : 19	151-52
9 : 5	84
Soṭah	
Chs. 2, 3	129
1 : 6	191
8 : 1-2	62
9 : 6	218
Sukkah	
2 : 1	147
2 : 2	147
Taʿanit	
1 : 4	189
2 : 4	181

4 : 1	96
Tamid	
3 : 1	228, 230, 232
3 : 2	111, 232
3 : 8	111
4 : 3	228, 230
4 : 2-3	229-30
5 : 2	231
Terumot	
1 : 1	248
1 : 4	236-39
1 : 8	236, 238, 240
1 : 9	238-40
6 : 5	175
Ṭohorot 9 : 1	53
Yadaim 4 : 3	64
Yevamot	
1 : 1	248
4 : 3	84
4 : 3-4	220
4 : 7	183
4 : 10	191
8 : 6	50n
9 : 3	187
Yoma	
1 : 1, 4	252
1 : 3	43
2 : 3	228, 230, 232
2 : 4	231-32
3 : 2, 4	252
5 : 1, 3-6	252
Zevaḥim 14 : 3	19

iii. Tosefta

Ahilot 14 : 4	171
ʿArakhin 3 : 15	112
Bava Batra 8 : 13	182
ʿEruvin	
1 : 23	43n
4 : 2	44
4 : 3	44
8 : 24	42
Giṭṭin	
1 : 4	95
6 : 8	172
Ḥagigah	
1 : 7-8	46
1 : 9	42, 43n
Hullin 8 : 6	51
Kelim 6 : 17	153
Ketuvot 3 : 2	195
Kilaʾim 1 : 2	49n

Makshirin	
2 : 9	49n
3 : 4	250
Maʿaser Sheni	
2 : 12	15
3 : 7	16
Negaʿim 5 : 3	172
Nezirot	
Ch. 1	189
1 : 5	189-90
4 : 1	185-86
Niddah 6 : 5-6	49n
Peʾah	
3 : 2	145
3 : 6	150
Qiddushin 1 : 7	203
Sanhedrin 6 : 6	95
Sukkah 1 : 1	148

Taʿanit	
2 : 4	96
3 : 1	96
Terumot	
3 : 14	236-38
3 : 16	238-39
Yevamot	
6 : 3	183
10 : 2	50n
Yom Kippurim 2 : 3	129
Zabim	
1 : 4-6	49n
1 : 5	173, 253
3 : 1	112
Zevaḥim	
1 : 4-6	49n
1 : 5	48
2 : 17	50n, 252
6 : 3	111

INDEX OF BIBLICAL AND TALMUDIC PASSAGES

iv. Palestinian Talmud

Berakhot		1 : 6	17	Shevi'it	
1 : 5	162	1 : 58a	17	1 : 1	31
1 : 7	2n	Megillah 4 : 1	65	1 : 33a	31
'Eruvin		Nedarim		2 : 1	31
1 : 1	31	2 : 1	194	Sotah	
1 : 18d	31	3 : 6	195	1 : 5	192
3 : 2	144	Shabbat		3 : 6	52n
3 : 20d	144n	1 : 2	162	3 : 19b	52n
7 : 9	144n	1 : 3a	18	Sukkah 4 : 10	17
7 : 24c	144n	1 : 5	18	Terumot 1 : 8	236, 237
Hagigah		Sheqalim		Yevamot	
1 : 8	43n	5 : 1	48, 160, 253	4 : 7	183
1 : 76c	43n	5 : 48c	48	13 : 2	160
Hallah		6 : 1	248	Yoma	
				1 : 13	228, 230, 232

v. Babylonian Talmud

'Avodah Zarah 19b	9n	13b	140n, 212	68a	158
Bava Batra		Hullin 85a	52n, 178	71a	100
33a	164	Ketuvot		86a	
130b	162	50a	9n		67, 114, 162, 172, 215
Bava Mesi'a'		93a	50n, 149	86b	67, 163
33a-b	4	101b	187	Shabbat	
59b	159	Makshirin 5b	95	15a	131
89a	146	Megillah		106a	95
Bava Qamma 82a	65	9b	178	138a	69
Berakhot		21a	126	142b	94
5a	1	Menahot		Shavu'ot 41b	92
25a	111	46b	213	Shevi'it 4a	66
28a	212	65b-66a	98n	Sotah	
47b	3n, 61, 94	Mo'ed Qatan 15a	95	8b	191
63a	94	Nedarim		27a	164
Besah 29a	93	14b	194	Ta'anit	
'Eruvin		41a	158n	16b	95
2b	31	Pesahim		26b	96
22a	78	3a	162	Yevamot	
Gittin		37b	17	30a	66
10a	95	70b	157	40a	183
15a	234	Qiddushin		42b	191
60b	2n	30a	9n	49b	128
67a	48, 160	49a	61	84a	50n
Hagigah		49a-b	79	Yoma	
3a	159	Sanhedrin		14b	111
10a	43n	21b	78	16a	111
10b	95	24a	9n	20b	214
Horayot		41a	129	Zevahim	
13a	111	48b	116	13a	95
				114b	19

vi. Compilations of Midrashim

Mekhilta of R.		Sifra 'Emor 12 : 1-9	98n	Exodus R., 47 : 1	2
Ishmael	172	Sifré Naso' 24	185	Lamentations R., 23	177
Sifré Deuteronomy	58	Avot de Rabbi Natan,		Leviticus R., 2 : 1	9n
	172n	Ch. 18	160, 253		

GENERAL INDEX

Abaye, R., 23-24, 34; Soṭah, 191-92
Abbahu, R., 248
Abba Saul, 49; guardian and orphan, 182-83
Abba Yosi b. Ḥanan, R., 42
Abraham, 99
Abraham b. David of Posquiéres, 5, 6
Abstract law, 60, 62
Abṭalion, 101, 156-58
Abtina, 251
Adulteress, 191-92
Afternoon offering, 219
Aggadah, 72, 81-82
Agrippa, 127, 214
Albeck, Ḥanoch, xix-xxii, 4n, 60, 143n, 153n, 225, 232; Epstein, comments of, 19n, 31n, 38n, 51, 52n, 53; *Halakkah*, 243-44, 253; "Hanoch Albeck on the Mishnah", 209-24; law code, 82; source material, 205
Alexander the Great, 62-63
Amoraim, 22-29, 31-33, 35; exegesis, 90, 92-97, 100, 103, 159, 166; formation and development of Mishnah, 107-108; *Halakhah*, 243, 248, 253-54; intermediate period, 136, 140, 151; law code, 88, 115; legal system and tradition, 176; oral law and first Mishnah, 123-24; positive-historical Judaism, 66, 69-70, 73; sayings, source of, 180-81, 188, 192-96; source criticism, 37-55; source material, 198, 200, 205-206
Amsterdam, 242
Antigonus of Sokho, 99
Atonement, Day of, 251-52
ʿAqiba, xiii, xix; broken vessels, 173-74; early editing, 215-16; exegesis, 97, 100-102, 160-65; *Halakhah*, 252-54; heave-offering and tithes, 239-40; intermediate period, 137, 140-41, 146; law code, 81-82, 89, 114, 169-73, 175-76; mixed produce, 174; oral law, 119-20, 123-24, 130, 132-33; organization of Mishnah, 226-27, 233, 235; positive-historical Judaism, 66-68; Passover offering, 110-11; scribal and oral law, 112-16; source criticism, 39-41, 45, 47-49; 55; teachings, 16, 35; wine and poll, 184-86
Aristobulus, 214
Ark and Shabbath, 94-95
Asher, R., 64
Asher b. Yeḥiel, 6
Ashi, R., 24
Auerbach, Benjamin, 74
Auerbach, Moshe, 136n
ʿAvodah Zarah, 70
Avot, 9; as first Mishnah, 122-34
Avot deR. Natan, 215

Babylonia, Palestine compared, 21-30; Talmud, source criticism, 37-55
Baer, Y., 39n
Bar Kokhba, 138
Bar Qappara, 177

GENERAL INDEX

Bassfreund, J., 51
Ben 'Azzai, 230, 232
Bené Bathyra, 158
Ben Sira, 142-43
Betar, 162
Bet Din, 64
Betrothals, 202-204, 220
Bird offering, 47
Bloch, Renée, 210n
Blumberg, Herman J., 232n
Bokser, Baruch Micah, "Jacob N. Epstein on the Formation of the Mishnah", 37-55; "Jacob N. Epstein's Introduction to the Text of the Mishnah", 13-36; "Y. I. Halevy", 135-54
Bomberg, D., 6
Bondwoman, testimony of, 194-95
Book of Jubilees, 143n
Broken vessels, 173-74
Brüll, Jacob, xix, 60; "Jacob Brüll: The Mishnah as a Law Code", 76-89

Clean and unclean, 42, 47, 53, 141; abstinence, 188-90; broken vessels, 173-74; locusts, 249-50
Cohen, Boaz, 205
Cohn, Haim, 2n
Commandments, 1, 2
Corpse, clean or unclean room, 141

Damages, law of, 112
Danby, Herbert, 1, 19, 127, 173-75, 182-88, 191, 193-95, 202-203, 219n, 220n, 221n, 222n, 251; divorce, 234; exegesis, 92-96; intermediate period, 141, 144, 147-48, 150, 152-53; Passover offering, 110; Tamid sacrifice, 111
Day of Atonement, 251-52
Debt, liability and exemption, 92
Dedications, 42
Defilement of woman, testimony, 194-95
DeVries, Benjamin, xii, xxii; "Benjamin DeVries", contributions to study, 242-255
DiLella, Alexander A., 143n
Dio Cassius, 136
Divorce, 112, 234; Samaritan as witness, 95-96
Domain, joining of, 143-44
Dough offering, 219, 248
Dual revelation, 1-10
Dumplings/flour paste, 16-17
Dünner, J. H., 51

'Eduyyot, xix, 111; *Halakhah*, 250; oral law, 120; teaching of, 212, 216-18
Eibenschutz, 155
Eleazar, R., 22, 30; *Halakhah*, 254; heave-offering and tithes, 239-40; source criticism, 49, 51
Eleazar ben 'Azariah, 111; exegesis, 159-60; oral law, 120; teachings of, 212; wine and poll, 185-86
Eleazar ben Diglai, 111
Eleazar ben Shammu'a, 177

GENERAL INDEX

Eleazar b. Simeon, R., 48-49, 52
Eliezer, R., 30; exegesis, 158; first Mishnah, 132; heave-offering, 239; law code, 115; organization of Mishnah, 226; positive-historical Judaism, 67; source criticism, 43-44, 47, 49
Eliezer ben Hyrcanus, 146, 252
Eliezer ben Jacob, 111, 221; first fruits, 128-29; limbs of sacrifice, 231-32
Elijah ben Solomon, 8
Elisha ben Abraham of Grodno, 8
Emancipation, Samaritan witnessing, 95-96
Enlightenment, xiv
Epiphanius, R., 41, 48
Epstein, Jacob N., xvii-xx, xxii, 62, 102n, 188n, 191n, 192, 252; on 'Eduyyot, 217; formation of Mishnah analyzed, 37-55; introduction to Mishnah analyzed, 13-36, source material, 198-99, 205
'Eruvin, 143-44
Eusebius, 136
Evening service, 159
Exemption from debt, 92
Ezekiel, 1, 210
Ezra, exegesis, 157; first Mishnah, 133; *Halakhah*, 245-47; law code, 89; oral law, 98, 109; oral Torah, xxi; positive-historical Judaism, 62; source criticism, 41; whole Torah, 1
Ezra the Scribe, 118

Fast days, prayer, 96-97
Feldblum, M., 199n, 201n, 205
Festival days, afternoon offering, 219; measuring on, 92-93; offerings, 44, 46
Finkelstein, Louis, 48n
First Commonwealth, 62
First fruits, 127-29
Fitzmyer, J. A., 17n
Flour paste dumplings, 16-17
Food laws, 112
Forbidden degrees, 42
Forgotten sheaf, 144-45, 149-50, 175, 219
Forty-five principles, 71-73
Fourth-year plantings, 219
Frankel, Zecharias, xviii-xxi, 4n, 77-78, 80, 88, 136, 255; "The Pioneer: Zecharias Frankel", 59-75; theories, 211, 215-16; source material, 205
Frankfurt-am-Main, 122
Frankfurt Rabbinical Conference, 59
Friedman, S., 36n

Gabini, Karoz, 214
Galatz, 90
Gamaliel, R., 31; divorce, Samaritan as witness, 95-96; exegesis, 159-60, 162; first Mishnah, 126, 130-31; intermediate period, 147, 153; Tamid sacrifice, 111
Gamaliel II, R., 131
Gamaliel III, R., 132
Garmu, House of, 251
Geiger, Abraham, 104n
Gentiles, aid to, 151-52
Gezerot, 61

275

GENERAL INDEX

Ginzberg, Louis, 18n, 45, 122n, 232n
Gleanings, 175, 219
Goldberg, Abraham, xxii, "Abraham Goldberg" and contributions to study, 225-41
Goldenberg, Robert, 13n, 34n
Golden jar, 17
Goldin, J., 47n, 253
Gold, tablet of, 129
Goodblatt, David, 135n, 138n
Grace after meals, 94-95
Graetz, Heinrich, 136, 211; formation and development of Mishnah, 107-108; law code, 117; oral and scribal law, 112-14
Great Ones of the Torah, 76-77, 82-83, 86
Grünberg, S., 122
Guardian of orphan, 182-83
Guilt offering, 19, 128

Ha-Cohen, Aryeh Leib, 2
Hadrian, 138
Halakhot, 77, 90, 109; exegesis, 156-58, 161, 163-64; formation, 242-56; intermediate period, 136-37, 140, 253; Maimonides, 5, 8; oral law, 119, 123-24, 126; positive-historical Judaism, 60-62, 65, 67, 74; source criticism, 38-55; source of sayings, 180-96; Zuri and legal system, 169-79
Halevy, Y. I., 125, 249; intermediate period, 135-54; oral law, 118-19; theories, 211
Halivni, David Weiss, 20n, 36n, 48n, 52, 91n, 96n, 104n; "David Weiss Halivni on the Mishnah", 180-96
Hallah, 70
Hamburg, 135
Hamburg Prayerbook dispute, 59
Hangings in Temple, 251
Hananel, R., 4
Hananiah b. Shilimy, 31
Hasmonean period, 64, 245
Hassidism, 108
Heave-offering, 64, 175, 219, 235-41, 248; moving objects, 93-94
Helene, 129, 147-48
Heller, R. Yom Tob Lippman, 7, 8
Herod, 63
Hieronymous, R., 41
Hildesheimer, Israel, 122
Hillel, xxi; exegesis, 97, 100-10, 158-59; flour paste/dumpling, 16-17; heave-offering and tithes, 237, 239-41; intermediate period, 137-38, 141-42, 144, 146; law code, 81-82, 88-89, 115; Levirate marriage, 220-21; oral law, 119, 123, 126-27, 130-32; order of law, 109-10, 112; positive-historical Judaism, 65-67; Shammai debates, 15-16; source criticism, 46, 49, 53; Tamid sacrifice, 111; teachings, 212-14, 216
Hirsch, Samson Raphael, 74, 122
Hisda, R., 23; intermediate period, 140-41
Hiyya, R., 18, 21, 31; Tosefta arrangement, 226-27
Höchberg, 122
Hoffmann, David, xxi, 255; "David Hoffmann's The First Mishnah", 122-34; theories, 211, 214
Holidays, laws of, 112; time for, 98-99
Horowitz, Lezar, R., 155
Hoshaiah, R., 21

GENERAL INDEX

Huna, R., 22, 187
Hyrcanus, 214

'Ila'i', R., 145, 252
Incense, 251
Isaac ibn Gabbai, 8
Isaac b. Jacob Alfassi, R., 70
Isaac b. Malkiṣedeq of Siponto, 4
Isaac b. Samuel, 6
Ishmael, R., 35, 43, 100, 173; Mekhilta, 172
Israelstam, J., 50

Jacob b. Qursi, R., 50
Jacob ben Samuel Hagiz, 8
Jamnitz, 155
Jastrow, S. V., 31n
Jawitz, Ze'ev, 107-108, 118-120
Jerusalem, 135
Jewish law, and antiquity, 59, 61
Jewish State, 169
Jonah, R., xvi, 160
Jonathan, 137
Joseph, R., 23, 34, 122; intermediate period, 140-41; legal system and traditions, 178
Josephus, 38, 63, 136, 251
Joshua, R., organization of Mishnah, 226, 230; Passover, 110, 115, 132, 159; positive-historical Judaism, 67; source criticism, 43, 47
Joshua b. Levi, R., 144
Joshua b. Peraḥiah, R., 250
Jubilees, Book of, 143
Judah, R., xii, 190; analysis by Epstein, 16, 18, 22, 24, 31; exegesis, 164-65; first fruits, 127-28; *Halakhah*, 254; intermediate period, 147-48; 153; *Ketuvah*, 187; law code, 115, 172; source criticism, 44, 49, 51; widow and marriage, 190-91
Judah b. Bathyra, R., 98n
Judah b. Ilai, R., 67, 164
Judah the Patriarch, Epstein and Rabbi, 14-16, 18-28; exegesis, 91-93, 95-96, 100-103, 159, 164-66; *Halakhah*, 246, 252-55; heave-offering and tithes, 239; history of Mishnah, xi-xiv; intermediate period, 137-41, 146, 149-51, 153; law code, 80, 82-87, 89, 115; legal system, 169, 171, 173, 176-79; Levirate marriage, 183-84; oral code of law, 119-20, 123, 132-33; order of law, 110-11; positive-historical Judaism, 61, 66, 68-70, 72-73; purpose of Mishnah organization, 226-27, 233; scribal and oral laws, 113-14, 116-17; source criticism, 37-55; source material, 192, 197-200, 204, 206; style and editing, 210-12, 215, 217-18, 221-23

Kanter, Shammai, 197n
Katz, Jacob, 9, 10n
Kaufman, Yeḥezkel, 246-47
Kelim, 67, 74-75
Ketuvah, 148-49, 186-88, 220-21
Klein, Shlomo, 74n
Kosovsky, C. Y., 224n
Krochmal, Naḥman, 136; formation and development of Mishnah, 107-108; oral law, 108-112; theories, 211, 213-15
Kutscher, Y., 27n, 36n

GENERAL INDEX

Lauterbach, J. Z., 248
Law code, 114-18; Scribes hiding meaning, 99-100
Law teachers, 109-112
Laying on of hands, xii, 46
Leazar, R., 145
Leazar b. 'Azariah, R., 145
Legal problems, xii
Legal system and traditions, 169-79
Leper, log of oil, 128
Levi bar Ḥamma, R., 1
Levirate marriage, 183-84, 220-21
Lewin, B. M., xiii
Liability for bed, 92
Lieberman, Saul, xvi, xvii, 3n, 96-97, 144-45, 148, 150, 236n; Epstein on formation of Mishnah, 18n, 27n, 29n, 36n, 38, 39n, 42, 43n, 44, 46n, 47, 48n, 49n, 50n, 51n, 54n, 55n; heave-offering, 237n, 238; Hillel-Shammai debates, 15-16
Limbs of sacrifice, 228-32
Lipschütz, Israel, 8
Literary questions, xii-xvii, xxi-xxiii
Locusts, 249
Löw, Leopold, 90n
Lydda, 149

Ma'aser Sheni, 42, 218-219
Maccabees, 136; positive-historical Judaism, 64-65
Maimonides, 30; law code, 78, 85; positive-historical Judaism, 70, 74; traditional study, 5-8, 9n, 10
Manah, R., 24
Manoah, 188
Mantel, Hugo, 142
Marcus, R., 41n
Marriage, Ketuvah, 186-88; laws of, 112; Levirate marriage, 183-84, 220-21; priestly stock, 221-22; Qiddushin and betrothals, 202-204; widow marrying, 190-91
Marx, A., 122n
Mar Zutra, 25
Matia ben Samuel, 111
Meat and milk, 50-51
Meir, R., xiii, 16-17; exegesis, 101-102, 162-66; flour paste/dumplings, 17; Halakhah, 254; intermediate period, 140, 153; law code, 80, 82, 86, 89, 114, 171-79; Levirate marriage, 221, Middot, 111, oral law, 119, 123, 130; Passover offering, 110; positive-historical Judaism, 66-68; scribal and oral laws, 113-17; source criticism, 47, 49, 51-52, 192; teachings, 212, 215
Mekhilta, 82, 89
Melamed, E. Z., 13, 28n, 35n, 37, 242n
Men of the Great Assembly, exegesis, 97, 103; Halakhah, 249; intermediate period, 137, 142-45; law code, 80-81, 89; oral law, 118-19; positive-historical Judaism, 60, 63-65, 74; R. Saadya Gaon and, 211, 213, 215
Milk and meat, 50-51
Mixed produce, 174
Moehring, Horst R., ix
Momigliano, A. D., xx
Money, return of, 92
Moral conduct, 202

GENERAL INDEX

Mordecai (Petaḥiah), 213-14
Moses b. Abraham of Pontoise, 4n
Mysticism, 46
Meyer, Rachel, 59

Naḥman b. Isaac, R., 24-25
Naḥman b. Jacob, R., 23
Nathan, R., 132; *Halakhah*, 254; intermediate period, 138, 140, 146-49, 152-53; law voided, 94; Middot, 111; source criticism, 49; teachings, 212
Nazirite, abstenance, 188-90; wine and poll, 184-86
Negaʿim, 82
Nehemiah, R., 162, 215
Neusner, Jacob, 1n; *Development of a Legend*, 15n, 43n, 65n; *The Formation of the Babylonian Talmud*, 13n, 91n, 107, 135n, 170n, 180n, 193, 197n, 209n, 232n; *The Rabbinic Traditions About the Pharisees Before 70*, 15n, 17n, 42n, 47n, 142n, 144n, 145, 210, 249-50
New Year, 44
Neziqin, 87
Niddah, 4-5

Oath affecting debt, 92
Obadiah ben Abraham of Bertinoro, 7-8
Ohalot, 82, 225
Olives, clean or unclean, 53
Oppenheim, Bernhard, R., 155
Oppenheim, Joachim, 155-66
Oral law, 209-10; DeVries on, 242-56; exegesis, 90-91, 97-98; First Mishnah, 123-25, 129; intermediate period, 136-37; Jawitz on, 118-20; N. Krochmal, 108-112; and scribal law, 112-14
Oral Mishnah, 14-15
Oral Torah, xii, xiii, xviii-xxi; law code, 78-80, 89; traditional study, 1-10
ʿOrlah, 70
Orphan and guardian, 182-83
ʿOshaya, R., 177, 226
Oven, clean or unclean, 152-3

Pairs, 60, 64
Palestine, Babylonia compared, 21-30; Talmud, 37-55
Pappa, R., 24; testimony of bondwoman, 194-95
Passover offering, 110
Peace offering, 128
Peʾah, 219
Petaḥiah (Mordecai), 213-14
Pharisees, xv, exegesis, 97, 99-100, 157-58; traditions, 245
Philo, 38
Pineles, Hirsch M., xi, 181n; "Hirsch Mendel Pineles: the First Critical Exegete", 90-104
Positive-historical Judaism, 59-75
Prague, 59
Prayers, Fast Days, 96-97
Produce mixed, 174
Property, 43, 112

GENERAL INDEX

Qaraism, xiii
Qeruspi, R., 31
Qiddushin, betrothals, 202-204
Qinim, 47

Raba, 191-92
Rabad, 5, 6
Rabbah b. Nahmani, 23
Rabin, C., 42n
Rabinowitz, Saul, R., 60n, 74n
Rabinowitz, S. P., 112n
Rappaport, Shlomo, 74, 136
Rashbam, 162
Rashi, law code, 85, 119, 160; positive-historical Judaism, 69-70; traditional study, 4, 7, 8
Rav, 22, 31; vows, 193-94
Rava, 23-26, 34
Ravina, R., 24
Rawidowicz, Simon, 109n
Resh Laqish, 22
Restitution, 175
Ritual obligations, 202
Rosh Hashanah, 70

Saadya, Gaon, R., 211, 212, 213
Sabbath law, 64, 112; intermediate period, 143, 171; moving objects, 93-94
Sadducees, 137; exegesis, 97, 99
Sages of the law, 60, 63, 65, 68
Samaritan as witness, 95-96
Samson, abstenance, 188-90
Samson b. Abraham of Sens, 4n, 5-6, 7, 70
Samuel, 22, 144, 193
Samuel b. Meir, R., 162
Sanctified property, 42
Sanhedrin, oral and scribal law, 112, 114; positive-historical Judaism, 60, 63-65, 70
Schechter, Solomon, 109n
Schorr, Joshua, 104n
Schrieber, Abraham, 122
Schück, Moses, 122
Schürer, E., 139
Schwartz, Adolf, 205
Scribes, exegesis, 97-100, 157-58, 163; *Halakhah*, 246, 248; intermediate period, 137; oral law, 108-14, 118-20; positive-historical Judaism, 61-62
Second Commonwealth, 62, 66, 245
Seder Toharot, xviii, 64; traditional study, 4-6
Seder Zeraʿim, 4-6
Segal, M. S., 143n
Seventh-Year law, 151-52
Shabbath and Ark, 95-95
Shammai, exegesis, 159; flour paste/dumplings, 16-17; heave-offering and tithes, 237, 239-41; Hillel debates, 15-16; intermediate period, 138, 141-42, 144, 146; law code, 81, 112, 115, 119; Levirate marriage, 220-21; oral law, 123, 126-27, 130-32; positive-historical Judaism, 65-67; source criticism, 46, 49, 53; teachings, 212, 216

GENERAL INDEX

Shavu'ot, 98
Shema'iah, 101, 156-58
Shema', reading of, 109
Sherira, xii-xiii, xvi, xviii-xix; exegesis, 161; first fruits, 129; *Halakhah*, 254-55; oral law, 118-19, 124; positive-historical Judaism, 70; theories, 211-12, 216
Sherira Gaon, Letter of, 136, 140
Sheshet, R., 13, 19
Shimshon of Chinon, 124
Simeon, R., 16, 48, 51-53; exegesis, 165; *Halakhah*, 254; intermediate period, 147; limbs of sacrifices, 229-30; scribal and oral law, 114-15
Simeon b. Azzai, 128
Simeon b. Eleazar, 176
Simeon b. Gamaliel, R., first Mishnah, 130-31; *Halakhah*, 254; intermediate period, 140, 150-51; Middot, 111; organization of Mishnah, 226-27; positive-historical Judaism, 65; source criticism, 49-50; teachings, 212
Simeon b. Gamaliel II, R., 131
Simeon b. Hillel, 130-131
Simeon ben Honi II, 109
Simeon b. Laqish, R., 1
Simeon b. Menasiah, 46
Simeon b. Yoḥai, R., 46, 115
Simeon of Mispeh, 111
Simeon the Righteous; exegesis, 99-100; oral law, 109, 117; oral Torah, xxi; positive-historical Judaism, 64
Simon, M., 126
Singer, Isidore, 76n, 122n
Sin-offering, 19, 128
Soferim, 91, 98-99, 101; scribes, 61-62
Sokolow, Nahum, 155n
Solomon, 99, 144
Sommer, Samuel, 122
Source criticism, 37-55
Source material, 197-206
Spira, 59
Strack, Hermann L., 41n, 51n
Sugya 197-98, 201, 205
Sukkah, 147

Tacitus, 136
Taḥalifa b. Ma'arava, 183
Tam, R., 4n, 6
Tamid, 45; limbs of sacrifices, 228-32; time of, 110-11
Tannaim, xi, 15, 21-27, 29, 34-35; Albeck on, 209, 211, 217, 222; exegesis, 91, 97, 99-103, 155-56, 161-62, 164, 166; formation and development of Mishnah, 107-108; *Halakhah*, 243, 247-48, 251, 253; intermediate period, 136, 140-41, 144, 146, 151-53; law code, 77-85, 87, 89, 169, 177-78; oral law, 119, 123-24, 130, 132-33; positive-historical Judaism, 63, 65-66, 68-70; source criticism, 37-55; source of sayings, 180-91, 198-200, 205-206
Taqqanot, 61, 65
Ṭarfon, R., 49, 254
Temple offerings, 47, 251
Temple service, 42-43
Ten Commandments, 1, 2

GENERAL INDEX

Testimony, defilement of woman, 194-95
Theft, 81
Tithes, 42, 175, 219, 235-41
Tobiad, Joseph, 137
Tohorot, 82, 87
Torah, xii, xiii, xviii-xxi, 1-10; law code, 78-80, 89; standing while learning, 126
Tosefta, xi, xvi; exegesis, 90-92, 161-62; *Halakhah*, 245, 254-55; heave-offering, 235-41; intermediate period, 140, R. Hiyya arranging, 226-30; law code, 82, 85, 89, 176; source criticism, 38, 40; source material, 200-201, 203; tithes, 235-41
Tosafot Yom Tov (Heller), R., 139
Traditions, xi-xiv, xviii; and legal system, 169-79
Twersky, I., 4n, 5

'Ulla, R., 247
'Uqsin, 82, 111, 140, 212
Urbach, Ephraim E., 6, 65n, 246
Usha, xix; intermediate period, 147-48

Valuations, 42
Vegetables, 50
Vermes, Geza, ix
Vessels, broken, 173-74
Vestments of Temple, 251
Vienna, 13, 59, 135
Vilna, 135
Volozhin, 135
Vows, release from, 42, 193-94

Water libation, 17
Weinberg, Yehiel Jacob, 136n
Weiss, Abraham, 197-206
Weiss, I. H., 122, 136, 157n; formation and development of Mishnah, 107-108; law code, 114-18; source material, 205
Widow and marriage, 190-91
Witness, defilement of woman, 194-95; Samaritan as, 95-96
Written law, 90; first Mishnah, 126
Written Mishnah, 14-15
Written Torah, 78-80

Yadin, Yigael, ix, 42
Yavneh, beginning of Mishnah, 226-27; 'Eduyyot created, xix, 111; *Halakhah*, 246, 249-50, 252; intermediate period, 139, 142, 144-45, 147; positive-historical Judaism, 67; teachings at, 216-17
Yesod HaMishnah, 136-38, 140, 142-45, 147, 149-51, 153
Yohanan, R., 215; *Halakhah*, 247; legal system and traditions, 178; source criticism, 52; teachings, 22, 31-32, 34; traditional study, 3, 4
Yohanan b. Beroqah, R., 192
Yohanan b. Gudgada, 46
Yohanan b. Nuri, 49
Yohanan b. Phineas, R., 251
Yohanan ben Zakkai, 131-32; exegesis, 100, 159, 164; first fruits, 129; legal system, 171, oral law, 119; positive-historical Judaism, 65; source criticism, 43, 46; student days, 212, 214; teachings, 226

GENERAL INDEX

Yoḥanan the High Priest, 157
Yoma, 251; limbs of sacrifices, 228-32
Yonah, R., 24, 32, 48, 253
Yosa, R., heave-offering, 237-38; limbs of sacrifices, 229
Yosi, R., 16-17; exegesis, 98n, 101; heave-offering and tithes, 236-41; intermediate period, 141, 153; legal system and traditions, 177; limbs of sacrifices, 230, 232; positive-historical Judaism, 67; scribal and oral laws, 112; source criticism, 44, 48-49, 51; widow and marriage, 191
Yosi b. Ḥanina, R., 22
Yosi b. Yo'ezer, R., 249-50

Zera'im, 70
Ze'iri, R., 19, 22
Zevid, R., 24
Zucker, M., 28n
Zuckermandel, 48, 51, 95, 152-53
Zuri, J. S., 169-79

www.ingramcontent.com/pod-product-compliance
Lightning Source LLC
Chambersburg PA
CBHW071233230426
43668CB00011B/1413